DEAR PALESTINE

Stanford Studies *in* Middle Eastern
and Islamic Societies *and* Cultures

DEAR PALESTINE

A Social History of the 1948 War

Shay Hazkani

STANFORD UNIVERSITY PRESS

Stanford, California

STANFORD UNIVERSITY PRESS
Stanford, California

Printed in the United States of America on acid-free, archival-quality paper

Library of Congress Cataloging-in-Publication Data

Names: Hazkani, Shay, author.

Title: Dear Palestine : a social history of the 1948 War / Shay Hazkani.

Other titles: Stanford studies in Middle Eastern and Islamic societies and cultures.

Description: Stanford, California : Stanford University Press, 2021. | Series: Stanford studies in Middle Eastern and Islamic societies and cultures | Includes bibliographical references and index.

Identifiers: LCCN 2020034448 (print) | LCCN 2020034449 (ebook) | ISBN 9781503614659 (cloth) | ISBN 9781503627659 (paperback) | ISBN 9781503627666 (ebook)

Subjects: LCSH: Israel. Tseva haganah le-Yiśra'el—Records and correspondence. | Arab Liberation Army—Records and correspondence. | Israel-Arab War, 1948–1949—Social aspects. | Jewish soldiers—Palestine—Correspondence. | Muslim soldiers—Palestine—Correspondence. | Nationalism—Palestine—History—20th century.

Classification: LCC DS126.9 .H39 2021 (print) | LCC DS126.9 (ebook) | DDC 956.04/21—dc23

LC record available at https://lccn.loc.gov/2020034448

LC ebook record available at https://lccn.loc.gov/2020034449

Cover design: Rob Ehle

Cover photo: Soldier of the Auxiliary Territorial Service (ATS), British Army, 1942. Photo by Zoltan Kluger. Courtesy of the Israel State Archives.

Typeset by Kevin Barrett Kane in 10.5/14.4 Brill

To Nitzan and Tom

Contents

Acknowledgments

From 2001 to 2008 I was a young—and somewhat naïve—radio and then TV correspondent, covering the Israeli military and the ongoing occupation of the West Bank and Gaza Strip. I was digging through records in the Israeli army archives for a short TV piece on the German-Israeli arms deal of 1958 when a strange document surfaced: it summarized the views of "ordinary" Israeli soldiers about the deal (a contentious issue given that Germany was boycotted for many years in Israel after the Holocaust). Their views were extracted from their personal letters, secretly copied by a massive Big Brother apparatus. I later learned that this was a very common practice, dating back to 1948, and that Israeli soldiers were a late addition to an operation which also copied letters by Palestinians and many others. After a back-and-forth with the archives, I was allowed to copy some of the sources, and a few months later, departed for the United States to pursue graduate studies with the letters in my suitcase.

I knew that these letters had an interesting story to tell, but what it was or how to tell it—I had no idea. It was the advice, help, and support I received from mentors, colleagues, and friends that eventually illuminated both the "what" and the "how" of this project.

I owe the greatest debt of gratitude to Zachary Lockman, who patiently guided me through the growing pains of this project over the past decade. His uncompromising standard for scholarship will continue to serve as a model for the rest of my academic career. I also benefited from excellent mentoring at

New York University and Georgetown University by many others. Ella Shohat blew my mind with the story of Arab Jews. Ronald Zweig reasoned with me that letters alone—without the story of the socialization of these people—made little sense. Judith Tucker was the first to believe something would come out of my work.

Many people graciously read this manuscript and provided invaluable feedback. Salim Tamari and Omer Bartov taught me how to write social history. Shira Robinson, Sherene Seikaly, Laila Parsons, and Hillel Cohen were very generous with their time and advice. I am grateful also to the two anonymous reviewers for their comments.

I am fortunate to have an intellectual home at the University of Maryland, College Park. Colleagues at the Joseph and Rebecca Meyerhoff Center for Jewish Studies and the History Department were immensely supportive of this project. Throughout my academic career I also have benefited from funding by Georgetown University's Center for Contemporary Arab Studies, NYU's Graduate School of Arts and Science and the Taub Center, the Middlebury Language School's Kathryn Davis Fellowship for Peace, the Israel Institute, and the Samuel Iwry Faculty Fellowship Fund at UMD.

Archives and archival decalcification policies have always been a topic close to my heart. Attorney Avner Pinchuk of the Association for Civil Rights in Israel shared this passion and then some. Thank you for sending dozens of letters and memos to help obtain the sources used for this study, and for taking my appeal against the Shin Bet to the Supreme Court. My work on this front would not have been possible without the work of many fellow travelers, and particularly Lior Yavne, Noam Hofstadter, and Adam Raz from Akevot. I also want to thank the staff at the various archives where I conducted research. I suspect that I caused them grief at times, but I want to recognize the dozens of hours they and their staff invested in processing my requests for documents. Special thanks to Doron Avi-Ad, Ilana Alon, Orly Levy, Yaacov Lozowick, Dorit Herman, Efrat Raz-Nagad, Avraham Zadok, and Eldad Harouvi.

Deciphering some of the handwritten Arabic letters used in this study would have not been possible without the assistance of Ali Adeeb Alnaemi and Khairuldeen Al Makhzoomi. Aharon Rose helped with Yiddish translations. Lee Rotbart assisted with the visual research. I also want to extend a heartfelt thanks to those who invited me to present my work at their institutions, who read parts of this study, or otherwise supported it ("can you just get me this one document from the archives?"): Emma Sharkey, David Tal, Avraham Sela, Reem Bailony, Kristen Alff, Yoav Alon, Israel Gershoni, Ahmad Amara, Orit Bashkin, Seth Anziska, Alon Confino, Nadim Bawalsa, Omar Boum, Guy Burak, Kfır Cohen, Henriette Dahan-Kalev, Amiram Azov, Jonathan Skolnik, Marsha Rozenblit, Peter Wien, Paul Scham, Arie Dubnov, Derek Penslar, Gil Rothschild, David Engel, Motti Golani, Aziza Khazoom, Orly Lael Netzer, Sarah Levin, Susan Miller, Emily Gottrich, Osama Abi-Mershed, Rochelle Davis, David Engel, Haim Saadon, Eugene Rogan, Joseph Sassoon, David Myers, Tom Pessah, Itmar Radai, Benny Morris, Orit Rozin, Gilad Sharvit, David Stenner, Gil-li Vardi, Alex Winder, Charles Anderson, Ori Yehudai, Assaf Banitt, Shahar Ben-Hur, and Rona Sela. I also want to thank my parents, Haya and Hagai Hazkani, for their continued support.

A special thank you to Kate Wahl from Stanford University Press, who had a wonderful vision for this project and helped make it a reality. Thanks also to Joel Beinin and Laleh Khalili, the series editors, and to Susan Karani, Paul Tyler, Tobiah Waldron, Caroline McKusick, and the rest of the team at the press for their hard work.

Finally, there are four people without whom this project could not have been completed. Samuel Dolbee and Fredrik Meiton whipped garbled sentences into coherent prose with great skill and offered critical advice at every juncture. Nitzan Goldberger, whom I was fortunate enough to meet a decade ago and who became my life partner, facilitated this project through challenging times. Tom, our son, has been a source of great strength.

DEAR PALESTINE

Introduction

MUSCULAR JEWS AND ARABS

IN 1948 VOLUNTEERS FROM ACROSS THE ARAB WORLD ASSEMBLED into a five-thousand-strong fighting force called the Arab Liberation Army (ALA), intent on joining with Palestinians to prevent the partition of Palestine and the establishment of the Jewish state. As one newspaper described:

> You find among them Saudis who jump fences like tigers, Yemenis who race with the gazelles, and robust Iraqis who are resolved and brave. You also find Syrians, Lebanese, Kuwaitis, Transjordanians, and fourteen-year-olds who left their school benches in Damascus and Baghdad and volunteered for the Arab Liberation Army.[1]

One of the "robust Iraqis" was Abdullah Dawud and he was Jewish. Born in 'Anah along the Euphrates river, Dawud served in the Iraqi brigade of the volunteer army and actually fought against fellow Jews in the ALA's attack on Kibbutz Mishmar ha-'Emek, south of Nazareth, on April 4, 1948.[2] In 1950 Dawud immigrated to Israel as part of the large wave of immigrants from Iraq that put an end to over two thousand years of Jewish civilization in Mesopotamia. For decades he kept his past in the ALA a secret, but shortly before his death, he decided it was time to come clean. A journalist, looking for a sensationalist story about Iraqi Jews in 1990—only months before the US-led military campaign to drive the Iraqis out of Kuwait—heard the rumor and tracked him down.³

At first Dawud insisted that he was forced to enlist, and that he feared for his life. But as the interview went on, it became clear that he was rather proud of his time with the ALA and especially of his talent as a sniper. "I was such a great soldier," he boasted, "that my officer, Husayn, who was a real bastard, told me: Abduallah, too bad you are Jewish." But the journalist interviewing him was not amused. She was baffled by Dawud's willingness to fight his core-ligionists. "Didn't you think of escaping to the kibbutz and joining the fighters there?" she pressed. Dawud explained that it was not an option: "I shot in the direction I was told to. I'm telling the truth. I'm not hiding anything. I knew I was shooting at Jews like me, but what could I have done? If I [acted] funny they would have killed me." But the journalist was not convinced, commenting that it appeared Dawud did not agonize about shooting Jews, not then and not now. To her, he appeared indifferent.⁴

The reason the reporter was irked with Dawud's response was that his story undermined the conventional narrative of the 1948 war, as one characterized predominantly by the dichotomy of Arab versus Jew. After all, hundreds, if not thousands, of books and articles have told this story. They point to clearly drawn battle lines with an age-old history, and an intractable present and future.

Abdullah Dawud's case was certainly exceptional—a "man bites dog" kind of story—but like the other stories told in this book, it complicates 1948, and suggests far messier battle lines than previously considered. Indeed, many Jews and Arabs were pitted against one another in 1948, but so were numerous other ethnic and class-based subgroups within those two categories: Ashke-nazi Jews, who came from Europe, saw Mizrahi Jews, who immigrated from Arab lands, as inferior, prompting the latter to reconsider their relationship to Zionism; American Jews saw Sabra Jews (who were born in Palestine) as violent, chauvinist nationalists, while the Sabras saw American Jews as soft-hearted and effeminate; Palestinians demanded that Arab leaders make good on their promise to save Palestine, while Arab leaders demanded that Pales-tinians stay put and not flee even in the face of the deadliest attacks against them; Arab volunteers became enraged with their leaders after discovering the ineffectiveness of the Arab League's volunteer army, while Arab leaders, in turn, were fearful the volunteers would try to force them out of office.

FIGURE 1. An Israeli soldier writing a letter during the 1948 war. Source: The Israel Defense Forces and Defense Establishment Archives (IDFA).

And on both sides, elites had very different aspirations and concerns than nonelites. However, it is not only the Arab/Jew binary that this book seeks to destabilize. Some of the seemingly opposing subgroups cited above actually had similar experiences in 1948, like young Arabs and Jews from the middle classes who were attracted to militarism, or Palestinians and Mizrahi Jews who both wished to return to their former homelands—Palestinians to Palestine and Moroccan Jews to Morocco. But 1948 not only occasioned conflicts and parallels between preformed groups who had made their way to Palestine. The war also rendered these categories meaningful in the first place, as its participants discovered what it meant to have their identity reduced to "Jew" or "Arab," in some cases for the first time.

These divisions and fractures, uncomfortable truths and surreal alliances have been downplayed and subordinated to a dominant ethnonational division between Jews and Arabs in the scholarship of the last several decades. This book seeks to bring these interactions to light through an examination of previously unseen personal letters of Jews and Arabs from the war, most of whom fought in the ranks of the Israel Defense Forces (IDF) or the Arab League's volunteer army, the ALA. The stories told by ordinary people about the war in these letters are far more diverse and complex than the nationalist fervor and unquestioning loyalty usually imputed to them.

Understanding what ordinary people said to one another in private letters, however, is impossible without also taking into account the efforts of elites (be they military, state, party, or tribal) to inculcate certain ideologies in them. To do so, this book also examines battle orders, pamphlets, army magazines, and radio broadcasts used to mobilize young men and women and to educate and indoctrinate them in their respective armies. Reading indoctrination materials alongside soldiers' letters reveals important and enduring fissures in the ideological edifices of Middle Eastern nationalisms precisely at the moment when, by most accounts, these conceptions of nationalism crystallized.[5] For example, the IDF command tried to teach Ashkenazi Jews that organized violence was in line with Jewish tradition. It tried to convince Mizrahi Jews that killing the Arab enemy in Palestine would be payback for their parents' suffering under Arab rule in the purported diaspora. But Ashkenazi soldiers were not easily convinced of the univocal view of violence in Judaism, and many Mizrahi soldiers did not feel that the Arabs were necessarily the enemy. This tension between the official narrative and lived experience also surfaced in the ALA. The army's propagandists aimed to restrict Arab volunteers' revolutionary zeal to fighting Jews by implanting the view that Jews transgressed the boundaries of their traditional place in Islamic society, only to discover that some volunteers and their families were not willing to separate the fight in Palestine from their struggle against their own corrupt governments.

ALL ROADS LEAD TO PALESTINE

The history of Palestine from the late nineteenth century until 1948 encapsulates more than the plight of Jews in Europe, their colonization of Palestine, and the resistance of Palestine's indigenous Arab population to that colonization.

It also demonstrates how younger generations of European Jews and the Arabs that came of age in the shadow of the Ottoman Empire's dissolution internalized the racist European gaze and envisioned similar solutions to combat it. The adoption of aspects of the antisemitic discourse about the "degenerate" Jew had brought some European Jews to embrace a masculine militarist culture in the hope of regenerating the "Jewish race." Meanwhile, European colonialism in Arab lands—and the Orientalist stereotyping associated with it—engendered a similar attraction to scouting and militarism among some Arabs. The adoption of a masculine militarist culture on both sides helps explain why thousands, Jews as well as Arabs, came to fight in Palestine in 1948. This is not to say that both sides bear equal blame for 1948, that there were no power imbalances that fundamentally shaped this history, or, indeed, that militarism is the underlying reason for the war. Rather, I wish to weave together the various strands of modern Jewish and Middle Eastern history to illuminate a salient parallelism in the response to European racist stereotyping, and to show the role of that thinking all the way up to and through 1948.

Zionism emerged in late nineteenth-century Europe, founded upon the conviction that Jews should be allowed to live as a "normal" people under their own sovereignty. The movement's emergence was closely related to the creation a few decades earlier of a "Jewish international." Like other forms of religious internationalism in the modern period, the "Jewish international" was characterized by the active participation of Jews in a newly created public sphere, mostly through the press.[6] Early espousers of Zionism, as nonobservant Jews, were on the fringes of the "Jewish international."[7] They were influenced by the Jewish Enlightenment (haskala)—an intellectual movement from the late eighteenth century inspired by its European predecessor—which weakened the traditional rabbinical leadership in Europe. Within this cultural revival, ideas like nationalism became popular among European Jews, as they did among non-Jews. When it became apparent that many European nation-states were not genuinely willing to integrate their Jewish populations on an equal basis, a minority of Jews turned to Zionism as a solution to European antisemitism. Some Zionists initially considered places outside of Palestine to establish Jewish sovereignty, but that idea was abandoned by 1905, and Palestine emerged in the movement as the sole destination for Jewish migration. This also allowed a small group of Orthodox Jews to become active participants in Zionism and see immigration to Palestine as part of the messianic process (they would come to be known as "religious Zionists"). Against those comparatively few, the majority of observant Jews in Europe opposed Zionism as a form of "false messianism." This was not the case among the Jews of Arab lands. Zionism was not seen as infringing on Jewish tenets, but neither did it generate much interest until the late 1940s.[8]

For many early Zionists, including the founding father of political Zionism, Theodor Herzl, European settler colonialism—especially the German experience before the First World War—was a model. In the German case, the Colonization Commission (*Ansiedlungskommission*), set up in 1886 by Otto von Bismarck, worked to transfer lands from Polish to German ownership in Poznan and West Prussia in order to transform the demographic balance there and reduce the Slavs to a minority population, subdued and depoliticized. The commission bought large farms from Poles, divided them into small parcels, and settled German farmers on them. Arthur Ruppin, who headed the Palestine office of the Zionist Organization (ZO), was born in Poznan and explicitly sought to replicate this model to transform the demographic balance in Palestine in favor of the Jews. To centralize the purchase of Arab lands and prevent the resale of Jewish-owned land to Arabs, the Jewish National Fund (JNF) was established in 1901. By 1907 Ruppin helped set up the Palestine Land Development Company (PLDC) along the lines of the German Colonization Commission, and even hired a former official from the German commission as a special advisor. The PLDC aimed to create homogeneous groups of Jewish farmers and support new agricultural settlements. Many of those farmers were Jews from eastern Europe, where antisemitic violence intensified in the late nineteenth century.[9]

In the Arab world, European expansion into the Ottoman Empire was a malady of similar magnitude. France sponsored autonomous Christian rule in Mount Lebanon in 1861; Algeria and Tunisia were occupied by the French in 1831 and 1881, respectively, and Libya by Italy in 1911. Most egregious in the eyes of many was Britain's occupation of Egypt in 1882. These crises spurred Arab intellectuals, religious scholars, and others to debate how to reverse what they saw as a long "decline" in Arab civilization, which had allowed its colonization. Many of the responses to this perceived decline were not in the realm of politics. In fact, much like the Jewish Enlightenment, the Arab renaissance, known as the *nahda*, was first and foremost an intellectual movement. However, like elsewhere in the non-Western world, the envisioned *political* solutions to the crisis included westernization, newly imagined forms of nationalism, religious reform, and ideologies like socialism, communism, and fascism, each incorporating varying degrees of anticolonialism. Many young men and women who espoused these ideologies belonged to a new urban middle class that was the product of several decades of Ottoman reforms. Some hailed from urban families; others were the first to be born in the big cities after their parents migrated there from the countryside for economic reasons. Many began their education in Ottoman institutions or mission schools, later to continue in state-sponsored schools of the colonial governments.[10]

For some early Zionists, projecting strength was appealing, as it became a few decades later for Arab nationalists. These early Zionists internalized certain aspects of European antisemitism, including the supposed emasculation, sickliness, and submissiveness of the *Ostjuden* (eastern European Jew)—and sought to reverse the decline.[11] Unlike European antisemites, however, prominent Zionist thinkers from the late nineteenth century maintained that the Jewish race could regenerate and restore its glory from biblical times, especially its military might.[12]

One can trace this Zionist aspiration to be "a nation like all other nations" (*ke-khol ha-goyim*) to Herzl himself. But the first Jewish thinkers to associate "normalcy" with the use of force were Micha Berdichevsky and (later) Shaul Tchernichovsky, who were active at the turn of the nineteenth century.[13] Both attempted, in their writings, to "rediscover" legends from the Jewish past that emphasized heroism, sacrifice, and militarism over "Jewish wisdom."[14] Berdichevsky's writings vilified rabbinic Judaism in particular because, in his view, it intentionally suppressed the Bible's militancy and replaced it with cowardice and weakness, which defined generations of Jews.[15] Adopting some of these views, Max Nordau, a Hungarian Zionist and a close confidant of Herzl, wanted to create a new "muscular Judaism" (*Muskeljudentum*), transforming the artisan and petty merchant into a soldier or a farmer.[16] "Let us take up our oldest traditions; let us once more become deep-chested, sturdy, sharp-eyed men," he wrote in a famous 1903 essay calling for the introduction of gymnastics into the Jewish education system.[17] Capitalizing on these ideas, European Zionist organizations (among others) began to offer physical education, bodybuilding, and eventually military training to young middle-class Jewish men. Although women were not initially envisioned as part of the Jewish "regeneration," many female Zionist settlers saw themselves as integral to the project early on.[18]

The idea of being "a nation like all other nations" was closely related to what many Zionists saw as the "negation of exile" (*shlilat ha-galut*). Berdichevsky, for example, maintained that Jewish life in the diaspora held no value and that the ultimate solution for antisemitism was immigration to Palestine.[19] Only modern Jewish nationalism—later equated with the struggle for political sovereignty in Palestine—could allow Jews to transcend two millennia of supposed passivity and "return to history" (*ha-shivah la-historiyah*).[20] Agency, among other things, was to be attained through the creation of a sovereign Jewish army.[21] Personal letters, showcased in this book, show that fifty years after these ideas were first introduced by the Zionist movement—and just as militarism ebbed elsewhere in the aftermath of the Second World War—most Jews in Palestine embraced them, with a few notable dissenters.

Like those who adopted militarism, the dissenters could also trace their views back to an ideological current from the late nineteenth and early twentieth centuries. This ideology rejected force as a means of advancing Zionist goals, emphasizing the moral aspects of Judaism and what its adherents saw as Judaism's nonviolent nature. Such school of thought was primarily associated with Asher Ginsberg, known by his pen name Ahad Ha'am ("one of the people").[22] Ahad Ha'am believed that what made the Jewish people distinct was their spiritual power, going back as far as the biblical prophets. To him, the Jews had a redemptive role to play, not just for their own sake but for humanity as a whole. Zion must become a "light unto nations" (*or la-goyim*, Isaiah 42:6) and serve as a spiritual center for the entire human race. It was only natural, in this view, that Zionists reject the gentile way of war.[23]

It took several decades of Zionist immigration to Palestine for these theoretical discussions to reemerge as policy. For the first thirty years of Zionist colonization, despite verbal protest, the Ottoman Empire generally tolerated the immigration of European Jews to Palestine as long as they did not call for secession. (A relatively small community of Ashkenazi and Mizrahi Jews had lived in Palestine continuously from ancient times, but they were not Zionist, and usually sought to live in the four cities most religiously significant for Jews.) The Ottomans also tolerated extensive land purchases by Zionist organizations in Palestine, even when it meant the dispossession of Palestine's indigenous Arab peasants, who worked the overwhelming majority of the land (this dispossession troubled Ahad Ha'am among others).[24] In fact, it was a new Ottoman land code in the mid-nineteenth century that, contrary to its intention, led many Arab peasants to lose the usufruct and other rights to their land in Palestine, thus putting that land on the market for Zionist organizations to buy.[25] Compounding the Arab landlessness crisis was a "conquest of labor" (*kibbush ha-'avoda*) policy adopted by Jewish settlers in the second wave of immigration to Palestine (the Second Aliyah, which extended from 1904 to 1914). Born of the realization that Jewish men and women could not effectively compete in the predominantly Arab labor market, the policy specified that only Jews could work in Zionist agricultural settlements, thereby eliminating the competition with Arab labor.[26] By the end of the first decade of the twentieth century, Zionist colonization and the ejection of Arab peasants had provoked armed clashes between individual Jews and Arabs on several occasions. Such clashes intensified with the lifting of Ottoman censorship and the development of the Arabic-language press in Palestine after the constitutional revolution of 1908. With a relatively free press, a far greater number of Arabs throughout the Ottoman Empire learned of the European Jewish settler project and its consequences.[27] This new Arab press was also instrumental in mobilizing volunteers to fight in 1948.

The 1908 Ottoman constitutional revolution—launched by reform-minded bureaucrats in Istanbul—inspired more than a free press. The reestablishment of the Ottoman parliament and the promise of citizenship, equality, and freedom attracted many middle-class Arabs (including some Jews) in Palestine to Ottomanism (*Osmanlılık*), a late nineteenth-century identification with the Ottoman state, inspired by European nationalism. But by the time the First World War was under way, the support for Ottomanism had faded, largely because of the brutality of the Ottoman military in Greater Syria (which included parts of modern-day Syria, Lebanon, Jordan, and Palestine/Israel). A British-sponsored revolt in the name of Arab nationalism against the Ottoman Empire in 1916 may have also played a role in the evolution of new identities in the region. In fact, the British had made wartime promises to leave the Arab domains united under the leadership of the Hashemites, the Hijazi family of notables that led the revolt. These promises for a pan-Arab kingdom were not kept. The dismantling of the empire at the end of the war delivered a last blow to the fledgling Ottoman identity in Greater Syria, and by 1919 Syrian nationalism became popular, especially among urban elites.[28]

Arab nationalism in Greater Syria received a major boost in 1917 when the British announced they would sponsor Zionism. Herzl had already envisioned sponsorship by a Great Power, but he failed to convince any world power to embrace Zionism.[29] The 1917 Balfour Declaration, thirteen years after Herzl's death, was the realization of his dream. According to the British cabinet, "His Majesty's Government view with favor the establishment in Palestine of a national home for the Jewish people."[30] Although Jews (Zionist and non-Zionist) were only 9 percent of Palestine's population (numbering 60,000), the declaration did not explicitly mention the Arab majority (numbering 640,000), but only referred to them as "non-Jewish communities." This was purposeful, since—in the words of Foreign Secretary Balfour—"in Palestine we do not propose even to go through the form of consulting the wishes of the present inhabitants of the country."[31]

In the aftermath of the World War, Britain and France divided the Arab domains of the Ottoman Empire between them. Under the auspices of the League of Nations (the predecessor to the United Nations), the Great Powers imposed an arrangement known as the "mandates system." While promising "administrative advice and assistance" to prepare nations for self-rule, in practice the mandates were a thinly veiled form of colonialism.[32] In Palestine the British mandate charter of 1922 included the Balfour Declaration, which the majority of the region's Arab inhabitants vehemently opposed. Some continued to regard Palestine as "southern Syria," an indivisible part of Greater Syria, but the breakup of the region into different mandates made a Palestine-centric national identity popular among Palestine's Arab inhabitants.[33]

Nearby, former Arab officers in the Ottoman army led revolts in the mandated territories of Iraq and Syria in 1919 and 1925, respectively. (Local notables in Egypt also led a revolt in 1919.) These revolts brought together grassroots agendas and the political ambition of the former Ottoman officers. A source of inspiration was also the success of an Ottoman officer, Mustafa Kemal, in the Turkish war of independence. Kemal's army forced militarily superior European empires to abandon their plans to colonize parts of Anatolia following the Ottoman defeat in the First World War. Many of the Arab officers who led the revolts, dubbed by one scholar as "the last Ottoman generation," knew each other, and Kemal, personally from their time at the Ottoman military academies. They demanded Arab unity and attracted a considerable following, even if those whom they led did not all agree on the precise borders, economic schemes, and system of governance for the Arab domains.[34] Ultimately, the revolts were crushed by Britain's and France's superior military power, but the insurgents did manage to extract concessions, including border correc- tions and constitutions. Subsequently, most of the revolts' leaders joined the postrevolutionary dual-government system, where national elites worked alongside colonial officials to govern the mandates. Still, many middle-class young people saw "the last Ottoman generation" as heroes who dared to con- front colonialism, and some former Ottoman officers continued to harbor desires to overthrow the colonial administrations and unify the Arab world.[35]

Some of the young sympathizers of the former Ottoman officers from Syria, Lebanon, Egypt, and Iraq joined paramilitary youth organizations in the interwar years. Scouting troops had existed in the Middle East since at least 1912. They were based on principles embraced around the world, such as chivalrous masculinity and national service, introduced by a British general, Robert Baden-Powell, in his 1909 book *Scouting for Boys*. Scouting in the British Commonwealth also directed young men to remain loyal to God and king, a quality colonial officials sought to embed in Middle East scouting troops. Local elites, however, quickly appropriated scouting, like many other institutions, for a variety of reasons, including challenging colonialism.[36] In fact, for some nationalists, the Baden-Powell model of masculinity was insufficient. Akram Zuʻaytir, a prominent Palestinian pan-Arabist, advocated in 1933 that the Arab scouts should "become a strong military organization—not boys like those of Baden-Powell, but young men who would save the country and enjoy the confidence of the people."[37]

Several scholars have pointed out how the Axis powers—and especially Fascist Italy and Nazi Germany—inspired paramilitary groups in the Middle East, such as in the use of names, salutes, uniforms, and chants.[38] Without downplaying these important crossovers, I argue these were *not* textbook Fas- cist movements as they neither advanced a radical agenda nor rejected liberal ideology nor even adhered to one strong leader.[39] In fact, a close examination of paramilitary movements in the Arab world reveals striking similarities to

Zionist militarism and its underlying anxieties regarding impaired masculinity. Not unlike European Jews, some Arab intellectuals internalized the European colonial gaze that saw them as emasculated and submissive. Racial decline, some believed, was the reason for their colonization by Europe.[40] By focusing on bodybuilding, discipline, and military parades in the streets of Cairo, Baghdad, Damascus, Nablus, and Aleppo, young Arab men believed they could restore Arab masculinity, and by extension the Arab nation. Some reminisced about the glory days of the early Islamic conquests as an inspiration for true militancy.[41] While not yet ready to take on colonialism, these paramilitary groups were preparing for such a day, or so many believed. National elites who worked inside the dual-government system and cooperated with the colonial administrations also supported this form of organizing because it allowed them to contain the activism of the middle classes who would otherwise turn their energy to revolting against the system.[42] As we will see, fear that the younger generations would try to change the rules of the game and seize power continued to preoccupy Arab regimes even after independence and in the midst of trying to prevent the creation of a Jewish state.

Among Zionist leaders in the 1930s, growing Arab resistance to the British mandate and to continued Zionist land purchases reinvigorated earlier discussions about Judaism and violence. For the majority of Zionist leaders from the Second Aliyah, neither the pacifist nor the militaristic approach appeared to meet the needs of Jews on the ground. Prominent Zionist leaders on the left, like Yitzhak Tabenkin, a leader of the kibbutz movement, and David Ben-Gurion, head of Mapai, the largest Zionist party in Palestine, adopted a middle ground on the use of force. Chaim Weizmann, who headed the ZO from London and was instrumental in securing the Balfour Declaration, adopted a similar stance.[43] Termed "the defensive ethos" by one prominent scholar, this philosophy saw the use of force as justified only in response to attacks, and that the amount of force used should be limited to fending off such attacks.[44] The defensive ethos was justified as both practical (because the Zionist community in Palestine was still small and weak) and moral. In fact, the Zionist leadership encouraged the Jews in Palestine to invest their time in settlement and agriculture and not in military training.[45]

But a final ruling on the use of force was not yet necessary, as long as the British were willing to use their military might to support Zionism. With British protection, Zionist colonization achieved immense success. Within the mandate's first decade, the Jewish community in Palestine (known as the Yishuv) not only nearly doubled in size (from 12 percent of the total population in 1922 to 20 percent in 1931) but also developed an array of institutions, including a school system, labor organizations, and healthcare infrastructure, all under the banner of socialism and Labor Zionism. Alongside them, a loosely organized paramilitary organization called the Haganah ("defense") focused initially on defending Zionist settlements. Established in 1920 from a nucleus of settlement watchmen (which dated back to 1907), the Haganah gradually professionalized with each wave of Arab resistance and began to receive British assistance in the mid-1930s.[46] The Arab population also grew in this period (from 680,000 in 1922 to 860,000 in 1931), but Palestinians did not build parallel institutions for reasons that are still debated among historians. In the initial years of Zionist colonization, it appears Palestinians did not feel a strong sense of urgency. When this changed, Palestinians discovered they were structurally excluded by the mandate state. In part due to this exclusion, the Arab economy lagged behind that of the Yishuv. Some prominent Palestinians were also reluctant to cooperate with the British for fear it would be constituted as legitimizing the mandate.[47] In 1921 the British appointed Amin al-Husayni, a member of one of the most notable families in Palestine, as Grand Mufti of Jerusalem. Shortly thereafter, the British established the Supreme Muslim Council and installed al-Husayni as its head. The council replaced the previous Ottoman religious administration and oversaw an immense source of revenue: all Islamic endowments (*awqaf*) in Palestine. The British wanted to shed responsibility for Muslim religious affairs and hoped that al-Husayni (whom they had just pardoned for nationalist activities) would be easy to control.[48]

This assumption proved correct during violent conflagrations between Palestinians and Jews in 1920–21 and 1929, when al-Husayni worked with the British to contain violence. But by the mid-1930s, Zionist land purchases and the global Great Depression had brought massive dispossession among Arab peasants in Palestine. In 1936, following a large immigration wave of Jews from Germany after Hitler's ascendance to power, Palestinians launched a general strike, followed by an armed insurrection against the British and the Yishuv alike. Initially reluctant to act against the British, al-Husayni eventually assumed a leading role in what became known as the "Great Arab Revolt." Under pressure from other political stakeholders, he established the Arab Higher Committee (AHC) to represent Palestine's Arabs (Muslim and Christian) and command the uprising. Nevertheless, the uprising was brutally crushed by the British army, with an estimated 3,800 Palestinians killed by 1939. Three hundred Jews were killed in the revolt. As factionalism intensified, the rebels themselves killed an additional 1,200 Palestinians.[49] For Mizrahi Jews who were native to Palestine and often spoke Arabic—including many who were not Zionists—these violent conflagrations were a turning point. As early as 1929, the killing of Mizrahi Jews in attacks in the mixed towns disrupted the coexistence between native Jews and Arabs and made many Mizrahi Jews turn to Zionism.[50]

Anticolonial resistance in Palestine was not only an internal Palestinian matter. Fawzi al-Qawuqji, a poster child for the "last Ottoman generation" who would lead the ALA volunteer army in 1948, provided outside help for the Palestinian revolt in 1936–39. Born in Tripoli, Lebanon, al-Qawuqji was trained in the Ottoman military school in Istanbul. He fought with the Ottoman army in the First World War, and then with King Faysal, of the Hashemite family, against the French in the short-lived Arab kingdom in Syria in 1920. Al-Qawuqji returned to fight the French in Syria in 1925.[51] Following the suppression of that revolt, he settled temporarily in Iraq, biding his time until rebellion could be resumed and Greater Syria freed and reunited. He was planning a two-pronged revolt in Syria and Palestine in the mid-1930s when he learned from his Syrian allies that an independent Syria would likely emerge from direct negotiations with the French, following a long strike organized by the nationalist opposition.[52] Reluctantly, he focused his efforts on the anti-British insurgency already under way in Palestine, but without giving up his pan-Arab rhetoric. He referred to himself as "Commander-in-Chief of the Arab Revolt in Southern Syria," which possibly strained his relationship with Amin al-Husayni, who no longer espoused a unified Syria and Palestine.[53] With the help of Yasin al-Hashimi, another ex-Ottoman officer who became the Iraqi army's chief of staff, al-Qawuqji secured weapons and ammunition for the revolt. He then sought out his comrades from the 1925–27 Syrian revolt and brought them to fight in Palestine. He recruited three hundred men in Baghdad alone, and relied on two close confidants in Damascus and Amman to help recruit several more bands.[54] Some of these people would also report for duty during later anticolonial revolts, including Palestine in 1948. As their personal letters suggest, they came to see the Arab anticolonial struggles as interconnected, whether in Baghdad, Damascus, Benghazi, or Haifa.

With the Palestinian anticolonial revolt under way, a more actively militaristic approach was also gaining momentum among Zionists, especially the so-called Sabras, the first generation of Zionist Jews born in Palestine. During the 1936–39 Arab Revolt, some of these young men and women began to publicly criticize the Yishuv leadership's official policy of *havlagah* ("restraint")—not targeting Arab civilians after the killing of Jews—which was seen as a natural extension of the defensive ethos.[55] These youth found an unlikely leader in the image of Orde Wingate, a British officer, who recruited the Yishuv's youth for a British-sponsored counterinsurgency unit known as the Special Night Squads. The unit staged raids on Palestinian villages from which attacks on Jews had been launched, but also on villages that did not participate in attacks; they killed Palestinian rebels but also civilians, including women and children. When Wingate was transferred from Palestine and his Special Night Squads disbanded, his work was continued by military leaders such as Yitzhak Sade and Yigal Allon, who would both later serve as commanders of the elite strike force of the Yishuv, the Palmach (established in 1941).[56] *Zemer ha-Plugot* ("song of the platoons"), a 1938 hymn by Nathan Alterman, the foremost poet of Labor Zionism, marked this shift from farmer to fighter: "Your boys once brought you peace by the plow / Today they bring you peace by the rifle!"[57]

For most of the 1930s, only the Revisionists, the Yishuv's organized right-wing opposition to Ben-Gurion's leadership and the defensive ethos of the Labor Zionist majority, publicly articulated a "longing to shoot."[58] By the end of the Arab Revolt, however, a handful of Second Aliyah leaders from the Left changed orientation and publicly endorsed the use of force against Palestinians. The most prominent among them was Yitzhak Tabenkin of the kibbutz movement, who exerted influence on the youth of the Palmach throughout the 1940s. Taking the Soviet Union as a role model, Tabenkin explained that it was possible to marry socialism and militarism. He assured the Sabra youth that there was no conflict between helping Arab peasants and laborers in Palestine in their supposed class struggle,[59] and at the same time establishing a Jewish armed force ready to fight these Palestinians and redeem Jewish honor.[60] Still, on the discursive level, Labor Zionism remained committed to the defensive ethos. Some scholars have argued that it never wavered in this commitment.[61] But as this book chronicles, 1948 saw a major realignment: Haganah (and later IDF) propaganda came to mimic that of the Revisionists, calling for what amounted to a celebration of violence.

On the eve of the Second World War, the British sought to reverse their pro-Zionist policy to placate Arab public opinion. Armed revolts of the kind they had encountered in Palestine from 1936 to 1939 were a major concern, and distancing themselves from Zionism presented itself as the best strategic move. The British policy paper of 1939 not only limited Jewish immigration and land purchases but also retracted a British proposal from 1937 to partition Palestine into an Arab and a Jewish state.[62] This prompted the Yishuv to openly oppose British rule, sometimes by force. In 1942, under Ben-Gurion's influence, the Zionist leadership officially declared its intentions to establish a "Jewish Commonwealth" at the end of the World War, with the understanding that such a move would inevitably mean war with the Arabs.[63]

In the aftermath of the Second World War, Palestinian nationalists moved to transform existing scouting troops into organized paramilitary youth movements.[64] In 1945 a relatively unknown attorney from Nazareth named Muhammad Nimr al-Hawari formed al-Najjada ("bravery") on the model of a similar Lebanese organization.[65] Al-Hawari sought to create a counter to the Haganah, preparing Arab youth to take military action, if necessary. Unlike the Haganah, however, al-Najjada emphasized drilling, marching, and hierarchy more broadly. Many of its commanding officers were former Arab soldiers or officers in the British army during the World War. Recruits came almost exclusively from the urban centers, rather than the countryside, which had been the main source of mobilization in the 1936–39 revolt. Although al-Najjada was not explicitly affiliated with any political group, Amin al-Husayni and his supporters saw the movement as a rival force. To counter it, they created another paramilitary organization, al-Futuwwa ("chivalry"), in 1946.[66] By late 1947 Amin al-Husayni sought to force the unification of the organizations under the leadership of one of his confidants. However, friction with al-Hawari—who may have harbored his own political ambitions—and British sabotage guaranteed that the merger never materialized.[67]

By that point the British had decided to leave Palestine. Imperial over-stretch and immense financial debt after the Second World War motivated the decision, as did concerns over Arab public opinion and the inability to reach an agreement with the United States on Palestine's future. Jewish guerrilla attacks against the British in Palestine may have also played a small role.[68] In February 1947 Britain announced that it would relinquish its mandate and referred the matter to the newly formed United Nations (UN), which in turn established the UN Special Committee on Palestine (UNSCOP) to examine the situation in the country and make recommendations about its future. While the Yishuv closely cooperated with UNSCOP, the AHC under al-Husayni's influence was reluctant, holding that "Palestine Arabs' natural rights are self-evident and cannot continue to be subject to investigation but deserve to be recognized on the basis of principles of United Nations charter ends."[69] On November 29, 1947, the UN General Assembly approved UNSCOP's plan to partition Palestine into Jewish and Arab states. Although Arabs constituted two-thirds of the population of Mandate Palestine, the Arab state was allocated only 43 percent of Palestine's territory; meanwhile, the Jewish state was allocated 56 percent of Palestine's territory, in which 45 percent of the population would be Arab. Not surprisingly, the plan was endorsed by the Yishuv but rejected by the Palestinian leadership and all Arab states.[70] The day after the UN approved partition, fighting reignited between Jews and Arabs, with the understanding that British departure would inaugurate the ultimate battle for Palestine.

A TURF WAR

The 1948 war lasted twenty months and resulted in the permanent displacement of three-quarters of Palestine's Arabs from their homes. A Jewish state was established over 80 percent of Palestine's territory, and an Arab state was not founded. On the Zionist side, the war was led by the Sabra generation and a select group of Second Aliyah veterans who had already converted to militarism. Even in the early stages of the war, their influence on Ben-Gurion was immense, and he may have feared their political power.[71] In December 1947 Ben-Gurion ordered the Haganah to switch to what he called "aggressive defense," whereby every attack would be answered by "a decisive blow," including "destroying the place [from which an attack originated] or chasing out the Arabs and taking their place."[72] In January 1948 he approved a policy suggestion by an advisor for "a vicious and forceful response" to attacks, "including [targeting of] women

and children" who were family members of militants.[73] Historians still debate
whether the depopulation of Palestine was "by design," or the impromptu initiative of local military commanders with Ben-Gurion's tacit approval.[74] His
speech to Mapai's executive leadership on February 7—just as the Palestinian
exodus started—sounds suspiciously ominous: "what happened in Jerusalem
and Haifa [the departure of Palestinians]—may happen in many other parts of
the country.... It is very much possible that in the next six, eight or ten months
of war, major changes will take place in the country, not all of which to our
disadvantage. It is certain that there would be major shifts in the composition
of the population in the country."[75] Indeed, by June 1948, under Ben-Gurion's
directive, it had become clear that the Yishuv would fight to expand the borders of the Jewish state beyond those of partition, that Palestinians who were
expelled or fled would not be allowed to return, and that their houses would
either be given to new immigrants or blown up.[76]

Younger, more militant generations also pressured Syrian president Shukri
al-Quwwatli into action in 1948. Al-Quwwatli feared losing the allegiance of
young nationalists, some of whom saw him as a relic of a distant Ottoman order.[77] And in some ways he was just such a relic: a member of a wealthy merchant
family with large land holdings, al-Quwwatli graduated from the Ottoman
school for civil servants in Istanbul in 1913. Shortly before the dissolution of
the empire, al-Quwwatli converted to Arab nationalism and supported Faysal's
short-lived Arab kingdom. The French exiled al-Quwwatli from Syria, but eventually pardoned him and allowed his return in 1930. Soon thereafter, he joined
the coalition of parties known as the National Bloc (*al-kutla al-wataniyya*),
which he eventually came to lead in 1940. Most of the bloc members, like al-
Quwwatli, were Ottoman notables and large landowners turned nationalists.
While the bloc and al-Quwwatli himself initially espoused a pan-Arab platform,
by the 1940s they had distanced themselves from the dream of Arab unification and focused on local patriotism in what had become the Syrian state. Not
altogether reluctant to cooperate with colonial powers, the bloc oversaw the
negotiations with the French for Syrian independence in 1946.[78]

The National Bloc initially attracted young middle-class men by incorporating them into an affiliated paramilitary organization, the Steel Shirts
(*al-qumsan al-hadidiyya*). The organization proved useful in containing the
activism of the middle classes, especially after the abrupt end of the Syrian

general strike in 1936. The Steel Shirts also coerced donations from merchants and provided fanfare at public rallies. But by the late 1930s, al-Quwwatli and others feared the paramilitary organization would turn against the party's leadership and decided to dismantle it.[79] With the Steel Shirts gone, many young men formerly affiliated with the bloc turned to more radical organizations like the League of Nationalist Action (ʿuṣbat al-ʿamal al-qawmi). Established in 1933 by a group of Western-educated young nationalists, the league was staunchly pan-Arab, calling for Arab states' independence from colonial rule and their unification in one Arab kingdom. Unlike the National Bloc, the league rejected any cooperation with Western powers until they renounced their imperialist designs.[80]

Largely disbanded by the end of the Second World War, some league members continued their political activism and became involved in parties like the Baʿth (established in 1947), which was instrumental in pushing now-president Quwwatli to action in Palestine in 1948.[81] Even before the UN approved the Partition Plan, the Baʿth ("revival") and other parties in Syria staged mass demonstrations and also acted in parliament to guarantee that Syria would not remain idle.[82] The day after partition was approved, on November 30, 1947, Radio Damascus reported on a large youth rally outside the presidential palace in Damascus:

> At dawn, Damascus was silent. But, later, defiance was voiced by the youth inspired by the mission of their Arab forefathers. They were heard crying: "We are at your service, Palestine! We will die for you! You will remain Arab even in the face of the opposition of all the nations of the earth!"[83]

According to the report, the youth complained that "the new political world has no conscience" and threatened to "transform the schools into barracks for the armies of Arabism."[84] As in the case of Zionism, projecting Syrian nationalism meant willingness to exercise violence to defend Arab honor. Under colonial rule, collective violence against the French had been heavily restricted. Personal letters reveal that with independence, this sort of violence was seen as possible, and exercising it to help Arabs in Palestine, who remained under the yoke of colonialism, held immense appeal.

Hearing the slogans of the youth from his office, al-Quwwatli eventually went to face the demonstrators, promising them that he would open a recruitment center for volunteers the next day in Damascus. But according to Syrian radio, his words also carried a chilling effect, aimed at keeping at least some of the youth out of the ranks of fighters: "Every able-bodied man should prepare for the defence, but those too young to serve must remain in school, to form a reserve to be drawn upon as the necessity arises."[85] Still, the next day, an official communiqué stressed that the Syrian government "shares the people's feelings" and "will participate in the fighting against the unjust, tyrannical, decision of the UN." Students and youth were asked to be ready to take up arms.[86]

The pressure on al-Quwwatli for military action in Palestine aligned well with his own desire to prevent his longtime political rival, the Hashemite King Abdullah of Transjordan (Faysal's brother), from resurrecting his family's aborted plan for a "Greater Syria." Al-Quwwatli correctly assumed that Abdullah was planning to use the crisis to take over the central hill country of Palestine (today's West Bank) as a first step. Acknowledging that the British-led Transjordanian army was far superior to his own, al-Quwwatli had to thwart Abdullah's plan without instigating a direct confrontation.[87] He also feared that Iraqi regent 'Abd al-Ilah, King Abdullah's nephew, would dispatch forces to Palestine, easing Abdullah's takeover.[88] Al-Quwwatli therefore desired an immediate military intervention, although preferably not by his own army, which was ill-equipped, untrained, and disloyal. In fact, the Syrian army was designed by French mandate authorities specifically to fight Syrian nationalism, and its officer corps was drawn from minorities and rural communities, precisely because the French believed they were the least likely to harbor nationalist sentiments.[89] A volunteer army, al-Quwwatli figured, would ease public pressure for immediate action to save Palestine without exposing the Syrian army to the threat of defeat and annihilation.[90] A volunteer army would also allow al-Quwwatli some degree of deniability and keep him from direct confrontation with the British, who were instrumental in securing Syrian independence and were still in control of Palestine.[91]

The Arab League formally announced the establishment of Jaysh al-Inqadh ("the Army of Salvation"), often referred to in English as the Arab Liberation Army (ALA), at an emergency meeting in the first week of December 1947. It was one of the first operational decisions taken by the league after its establishment in 1945.[92] The Grand Mufti of Jerusalem, Amin al-Husayni, insisted that command of the volunteer army be in Palestinian hands, namely those of his confidant and nephew, 'Abd al-Qadir al-Husayni, who would be the supreme commander of all armed forces in Palestine. Al-Quwwatli, however, had other plans. His pan-Arab army was founded to thwart certain Arab designs on Palestine as much as Zionist ones. With the support of the Arab League, 'Abd al-Qadir al-Husayni assumed leadership only of the Palestinian militia forces operating in the Jerusalem district, while the volunteer army would oversee the Galilee and the central hill country of Palestine under a different commander. Amin al-Husayni's protest was ignored.[93]

Al-Quwwatli wanted to appoint an "outsider" to command the ALA, and Fawzi al-Qawuqji was believed to be a perfect fit. Unlike many of the "last Ottoman generation," al-Qawuqji refused to settle down permanently in one Arab state; nor had he taken up a position in the dual-government system of the mandates. His participation in previous anti-British insurgencies in Palestine (from 1936 to 1939) and Iraq (in 1941) had already earned him recognition as an Arab national hero. After the British suppressed the latter revolt, al-Qawuqji found himself in Syria, where he briefly lent his services to Vichy France. Injured by British fire, he was flown to Berlin for treatment. Warmly received by Nazi officials, al-Qawuqji recuperated and helped the German war effort.[94] Six years after arriving in Germany, after the war's end, al-Qawuqji was sent to a Soviet POW camp, where he spent a few months before fleeing to liberated France. On March 2, 1947, al-Qawuqji finally returned home to Lebanon, where he found cheering crowds imploring him to save Palestine. An informant for the Haganah, assigned to monitor al-Qawuqji in Lebanon, reported on his arrival:

> Together with many other Syrians, I came to the Beirut airport to greet al-Qawuqji . . . As he stepped out of the airplane, a few Syrians asked him: "What about Palestine, o hero?", and he answered: "I devoted my blood to the Arabs, and soon you will see that the cry out of Palestine has found an echo, but I request that you not ask too many questions about this because I cannot answer these questions coming from just anyone."[95]

From Beirut, al-Qawuqji went to Tripoli, his hometown, where hundreds of people greeted him with "Welcome! We want Palestine."[96] Al-Qawuqji's appointment as ALA commander was widely popular with militant youth (among others) in Syria, Lebanon, and to some degree even in Palestine. His most vocal detractor was Amin al-Husayni, who had a long-standing quarrel with al-Qawuqji from the 1936–39 revolt and their days in Berlin during the Second World War.[97]

Al-Quwwatli also appointed Ṭaha al-Hashimi, an Iraqi army general (and Yasin al-Hashimi's younger brother), as Inspector-General of Volunteers. From his office in the Syrian Ministry of Defense, al-Hashimi controlled the enlistment, training, and transportation of volunteers to Palestine.[98] Training took place in Qatana army base near Damascus, with the vast majority arriving there in December 1947.[99] According to figures recorded at the time, 4,976 volunteers passed through Qatana by February 1948, including 2,987 Syrians, 800 Iraqis, 304 Lebanese, and 800 Palestinians who volunteered early and received training in Syria.[100] The rest were from other parts of the Arab and Islamic world, including Egypt, Sudan, Libya, Turkey, and even Saudi Arabia, Algeria and Yugoslavia. In all, the ALA volunteer army reached the size of four regular-sized battalions, although it was actually divided into eight battalions and many smaller units.[101]

Transportation to Palestine proved especially difficult because of France's and Britain's attempts to prevent the dispatch of volunteers from their former mandates.[102] Despite these efforts, several hundred ALA soldiers—primarily Syrian volunteers—first crossed into Palestine in mid-January 1948. They joined local Palestinian militia forces already engaged in fighting. The rest of the ALA, including al-Qawuqji himself, entered Palestine during the following two months. The volunteer army was most active during the first six and a half months of the war, when the British were still nominally in control of Palestine. Yet the British mostly stayed clear of the ALA, and ALA soldiers were instructed to keep their distance from the British.[103] On May 15, 1948, immediately following the final withdrawal of the British forces from Palestine and David Ben-Gurion's declaration of Israel's independence, Egyptian regular military forces invaded southern Palestine; they were followed by forces from the Transjordanian, Syrian, and Iraqi armies. (Lebanon also declared war on Israel, but its forces never crossed into Palestine.)

These armies fought the newly established Israel Defense Forces (IDF), built on the foundation of the Haganah, on multiple fronts until they were largely defeated and forced to sign armistice agreements (the first of which was signed in February 1949 with Egypt, and the last in July 1949 with Syria). At the height of the war, in October 1948, Israel had 88,000 troops, while the Arab states combined had a total of 68,000 soldiers inside Palestine. Israelis killed in the fighting amounted to between 5,700 and 5,800 civilians and soldiers, slightly less than one percent of the total Jewish population in late 1947, which stood at 628,000. The number of Palestinian fatalities is estimated at about 13,000—also about one percent of the total Arab population in Palestine at the war's start (an estimated 1.4 million people). The combined Arab armies lost about 3,500 men, the vast majority of whom were Egyptian. During the war, some 530 Palestinian villages and towns were occupied, and roughly 750,000 of Palestine's Arabs became refugees.[104]

SOURCES FROM THE CENSOR'S DESK AND THE BODIES OF THE SLAIN

The figures quoted above are certainly important for understanding the history of 1948. Yet the neat divide into sides and camps risks "adopt[ing] nationalism's own language and way of seeing the world."[105] Conversely, this book depicts identities and spaces *in formation*, as well as normal, everyday people's fear, bravery, failure, arrogance, cruelty, lies, and exaggerations. To do so, I rely principally on two types of primary sources: propaganda materials used to mobilize, educate, and indoctrinate Arab soldiers in the ALA and Jewish soldiers in the IDF during the 1948 war; and correspondence between soldiers and their families and friends from the same period (in addition to some correspondence by civilians). The origins of the propaganda materials are relatively straightforward, with many of the sources pertaining to the ALA originating from the IDF archives, where they ended up in the 1950s after Haganah soldiers took them from ALA compounds in 1948.[106] Other education and mobilization propaganda was located in libraries around the world, and especially in the Middle East.

The origins of the letters used in this book are somewhat less conventional, and very much shaped by state archival patterns. Several of the files in the ALA collection in the IDF archives, labeled "private letters" or "unidentified material," contained letters and a handful of diaries by ALA volunteers from around the Arab world and by Palestinians. It appears that the letters and diaries that ended up in the IDF archives were found by Haganah forces in the ALA headquarters, in post offices in Arab villages and towns, and on the dead bodies of enemy soldiers. These sources constitute part of the "Palestinian archive," the documents captured or looted during the 1948 war and for decades afterward in Palestine and Lebanon. These documents were later scattered in various Israeli archives, where they remain today. Initially available only to a handpicked group of scholars who were veterans of the Israeli intelligence apparatus, the "Palestinian archive" opened up in recent decades—at least partially—to the general public (but only to those not barred from visiting Israel on political grounds).[107] Indeed, as of today, Israel has liberal declassification policies (certainly compared to surrounding Arab countries). Still, obtaining access to the files used in this study entailed a decade-long legal struggle against the archives in Israel, which is still ongoing. The never-ending exchange of correspondence with a branch of the state bureaucracy is always frustrating. Compounding this has been the disingenuous use of "privacy concerns" to block access to documents written by Palestinians and seized by Jewish forces in 1948.[108] Rather than protecting the privacy of these Palestinians, I suspect that the real purpose is to obscure Israel's involvement in Palestinian displacement and maintain the officially sanctioned Israeli narrative on 1948. The chief Israeli archivist even admitted as much in a rare moment of candor in January of 2018, noting that choices of what to declassify sometimes involve "an attempt to conceal part of the historical truth in order to build a more convenient narrative," particularly those materials that might "incite the Arab population" or "be interpreted as Israeli war crimes."[109]

The other provenance of letters used for this book is the files of the Israeli censorship bureau, which secretly intercepted and copied letters by Israeli soldiers and civilians, as well as letters by Palestinians. The Israeli censorship bureau drew much of its infrastructure and methods from its British predecessor, the Imperial Censorship in Palestine, established in September 1939, as part of the network of postal censorship bureaus in all parts of the British empire.[110] The bureau in Palestine had three branches, in Haifa, Tel Aviv, and Jerusalem, where censors read letters and telegrams in a staggering eighty-six languages.[111] While the primary goals of the British postal censorship bureau were to prevent the Axis from obtaining information from letters, and to collect information helpful to the Allies from those same letters, at least some of the activity of the Palestine bureau was geared toward issues inside Palestine, such as "terrorism," "unlawful assembly," "illegal immigration [of Jews]," "drug

FIGURE 2. Mail distribution to Arab POWs during the 1948 war. Source: Israeli Defence Forces Liaison Office to the International Red Cross, *Arab Prisoners-of-War in Israel*, April 1949. Courtesy of the IDFA.

traffic," and "prostitution."[112] The censorship bureau periodically published an assortment of top-secret reports based on the letters it intercepted, some related to the war with Germany and others to Palestine.[113] Operating from within the Palestine bureau was also a military censor who would examine (and censor) the letters of British soldiers stationed in Palestine, including letters by Jewish and Arab soldiers from Palestine who had enlisted in the British army.[114] The military censor would copy excerpts from those letters and combine them into a bimonthly report, which included hundreds of excerpts from British soldiers' letters in the Middle East theatre.[115]

Long before the establishment of the State of Israel, the Haganah intelligence department, known as Shai (the Hebrew acronym for "intelligence service"), enjoyed a constant stream of many of the same letters that the British postal censorship bureau intercepted from Arabs and Jews. The demographics of the Palestine bureau may explain some of the cross-fertilization: in 1945, of the 262 people employed by the British, 198 were Jewish.[116] Although the British had staffed the bureau with such a high proportion of Jewish censors, they remained wary of the latter's loyalty. According to one audit, there was great fear in London that the chief censor in Palestine who was "married to an active Zionist and is himself a Zionist" was providing intelligence to the Haganah.[117] Whether the chief censor, Edwin Samuel, who was the son of Herbert Samuel, the first high commissioner for Palestine, ever disclosed information from the censorship bureau to the Haganah is unknown. But it was also of little importance: the Haganah managed to penetrate the British censorship bureau early on, and hundreds of documents found their way from the desks of the Jewish censors employed by the British to those of Haganah intelligence officers.[118]

One Jewish censor who was constantly on the Haganah's radar was Gershon Dror (Schwalbe), an assistant censor and the deputy head of the Haifa branch of the Imperial Censorship.[119] Dror stayed with the Palestine censorship bureau all the way to 1948, and when the British left and the Israelis came in their place, as the most senior Jewish censor, he was put in charge, guaranteeing the continuity of the imperial surveillance and record-keeping system. Officially appointed by Ben-Gurion on July 12, 1948, Dror became the chief censor of Israel, responsible for all mail, civilian and military.[120]

The Israeli incarnation of the postal censorship bureau was housed inside the Intelligence Department of the IDF and was named the Military Censor (*ha-tsenzura ha-tsva'it*). Dror himself received the rank of major and was also put in charge of press censorship in Israel, something he was unfamiliar with.[121] During a visit by Edwin Samuel, the former British chief censor, to the Tel Aviv branch of the Israeli censorship bureau in October 1949, he noted that it was "organized almost entirely on British lines" and therefore was "highly efficient."[122] He was also happy to find many of his former Jewish employees among the staff.[123] Indeed, the three branches of the Israeli censorship bureau, in Tel Aviv, Haifa, and Jerusalem, operated much as they did during the British era. Each had a staff of several dozen people, headed by a regional director, who were assigned to a part of the mail volume sent from Israel to overseas, or received from abroad.[124] Each branch compiled periodic reports on various topics of interest to the state's leaders, like the mail of Palestinian refugees, political views among Israeli citizens, the letters of new Jewish immigrants to Israel, letters by foreign correspondents stationed in Israel, and the views of tourists visiting Israel.[125] Some of these reports are used in this book.

Also under Dror's supervision was the military postal censorship, in charge of reading all letters written by IDF soldiers, formally in order to remove military secrets from them. But starting in September 1948, in addition to redacting sensitive information, the censors were instructed to copy excerpts from soldiers' letters before sending them out for delivery to their recipients. The censors were told to pay special attention to soldiers' reflections on morale, the opinions of commanding officers, food and equipment, training, cultural activity, discipline, and combat engagement.[126] In their internal memos, censors indicated that they were looking for representative letters but also for "anecdotes . . . with a high literary-artistic level, or serious and mature expression of opinions."[127] Every two weeks, the censor for military mail would go through the quotations and search for trends. He or she (the position was often filled by a female officer) would then mark specific excerpts to include in the final report, and after reviewing the decisions with the chief censor and writing a short commentary, a report was typed up and published under the title *The Soldier's Opinion (da'ato shel*

FIGURE 3. The Israeli postal censorship bureau. 4 February 1954. Photo by Avraham Vered. Source: *Bamahane*. Courtesy of the IDFA.

ha-hayal).[128] Each of these reports included several dozen relatively long excerpts from male and female soldiers' letters (some of which never made it to their recipients because they were deemed to include secret information). The reports did not include the soldiers' names or their ethnic backgrounds, but only the date on which the letters were written—and over time—their language and the soldiers' units. The first report from September 26, 1948, addressed senior political and army leaders: "We hereby submit to you the first report to express the perspectives of the most important individual in the army—the soldier—as they are reflected in his letters."[129] Dror, the chief censor, was apparently the one to devise the idea of publishing the *Soldier's Opinion* reports, another idea he borrowed from the British. In fact, the Hebrew warning that opened each *Soldier's Opinion* report—that the officers may use the information included therein provided they did not disclose the source—was copied almost verbatim from its British predecessor.[130] It is the extracts of letters included in these reports that make up part of the source material used in this book.

METHODOLOGICAL CONCERNS

Neither the British nor the Israelis were the first to spy on soldiers by monitoring their personal correspondence and reproducing it in special reports. Military postal censorship bureaus in France, Russia, Britain, the United States, and Germany engaged in similar practices starting in the First World War, and the reports they produced have served as the source material for a number of studies. The use of such sources for "history from below" raises several methodological questions. The first question is whether one can argue that letters by soldiers who were aware of the existence of censorship are an authentic reflection of their identity, or of their individual or collective "moods" more broadly. Second is the question of mediation: What role did the censors have in choosing letters to include in their reports, and were their selections predicated on their desire to please their superiors, or fear that they would be punished if they included letters that did not conform with the official "party line," or other considerations? In other words, when we read the excerpts of soldiers' letters in the censorship bureau's reports, are we reading the soldiers' voices alone? This question is pertinent, especially considering that the censors translated letters written in any language other than Hebrew, and they did not include copies of the originals.

Indeed, the authenticity of the censors' reports varied greatly from one country to another. Due to the fact that copies of the original letters (reproduced inside the reports) were available to scholars, we can surmise that the British and American censors reliably reflected the views of soldiers in their reports. Meanwhile, French and Russian censors often tailored their reports to the views of their superiors (at least in the Russian case because these censors feared for their lives).[131] I argue that the Israeli case is more akin to the organizational culture of British and American censorship bureaus than the French and Russian ones, especially during Dror's tenure as chief censor. The best evidence for the trustworthiness of the Israeli *Soldier's Opinion* reports is the relatively high number of letters critical of the army, the ruling elite, and the very existence of the state that were published by the censors and are explored in this book. Although Chief Censor Dror was not concerned about infringing on people's privacy, he saw the integrity of his reports as one of the censorship bureau's most important tasks.

In fact, in response to objections from commanders about the representativeness of the *Soldier's Opinion* report in 1950, Dror noted that his reports were not spiced up in any way and did not contain any of the censors' personal views. "We collect quotations, and I am extremely sorry that I cannot present them through rose-colored glasses, but only as they are," Dror wrote to his commanding officer.[132] The chief censor also suggested, rather brashly, that the chief of staff of the IDF call the soldiers whose letters were quoted in one of the controversial reports and "hear from them in person whether what they had written was true, or if they had made it up in their heads."[133]

At the same time that this was unfolding, the *Soldier's Opinion* report was undergoing an external review at the behest of the chief of staff of the IDF, Yigael Yadin. A specialist on public opinion, Louis Guttman of the Center for Applied Social Research, an independent institute that had been a unit inside the IDF, examined the report to assess how representative it was of the soldiers' views from a social sciences perspective. Dror had argued as early as 1949 that, "though only a small percentage of soldiers' letters is read, we believe that this small percentage faithfully reflects the soldiers' mail in its entirety."[134] The specialist on public opinion, Guttman, disagreed. He concluded that while the reports allowed for a rather cost-effective evaluation of morale in the army, they also posed several problems:

> a. Only the opinions of the soldiers are included in the reports, and it is unknown to what degree they reflect the state of mind of the rest of the soldiers [who cannot write]; b. It is hard to match the views and the personal background of the writer, as it is not mentioned in the letter . . . ; c. It is unknown to what degree the letter reflects the opinion of the writer: he might want to calm his parents, and that is why he is not complaining. Or the other way around, he might want to impress his friends by exaggeration.[135]

Still, Guttman thought that the evaluation of soldiers' morale through their correspondence was a useful tool, and that it should continue together with more "scientific" means of studying soldiers' opinions, especially using questionnaires.[136] The director of military intelligence, who also read Guttman's report, nevertheless decided to retaliate against Dror (possibly because of Dror's earlier brashness) and shut down the entire operation of producing reports based on soldiers' letters. Conveniently withholding Guttman's recommendation to continue the production of the report, the director recommended to the deputy chief of staff that the plug should be pulled on Dror's operation.[137]

The deputy chief of staff was not convinced. He ordered the publication of the *Soldier's Opinion* report to continue in more or less the same manner (which it would do until 1998).[138] But Dror did make some changes. He asked his staff to note henceforth in the reports the personal background of the soldier concerned (new immigrant, Sabra, etc.) to the degree known, identify the recipient of the letter, and—most important—state the relative prevalence of the opinions in letters that made their way into the reports.[139] Since most of these instructions were only incorporated into the report after the 1948 war had ended, I make no claim that the views of the soldiers surveyed in the following chapters are in any way representative of the entire population of soldiers (with the exception of Moroccan soldiers for whom there is data on the sample size of letters). Rather, the significance of these views is in their existence, even if there is no way to determine their statistical prevalence.

A second methodological concern, about the authenticity of the letters themselves and their ability to reflect the soldiers' cultural, ethnic, religious, or political identities, is harder to address. Israeli soldiers who wrote home in

1948 knew very well that there was another pair of eyes reading their personal letters before they reached their intended recipients. The emblem "inspected by the censor" stamped onto the envelopes was straightforward; however, it seems that most soldiers thought their letters were quickly scanned for military secrets and then passed along in a mechanized routine. The chief censor himself promoted such a belief in pamphlets distributed to soldiers:

> Rest assured that the censor, who reads your letter, knows how to keep your personal secrets. *He and only he* [emphasis in original] opens and looks at your letters, and all your personal matters that appear there are kept with him as a closely guarded secret.[140]

Officers who were in charge of composing the *Soldier's Opinion* reports in the 1950s, 1960s, and 1970s remain convinced to this day that the soldiers did not know their letters were being used for research, and so expressed themselves freely.[141] As mentioned, the writing of the soldiers themselves seems to corroborate this, for the most part. Soldiers during the 1948 war and its aftermath either ignored the censorship or at least were not fearful of it, as indicated by the critical voice adopted by many of them in their letters. This holds true for Palestinians as well, although their letters present other methodological challenges (discussed in chapter 5). In any case, I recognize that the voices of letter writers are only available to us through the filter of the censor, especially when the letters were written in a language other than Hebrew and translated inside the reports. Although I cannot speak to the level of filtration in the reports (because I do not have the original letters), the voices captured in them are still worth unearthing because they tell a story that departs significantly from the one commonly told of the war.

This new story owes a great debt to Palestinian oral history of the *nakba* ("catastrophe"). Beginning in the 1970s, studies based on interviews with Palestinians opened up a new set of questions and helped unearth marginalized narratives. The paucity of contemporaneous Arabic documents makes oral history and memoirs crucial for offsetting the dominance of the Zionist archives.[142] Still, oral histories and memoirs, often recorded decades after the fact, present their own set of challenges. In this book, which is interested primarily in the visceral reactions that events provoked in real time, I focus on archival sources that have hitherto been inaccessible (i.e., not declassified) and thus essentially unknown.[143] While I occasionally compare letters and diaries to later recollections, future work that incorporates memoirs and oral histories in a more sustained manner will enrich our understanding of 1948.

A NOTE ABOUT NAMES

The names of letter writers in this book are often fictional. There are no names in the postal censorship bureau's reports that included letters by Israeli soldiers and Palestinians from 1948–49. Therefore, all the names of letter writers derived from these sources are pseudonyms and only include a first name.[144] Meanwhile, the letters by ALA soldiers used in this study are by and large my translations from the original Arabic handwritten letters. If the original name was included in the letter, I used the full name of the author as it appeared.

WHAT'S AHEAD

This book is not an exhaustive blow-by-blow account of the 1948 war. It focuses on a handful of selected episodes from the war. It also limits the analysis to the IDF and ALA, leaving out all other Arab armies that participated in the war, for which relevant primary sources are scarce.[145] Interested readers may find more comprehensive military or diplomatic histories of 1948 readily available elsewhere.[146] Those studies, however, give little or no attention to the lived experience of the war's participants and victims. Perhaps the most acclaimed historian of the war, Benny Morris, claimed that "for all intents and purposes, the masses were silent. . . . We have no records, or almost no records, about what the masses of peasants and urban poor and soldiery thought or felt, certainly not from their own pens or mouths."[147] My analysis challenges this assertion as it takes the reader on an extended journey that explores not "what really happened," but rather what sense Arab and Jewish soldiers (and some civilians) made of 1948 as it was unfolding, or, more accurately, what sense *some* soldiers and civilians made of the war.

Chapter 1 traces the little-known grassroots activity carried out by societies, parties, and tribes to recruit men and women to fight in Palestine in 1948. Arab mobilizers appealed to pan-Arabism, and in the Jewish world, Zionist mobilizers appealed to a "pan-Judaic" sense of duty they believed all Jews should possess. The Palestine cause created a major transnational mobilization, but what that cause symbolized was radically different in Morocco, the United States, Syria, Lebanon, Iraq, and in European Displaced Persons (DP) camps where Holocaust survivors were concentrated in the aftermath of the Second World War. In fact, mobilization did not simply call on latent identities for either Jews or Arabs. It also helped mold them, creating new visions of political possibility.

In chapter 2, the focus shifts back to Palestine, where thousands of Jews and Arabs arrived in 1948 and underwent rigorous ideological training, alongside the Jews and Arabs who were already there. Propaganda answered the critical question of "who is the enemy?" and pressured soldiers to repress competing interpretations not in accord with the officially sanctioned understanding of Zionism or the brand of Arab nationalism espoused by the ALA. The chapter argues that Zionist army education officers made novel use of biblical ideas that dealt with exterminating the enemy, long suppressed in Western rabbinical tradition. In so doing, they bridged the gap between the brutal ideology of the Revisionist Right and the supposed moderate view of Labor Zionism and the Haganah. The ALA leadership also drew on religious traditions, but more pressing for them was keeping Palestine at bay and taming the enthusiasm of Arab volunteers lest their anticolonial fervor extend to fighting the Arab regimes themselves.

From the ideological training of volunteers, the book turns in chapter 3 to the Jewish and Arab recruits themselves, who explain in their own words what brought them to Palestine, and what being there meant for them and their loved ones back home. Rather than the assertion that "jihad" was the primary motivation for Arab volunteers, or that an uncomplicated sense of Jewish solidarity was behind Jewish mobilization, the chapter argues that the participation in the 1948 war was driven by complex, and often surprising, interests and causes. Chapter 4 explores the reflections on violence among perpetrators and victims, and the ways that violence brought about a revaluation of the role of community in their lives. Jewish soldiers wondered what it meant to be Jewish in an era of national sovereignty, and whether Jews, like soldiers of other nations, should enjoy the blood drawn from their enemies. Meanwhile, Palestinians and their allies wondered about the worth of pan-Arabism if it failed to save Palestine.

The last stop on the book's journey, chapter 5, captures the moment when the chaos cleared in 1949, and the results of the war became apparent: the loss of a homeland for Palestinians, and the creation of a new homeland for at least some Jews. It was then that several subgroups of Jews and Arabs wished to undo the results of the war, and go back to how things used to be: a return to Palestine for Palestinians, and a return to the comforts of the diaspora for Moroccan and some Western Jews. Other Jews were content with the revolution that 1948 had brought about: they felt they had regained their place in world history and won a seat at the table of Western nations through constitutive violence.

Chapter 1

PAN-ARAB AND
PAN-JUDAIC MOBILIZATION

IN NOVEMBER 1947, AS THE CLOUDS OF WAR DARKENED OVER Palestine and shortly before the United Nations vote on the Partition Plan, both Zionist and Palestinian leaders became increasingly concerned about securing fighters for their respective sides. The Yishuv leadership focused on mobilizing all able-bodied Jewish men and women in anticipation of the fighting. Mobilization also took part on the Palestinian side; however, weak institutions meant that the leadership there pinned most of their hopes on local recruitment in villages and neighborhoods and the enlistment of those with special skills, rather than the systematic drafting of all able-bodied men on a national scale. But the mobilization in Palestine itself was only part of the picture. For both Zionists and Palestinians, enlisting members of their ethnic/religious/national community from around the world was crucial to their respective war efforts. Indeed, recruiters were able to convince thousands of Jews and Arabs to leave their place of dwelling and travel, sometimes across significant distances, to fight in a war they knew very little about.

Both Zionist and Arab mobilizers appealed to a certain collective logic they believed existed among potential recruits: Arab mobilizers appealed to a pan-Arab sentiment, and in the Jewish world, Zionist mobilizers tried to capitalize on the public sphere inaugurated by the "Jewish international" in the mid-nineteenth century. The latter called on the sense of duty they believed

Jews ought to harbor, whether they were Zionists or not. In that sense, Zionist mobilizers tried to capitalize on a "pan-Judaic" sentiment. This chapter looks at some of those mobilization efforts, demonstrating how malleable the meaning of "Palestine" became for many of the groups seeking to recruit volunteers: being a good American Jew meant, at a minimum, generously donating to the war effort in Palestine, if not going to fight (and possibly die) alongside its Jews; being a Francophile freedom-loving Jew in colonial North Africa meant fighting for the liberty of the Yishuv; and most crucially, being a Holocaust survivor hell-bent on fighting Nazism meant becoming an Israeli citizen while still in Displaced Persons (DP) camps in Europe, and quickly shipping out to fight Nazism's newest incarnation in the form of Arab nationalism in Palestine (or so the message went). The same basic logic was at play for the mobilization of Arabs: bolstering your patriotic credentials as a Syrian or a Lebanese—especially if your reputation had been tarnished by selling land to the Zionist movement—meant sending members of your family or clan to fight partition in Palestine; and if you were a radical Syrian or Lebanese nationalist seeking to end the reign of those collaborating with colonialism while masquerading as nationalists, your first fight was in Palestine. But the opposite was also true—for Iraqi elites seeking to prolong British colonial influence in the monarchy it had installed in their country, Palestine became an ideal location to send rebellious elements.

Despite some of these fundamental similarities, the Zionist and Arab mobilizations were far from equivalent. Zionist organizations and later the State of Israel secured extensive funds and used them to bring Jews from all over the world to fight in Palestine. Meanwhile, the ALA relied of disparate societies, parties, and tribes with little state backing or funding. In fact, due to British and French pressure, Arab leaders often deliberately placed obstacles for the purpose of impeding volunteer mobilization and transportation to Palestine. Some leaders also feared that the revolutionary spirit of volunteers would eventually be turned against them.

ZIONIST AND ARAB MOBILIZATION IN PALESTINE

The Haganah began mobilizing for war in early November 1947. That month it established a recruitment center, ordering all men aged 17 to 25 to come forward and register. "These days, the vision and yearnings of eighty generations is being realized," proclaimed one recruitment poster, demanding that the youth enlist immediately because they "were honored to be the ones realizing the creation of the Hebrew state."[1] By February 1948 a general draft of all men aged 18 to 25 was announced, and by the end of the month the draft was extended for all men up to the age of 35. Even (presumably non-Zionist) ultra-Orthodox (*haredi*) men were called up. They were reassured by their leadership that all their religious needs would be met, including the observance of Sabbath, dietary restrictions, and special units composed solely of Orthodox men.[2] By April, unmarried women and married women without children aged 18 to 25 were also asked to report for noncombat duty, under the banner that each female who enlisted "releases one male soldier to the front."[3] Only the Palmach had a significant number of "combat-fit females" who were trained in sabotage and scouting, but even most of them were withdrawn from the frontlines by early 1948.[4]

Before Israel's independence on May 14, some 105,000 people had reported for conscription, of which 25,000 were drafted for active service. By the end of the month, the number grew to 45,574. In an attempt to enlist an additional 19,000 draft evaders (about 20 percent of the total men called for service) the Yishuv, and later the State of Israel, employed a series of measures including dismissal from work, fines for employers who hired draft dodgers, and restriction on overseas travel. Later, a special tribunal tried some of the evaders and jailed them.[5] Indeed, the mobilization on the Zionist side was highly effective.

Among Palestinians, mobilization was less systematic, and less effective. Declarations were grand. 'Abd al-Qadir al-Husayni, the commander of the Army of the Holy Jihad (*jaysh al-jihad al-muqaddas*), the primary military force composed almost solely of Palestinians, promised to "conquer every inch of Palestine" but in fact only mobilized men from the countryside, relying on a small group of commanders with whom he had fought during the 1936–39 Arab Revolt.[6] He also hoped that the technique of *faz'a* (alert)— where fighters would rapidly summon auxiliary forces from nearby to help a village under attack—would prove useful in blocking Jewish advances in 1948. This technique had worked well for Palestinians during the revolt, and it is possible 'Abd al-Qadir al-Husayni believed that it was more likely to attract peasants because it allowed them to continue tilling their lands until called for service.[7]

The evidence available suggests that 'Abd al-Qadir al-Husayni made only limited efforts to draw fighters from the big cities, with the exception of Jerusalem where—according to Haganah intelligence—a recruitment center was set up inside a youth club.[8] One attempt to draw in volunteers was carried out shortly before the British withdrawal from Palestine, when the Army of the Holy Jihad attempted to mobilize clerks who formally worked for the mandate authorities. Now that "a large group of these officials is released from the shackles with which they were bound," declared one pamphlet, they must step forward and enlist. Specifically, the pamphlet urged "those who are suitable for armed service" to be ready "to enter battle when asked," since "it is unreasonable that the Palestinian-educated youth avoid joining the armed activity when we see that even parliament delegates in many Arab states have registered themselves in volunteer groups."[9] Perhaps due to limited response from the educated middle class, and critique in the Palestinian press about the leadership's lackluster preparations for war,[10] the AHC made an attempt to train new cadres of Palestinian commanders from among the lower classes. In March 1948 it issued a call for young Palestinian men aged 18–30 to volunteer for special officers' training in Syria, sponsored by the Arab League. The local governing assemblies of Palestinians, known as the national committees (sing. *al-lajna al-qawmiyya*[11]) in Jaffa, Jerusalem, and Nablus, were quick to advertise the call in local newspapers.[12] Many apparently applied, but only ten young men from notable families were eventually admitted and sent for training in Damascus.[13]

The defense front was spearheaded by local initiative rather than by the AHC. Immediately after partition was endorsed by the UN, the Committee for Arab Jihad (*lajnat al-jihad al-'arabi*), an organization about which little is known, issued a call for all Palestinians "to arm up" in order to defend themselves and "the inhabitants of every neighborhood and village." The organization stipulated that all young men had to be ready to fight "at any moment, without being asked," and promised that further instructions on military engagement would be provided by a new radio station.[14] Towns and neighborhoods also started their own mobilization campaigns, including the Musrara neighborhood in Jerusalem, Nablus, Jenin, Tulkarm, Jaffa, and Tiberias. In Tiberias the national committee ordered all men between the ages of 17 and 40 to report to the local branch of the unified al-Najjada and al-Futuwwa organization to register their names for military service.[15] The national committee even wrote Syrian authorities in March 1948, requesting their help in returning a number of young men who ran away "to escape their difficult duty."[16] In Jaffa the city's security council, headed by Muhammad Nimr al-Hawari, who was also the director of al-Najjada, issued a call to all residents, urging them to participate in the defense of the city. The Zionists, one pamphlet stressed, planned "to colonize our souls, rule our country, destroy our holy places and control our future generations."[17] To stop them, Jaffa's leadership emphasized, the inhabitants must form "an impervious dam." Those who had useful skills were ordered to step forward and present themselves to the authorities. However, the city's inhabitants were also warned to "limit their efforts individually and collectively only to defense and warding off attacks" while leaving "general politics" and "jihad for the sake of God" to the leadership. In other words, the mobilization was for defensive purposes only, not for all-out war.[18]

A more systematic effort to mobilize Palestinian fighters was made by the Arab Liberation Army, but with limited success, perhaps because of Amin al-Husayni's call to Palestinians in pamphlets not to cooperate with the volunteer army.[19] Like 'Abd al-Qadir al-Husayni, al-Qawuqji too had hoped to leverage his reputation from fighting in Palestine during the 1936–39 Arab Revolt to attract young Palestinian fighters. On March 13, 1948, he issued guidelines for drafting Palestinian men: A recruit must be between the ages of 18 and 40, with a clean bill of health and no criminal record. The most important condition, however, was that the recruit "be known for his national aspirations and lack of cooperation with the enemies of the land, and that this be certified by the national committees."[20] Al-Qawuqji assured the Palestinian recruits that they would be assigned to protect their own villages, or nearby ones, and that their pay would be equivalent to that of other Arab volunteers, with the exception of food allowances.[21] By late April, al-Qawuqji, in desperation, tried to impose a draft on Palestinian men by calling on the mayors, chairmen of national committees, and other officials to send five men for every thousand inhabitants with a weapon and a hundred bullets each within a week.[22] That measure too was only partially successful, perhaps due to limited cooperation from the national committees, prompting al-Qawuqji on April 30 to try yet another approach of subordinating Palestinians serving in the Palestine police to the ALA. Al-Qawuqji promised the policemen—still in British employment—that their pay would remain the same if they agreed to enlist and demanded that they give up their weapons if they refused. Those who failed to join or yield their weapons would be required to pay a fine, to be collected from the officer or "his family or clan." Moreover, these draft evaders would "be completely prevented from being employed in any capacity when the Palestinian government is formed"—that is, after Zionism was defeated.[23]

Even if most of the Palestinian elite sided with Amin al-Husayni and were reluctant to join the ALA, some local leaders actually called their followers to join the volunteer force precisely because of al-Qawuqji's strained relationship with the mufti.[24] The resistance to al-Husayni and his sectarian and authoritarian rule dated back to the 1930s. The mufti not only exclusively funneled money through the Supreme Muslim Council to a select group of elites affiliated with the Husayni clan but also was reluctant to act against the British well into the Arab Revolt of 1936–39. When he finally assumed the leadership of the revolt, his supporters resorted to violence against those who defied his rule.[25] Alluding to those difficult times in Palestine, a notable from Haifa, Hanna Badr Salim, wrote the editor of *al-Difa'* (Defense) in February 1948 that "we waged war on Zionism, but we were unprepared" because "we were busy fighting one another, which distracted us from the danger."[26] Now, he reassured the readers, Palestinians had sufficient weapons for defense purposes, "but the upsetting thing is that the armed men in this country are unorganized and lack a general command to guide them." This made the defense strategy of Palestinians haphazard and encouraged a lack of initiative. The solution, according to Salim, was the ALA, "which had proven to be well-trained, knows the art of war, and specializes in lethal strikes against the enemy." This orderly conduct, Salim insisted, was the only way to strike back at the organized Yishuv:

> We advise everyone who truly wishes to take part in the defense of Arab Palestine to join the ALA, and by doing so to guarantee victory and save ourselves from many of the hardships of war. A revolution on its own will not be enough against an enemy whose virtues are punctuality and order.[27]

As we will see, Salim was not the only notable to give an accurate assessment of the strength of the Yishuv in real time. This danger prompted some prominent Palestinians to have second thoughts about sectarianism (ultimately, too late). Even Amin al-Husayni himself may have realized that his rivalry with al-Qawuqji and internal opposition were detrimental to the war effort. According to a Palestinian informant—placed by the Haganah inside the ALA training camp in Qatana—the mufti had visited the camp in early 1948 and delivered a surprising speech, given his own role in promoting sectarianism in Palestine. In Qatana, the mufti warned volunteers not to repeat the mistakes of 1936–39, when Palestinians turned against one another, informed on rebels, "stole and exhorted money, and received bribes from the Zionists."[28] But the last part of his speech was perhaps the most remarkable considering the mufti's own attempts in the early 1940s to destroy al-Qawuqji's public image by alleging he was a British spy. In his speech the mufti admonished "those who plotted to kill the commander, Fawzi al-Qawuqji, who escaped them."[29]

In any case, whatever the mufti's true intentions in his speech, in Palestine, 'Abd al-Qadir al-Husayni's Army of the Holy Jihad still tried to poach those Palestinians who ended up joining the ALA and had gone through training in Qatana.[30] But even those Palestinians fighters who stayed with the ALA were not fully utilized by the volunteer army in battle. Some of the ALA field commanders, themselves career officers from other Arab states, did not trust the Palestinian recruits. They assumed Palestinians would primarily be motivated by personal and clan-based vendettas going back to the internal rivalries in Palestine during the 1936–39 revolt.[31] "I cannot control the Palestinian soldiers," warned a company commander in a letter to the commander of Hittin battalion, the unit with the most Palestinian recruits.[32] In internal correspondence between the battalion, stationed in Tulkarm, and al-Qawuqji's headquarters, another officer recommended that the local Palestinian units be led by Syrian, Egyptian, or Iraqi officers and not by Palestinians, "so that there would not be jealousy and hatred between the residents."[33] If such officers could not be found, and no other option existed, then "it will be possible to choose people of the educated youth that have gone through military training, on the condition that they will not come from the residents of Tulkarm."[34] In other words, Palestinians were only to be stationed to defend areas with which they did not have a direct connection. But even with officers from the Palestinian "educated youth," ALA commanders still believed that the Palestinian units "cannot be trusted to carry out operations for the greater good," and ALA officers continued to express fear that Palestinians would act in their own self-interest, carrying out robberies.[35]

There are no reliable figures for the number of Palestinians who fought with the ALA besides the 800 Palestinians who trained in Qatana. Apparently, most Palestinians joined the ALA in fighting only on a temporarily basis.[36] Meanwhile, 'Abd al-Qadir al-Husayni's Army of the Holy Jihad, and other smaller forces ostensibly under his command, are estimated at about 1,600 men. Independent Palestinian militias had about 750 men, and local town garrisons that existed in some cities numbered around 1,500 people.[37] Several hundred additional young men also fought as part of scout movements, primarily al-Najjada and al-Futuwwa. However, rivalry between the two organizations and the ousting of al-Najjada's director, Nimr al-Hawari, by Amin al-Husayni in December 1947 made their fighting ineffective throughout the war.[38]

COMPULSORY CONSCRIPTION IN DP CAMPS

The Displaced Persons (DP) camps in the American zone in Germany, where hundreds of thousands of Holocaust survivors were concentrated in the immediate aftermath of the Second World War, were an ideal location for recruiting fighters for the new Jewish state. There were virtually no restrictions there, with Haganah recruiters accorded free rein by the American authorities. Of the 23,300 recruits among Holocaust survivors (known as *giyus huts la-'arets* or "recruitment outside Israel" and by the Hebrew initials *Gahal*), thousands were members of the youth movements who willingly volunteered, either out of a sense of Jewish solidarity and/or their Zionist convictions. But many Holocaust survivors, even Zionist ones, were not necessarily interested in going to fight in Palestine shortly after surviving the Nazi extermination campaign. To convince them, the Zionist movement launched a massive propaganda campaign, stressing a "pan-Judaic" duty to fight in Palestine, and eventually claiming Holocaust survivors in camps as *de jure* Israeli citizens, subject to mandatory conscription by the IDF.[39]

Zionism was initially very influential in the DP camps established in the American zone in Germany. Many members of youth movements were eager to immigrate to Palestine from 1945 onward. Some had intended to establish kibbutzim upon their arrival.[40] Those who were able to embark on the journey were often captured by the British and deported to internment camps in Cyprus. Others, like the 4,052 men, women, and children aboard the ship *Exodus 1947* (also known as *yetsi'at eyropah*), were prevented from landing on the shores of Palestine and sent back to Europe, while the entire international community was watching.[41] Knowledge of the six million Jews exterminated by Nazi Germany made little difference to the British. By late 1947, realizing that immigration to Palestine would be extremely difficult, many Holocaust survivors started contemplating going elsewhere. An atmosphere of depression was widespread.[42] The Palestine Partition Plan gave new hope to tens of thousands of survivors lingering in DP camps that their immigration to Palestine would soon become possible.[43] It was exactly at that point that Haganah commanders also started to look to the survivors in DP camps as potential recruits for the Yishuv armed forces.

The Haganah was well placed to start a massive recruitment campaign in late 1947. Since 1946 Haganah instructors, led by an army officer, Nahum Shadmi, had worked to train young men and women in DP camps in self-defense.[44] When partition was approved by the UN, Shadmi, on his own volition, started to promote the drafting of Holocaust survivors. Ben-Gurion only came around to the idea in February 1948, instructing all officials dealing with immigration of European Holocaust survivors to focus solely on the immigration of young men and women of military age.[45] But when the necessary funds for such a massive recruitment operation failed to arrive from Palestine, Shadmi decided he would collect at least some of the money from Holocaust survivors themselves. He launched a fundraising campaign in three occupied zones in Germany (and in Italy) and managed to raise a staggering sum of 330,000 dollars (more than 3.1 million in 2020 dollars).[46] This money presumably came from personal funds recovered by Holocaust survivors in the aftermath of war, or money earned from work inside and outside DP camps.

The funds collected by Shadmi were used to set up recruitment and training centers in DP camps. Although overseen by the Haganah, much of the enlistment was carried out by the five major youth movements operating in the camps.[47] The stated aim was to recruit every able-bodied young man and woman between the ages of 17 and 32.[48] At first, an appeal to Jewish solidarity was aimed at convincing the youth of DP camps to volunteer to fight for a Jewish state in Palestine. This was not a new approach—Jewish solidarity had been an effective mobilization technique for collecting donations for Jewish communities in crisis for centuries. But the Zionist emissaries working in DP camps in 1947–49 wanted to make sure that the youth realized that donations were no longer sufficient, and actual fighting was necessary. One pamphlet stressed that the youth "know that they are not only fighting for themselves, but for the [entire] long-suffering Jewish people."[49] Jews around the world needed to reinforce their solidarity to protect the Jews of the Arab world "who are under the threat of extermination" but also to protect Jews who were currently living comfortably but whose fortunes could change at any time. "Will we let Palestine's youth fight on their own for our struggle? Will we look indifferently at the bloody struggle in Palestine, only to be the first to enjoy victory when it is all over?" asked another pamphlet. For any who were hesitant, Zionist youth movements added that it was "a duty of honor" and "a Jewish holy work" from which no one may escape.[50] Other slogans distributed in DP camps carried a similar "pan-Judaic" logic, proclaiming that "Generations have waited, you won, fulfill your duty!" and "Go today, tomorrow may be too late!"[51] Some 40,000 Zionist youth in DP camps who were nominally Haganah members (but did not necessarily intend to immigrate to Palestine immediately) were likely also reminded of the oath they were required to take several years earlier when the Haganah first started operating in DP camps.[52] With one hand on the Hebrew bible, both men and women swore "to defend the lives, well-being and honor of Jewish brethren everywhere, and in compliance with orders of my superiors and to devote my life to the Zionist-pioneering war for the national independence of the People of Israel."[53]

The call to become "a nation like all other nations" and normalize the use of force became a crucial theme in the indoctrination of soldiers after arriving in Israel, as the next chapter demonstrates. But the efforts to convince Holocaust survivors that force was the only way to solve the problems facing the Jewish people had already begun in the DP camps. As another pamphlet explained, in denigration of what had been taught in the past: "The doctrine of exile stipulated that you lower your head and wait until the storm passes. The doctrine of exile commanded us to cry over the victims but not to defend them, not to avenge." Then came the first organization for Jewish self-defenders, responding to the Kishinev pogrom of 1903. Members of the organization decided to take up "guns, knives, stones and sticks" and strike back against the assailants. "It was then that the free Jew was reborn, a proud Jew, who cares about honor as much as he cares for his own life. It was then that the spirit of pioneering and defense was born. This is the spirit we use to build our old-new homeland."[54] Indeed, proud Jews "decided not to be passive anymore in the Jewish struggle for freedom".[55] If Holocaust survivors also wanted to abandon passivity, they must join the fight in Palestine.[56]

While many members of youth movements were quick to present themselves for recruitment, the optimism that thousands of young men and women would seize the opportunity to be drafted and shipped to Palestine began to dissipate.[57] One youth movement assessed that hundreds of its members evaded conscription.[58] "Our efforts are not commensurate with the severity of the moment," explained an internal memo, suggesting that the youth be told that the Jews of Palestine have already sacrificed for the sake of Holocaust survivors, and therefore it was now the time to repay in kind.[59] But when that tactic too failed in late February 1948, Shadmi, the Haganah commander in Europe, offered Ben-Gurion a revolutionary idea: declare that all DP residents were now *de jure* under the jurisdiction of the Yishuv's Jewish National Council and hence subject to the mandatory conscription already enforced in Palestine. In the words of Shadmi, years later:

> We are demanding compulsory conscription of the Jews in the camps, as if they were citizens of Israel and not of Germany. . . . They are citizens of Israel who are prevented from coming to Israel, but they are still citizens of Israel. The moment compulsory conscription is applied to Jews in Israel of a certain age, the same must be applied among the Holocaust survivors.[60]

This was no abstract idea. Indeed, by May 1948, DP camp residents received draft orders signed by the State of Israel, where each individual was ordered to report for conscription, and threatened that "failing to report for duty in the specified time would be interpreted by us as defection and we will take the appropriate measures."[61]

Shadmi and others failed to realize that the fact many Holocaust survivors declared themselves as Zionists or voted for Zionist delegates in DP camps elections did not mean they were willing to go fight for the new Jewish state just three years after the end of the Second World War.[62] Indeed, many attempted to evade conscription by any means possible. The "draft-dodgers" were a primary target for propaganda campaigns in the camps.[63] One pamphlet distributed in German DP camps, "Trial of a Dodger," included an entire theatrical play of a trial against a Holocaust survivor who refused to be sent to fight in Palestine.[64] This time the language was far more radicalized: "The same Nazi hand, in a new garb, started to extinguish the only illuminating torch [the Jewish state] for the sons of Zion." Not only were the Arabs the new Nazis, "the Jewish Yishuv is facing a cruel reality: be exterminated or fight till the last man for the future of the country and the Jewish people."[65] Indeed, the pamphlet repeated again and again that the current war was the ultimate battle for the Jewish people, and therefore the decision of the defendant to evade conscription was unacceptable.

According to the narrative related in the play, the defendant had lost his entire family in the Holocaust and had several other personal circumstances preventing him from enlisting despite having declared himself a Zionist. The prosecutor dismissed these explanations, and insisted that the defector had to be punished severely: "If we were a state like all others we would have sentenced a defector as all states do." What such a sentence in other states entailed was not laid out in the text. But the implication was clear: jail or even death, the common sentences for defectors in many armies at the time, was what the defector deserved. "But since we do not have the power of a state, I suggest we put the defendant in the shame corner as a coward. And after the war, when the gates of the Land of Israel open, we would discuss whether the defendant has a right to come to Israel or whether he be sentenced to eternal exile."[66]

To convince the defector-defendant to enlist, several witnesses appeared: a bereaved mother of a soldier urged him to "take up the banner" that fell from the hands of her dead son; a Haganah fighter explained that in Palestine even elderly and teenagers fight, and therefore the defendant cannot be excused. "Tomorrow this very well may be pointless," the fighter stated, warning the defendant of a possible Jewish defeat. A partisan was also summoned to show the defendant that other Holocaust survivors did not evade their duty to the Jews of Palestine, even shortly after fighting the Nazis in the forests. The partisan apologized that he had so little time to talk, "as a car is waiting to take me to the recruiting office." When the witnesses finished their testimonies without the defendant changing his mind, the prosecutor pleaded with the court for a verdict that would be severe "so as to serve as a warning for all the youth survivors in DP camps." But a verdict was unnecessary, at least in this imaginary trial, because the defendant changed his mind: "I ask that the jury release me immediately because I am going straight to the recruiting station."[67] These theatrics, no doubt, would have been immensely traumatizing for Holocaust survivors. One can only imagine the pressure felt by those who viewed the play.

At the same time, more violent steps were taken to convince those who refused to enlist. Already in March 1948 the third congress of Holocaust survivors in DP camps decided that those who evaded the draft "would be excluded from social and political life."[68] By mid-April those who refused to present themselves for conscription were fired from their jobs and many were fined; some had their apartments taken from them, and others were denied additional food rations. Quite a few, apparently, were beaten by Zionist activists in the camps. Finally, the conscription committees in DP camps published "shame lists" with the names of those who refused to enlist.[69] This abuse was made possible by the fact that the American authorities allowed much of the DP camps to be self-governed by camp committees, which were largely Zionist. Apparently, only after complaints to the American administration did some of the harassment stop.[70]

Conscription and the coercive measures that accompanied it continued until April 1949, when the IDF delegation (which replaced that of the Haganah in June 1948) returned to Israel.[71] The delegation's activities in DP camps were considered a major success. All told, 23,300 Holocaust survivors had enlisted in the IDF by the end of the war. The majority came from DP camps, but several thousand were drafted in eastern Europe or in the British internment camps in Cyprus. Some were briefly trained in Marseille or Cyprus before their departure to Israel by ship.[72] On board the ship, Holocaust survivors were told they were about to join "one of the world's best armies."[73] The reason for the success was neither equipment nor the number of soldiers, but rather "its victories came to it only because of the immortal bravery of its fighters, because of their willingness to make any sacrifice necessary." The survivors were asked to make the same kind of sacrifice. Upon their arrival, many were immediately assigned to fighting units, with little or no training.[74]

DYING FOR AMERICA, DYING FOR ISRAEL

Recruitment of Jews in other Western countries was far more difficult, since the laws of most nations prohibited serving in a foreign army.[75] Still, in the course of the war, 3,500 Jews from wealthy countries traveled to Palestine to join the fighting.[76] They were referred to collectively in Hebrew as *mitnadvey huts la-'arets* (volunteers from overseas), and were known by the Hebrew initials *Mahal*. While about 40 percent of these volunteers came from the United States, recruitment also took place in Latin America, Canada, South Africa, Britain, France, and elsewhere.[77] In the US the Haganah had a major propaganda arm and a small clandestine recruitment agency. Those who volunteered did so at significant risk and were sometimes the target of FBI investigations (even if eventually no action was taken against most of them).[78]

The focus of the Haganah in the United States was not volunteers. An organization known as the Sonneborn Institute primarily dealt with securing weapons and trying to bypass the arms embargo imposed on Palestine by the US State Department in December 1947. A separate venture, created jointly by several Jewish organizations and headed by the wealthy businessman and philanthropist Abraham Feinberg, was named Americans for Haganah. Formally affiliated with the Haganah in Palestine, it focused on collecting donations and publishing a bimonthly subscription-based magazine, *Americans for Haganah* (later, *Haganah Speaks*), which was in wide circulation from August 1947 and also published in Yiddish.[79] For the most part, the magazine did not directly urge American Jews to join the fighting in Palestine, likely because such recruitment would have been considered illegal under US law.[80] Rather, it provided extensive news coverage of the war and the attempts of Holocaust survivors to immigrate to Palestine.[81] The magazine presented itself as a dependable source of information, compared with British news outlets that relied on the mandate authorities. "To be of help in the present crisis, you must get the facts straight. Read *Haganah Speaks*. Pass it to your friends. Get them to subscribe. Use it to win new friends for Haganah," entreated one advertisement.[82] The magazine also initiated several donation campaigns, both for equipment and funds, and called on American Jews to pressure their government to lift the arms embargo and recognize the State of Israel.[83]

As was done to mobilize Jews elsewhere in the world, *Americans for Haganah* emphasized a theme of "pan-Judaic" solidarity, and often provided news from other Jewish communities, like the Jews of Arab lands whom the magazine insisted were "hostages" who "sit on an active volcano."[84] "The Jews of Palestine rely on the Jews of the world to make available sufficient arms and manpower to defend the new state," another piece explained.[85] Arabs were presented as Nazi sympathizers and collaborators, and pictures of severed corpses of Jewish soldiers were printed under headlines such as "They Mutilate the Dead."[86]

As early as the first issue, the Haganah headquarters sent a greeting to the new magazine emphasizing that Haganah is "the democratic voluntary army of the Jewish people. To its ranks belong all able-bodied young Jewish men and women of all classes and political parties."[87] Indeed, this was a novel claim, suggesting that the Haganah was the army of the entire Jewish people, not just those living in Palestine. Not unlike the tactic used in DP camps—but much more subtly—this too was a claim on American Jews' national belonging, and perhaps even citizenship. While the authors likely did not believe that many American Jews would give up their American citizenship (to allow for their lawful enlistment), the principle still stood: as *de facto* nationals of a Jewish polity, they must do their part.

The magazine often commemorated American Jews who died fighting in Palestine, but without explicitly calling for readers to follow suit.[88] Several stories were devoted to David "Mickey" Marcus, a Second World War colonel with the US army who volunteered as part of Mahal and was accidentally killed by an IDF soldier prior to the first truce in June 1948. One article emphasized the impact visiting the Nazi concentration camp in Dachau had on Marcus: "What he saw there brought home to him with terrible impact the need for a Jewish State where Jews would never again be subjected to such inhumanity."[89] His death, the magazine made clear, should serve as an example: "Colonel Marcus believed in America, he loved America, he was ready to die for America. In dying for Israel, he truly died for America."[90] Indeed, to be considered an exemplary American Jew, one had to pledge his or her allegiance not just to America but also to Israel, since the two shared common values.

The magazine heavily advertised its speaking bureau, which supplied "American and Palestinian [Jewish] speakers for non-sectarian, Zionist and non-Zionist groups and organizations."[91] By July 1948 these talks were often accompanied by the screening of a Haganah-produced film, *The Illegals*, which portrayed the journey of Holocaust survivors to Palestine and their capture by the British mandate authorities.[92] It was in these talks and screenings in synagogues and community centers that volunteers were recruited. In fact, Zionist activists in the United States managed to get their hands on a list of Jewish recruits in the American armed forces during the Second World War, which included not only names but ranks, military professions, and addresses. Some of these men were approached and invited to talks by the Haganah in their hometowns, where they were eventually asked if they were willing to volunteer for the Jewish armed forces in Palestine.[93] Other times it was young Jewish men themselves who actively sought to volunteer. They would call various Zionist societies operating in the United States and also approach speakers who came to their communities to give talks.[94]

Much of the actual recruitment process was overseen by Land and Labor for Palestine, an organization that disguised itself as a society to bring agricultural workers to Palestine. Staffers in the Jewish Agency[95] office in New York were told that whenever phone inquiries were made about volunteering to fight, they should answer: "You realize that there is not [*sic*] recruiting in the USA for military service in Palestine. However, would you care to go to Palestine and work and carry out whatever duties you may have to as a volunteer worker?" Those who answered affirmatively were sent to the local office of Land and Labor.[96] After a personal interview, medical examination, and a psychological evaluation, the volunteers were given equipment and flown to Palestine. The necessary documentation often had to be forged to circumvent the State Department's prohibition on US citizens serving in foreign armies.[97] Polling data for the North American volunteers suggests that their average age was 25.3 years.[98] The North American volunteer community was highly educated: 61 percent of all volunteers had postprimary education, and half were college students at the time they volunteered.[99]

MOROCCAN LOVERS OF LIBERTY

In North Africa, recruitment in 1948 was centered in Morocco, a French protectorate since 1912, which preserved the country's Islamic sultanate, dating back to the seventeenth century. Between 645 and 1,600 North African Jews, the overwhelming majority of them Moroccan, came to Israel and served in the IDF during the war. They were part of a group of 20,000 Moroccan Jews (out of a community of 250,000) who immigrated to Israel in 1948–49. Like European Holocaust survivors, the Moroccan soldiers in the IDF were part of the *giyus huts la-'arets* (recruitment outside Israel), known by the Hebrew initials Gahal.[100] However, unlike in DP camps, recruitment in Morocco was carried out at considerable risk to volunteers, as both Moroccan nationalists and the French police were looking to stop them. In June 1948 the tension following the departure of volunteers to Israel exploded in the form of a massacre of forty-four Jews in Oujda and Jerada, border towns used by the Haganah for the departure of young Moroccan Jews to Israel.

As in most struggles for national liberation from colonial rule in the Middle East and North Africa, the anticolonial and nationalist fronts in Morocco also stressed their opposition to Zionism from the mid-1930s as part of their alliance with the Arab and Islamic world. The Palestine question gradually became visible in Morocco in the form of solidarity movements and donation campaigns.[101] The Arabic press in the country played a key role in this process. While news from Palestine was often used as a rallying cause for pan-Arabism, virulent anti-Zionist publications were rather rare due to the heavy censorship imposed by the French colonial authorities.[102] A November 1945 article in the newspaper *al-Wahda al-Maghribiya* (North African Unity) called on Muslims and Arabs to mobilize to defend Palestine and warned that "if Palestine is gone from our hands, it would be like the explosion of an atomic bomb inside the body of the Arab and Islamic world."[103] Although most articles attempted to distinguish between Moroccan Jews and Zionists (in Palestine and in Morocco), not all newspapers kept this distinction. One article from June 1947 in *al-Shabab al-Maghribi* (The Moroccan Youth) resorted to European-style antisemitic propaganda: "The truth is that they rise up against us secretly by transferring the wealth of Morocco to their pockets without us sensing the danger that threatens our Moroccan homeland."[104] The author explained that "the Jew" used every means of fraud and seduction to collect money because "money is his homeland and his dignity."[105] Because Jews were supposedly transferring a portion of their earnings to fund the Zionist movement, and because Jews in Palestine were boycotting Arab goods, the article proposed a boycott of Jewish businesses in Morocco.[106]

Tension in Morocco rose considerably with the vote on partition in the UN. Concerned for the safety of their communities, Jewish leaders demanded increased protection, and these requests were reportedly answered by the sultan's government (Makhzan) and the French authorities. During the month of December 1947, the sultan, Muhammad V, warned the nationalist leadership not to exploit the war in Palestine to destabilize Morocco. To Jewish leaders he stressed the importance of cooperation with Muslims in Morocco.[107] It is likely that these measures influenced the actions of nationalists, especially those of Istiqlal, the largest political party. In the first months of 1948, the party, which emphasized Morocco's pan-Arab identity, published a proclamation denouncing partition and criticizing the government's decision not to send Moroccan soldiers to Palestine. However, the proclamation also called for restraint inside Morocco, and to not allow tensions to escalate into violence. "Our goal is only the struggle against Zionism, without any resentment towards our fellow Jews who are of Moroccan nationality just like we are, and who are subject to the authority of the sultan like us."[108]

The press coverage of partition and the war that ensued was less nuanced. An article in Istiqlal's mouthpiece, *al-'Alam* (The Flag), warned that the partition of Palestine threatened not only Arab achievements up to that point but the survival of Arabs as a nation.[109] The smaller nationalist party, Parti Démocratique pour l'Independence (Democratic Party for Independence or PDI), composed of middle-class businessmen and merchants, was more aggressive in its response. On January 1948 the party mouthpiece, *al-Rai al-'Amm* (Public Opinion), published a call to boycott all Jewish businesses:

> You noble Moroccan, know that when you give one dirham to a Zionist you destroy an Arab house and fund the treacherous Zionist state. . . . Don't buy your medicine in a Zionist pharmacy, don't seek treatment with a Zionist [doctor], don't give your cloth to a Zionist tailor, don't cut your hair at a Zionist [barber], don't take your photo with a Zionist photographer . . . and remember that every Jew is a supporter of Zion.[110]

The press also printed rumors from Palestine about Jewish forces poisoning wells and reports about massacres and the rape of Arab women.[111]

Faced with escalating tension after Israeli independence was declared, the sultan published another proclamation on May 28, 1948, stressing his support for the Arab League's decision to send the regular Arab armies into Palestine in order to defend its inhabitants against Zionist aggression. After paying lip service to pan-Arabism, the sultan made a special effort to distinguish between Jews and Zionists: "The Arabs do not bear a grudge against Jews and do not hate them . . . Their goal is to defend Islam's first Qibla,[[112]] and to establish peace and justice in the Holy Land, while Jews remain in their customary position since the Islamic conquest."[113] This "customary position" was the classical Islamic principle of *ahl al-dhimma*, which referred to Jewish and Christian residents of an Islamic state who were entitled to protection in return for submission to Muslim rule and paying a special tax. Unlike other localities that were under direct French or British rule, the lingering existence of the Moroccan sultanate from before the French occupation ensured that this concept was still relevant in Morocco in 1948.[114] The sultan wanted to make sure the Muslim population in his kingdom remembered the Jews' "customary position," to avoid outbreaks of violence:

> We order our Muslim subjects not to be caught, because of what the Jews do to their Arab brothers in Palestine, doing any act that compromises the regime or disturbs security and peace. They must know that these Moroccan Jews settled in this country centuries ago as protected subjects [*dhimma*], and they found it to be the best place for dwelling and were completely loyal to the Moroccan throne. These are not the wandering Jews who traveled to Palestine from around the world and wanted to violently and unjustly seize it.[115]

Finally, the sultan warned his Jewish subjects against extending support to Zionists in Palestine or Morocco. Doing so, he warned, would jeopardize their civil rights and their Moroccan citizenship.[116]

Even with tensions rising after the approval of the partition plan, very few Moroccan Jews actually considered leaving Morocco and immigrating to Israel, and even fewer considered fighting for the new Jewish state. Some Moroccan Jews saw themselves as loyal Moroccan patriots, others as committed communists, and both resisted the influence of Zionist activists in the country.[117] But as noted, within less than a month after the establishment of the State of Israel, the situation in Morocco dramatically changed with the June 7 riots in the towns of Oujda and Jerada, where forty-four Jews were killed.[118] Most scholars agree that the riots were fueled by the war in Palestine, although whether the attacks were premeditated remains a point of controversy.[119] The two towns were a transfer point for trafficking goods and people in and out of Morocco, and Zionist activists often smuggled immigrants through the area en route to Palestine. While some benefited from the smuggling business, for many in the Muslim community the departure of Jews to aid the Yishuv in Palestine was seen as a great threat. In fact, nationalists from the eastern province, where Oujda and Jerada are located, often used the crossing of Jews as a pretext to attack the French colonial authorities, alleging that they were turning a blind eye to the border crossings.[120] In the weeks preceding the riots, Istiqlal mobilized the local community for a general strike, calling for the boycott of Jewish merchants and holding rallies in support of Palestinians.[121]

Under the influence of the Makhzan, most of the Moroccan general press sought to downplay the importance of the killings in Oujda and Jerada and their intercommunal nature. The number of casualties was not reported, and some newspapers portrayed the events as local disputes between Jews and Muslims. The nationalist opposition, on the other hand, blamed the French colonial authorities for the violence and for allowing the smuggling of Jews into Palestine through the eastern province.[122] The newspaper of the smaller nationalist party, PDI, justified the attacks, stating that it was aimed at stopping young Moroccan Jews from joining the fighting in Palestine:

> The Moroccan people cannot continue sitting around doing nothing in the face of the recruitment of Jewish volunteers and their departure to Palestine . . . Jews must understand that in Morocco they are in an unusual situation which does not allow them to hurt the feelings of Muslims and provoke them.[123]

Jewish organizations around the world condemned the killings and attempted to put pressure on the Makhzan and the French authorities to better protect their Jewish subjects.[124]

The anxiety of the Jewish population following the Oujda and Jerada massacre provided an opportunity for extensive Zionist activity, and especially attempts to recruit Moroccan Jewish youth to the IDF as part of Gahal.[125] Spearheading that effort were the Zionist youth movements that redoubled their activity in North Africa following the establishment of the State of Israel. By late 1948 about 6,000 young Jews were registered in those youth movements throughout North Africa, the majority in Morocco.[126] French intelligence indicated that it was the Charles Netter youth movement that worked most diligently to bring young Moroccan Jews to fight in Israel.[127]

Even with the involvement of youth movements, however, much of the mobilization of volunteers was not done in an organized manner. Instead, Hebrew teachers, community leaders, and even some Alliance Israélite Universelle (Jewish Universal Alliance) officials acting independently (since the organization was not officially pro-Zionist) worked to convince families to send young men to join the fight for Israel's independence, suggesting that would increase the family's honor.[128] Few records of that mobilization campaign survived, but fragments in the French and Israeli archives tell some of the story. In September 1948 a pamphlet written in French and distributed in Casablanca explained to the youth of Morocco that although the Haganah "writes glorious pages of a rare heroism," it needed their help:

> The Jews of Palestine cannot remain alone in this fight. They need immediate help from all of the Jewish people, and particularly from the Jewish youth who join the ranks of the Haganah in great numbers and with enthusiasm.[129]

This was a concrete call for duty that also echoed "pan-Judaic" themes. The Zionist activists who authored the pamphlet were hoping that those reading would join the clandestine movement in Morocco and would soon be on their way to fight in Palestine:

> Young Jew of France and of North Africa:
>
> Do not remain at a distance any longer, in these days when the fate of your people is being decided.
>
> You, whose spirit is impregnated with love of liberty, you who have participated with ardor in all of the fights for the happiness of humankind, join the ranks of those who fight for YOUR liberty, for the liberty of YOUR PEOPLE and of YOUR COUNTRY.
>
> The fighters for Jewish liberation await you.
>
> Without waiting any longer, respond to their call.[130]

The pamphlet clearly sought to appeal to Francophile Jews, especially the graduates of the Alliance schools who were intimately familiar with the heritage of the French Revolution. Palestine, the reasoning went, was another cause for those "impregnated with love of liberty," interested in "the happiness of humankind." Still, using phrases such as "your people" and "your country" was clearly aimed at dispelling any notions that Morocco (or France) was the homeland of Moroccan Jews, or that Morocco's Muslims were the Jews' compatriots. Instead, like in DP camps and the United States, this was a claim for Moroccan Jews' national belonging and citizenship, transforming them into *de facto* Israeli citizens. Judging by the hundreds of people who came forward to enlist, both from among the poor and the middle classes, this sort of propaganda was effective. In fact, the Zionist emissaries established a rigorous selection process, where preference was given to men aged 17 to 20 of a certain height. Only those determined to be of adequate physical strength were allowed to enlist.[131]

Instruction manuals found in the possession of those arrested by the French authorities suggest that volunteers may have received some army training while still in Morocco, including physical education, judo, and the use of weapons and hand grenades. In one manual confiscated by the French police, the fundamentals of the IDF were explained to volunteers, and especially the Hebrew words commonly used in battle and on the training ground. The volunteers were instructed to carry the means to burn the manual if arrested and were threatened with court martial if they violated any of the orders given to them.[132] French intelligence noted that the young men they arrested were told what answers they should provide when interrogated so that they did not reveal any secret information about the activities of the Zionist movement to draft young Moroccan Jews.[133] Zionist activists reportedly reassured the young volunteers that "in the event that you are arrested, you will not risk any punishment. Numerous are your comrades who have succeeded in crossing the borders: letters received from Palestine prove it."[134] Before crossing the border by foot, some volunteers were apparently required to sign a detailed contract, stating that they understood the dangers of such a journey, that they would follow the instructions of the Jewish Agency throughout their time in Israel, and would refrain from contacting the French authorities. Finally, immigrants had to pledge to work in agriculture once in Israel (presumably after their army service). Parents were required to sign for underaged volunteers.[135]

According to French data, from June to December 1948 approximately 9,000 Jews left Morocco, reportedly to Israel.[136] The French distinguished between immigration of volunteers to join the fighting in Israel and immigration of Moroccan Jews to Israel that was not for military purposes. While trying to block the former, they tolerated the latter. In fact, a secret agreement between the Jewish Agency and the French authorities in 1949 allowed Moroccan Jews to immigrate to Palestine for nonmilitary purposes without attempts to block their transfer, as long as it did not embarrass the French government.[137] To curb mobilization for military purposes, the French authorities attempted to block the travel of young Jewish men through Oujda, and increased security at the border. They also pressured the heads of the Jewish communities to influence the youth. Still, those volunteers who were arrested often were immediately let go.[138] Volunteers were transferred via Oujda by foot into Algeria, where it was much easier to operate because of French direct rule. From Algeria, Moroccan volunteers sailed either straight to Haifa or to training camps near Lyon or Marseille, France, and from there on to Israel.[139]

A PALESTINE FRENZY IN SYRIA

Arab volunteers enlisted with the same vigor. From Hama to Homs, to the Golan Heights, to Jabal Druze, to Damascus itself, "all of Syria is in the midst of conscription and a Palestine frenzy; this is the top news everywhere you go," reported an informant for the Haganah in December 1947 from Syria.[140] Those volunteering, one radio ad stipulated, should be able-bodied, without dependents, and produce documents to prove their "Arabism" and integrity.[141] Although only about 3,000 Syrians ended up fighting for the ALA, many times that number came forward to register their names.[142] Mobilization for Palestine in Syria became the litmus test for Syrian patriotism, and local and national leaders realized that the number of volunteers they registered served as a barometer of the power they wielded in the country. It is in this context that we meet many of Syria's luminaries in the second half of the twentieth century—firebrand nationalists, pan-Arabists, large landowners, regime supporters, and tribal leaders—competing with one another for volunteer mobilization.

In rural Syria, mobilization was carried out by tribal leaders in a bid to bolster nationalist credentials and repent for earlier collaboration with Zionism. In Quneitra, in the Syrian Golan Heights, the aforementioned Haganah informant witnessed the celebrations that followed the voluntary enlistment of hundreds of tribesmen of the Arab al-Fadl tribe of Amir al-Faʿur in the ALA.[143] The volunteers paraded inside the square of the cattle market. Some were carrying weapons; others, sticks. The informant recorded that many in the audience laughed at the sight. "I have the impression that the mass drafting of the Faʿur Arab was mostly for show. Or as the residents say: to encourage drafting."[144] The suspicion about the sincerity of Amir al-Faʿur's intentions was not implausible. The amir was famous for selling land to the Zionist movement in the Hula Valley in the 1930s and 1940s, making his sudden mobilization to save Palestine surprising.[145] But since the 1948 war brought with it unparalleled support for Palestine in the Syrian parliament—where the amir was a delegate—he could hardly stay idle.[146] Moreover, Amir al-Faʿur was previously denounced as a traitor after refusing Amin al-Husayni's request to send his men to help the Palestinian revolt of 1936–39, which made his need to make amends even more critical.[147] It appears that the amir saw 1948 as an opportunity to repent, and there is evidence his men actually took part in fighting.[148]

In southern Syria's region of Jabal Druze, calls to volunteer for the ALA apparently only drew minor interest at first, possibly due to the fact that the Zionist movement had worked for decades to develop links with the community.[149] A December 19, 1947, article in *Jabal* (Mountain), a Druze newspaper, reported that al-Qawuqji himself had attempted to convince the Druze to join the ALA. Apparently, he arrived in Druze territory but was disappointed that no one came out to greet him. Schoolchildren and officials had to be dragged out to serve as a makeshift reception committee. In his speech to them, al-Qawuqji said: "When I see the faces of Druze here I am assured of victory in Palestine . . . This is a battle in which the fate of the aggressive Jews will be decided exactly as it was decided three thousand years ago by Nebuchadnezzer."[150] When he realized that invoking the Babylonian king who destroyed the Israelite temple in 586 BC failed to achieve the desired impression, al-Qawuqji reportedly promised the Druze that Palestine had much loot for them.[151] This may have been compelling enough for some young Druze, but not for the leader of Jabal Druze (and the 1925–27 Syrian revolt), Sultan al-Atrash. Eventually, however, al-Atrash did acquiesce to the enlistment of the Druze and the establishment of a Druze battalion inside the ALA.[152]

It is possible that al-Atrash's decision was tied to the conflict in Jabal Druze itself. When the mobilization for the ALA started in December 1947, al-Atrash's

forces were engaged in fierce fighting with other Druze clans that were armed
and funded by Syrian president al-Quwwatli, who in turn wanted to do away
with the Druze aspirations for an autonomy once and for all.[153] An unofficial
Druze autonomy had existed on and off from Ottoman times, owing to the
excellent fighting skills of the Druze and to the mountainous terrain of Jabal
Druze. In 1921 the French mandate formally established an autonomous Druze
state, which was reincorporated into Syria in 1936.[154] But even a decade later,
in 1947, al-Quwwatli was still fighting Druze separatism in a bid to consolidate
his power. Censured by rival clans for betraying the Syrian national cause and
conspiring with King Abdullah, al-Atrash likely wished to bolster his patriotic
credentials in Syria. Allowing his men to enlist in the ALA would achieve just
that. In fact, at al-Atrash's insistence, the ALA Druze battalion was not called
Jabal al-Druze but rather operated under the title *Jabal al-'Arab*, a name coined
for the Druze mountain in 1937 to emphasize that it was part of the Arab homeland.[155] In the context of 1947, the name Jabal al-'Arab for the ALA battalion
stressed that Druze were part of a pan-Arab endeavor to save Palestine, and
the battalion's orders repeatedly stressed that "there was no Druze purpose
in this war" and that any Druze politics were strictly forbidden.[156]

In Hama it was the charisma and organizational skills of two cousins that
were behind the mobilization of the largest number of volunteers anywhere in
the Arab world (between 450 and 600 men).[157] 'Uthman al-Hurani, a nationalist
schoolteacher with a long history of revolution, provided the infrastructure for
recruitment through the local branches of the Association for the Liberation
of Palestine (*jam'iyat tahrir filastin*) and the Committee for the Defense of
Palestine (*lajnat al-difa' 'an filastin*), which he headed.[158] His cousin, Akram
al-Hurani, who was a parliament delegate and a rising star in Syrian politics,
provided the charisma. Akram used his Youth Party (*hizb al-shabab*) as a
platform to encourage middle-class professionals—students, teachers, and
even doctors—to join him in Palestine.[159] Both 'Uthman's organizations and
Akram's party exhibited a clear pan-Arab stance, using religious discourse but
primarily focusing on a struggle "for Palestine's Arabness."[160]

By forming the unit in Hama, Akram al-Hurani intended to pressure President al-Quwwatli and the Syrian parliament to take more decisive action on
the Palestine question. Al-Quwwatli, for his part, tried his best to prevent
the departure of al-Hurani's unit to Palestine because he feared the young

FIGURE 4. Men outside Arab recruiting office of the Syrian Association for the Liberation of Palestine (*jam'iyat tahrir filastin*). 1 March 1948. Photo by John Phillips. Source: The LIFE Picture Collection via Getty Images.

politician had become too powerful. But the pressure was ultimately too great and al-Quwwatli relented.[161] Adib al-Shishakli, a native of Hama, a career officer in the Syrian army and later the president of Syria, was installed as the commander of the unit, and it was allowed to leave for Palestine.[162] In a letter to the delegates of the Syrian parliament, al-Hurani explained, shortly after his departure: "I consider fighting in Palestine equal to or more important than my service in Parliament, because the establishment of a Jewish state not only threatens Palestine but all the Arab East and the Arab race."[163]

In Aleppo too, most mobilization was done on a basis of local patriotism. This was reflected in the names given to units: the "Lions of Ibrahim Hananu" were named after one of the leaders of the 1925–27 revolt against the French who originated from the town, and the "Lionesses of Sayf al-Dawla" commemorated the tenth-century founder of the Emirate of Aleppo.[164] Trying to secure donations and weapons for their units, one of the Aleppo groups urged the town's residents on the pages of a local newspaper: "Please do not tighten your fist [when donating]. You'll give money, and we will give our lives."[165] The volunteers also promised to bring glory to the name of Aleppo for the entire Arab world to see.[166]

Of the political parties working to mobilize their base for Palestine on a national level, the newly incorporated Ba'th party stood out. A founding member of the Association for the Liberation of Palestine, the party decided to send volunteers to Palestine as early as November 1947, even before the formal establishment of the ALA.[167] An ad in the party's mouthpiece al-Ba'th on November 16, 1947, called interested men "to hurry up and register their name for volunteering in the salvation battalions which are being prepared for saving Palestine."[168] Those coming to "free the sacred land from the burden of colonialism and Zionism" needed to be ready "to pay the necessary tax of blood for freedom and honor."[169] In a meeting on January 15–16, 1948, the party decided to mandate that all its members volunteer to fight in Palestine, and the party leaders were the first to leave for Palestine.[170] But the party was not just targeting its own members in its volunteer recruiting efforts. To attract people who were not affiliated with the party, a separate office was created, the Permanent Palestine Office (maktab filastin al-da'im), which was active both in Syria and in Lebanon to recruit young men and collect donations.[171]

Of course, Palestine was not the only item on the Ba'th's agenda in late 1947.

One of the party's primary goals was to block the modification of the constitution that would have allowed al-Quwwatli to be reelected in the April 1948 elections.[172] Michel ʿAflaq, one of the party's founders, found many similarities between Palestine's partition and the proposed change to the constitution. Both, he explained in an article in the party's mouthpiece on November 16, necessitated a two-thirds vote, one in the UN, the other in the Syrian parliament, and both were tests for the principles of freedom and democracy in the post–Second World War era.[173] Thus, in another display of the cross-purposes at work amidst this mass mobilization, ʿAflaq encouraged Baʿth members to fight for Palestine as part of opposition to al-Quwwatli, who had himself established the ALA in the first place to secure his grip on power. Indeed, Palestine meant different things to different political players in Syria.

Unsurprisingly, it was the party's attempt to prevent his second term that turned al-Quwwatli against the Baʿth, including all its activities to mobilize people for the ALA. Al-Quwwatli not only ordered the party's paper shut down in March 1948, he also ordered the dispersal of meetings organized by the party.[174] By May 1948 ʿAflaq himself was arrested after supposedly agitating to overthrow the government.[175] But before the closure of its mouthpiece (and possibly its printing press) in March, the party managed to publish five pamphlets calling for volunteers to fight to liberate Palestine as well as several lengthy essays on the dangers of partition. These publications, though, included much more than the party's view on Palestine and the Jews. They were aimed at fomenting a revolution of which the fight in Palestine was merely the opening gambit. In that, the Baʿth was part of a limited number of revolutionary movements in the Arab world that did not simply call for reforms but for an overhaul of the rules of the game. These movements refused to operate inside the dual-government system, where national elites worked alongside colonial officials.[176]

The recurring theme running through all Baʿth publications from 1948 was a warning against Western colonialism conspiring with Zionism to take Palestine from the Arabs, each for their own designs.[177] But anticolonial rhetoric often also carried an indictment of forces closer to home. What enabled the Zionist success, some pamphlets contended, was actually the incompetence of Arab regimes—especially the post-independence Syrian one—which had wasted valuable time in waiting and negotiating with the superpowers, choosing compromise over war.[178] The Arab League was also criticized for its neglect of the Palestine question and its preference for proclamations over action. In fact, Ba'th contended that the league was not sincerely opposed to partition but only opposed to the borders specified in the UN's plan.[179]

This link between opposition to Zionism in Palestine and opposition to Arab regimes themselves was further elucidated in another of the Ba'th's key pamphlets. In this tract, one of the party's founders, Salah al-Din al-Bitar, called on Arab governments to "sever all economic, cultural and diplomatic ties" with the foreign powers that supported partition.[180] But within a month, in January 1948, when it became clear that not only were the ties with the superpowers not severed but even the boycott of goods imported from the Yishuv was not being fully enforced, the party called for more radical action:

> Arab states are still capitulating to the colonial powers which was the reason for Palestine's catastrophe [*nakbat filastin*], and they are avoiding threatening the colonial powers with the only weapon that will affect their economic interest, that is, the cancellation of oil contracts.[181]

Al-Bitar appears to be the first to use the term *nakba* (catastrophe) to describe the 1948 war. He also provided concrete suggestions on how to avoid it by reforming the Arab economy so it could support the war effort and the acquisition of modern arms.[182]

The Ba'th party's propaganda campaign attempted to convince potential volunteers that fighting for Palestine would help secure personal and political freedoms for all Arabs, not only Palestinians.[183] Yet the party did not simply aim to force Arab regimes to change; rather, it considered the fight in Palestine as a means toward the creation of a new Arab civilization. Shakir al-'As, who was the representative of Ba'th in the Association for the Liberation of Palestine, explained that in order to rescue Palestine, the Arabs must strengthen their national consciousness and rid themselves of the "primitive [*ibtidā'ī*] Bedouin mentality."[184] According to al-'As, "the strong reaction and the expressions of violent excitement are qualities of this primitive mentality and are most dangerous to the society, in general, and to the calculated and reasoned actions more specifically."[185] One of the main things those wishing to overcome this mentality had to realize was "the difference between actions and words." The primitive nations, and among them the Arabs, he explained, were often mollified simply by hollow declarations and speeches of their politicians that were not followed by action. In order to move beyond this mentality and avoid disaster in Palestine, Arabs had to sideline "the professional politicians" and have "educators" lead the change.[186]

Ba'th party leaders repeatedly claimed that the old political structures had molded Arab citizens into a subservient lot, and only a complete transformation of Arab civilization could guarantee victory in Palestine. A January 1948 article asked, "Why the Arabs, who are the majority, with many governments, princes and kings, are the weak ones, while Jews who are few, with no kings and princes, are the strong ones?"[187] After considering several reasons, the unidentified author explained that "the source of the strength [of Jews] is in spirit and not in matter, in thought and not in land, in hearts filled with belief and not in spreading out to more territories."[188] The Arabs, the author elaborated, had once built a great civilization but then had locked themselves within its confines. The refusal to allow any outside influence had stifled the Arab civilization. "The conflict with Zionism is not but a conflict between two souls, and a war between two civilizations. This is a conflict between a frozen soul [i.e., Arab civilization], and another one that is liberal [i.e., Zionism], and a war between an ancient civilization, and another modern one."[189] The Arabs, the author concluded, must reform themselves or cease to exist:

> This is the problem the Arabs are facing in Palestine, and it is the one which will awaken the Arab spirit, until its ancient civilization is destroyed, and ruin is spread in its midst, and until it abandons its ruined nest [and moves] to a new spacious land, and returns the structure of its fortress once again. That is the beginning of the Arab resurrection [ba'th].[190]

Other articles endorsed this message of struggle on multiple fronts, explaining, for example, that the first step in this resurrection was realizing that there was "colonialism in the internal life of the nation" which used a variety of means to enslave and exploit the people, including the constitution.[191] In other words, al-Quwwatli's government, and other governments established in the Arab world after the end of the mandate regime, were not necessarily a break from colonialism, even if they claimed to be so by introducing constitutions.

Much of Ba'th propaganda also included anti-Zionist rhetoric, which sometimes blurred the line between anticolonialism and antisemitic tropes.

One pamphlet, for example, referred to the Yishuv as "the poisonous bayonet" and stipulated that Zionist wealth was attempting to secure Palestine for the Jews.[192] Another pamphlet, authored by al-Bitar, explained that Palestine was just the first step for the Zionists who wished to take over the entire Arab world.[193] Conflating Zionists with Jews, al-Bitar explained that the latter were "the ones known for sowing discord in every society," and that they would work to weaken Arab morals and eventually bring about the disintegration and collapse of the Arab people.[194]

It is worth noting that, true to the Ba'th's vision of secularism, notably missing from their mobilization efforts are references to jihad, or any religious discourse for that matter.[195] But religion and ethnicity did matter for ALA mobilization: several Syrian ALA units were solely composed of religious or ethnic minorities. This was the legacy of colonialism in Syria. It was the French mandate authorities who had designed the Syrian army in such a manner. In the ALA, a Syrian Christian unit was named "Faris al-Khoury Platoon" after the Greek Orthodox Christian who was Syria's representative to the UN (and later the prime minister), and an "Alawite Battalion" was composed of former Alawite recruits from the Syrian army.[196]

ACTION INSTEAD OF TALK IN LEBANON

The mobilization of volunteers in Lebanon was less organized, and also less effective, with only 304 Lebanese joining the ALA fight in Palestine.[197] One of the first calls for mobilization was published in a journal dedicated to educational and cultural reform.[198] On the front page of its December 1947 issue, *Al-Ma'had* (The Institute) urged readers to stop talking about Palestine and go fight on its behalf:

> O Arabs. The time has come. Whoever can fight, and does not fight, is a coward. Whoever can fight, and is called to fight and does not fight, is a coward and despicable. And whoever can fight, and is called to fight and does not fight, and he does not allow fighting to start—even though he can—he is a coward and despicable and a forbidden, renegade charlatan [*dajjal*].[199]

The proclamation continued by stipulating that the only way to solve the Palestine problem was a daily dosage of blood.[200] The fact that copies of this proclamation were found in ALA bases in Palestine suggests that it was widely circulated, reprinted, and likely distributed in the streets of Beirut. The reprints of the article stated that "an elite group of Arab nationalist youth . . . published these words in a special publication so that it would come to those who did not have the chance to read *al-Ma'had* magazine."[201] This call and others apparently made an impression on prospective volunteers. According to British intelligence, 3,000 Lebanese registered as volunteers during the month of December 1947, but as the reporting British officer (accurately) cautioned, "it is reliably estimated that not more than a few hundred of these will ever take to the field."[202]

The original piece in *al-Ma'had* was authored by 'Ali Nasir al-Din, the director of the ALA propaganda department, whose biography typifies the diverse and geographically expansive genealogies of this generation of Arab nationalists.[203] Born in 1888 to a prominent Druze family in Bmariam in Jabal Druze, Nasir al-Din attended an Ottoman school in Beirut and became a Francophile, believing that France would bring emancipation to the Arabs. He even joined a French-sponsored military force during the First World War and fought in North Africa before returning to Lebanon with the French forces in 1918. When Nasir al-Din learned that French intentions for Syria and Lebanon did not include emancipation or independence, he quickly shifted his alliance to Faysal and his short-lived Arab kingdom in Syria (where he likely met al-Qawuqji). With the end of Faysal's kingdom, Nasir al-Din returned to Beirut to continue advocating for Arab independence. Unlike al-Qawuqji, Nasir al-Din was not much of an army man and instead focused on the written word. He published several newspapers centered on anti-French propaganda, which eventually led to his imprisonment by the French in 1923. Subsequently, Nasir al-Din was forced into exile and ended up in British-controlled Haifa in Palestine, where he first learned of the dangers facing Palestine.[204] Over the next two decades, Nasir al-Din remained active on the Palestine question and was involved in pan-Arab circles in Lebanon and Syria as a member of the League of Nationalist Action, calling for independence of Arab states from colonial rule and their unification into one Arab kingdom.[205]

It is therefore hardly surprising that the articles he authored in his attempt to mobilize the Lebanese youth for the Palestine cause echoed pan-Arab and militant themes. In another article from the January 1948 edition of *al-Ma'had*, Nasir al-Din criticized what he saw as the Arab states' overreliance on diplomacy.[206] Diplomacy, Nasir al-Din explained, had been the art of lying and backstabbing for centuries, and as such was not fit for solving the Palestine problem. Instead, Nasir al-Din suggested that the Arab nation adopt a new interpretation of "diplomacy" that relied on action rather than talk.[207] Like the Ba'thists, his strongest criticism was directed at certain unspecified individuals who advocated waiting and spread defeatism. For those people, and for Arab diplomats who were at a loss, Nasir al-Din suggested that they raise their heads and see "Fawzi al-Qawuqji, the leader of the revolution whose legs are in the soil and whose nose is in the clouds."[208] This mythic depiction of al-Qawuqji, as a giant both well grounded but able to view everything from above, sought to convey that he was the only one who could save Palestine and that the diplomats should give way to him.

Elsewhere in Lebanon, mobilization of volunteers assumed a more communal or tribal cast. In southern Lebanon, Shi'a from the region of Jabal 'Amil—stretching between the Awwali river in the north and the Galilee to the south, including the towns of Sidon, Tyre, Nabatieh, Jezzine, Bint Jbeil, and Tibnine—were mobilized to volunteer for Palestine by Ahmad al-As'ad, the powerful leader of the region (not to be confused with Syria's ruling Asad dynasty).[209] Al-As'ad wanted to make sure the Shi'a of Jabal 'Amil stopped seeing Jews as protected subjects (*dhimma*) and started seeing them as enemies of Islam more broadly, and the Shi'a of Lebanon more specifically. This is perhaps because, like the Syrian Amir Fa'ur, Ahmad al-As'ad also needed to bolster his patriotic credentials after decades of cooperating with the Zionist movement.

Contact between the Yishuv and the al-As'ads had been long-running. In the early twentieth century, young Shi'a men, under contract with the al-As'ad family, were sometimes hired to guard Jewish settlements in northern Palestine.[210] In March 1920 Kamil al-As'ad—Ahmad's uncle and for many years the patriarch of the family—was instrumental in rescuing Jewish settlers from attack by Bedouins in the Upper Galilee. The famous incident occurred after a group of Bedouins who supported King Faysal's kingdom attacked several settlements in the area; the most well-known among them was Tel Hai, which came to occupy a key place in Zionist mythology after some of its defenders were killed.[211] The Jews of Palestine, for their part, paid back in kind when the French were after Kamil al-As'ad for his involvement in attacking a Maronite village in May 1920. He was allowed to take refuge in the settlement of Rosh Pinna, where he was hosted by a prominent Zionist leader.[212]

In the 1930s, when Ahmad al-As'ad, Kamil's nephew, started to rise in prominence, close contact with the Zionist movement continued. Ahmad too took refuge inside Mandate Palestine when the French sought to arrest him. Memoirs of Zionist settlers reveal that he, his wives, and his children spent a total of eight months in Kfar Giladi in 1934–35. Al-As'ad's relations with the Yishuv during the 1936–39 Arab Revolt in Palestine were murkier. On the one hand, Haganah officers reported they were in regular contact with him and that he provided intelligence on the actions of rebels in Lebanon while serving in the Lebanese government. On the other hand, in a meeting with a friend from Kfar Giladi, al-As'ad reportedly admitted that he had met Amin al-Husayni, and even sent young men from Jabal 'Amil to fight alongside Palestinian rebels, after al-Husayni promised him that his fighters would not target Kfar Giladi.[213]

Ahmad al-As'ad also sold land that his family owned in Palestine to the Jewish National Fund. Negotiations for the sale of land in the Upper Galilee (where Kibbutz Menara is located today) started in September 1939 and were concluded in October 1942. Al-As'ad sold the JNF a total of 800 dunams (a dunam measures approximately a fourth of an acre) for 4.5 liras per dunam.[214] When a rival of the al-As'ads got his hands on the deed of sale and published it in the Lebanese press in 1945, al-As'ad was condemned for betraying the national cause. He claimed in his defense that the sale was carried out by his father and that he had known nothing about it, but even after this incident he continued to assist the JNF with purchasing lands owned by his family and their clients in Palestine.[215]

The relationship between Ahmad al-As'ad and the Zionist movement ended (at least for the time being) in late 1947. Starting in August, reports about al-As'ad's anti-Zionist rhetoric started flowing to the Haganah. Apparently, he held a party at his residence in the company of the American consul in Beirut and expressed his dissatisfaction with American support for Zionism, saying that Zionism was a source of turmoil in the Middle East.[216] Even Ben-Gurion noted his concern over al-As'ad's change of heart in his diary, writing that al-As'ad, "who was moderate, has now become zealous."[217]

Action quickly followed: on January 3, 1948, al-As'ad published a pamphlet calling on the youth of Jabal 'Amil to volunteer for the ALA. The pamphlet was a curious mix: demands for the protection of Arabism, jihad, Shi'i symbols, anger with the Jews, and lineage-based mobilization. The invocation of jihad was rather conventional, and not unlike the way the Ottoman sultan-caliph presented the fight against the Triple Entente during the First World War.[218] In the words of al-As'ad from 1948, "the assault on Palestine is an assault on Arabism and religion," and the "sons of Jabal 'Amil must know that the war for Palestine is a holy duty that rests on your shoulders."[219] The justification given for mobilization was also rather standard—the threat Zionism posed to Palestine and the supposed plan of Zionists to destroy Islam:

> In the Zionist plans there is a section that commands the obliteration of Islam and destruction of the pure al-Ka'aba. And with God's help we will make Palestine a graveyard for Zionism.[220]

If the threat to Islam's most sacred structure in the al-Masjid al-Haram in Mecca was not enough to galvanize the young Shi'a, al-As'ad also invoked specific Shi'i Arab symbols: Al-As'ad referred to a Fatimid tradition according to which the village of Asqalan in Palestine was the first resting place of the head of Husayn ibn 'Ali, grandson of the prophet, after he was decapitated in the Battle of Karbala in 680 CE.[221] According to al-As'ad, Palestine, as the first place of burial for Husayn's head, merited the sacrifice of young Shi'a men.[222]

Arguably the most important tradition invoked by al-As'ad to mobilize the Shi'a youth for the ALA was his ancestors' fight against the Ottoman ruler of the Galilee, Ahmad Pasha al-Jazzar, in the eighteenth century. Jazzar Pasha was sent to restore Ottoman control over the area following the death of Dhahir al-'Umar, the warlord of Acre and the Galilee. When the leaders of Jabal 'Amil refused to submit to Jazzar Pasha's authority, he launched a punitive campaign against the Shi'a in 1781, razing many of their villages. Nevertheless, the Shi'a did not surrender and launched a series of revolts, which were ruthlessly suppressed by al-Jazzar. In fact, most Shi'i villages were practically decimated following al-Jazzar's retaliations.[223] Playing on the nickname given to the pasha, *al-Jazzar*, meaning "the butcher," al-As'ad explained that just as the Shi'a warded off the pasha, surely they could banish less dangerous "butchers," meaning the Zionists.[224] In other words, al-As'ad incited the young men of his region to fight for Palestine by likening the Yishuv to the oppressive and bloodthirsty Ottomans.

The final theme in the pamphlet of interest—what could most aptly be termed disappointment with the Jews' alleged dishonoring of past displays of hospitality—was intended to explain how Jews became the villains:

> A persecuted nation, one denigrated by God, is trying today to take over Palestine. Their victory over us is a victory of evil, and our victory over them is a victory of justice, honesty and faith. This nation, which our honor and nobleness made us pity as the hero pities the weak. The day we gave them shelter and defended them and protected them was a day of the ingrate when they bit the hand that fed them and tried to drive us out from our homes and lands.[225]

This account is likely a reference to the dhimmi status of Jews under Islam as protected subjects, as well as to the unique connection of the Shi'a of Jabal 'Amil—and the al-As'ads in particular—and Zionists in more recent history. The proclamation clearly articulates that whatever al-As'ad felt about the Jews in the past, he now called for a change in that perception. Jews, who had been protected subjects, had become enemies.

According to Haganah intelligence, al-As'ad continued his mobilization efforts at a party in al-Qawuqji's residence in January 1948 in the presence of thousands of tribesmen.[226] After a few fiery speeches, a parade of Shi'a volunteers was held, and the recruits passed in front of al-Qawuqji and al-As'ad with their weapons, chanting "Long live Palestine!" and "Down with Zionism!"[227] Indeed, a few months later, al-As'ad's men participated in the fighting against Jewish forces in Ramot Naftali in the Upper Galilee. The subsequent Israeli revenge was a painful one for al-As'ad.[228]

MOBILIZATION IN IRAQ

After Syria, Iraq was the country that sent the most volunteers to the ALA: 800 of the 15,000 Iraqis who initially registered their names for volunteering. One of those was 'Amir Hasik, a former mid-level army officer in the Iraqi army. On December 18, 1947, he was reading through the popular Baghdadi daily *al-Yaqza* (Vigilance) when his eyes landed on an article titled "The Zero Hour Had Arrived." That "zero hour" was the partition plan endorsed by the UN, and the expected British withdrawal from Palestine in May 1948. Until the British withdrawal, the article explained astutely, British protection "will give the Jews sufficient opportunity to bring great numbers of the world Jews into Palestine, and secure equipment and weapons."[229] This would provide a strategic advantage to the Jews in the ensuing war, and that was why Arabs had to act immediately. The article called on Iraqis to take up arms and fight alongside Palestine's Arabs. On the radio, Iraqi reserve officers under the age of 40 were specifically asked to volunteer.[230]

This boded well for Hasik. Ever since he was released from jail, following his arrest for participating in the Rashid 'Ali al-Gaylani anti-British revolt in 1941, he felt that his civil rights had not been fully restored to him. Volunteering to help Palestinians would not only bolster his patriotic standing in a country where one's alliance to Palestine determined the loyalty to the Iraqi nation but also provide him with some income. As Hasik's memoir relates, minutes after he read the article in *al-Yaqza*, he telegrammed the organization mentioned in the article and offered his services.[231] Many Iraqi officers, whether involved in the al-Gaylani revolt or not, did the same. At least some of them had also joined al-Qawuqji in Palestine during the 1936–39 Arab Revolt.[232]

Indeed, several associations in Iraq were active in 1947–49 for the Palestine cause. When he decided to enlist, Hasik contacted the Committee for the Defense of Palestine (*lajnat al-difaʿ ʿan filastin*), an organization about which not much is known. A British report from September 1947, discussing the Iraqi responses to the UNSCOP recommendations to partition Palestine, stated that the committee held several rallies in Kirkuk and Irbil, north of Baghdad. According to the author of the report, although only several dozen people showed up in Kirkuk, in Irbil "the rabble of the town was easily incited to massed demonstrations by a group of undesirable agitators."[233] The British official also noted that the markets were closed down for the day and that Jewish inhabitants of the town were attacked.[234]

Far more successful in recruiting Iraqi volunteers for the ALA was the Association for Saving Palestine (*jamʿiyat inqadh filastin*), which was established in October 1947 by a group of prominent Iraqis, including religious figures, retired army generals, and lawyers. It was headed by Husayn Fawzi, the former Iraqi chief of staff, who was an establishment figure, deeply involved in Iraqi politics.[235] Unlike the activity of the Baʿth in Syria, that of the Association for Saving Palestine and similar organizations in Iraq was in full coordination with the central government, itself interested in promoting pro-Palestinian activity in Iraq to deflect the attention of Iraqis from the signing of a new Anglo-Iraqi agreement (see chapter 3). The regent, 'Abd al-Ilah, met with activists from the association after the approval of the partition plan, and the Iraqi government headed by Salih Jabr approved the registration of the association in only two months, on December 7, 1947.[236] In the following thirteen months during which the association operated, its governing body met no less than seventy-six times.[237]

The association's goal, according to the official gazette of the Iraqi Ministry of Interior, was "saving Palestine from Zionism and enabling the establishment of an independent Arab government." This ambitious aim was to be achieved through the following measures: "Bringing [forward] a force and preparing it in different units, training them, organizing and supplying them so that they can participate in the work of rescue"; "helping the fighters of Palestine with money, equipment, and provisions to continue the struggle"; "cooperating with institutions, committees, and associations which see eye to eye with the Association on its goals inside and outside Iraq"; "broadcasting propaganda for the victory of Palestine"; and "collecting money and necessary donations to run the Association."[238]

Shortly after it was incorporated, the association launched a propaganda campaign, calling for donations and volunteers for Palestine. Three publications were distributed by activists in gatherings and clubs in Baghdad and other Iraqi cities, and over three thousand letters were sent to Iraqi decision-makers and other prominent figures. A weekly radio broadcast by the general secretary of the association, Muhammad Fawzi Darwish, on the situation in Palestine also helped to win hearts and minds.[239] But it seems that the association's most successful propaganda weapon was mass rallies, which often drew thousands of supporters, and where anti-Jewish Islamic rhetoric was apparently often used. One of the association's star propagandists was Muhammad Mahmud al-Sawwaf, an Islamist activist from Mosul, who was affiliated with the Egyptian Muslim Brotherhood, and was one of the fifteen founding members of the Association for Saving Palestine.[240] Al-Sawwaf, according to his own admission, would orchestrate week-long rallies where he would speak for five hours straight.[241] According to a former Jewish-Iraqi parliament member, Salman Shina, in one of al-Sawwaf's mass rallies in front of the prime minister's office, the fiery propagandist rallied the audience in the street by quoting a famous prophetic oral tradition (*hadith*) attributed to Prophet Muhammad about the treachery of the Jews.[242] According to Shina, Sawwaf screamed at the entranced audience: "A day will come and we will wipe out all the Jews, and if anyone among them tries to hide behind a stone, the stone shall scream: A Jew is hiding behind me, get up and kill him! . . . This is what Islam's religious scholars commanded us."[243] Coming out to face the demonstrators, the Iraqi prime minister, Salih Jabr, promised to do everything in order to save Palestine. Then the masses went into the nearby mosque to register as volunteers.[244]

Indeed, eight registration centers were opened in Baghdad's large mosques by the association, and several additional ones were set up in other cities. According to the official report of the association, published after the war in 1949, 15,000 people came forward and registered, although only 800 eventually made it to Palestine.[245] Iraqi men and women also donated money, jewelry, and other valuables, and many of the Iraqi tribes, including Kurdish tribes, donated weapons for the volunteers.[246] Over 70,000 dinars were collected, which allowed the association not only to recruit volunteers but to equip, organize, and even partially train them.[247] According to British intelligence, the 450 men who left for Syria on January 20, 1948, "all were ex-army and police and 215 were ex-non-commissioned officers."[248] They were wearing "olive-khaki battledress, head cloth and agal with green flashes to indicate N.C.O. rank." Each man also carried a haversack with a water bottle and a dagger.[249] As the Iraqi volunteers were driven through Fallujah and Ramadi on their way to Damascus, thousands of bystanders cheered and fired into the air in celebration.[250] British officials were unhappy about the crossing of Iraqi volunteers from Syria into Palestine, and requested the Iraqi government to intervene to stop volunteers in order to "refrain from causing embarrassment to His Majesty's Government."[251] Explaining the purpose of the mobilization in Iraq, Salah Jabr, the Iraqi prime minister, told a reporter that "the aim of our interference would not be to murder Jews, but to keep order in the Arab zone."[252] If the Jews of Palestine chose war, he warned, he would send two million Iraqi tribesmen to fight in Palestine, but if they agreed to reject partition, then they would be granted the same rights as Iraqi and Egyptian Jews.[253]

BECOMING A PATRIOT

Zionist and Arab mobilizers who sought to bring volunteers to Palestine offered a fast-track to unblemished patriotic credentials, and inadvertently also
gave new meanings to several categories of identity. The journey to become an
exemplary American Jew, Holocaust survivor, or Francophile North African
Jew meant fighting for the Yishuv in Palestine and, at the least, tacitly acknowledging the legitimacy of Israel to claim that individual as part of its citizenry.
Loyalty to coreligionists—not new in and of itself—now required more than
donations. One had to be willing to sacrifice one's life for the Zionist cause.
Similarly, those who wished to present themselves as true Lebanese, Syrian,
or Iraqi nationalists were required to send their supporters to fight Palestine's
partition alongside Palestinians. But there was far more ambiguity in what
fighting for Palestine actually meant in the Arab world: one could fight for
Palestine to atone for earlier collaboration with Zionism; fight for Palestine
as a first step in overthrowing corrupt Arab regimes that supported Western colonialism; or just the opposite—send rebellious and antigovernment
activists to fight for Palestine in order to mitigate their influence and allow
colonialism to continue.[254]

Many of the appeals to Jews and Arabs to enlist surveyed here were an-
chored in recent traumas, and promoted a new muscular way of being in
the world as the only response to subjugation by others. Zionist mobilizers
benefited from presenting the war in Palestine as a possible second Holocaust.
Arab mobilizers presented the Palestine question in similarly catastrophic
terms, as another case of colonial usurpation, but one more galling since it
was by a former subjected people. Like the British in Iraq and Egypt or the
French in North Africa and the Levant, Arabs had to come together to free
Palestine from the yoke of Zionism. For both Arab and Jewish mobilizers,
abandoning the supposed Arab/Jewish passivity and adopting the use of force
was presented as the only way to wrestle out of subjugation by others—be they
the Arabs as the new heirs to the Nazis, or the Yishuv as a tool in the hands
of Western colonialism.

Ordinary Jews and Arabs from around the world responded enthusiastically
to the call to fight in Palestine. Tens of thousands came forward to volunteer
(or were compelled to enlist in DP camps) even when this call included claims
for their national identity. However, it was at that point that the centralization

of the Zionist organization, and later the State of Israel, proved immensely advantageous. The tens of thousands of Arabs—not only in Syria, Lebanon, and Iraq but also in Saudi Arabia, Algeria, Egypt, Libya, and Sudan—who came forward to volunteer, lacked the means to travel to Palestine, and no state was willing to pay their way. In fact, many Arab states, under British and French influence, actively tried to prevent the departure of volunteers to Palestine, while the small societies and associations that mobilized the volunteers to begin with often lacked the funds to pay for their travel.[255] Meanwhile, no such problem was encountered on the Zionist side, where Jewish organizations and later the State of Israel itself had ample funds to make sure volunteers made it to Palestine and were sent immediately to the battlefield. The state-centric efforts also made it much easier to educate and indoctrinate the masses of volunteers once they arrived in Palestine.

Chapter 2

TOE THE LINE

ONCE VOLUNTEERS FROM ALL OVER THE WORLD MADE IT TO Palestine, joining those already there, ideological instruction supplemented conventional military training for the new recruits. This form of political indoctrination to the official party line is rarely acknowledged in scholarship about the modern Middle East. It is certainly not part of the histories of the 1948 war.[1] In fact, beyond the polemical assertion that Arab leaders "incited" against the Jews,[2] scholars have paid scant attention to the actual themes of soldiers' education. This chapter chronicles the way that the IDF and the ALA each sought to tell Jews and Arabs who the enemy was, and what was permissible to do to him or her in the heat of battle and afterwards.[3] To cement some of these ideas, the patrons of the two armies relied on Jewish and Islamic religious traditions, while also invoking more recent experiences that could resonate with the diverse groups of soldiers coming from different places for different reasons. Both armies also worked hard to censor politically provocative rhetoric and radical discourse because they were fearful that such thinking would eventually backfire and turn against the political leadership in Israel and the Arab world.

In the messages they advanced in 1948, I argue, the Haganah and IDF bridged the gap between the Left and Right in the Yishuv. It was common at the time—and still is today—to differentiate between the brutal ideology of the two militias associated with the Revisionist Right, the Irgun (Etsel) and the Stern Gang (Lehi), and the main military force, the Haganah, affiliated with Ben-Gurion's Labor Zionism.[4] Members of the latter insisted that they espoused humanistic values and never expressed hatred for the enemy. In fact, Labor Zionists labeled their Revisionist opponents as "fascists," "terrorists," or "Jewish Nazis."[5] But the 1948 war brought about unprecedented convergence. By adopting the Revisionist narrative, which presented the Arabs as descendants of the arch-nemesis of the Israelites, Amalek and the Seven Nations of Canaan, the Haganah and IDF offered soldiers a moral justification for fighting, killing, and expelling Arabs.[6] Meanwhile, fearful that the antimilitaristic stances of Ashkenazi volunteers from North America would interfere with the Yishuv's strategy, army officials sought to delegitimize the former's views and make sure they did not feel safe expressing them in public. Finally, IDF officers tried to convince Jewish recruits from Arab lands that fighting the Arabs in Palestine would constitute payback for the persecution of their families by Muslims in their countries of birth. With the exception of a few dissenters, to the extent that officers set any limits on stoking hatred of the enemy, they did so out of fear that this hatred could not be contained at war's end and would come to define the new Jewish state, creating anarchy.

The task of the ALA was as complicated as that of the IDF. As discussed in the previous chapter, during the mobilization phase the many actors involved often used anticolonial and pan-Arab rhetoric to recruit volunteers. Meanwhile, when in Palestine, the patrons of the ALA from Arab governments produced very different propaganda. Volunteers were told that the Jews had trespassed on their status as dhimmis in accordance with Islamic tradition and therefore had to be subdued. But contrary to wartime Zionist propaganda that the Arab war objective was to kill Palestine's Jews in a systematic or organized manner, there was no instruction to this effect. This point is significant, since scholars continue to debate whether Nazi and antisemitic propaganda made headway in the Arab world throughout the 1940s.[7] My findings suggest that antisemitism was negligible in ALA propaganda, but I am unable to make a more generalized assertion about Palestine at large or the rest of the Arab world. The Library of Congress has recently made available pamphlets that circulated in and beyond Palestine in 1948 that contain clear antisemitic tropes as well as selective Islamic traditions about Jews as debased humans.[8] Publications by the Egyptian Muslim Brotherhood and the Young Egypt Party (*misr al-fatah*) also traded in antisemitic themes. It is noteworthy, however, that antisemitic publications were largely self-published, and not officially endorsed by the AHC, the Arab League, or the ALA itself.[9]

Indeed, ALA propaganda was very restrictive. Even the term "colonialism" was absent from it for fear that the volunteers would connect Palestine to the oppression of the colonial system that they were so intimately familiar with from home. This was especially true for Iraqi volunteers, whose country was still in many ways a British client. If such a connection were to be made—and volunteers realized that the elites who sent them off to fight were very much implicated in colonialism—there was a chance that volunteers could turn against their own governments upon their return. That is something the patrons of the ALA sought to prevent at all costs. ALA propaganda even censored aspirations for the unification of all Arabs in one kingdom, along the lines of what the Ba'th had suggested, since such plans went against what the chief sponsor of the ALA, Syrian president Shukri al-Quwwatli, saw as acceptable.

Unmet expectations were also a concern in the ALA's dealings with Palestinian civilians. The volunteer army had entered Palestine with grandiose promises of a swift victory against the Jews and minimal intervention in Palestinian daily lives. But as victory became less likely, the noninterference strategy was abandoned. The ALA sought to control every aspect of Palestinian daily lives in order to legitimize itself, and used coercion against those unwilling to cooperate.

RATIONAL HATRED IN THE HAGANAH AND IDF

The Haganah was engaged in sociopolitical training—commonly called *hasbara*—from its inception in 1920, but a specialized hasbara department was established only during the Second World War.[10] The department focused on both political indoctrination and military education,[11] and a special emphasis was placed on the question of restraint (*havlagah*)—the decision to cease Haganah attacks against the Arabs, so as not to antagonize the British empire.[12] By the early 1940s, the Haganah's hasbara department shifted its orientation and began agitating against the British policy paper of 1939, which limited Jewish immigration to Palestine.[13] The department also disseminated information about Palestine's Arab population.[14] In 1947 the Haganah weekly *Bamahane* (In the Base Camp) was placed under the supervision of the hasbara department, and gradually became a major tool in the education of armed Jewish men and women.[15] The Palmach had its own hasbara apparatus aimed at propagating its unique *esprit de corps*. Borrowing many of the institutions of the Red Army and especially that of the *politruk* (the so-called "political officer"), the Palmach saw political indoctrination as an integral part of soldiers' training.[16]

Following the announcement of mandatory conscription in November 1947, the Haganah General Staff sought to establish a propaganda apparatus for soldiers that would transcend the political divides within the Yishuv. In March–April 1948 a restructured hasbara department was created and referred to as the education department (*mahleket tarbut*), known by its Hebrew acronym *Mahtar*. The new department was put under the command of Yosef Karkoubi (later, Kariv), an intelligence officer who was familiar with hasbara through his work in the Haganah's underground radio stations.[17] The education department had several branches, including a publishing house, a broadcasting service, an art department, and a library.[18]

The new education apparatus of the IDF was a massive undertaking. In fact, less than a year after the IDF was officially incorporated in late May 1948, 746 education officers and sergeants were appointed in the division, battalion, and platoon levels throughout the armed forces. Some of those also wrote for the *Bamahane*.[19] A survey of eighteen rank-and-file officers in the department, based on biographical information I was able to locate, reveals that they were all of Ashkenazi origin, the majority of them born in either Russia or Poland. Education officers were older than the general soldier population, and their average age was 40. About half of the surveyed officers were from *moshavim* or kibbutzim (cooperative or collective agricultural settlements) and the other half were associated with the Labor movement in Palestine, either through membership in parties or by holding positions in the general organization of workers, the Histadrut. Many served in the Haganah or the Yishuv intelligence agencies before 1948.[20] Therefore, it is likely that these men were seen as politically reliable by the Zionist leadership and Ben-Gurion himself. This makes their adoption of views usually associated with the Irgun and Stern Gang about the Arab enemy all the more remarkable, given the trouble the Left in the Yishuv went through to distinguish itself from the Revisionists.

One of the most important tasks of the education department was to produce pamphlets with lesson plans that could be used to indoctrinate soldiers.
The pamphlets were sent to education officers and sergeants, to commanders
at company level and above, and to other staff officers. However, education
materials were also produced at the unit level, with the support of the education
department.[21] The pamphlets were almost never signed, and with the exception
of publications produced in specific units, there is also no record of which pamphlets went to which units. We also know very little about the nature of actual
interactions between education officers and soldiers during sessions referred
to as "hasbara talks." However, we do know some of the general contours of
these events. The chief hasbara officer, Dov Berger, authored guidelines for
education officers in August 1948. In them he stipulated that a talk should be no
more than forty-five minutes, followed by a fifteen-to-thirty-minute discussion.
The officer was to give the talk after his men had rested and eaten so that they
would pay attention. Berger emphasized the need for eye contact and required
that officers "converse" with the soldiers rather than read to them. "Convince
them that everything you explain concerns them and obligates them," Berger
concluded.[22] Education officers reported that capturing soldiers' attention was
hard but not impossible. One noted that he saw his work as the "social cement
that brings the servicemen together and creates bonds among them."[23]

One of the most effective "social cement" themes was the Bible, which had
been used already in Palmach education materials before 1948 to promote
the view that "activism"—a euphemism for militarism—was the only course
of action for the Jewish people.[24] Numerous education pamphlets in 1948–49
stressed the bravery of the Jews from biblical times to the present and their
mastery of the sword. Willingness to sacrifice oneself—like the defenders of
Masada had done when they committed suicide so as not to fall into the hands
of Romans—was hailed as one of the critical characteristics of the Jewish
soldier.[25] However, soldiers were also told that Jewish history had come to a
standstill in the diaspora and that only modern Jewish soldiers, such as those
who fought in the Jewish Legion in the First World War, represented the return
of the Jews to history and "the eradication of the Diaspora and its complete
negation [*shlilat ha-galut*]."[26]

But a simple resort to biblical tales was apparently insufficient to make soldiers remorseless and effective fighters. Early on in the war, education officers

from the Carmeli brigade reported having difficulties convincing soldiers to shoot at the enemy. It is not entirely clear what specific incidents sparked this concern. It is possible that one was the reprisal attack on the villages of Balad al-Shaykh and Hawassa, east of Haifa, on December 31, 1947, in response to the killing of thirty-nine Jews at the Haifa oil refinery (itself a retaliation for an Irgun attack on Arab workers that left six dead a day earlier).[27] The orders to Carmeli soldiers were to "kill as many men as possible" but also "to avoid hurting women and children as much as possible."[28] Indeed, several dozen men were taken out of their homes and executed, and some women and children were killed as well.[29]

Still, Carmeli commanders apparently felt their soldiers were not responsive enough to these sorts of commands. One education officer noted that his men "used to fire to the sides every time, but not at the target—they couldn't [do it]. Their Jewish heart would not let them."[30] In an effort to devise a solution, the officer consulted Soviet wartime propaganda, specifically the notorious *Volokolamsk Highway*, a novel by Alexander Bek about the defense of Moscow during the Second World War. The book was translated into Hebrew in 1946 and was viewed by many as a pivotal resource for promoting *esprit de corps* and combat readiness among soldiers.[31] The Carmeli education officer did not share in his account what parts of the novel he found most effective in convincing his men to overcome their reluctance to shoot at the enemy, but the novel's most famous story was about soldiers in a Soviet battalion who were goaded by their commander to execute a fellow sergeant who had deserted the line. Whatever lessons the Carmeli education officer ultimately chose from the novel, it was deemed effective. Showcasing his success in the pamphlet for all the battalion's soldiers to see, the education officer explained that "our people are too good. It is not a shortcoming, but when it comes to the enemy, we need to be a bit wild. I am not saying we need to target women and children, but the enemy's nature is such that if we don't show him our strength—he'll show us his."[32] An education officer from a unit stationed near Jerusalem felt this strength was measured by soldiers' willingness to kill as many as possible:

> The enemy is about to kill you and me too. I teach you, and I demand: Kill him. Know how to kill because I too want to live. Each one of us is ordering you, each and every one commends: Kill—We want to live! . . . Maybe a bullet will catch you, but first you kill! Destroy as much as you can![33]

Encouraging brutality was also attempted by resorting to a technique frequently used by propagandists in the Second World War to excite soldiers into battle: telling them that the bodies of their fallen comrades had been mutilated by the enemy.[34] Alluding to the Arabs as the descendants of biblical Ishmael, the education officers wrote, "The Ishmaelites raided the fallen men, abused their corpses, rejoiced and exulted, and were dancing and singing."[35]

The space devoted to killing in the various soldiers' publications suggests that convincing soldiers to do so was a major challenge for education officers early on in the war. Simple references to the bravery of biblical figures were not sufficient to encourage the kind of behavior the army desired. For that purpose a more suggestive language was required, and the biblical tales were abandoned for the trope about the Arabs as the descendants of Amalek and the Seven Nations of Canaan, the archenemies of the Israelites. One of the most intriguing and cryptic publications of the education department that dealt with the issue was an undated pamphlet titled "Morality in Israel's Army."[36] Morality, the education officers wrote, "is different in every period and every place ... Jewish morality is not the same as Christian morality, and the morality of peacetime is unlike that of wartime."[37] The last differentiation was crucial and it was repeated several times. The education officers wanted to make sure that in wartime, soldiers understood that killing was a necessity:

> In peacetime we say: "Whoever sheds the blood of man, by man shall his blood be shed" [Genesis 9:6]. And in a time of war "the more [killing] the merrier [Hebrew: *kol hamarbeh harei zeh meshubah*]." And it is said: "Thine eye shall not pity him" [Deuteronomy 19:13].[38]

The implication was clear: the soldier should not pity the enemy but kill him without hesitation. But who was the enemy? Here the education officers entered into an elaborate discussion of the different kinds of warfare in biblical times.

The first kind of war presented in the pamphlet was a war of complete extermination (*milhemet herem*) against the ancient nemesis of the Israelites in Canaan, Amalek. This people, the pamphlet narrated, attacked the Israelites for no apparent reason, coming from behind their camp. "That is why Israelite morality commands us to revenge. In an oath of revenge [*shvu'at nakam*] the Torah commands us 'the LORD will have war with Amalek from generation to generation' [Exodus 17:16]."[39] The pamphlet continues, "He demands a revenge of extermination without mercy to whoever tries to hurt us for no reason."[40] The education officers then explained that in biblical times Saul exterminated all of Amalek, men and women, youth and elderly, and even sheep and cattle.[41] Their possessions were burned because in a war of complete extermination it was unlawful to enjoy the loot.[42]

The other type of war mentioned in the pamphlet was a war of conquest (*milḥemet kibush*), which the authors also called a war by commandment or mandatory war (*milḥemet mitsyah*).[43] This war could only take place within the boundaries of the Land of Israel. The education officers stressed that this too was a war of annihilation: biblical Joshua was commended to annihilate the nations of the land and he was forbidden to make any treaties with them.[44] The pamphlet quotes Deuteronomy 7:1 referring to the Seven Nations of Canaan, whom the Bible instructs the Israelites to annihilate permanently. The pamphlet ends[45] by specifying, "In this case [war of occupation] the army is allowed to take spoils including women and children to be slaves and concubines. It is a must to kill the male captives in this sort of war."[46]

The suggestion that there were parallels between the war in 1948 and biblical wars of extermination was not a fringe view, but one repeated in *Bamahane* and even by Ben-Gurion himself.[47] It was also sanctioned by at least some in the religious-Zionist leadership (but not among the ultra-orthodox *haredi* leadership). Yitzhak HaLevi Herzog, the chief Ashkenazi rabbi of Palestine and later the State of Israel, wrote religious soldiers in February 1948 that the war against the Arabs "who wish to conquer our settlements" and "exterminate us completely" was indeed "a war by commandment."[48] Due to the war's special status according to biblical law, the rabbi reassured the soldiers that "miracles from heaven will occur to us."[49] Another article in the same publication (tailored specifically to religious-Zionist soldiers) brought up a question by "a veteran fighter" about the spoils in such a war by commandment:

> In every army, the soldier sees himself as entitled to the spoils and rape (of the enemy's women) [sic]. Why would the rights of our soldiers be different from that of any other soldier? And if we may also add that it is a known fact that our enemies are as cruel as an ostrich in the wilderness,[50] and that no stone is left unturned anywhere which falls into their hands! Should we not repay in

kind? Why should we be more righteous than our forefathers in biblical times? They too took pillage and even set rules to do so.[51]

In response to the query, the author—presumably a rabbi—explained that collecting loot distracted soldiers from fighting, and may be taken advantage of by the enemy. It was also stated that soldiers' behavior must be exemplary, and robbery may set a bad example for Jews. However, "since there is a reality that is difficult to fight against," where looting was very widespread, the author suggested that the spoils should be assembled collectively and later distributed evenly between soldiers and institutions. The part in the questions about rape was not addressed in the response, leaving open the possibility that such behavior was not altogether unacceptable.[52]

In the quest to encourage soldiers' ruthlessness, not only Amalek and the Seven Nations of Canaan were invoked but also the victims of the Holocaust and its perpetrators. A publication in a bulletin prepared for religious-Zionist soldiers showed on the top part of the page a picture of an Auschwitz gas chamber, with what appeared to be corpses of Jews, "taken through a hatch while the gas [chamber] operated."[53] Underneath the picture the headline stated that this was the commemoration day for those exterminated in the Holocaust, and verses from Deuteronomy 25:17–19 were quoted to remind the readers of the divine promise made to the Israelites that they shall inherit Canaan. To fulfill that promise, the Israelites must not forget the commandment to "blot out the name of Amalek from under heaven."[54] Bringing in the story of the Nazis as Amalek in this context was meant to encourage soldiers to fight:

> We need to remember them [the Holocaust victims] throughout this day. Their memory is blessed, but we must no longer cry. Our tears have dried out. From now on we will grind our teeth [i.e., hold back], and carry in our heart the holy commandment, "Remember what the Amalekites did to you." We shall remember that Jerusalem may not be under siege and distress because "that causes the destruction [of the temple] to prolong."[55]

Only liberating Jerusalem and the entire Land of Israel from the new Amalekites—the Arabs—could bring about the rebuilding of the Jewish temple and the coming of the messiah.

These publications discussing Amalek, the Seven Nations of Canaan, and a war by commandment in a distinctly modern context were the work of experts who had intimate knowledge of the biblical text and its exegesis in later periods.[56] They were not solely trying to convince religious soldiers but to sway the entire soldier population that indiscriminate use of force was the only course of action. The decision to include these biblical traditions in education materials is especially remarkable because Jewish religious law (*Halakha*) had tended to suppress them for centuries. In the context of Western rabbinical Judaism's renunciation of political power and the use of force in the diaspora, it was often stressed that the example of the war against the Seven Nations of Canaan and Amalek was no longer applicable because these nations had vanished, and even if individuals from these nations survived, it was impossible to identify them with certainty.[57] The revival of these traditions, at least in Palestine, probably should be attributed to the Revisionists: poet Uri Zvi Greenberg (1896–1981) saw the biblical story of the annihilation of the Amalekites as a roadmap to the Zionist struggle against the Arabs.[58] He argued against those in the Yishuv who said that Jewish morality prohibited vengeance and cruelty against the enemy.[59] Although scholars have downplayed the influence of the Revisionist ideology on the political leadership of the Yishuv—and especially on Labor Zionism—at least in education materials, the influence was very significant.[60]

Some education officers took the concept of a war of annihilation quite literally. The most famous of them was the poet Abba Kovner, who served as the education officer of the Givati brigade during the war. Kovner's brutal recommendations on how to deal with the enemy appeared in the education pamphlets he authored, which were known as "combat bulletins" (*daf kravi*). These bulletins were regularly read and distributed to soldiers, and were immensely popular among them.[61] All in all, Kovner published thirty-one combat bulletins during the war, with each printing consisting of about 7,000 copies. Nevertheless, the impact of the bulletins far exceeded their limited number, and they were in high demand all over the IDF.[62]

Kovner was a known figure in the Yishuv even before being appointed as Givati's education officer. He was one of the leaders of the Jewish underground in the Vilna Ghetto during the Second World War and later fought as a partisan alongside the Red Army. After the end of the war he immigrated to Palestine and assumed various leadership positions in Zionist and pro-Soviet Hashomer Hatz'air (Young Guard) youth movements.[63] Kovner remained convinced that the Jews faced a danger of extermination even after the defeat of the Nazis.[64] To him, the logic that drove the Arabs was the exact logic that had driven Hitler, and he believed that the 1948 war could be the ultimate victory of the Jews after their failure to save themselves during the Holocaust.[65]

The first bulletin Kovner published, dated June 9, 1948, did not yet discuss the ways to kill the enemy, but rather criticized IDF soldiers, in what became a major public debate in Israel for decades to come. Kovner harshly attacked the decision of members of Kibbutz Nitzanim and the Givati soldiers who were stationed there to surrender to the Egyptian army on June 7, 1948, calling their surrender "a failure and a disgrace." Kovner argued it was better to die than to surrender.[66] A month later, the situation on the ground changed and the IDF became more successful on the battlefield. Worried about the complacency of the soldiers, Kovner implored them in his bulletin of July 12, 1948: "Yes, we have broken their spirit. We also cracked their bodies. But they still have strength. . . . And even if we are certain that the manure of the invaders' corpses will make our fields bloom, for now—we are called to be ready, to have valor and to be prepared to sacrifice ourselves."[67] Two days later, Kovner used even more explicit language, exalting revenge:

> The Anglo-Faroukian[68] dogs are under our wheels! . . . This night will be the night of the Plague of Blood. Samson's Foxes (the brigade's mechanized commando unit) pushed forward! And suddenly—the land was soft—corpses! Dozens of corpses under their wheels. The driver flinched: human beings are under his wheels! Wait. Remember Negba[69] and Bayt Daras[70]—and run them over![71] Don't flinch, sons, these are murder dogs—their sentence is blood! . . . Buckle down, boys, as our jeeps will turn into amphibious vehicles and we will march in the stream. The stream of the invaders' blood . . . Run them over![72]

By invoking the biblical story of the Plague of Blood (*makat dam*) from the Ten Plagues of Egypt in the book of Exodus, Kovner equated modern-day Egypt with ancient Egypt and presented Givati soldiers as victims of Egyptian oppression. He hoped that making the soldiers conflate the two would render the mass killing of Egyptian soldiers morally palatable.

For the few Israeli soldiers who still might have thought his injunction to be allegorical, Kovner adopted a more explicit tone in his bulletin of July 17, 1948: "Around you, the eyes of the Nile dogs glimmer. Into the Nile, you dogs! Into the Nile! In curse, in prayer, and in love—pull the trigger, slaughter, slaughter, slaughter."[73] Indeed, for Kovner, revenge could engender a love of freedom: "As you improve in killing the murderous dogs, so would you improve in your love for what is beautiful, what is good and for freedom."[74] Kovner's view that love and hatred were inextricably bound through revenge could be directly tied to Soviet propaganda during the Second World War, propaganda he knew very well from his time as a partisan.[75]

In the decades since the 1948 war, both veterans and scholars have argued that few took Kovner's writings seriously and that the combat bulletins were not regarded as instructions on how to deal with the enemy.[76] However, the backlash against Kovner's writing at the time belies these claims.[77] In fact, Kovner's gory language in his combat bulletins prompted his peers in the education department to address head-on the delicate topic that had hitherto been left unaddressed in official deliberations: hatred of the enemy. On August 4, 1948, all brigade-level education officers convened to talk about Givati's combat bulletins, and about hate indoctrination more broadly. The discussion was led by Yosef Karkoubi, the head of the education department, who was tasked with making a final decision on the subject. Few education officers believed that encouraging soldiers to hate the Arab enemy was problematic, but most objected to the graphic language in Givati's combat bulletins.

Quoting the call to make "a sea of blood" of the Egyptian soldiers, a staff officer from the education department argued: "We should excite them [the Israeli soldiers] into battle but we must maintain some limits of expression." Another officer replied that since the Egyptians were foreign invaders, one was allowed to be particularly brutal. Then the education officer of the Carmeli brigade intervened,[78] offering a more nuanced understanding of the psychology of the soldier: "There are bestial instincts in the human heart. On top of them there is a thin layer of civilization. If we give room to those instincts, we won't be able to stop them. If we say slaughter, we condone rape." The navy's chief education officer did not agree. He stressed the importance of hatred, especially when "defeatist" voices in the press were calling to let the Palestinian refugees return to their villages (as Palestinians were doing en masse at the time). "The Givati Brigade combat bulletins border on sadism," objected the Golani brigade education officer. "We know well what slaughter is, and we cannot be cavalier about it . . . A soldier does not slaughter, he kills if and when there's a need."[79] Along similar lines, the IDF chief hasbara officer, Dov Berger, objected to hate indoctrination and warned that a call to step on the corpses of the enemy would not stay within the confines of war but would influence the character of the new state as well.[80]

Quoting some of the ideas presented in "Morality in Israel's Army," the education officer for the public works brigade eventually stepped in, saying that the Hebrew Bible contained crueler depictions of warfare and mass killing, ones that should be followed.[81] "There is no basis for panic," he ridiculed his fellow officers. "The Bible has harsher expressions than Givati's combat bulletins, and the Bible books were edited [i.e., before canonization] and these expressions were specifically not omitted." The officer then said what others did not dare to say: "The orders pertaining to the murder and extermination of the enemy in the Bible were written with discretion, and not during times of emergency. It was written for coming generations. We have to make the enemy hated using all the tools at our disposal."[82] It is unclear whether the officer was also advocating the murder of women and children along the lines of the biblical story mentioned in the "Morality in Israel's Army" pamphlet. It is clear these views echoed to a large extent those of the militias associated with the Revisionists, the Irgun and Stern Gang.

Karkoubi, head of the education service, was only partially convinced by his officers:

> There is a danger that we would be overly influenced by the Jewish tradition that rules out crude hatred. We need to adjust our state of mind to the new conditions. . . . That is why we need to nurture the hate instinct. [But] we need to put limits to hatred. It has to be rational. We must explain to the soldiers why they have to hate the enemy, and they would hate him as long as there is a reason. This is a rational hatred that fits the Jewish nature.[83]

Karkoubi was at least partially correct in suggesting that modern European Jewish tradition "rules out crude hatred." Indeed, Jewish religious leaders from the nineteenth century onward were sometimes hesitant to vilify the enemy with which their state was at war. With Jews dispersed across the European continent, there was fear that Jews from one nation would fight Jews from another, and Jewish religious leaders were not willing to entertain the possibility of Jews killing other Jews.[84] But as there were very few Jews fighting

for the Arab armies this was not a concern in 1948.[85] Thus, the debate among
education officers concluded that hatred of the enemy was permitted, but
on a limited scale in keeping with what Karkoubi considered to be "Jewish
nature." This nature, Karkoubi felt, would ensure balance between the need
to create effective fighters and the desire that "hatred," in its abstract sense,
did not bring anarchy to the new Israeli society. Indeed, field-level commanders reported that instilling hatred for the enemy in their soldiers was quite
effective in combating fear during battle.[86]

A different kind of problem presented itself when trying to convince Jews
from Arab lands to exhibit the sort of hatred for Arabs that Karkoubi and
others were interested in. In a meeting between the chief of staff of the IDF,
Yigael Yadin, and the IDF high command, Yadin read to the officers excerpts
intercepted from letters sent by soldiers who were recent immigrants from
Iraq. Yadin expressed his concern that most did not show the level of animosity
to Arabs he had expected.[87] He nevertheless was excited to find one letter in
the collection, where an Iraqi Jewish soldier wrote to his family that those who
complained about the hardships of army training were the ones "who don't
have in their hearts the burning fire we have, because they did not suffer as
we did." The soldier explained that he devoted himself completely to the study
of war "out of cognition and also out of a feeling of revenge." [88] For Yadin, that
sentiment needed to be instilled in all soldiers from Arab lands:

> Jews who lived in Iraq and were humiliated all the time, in them of all people
> we need to stimulate this sentiment: *hatred of the Iraqi Arabs*; even in times of
> peace. We don't have times of peace. And even more than that—as that sol-
> dier is saying—*a possibility of revenge against the Iraqis*. Because that is what
> he can fathom at the moment; and I don't care if a commander, before going
> into battle, would tell his soldiers: "We have Iraqi soldiers there; that is your
> chance" [emphasis in original].[89]

Yadin alluded to what would become a deeply entrenched Israeli belief that
peace with the Arabs could never be realized.[90] Therefore, a constant state of
alert—based on hatred of the enemy—was essential. Yadin did not shy away
from tricking his soldiers to achieve it, and he also echoed racist views about
Mizrahi soldiers' primitivism.[91] But he also knew that not all Mizrahi soldiers
were cut from the same cloth: many North African soldiers (whose number

was much higher than Iraqi soldiers in the ranks of the IDF at the time) "did not really suffer [in their place of origin]," and therefore took no pride in killing Arabs.[92] This insufficient hatred for Arabs alarmed him and the IDF leadership, and the various education publications were aimed at addressing it, in accordance with what Karkoubi considered the "Jewish nature."

To do so required walking a fine line between encouraging brutality and censuring it. In Brigade Seven's bulletin, written after the capture of Nazareth in July 1948, one author explained that "the Hebrew soldier is not capable of murder and bloody revenge. At the end of battle, as an occupier, he demonstrates kindness and compassion, even if he announces (out of shame of being caught in the 'sin of softheartedness') his hatred of the enemy."[93] In other words, the expression of hatred was not organic to Jewish soldiers and thus there was little risk of it interfering with daily life at the war's end. On the pages of the weekly *Bamahane*, with wider circulation, the message was more forceful. Soldiers were told that one of the core elements in any unit's *esprit de corps* was hatred for the enemy "with eyes wide open . . . efficient, but passionate, and unyielding." The outlet for that hatred was also made clear: "We destine *death to the invaders* and nothing less. Death and defeat and extermination, one from which there is no resurgence."[94] Although the article was not authored by Kovner, it used the slogan most famously associated with him: "death to the invaders."[95]

In fact, Kovner did not bother following the guidelines set by Karkoubi. He continued to write as he pleased, almost until the end of the war. On October 1948 Givati soldiers were once again told that they were allowed to take revenge on the enemy using bayonets.[96] During the IDF's brief incursion into Gaza that month, Kovner criticized those around the world who bemoaned Gaza's imminent destruction. He explained that the Arabs were responsible for any death and destruction because they wanted to destroy the Jewish state.[97] He warned his soldiers against showing mercy to the enemy:

> We must not be vulnerable to the tears of the enemy and the mourning of his leaders. The only thing we can send Gaza now is not our condolences, but lead [bullets]. Because there is no voice that the Arab East understands better than lead, and no lead speaks as clearly . . . as that of the Israeli army.[98]

To keep hatred out of their own society, however, the education officers also saw a need to target plunder. In an article calling on them not to loot

Palestinian property, soldiers were told they could not possibly know if the person they were stealing from was innocent or not. Invoking the character of the new Jewish society, the author explained:

> The one who lets himself run wild with Arab property would end up taking Jewish property lightly [too]; the one who abuses our neighboring people will mistreat his own people ... Plunder, more than it hurts the victim, corrupts the soul of the offender.[99]

In fact, looting was one of the only criminal behaviors systematically addressed in education materials. Harsh warnings against looting were issued on numerous occasions, and criticism of the continued practice often appeared in army publications, relying on the reasoning that looting led to a collapse in discipline and combat readiness.[100] Palmach publications sometimes invoked Jewish morality and *tohar ha-neshek* ("the purity of arms") as reasons to resist looting. At other times, soldiers were warned that looting disrupts military operations and corrupts the character of the new Israeli society, and that all the spoils belonged to the Israeli government.[101] Judging by the widespread extent of looting, and by the fact that senior officers also took part in it, it would appear these pamphlets only had limited resonance.[102]

Education materials also devoted some attention to the treatment of POWs in Israeli captivity. On the one hand, *Bamahane* stressed that the IDF was obliged by the international conventions on POW treatment.[103] But even that message was vague: another article quoted a POW saying that he was told that the Jews would kill every captured Arab. "We thought you would be right to do so," the prisoner ostensibly told the reporter.[104] Soldiers were reassured that many POWs were in fact happy to be in Israeli captivity, especially Palestinians. This supposed joy, one pamphlet explained,

> shows the liberating nature of our army. The Jewish Land of Israel is the only advanced and progressive corner in the entire Middle East, where every person can fight for his elementary rights. Without noticing, we carry the word of progress and freedom to backwards and feudal Arab countries as well.[105]

This idea that Zionism was fighting for the liberation of Arabs in addition to that of Jews was a hasbara theme used from the beginning of Zionism and for decades after the 1948 war.[106] It is hard to assess how soldiers regarded such ideas.

Only Palmach education materials cautioned soldiers about committing war crimes, but not always in a consistent manner.[107] During the discussion about *havlagah* ("restraint") in the final stages of the Second World War, Palmach education materials warned soldiers against abusing innocent Arabs, and before war started in late 1947, apologies were often published when Arab women and children were killed during reprisal raids.[108] After the start of hostilities, Palmach education materials occasionally cautioned soldiers against indiscriminate violence. In August 1948 the Palmach published a pamphlet warning soldiers to keep their weapons pure so that they would not stain the name of the Hebrew soldier. "Every man is responsible for the results of his actions. . . . Your friends . . . are the ones who will demand explanations for your actions. . . . The IDF will not have felons and criminals among its ranks."[109]

One technique to discourage random killing of Arabs was to convince soldiers that revenge and murder did not bring relief. In November 1948 the story of the thirty-five Haganah men who were killed in January 1948 on their way to supply the besieged kibbutzim of Gush Etzion was presented in the Palmach bulletin, including a portrayal of the men's mutilated bodies.[110] According to the narrative provided, comrades of the thirty-five avenged their friends' death by killing "Arab murderers." However, as the article stated, revenge did not make the soldiers feel any better and did not serve as proper atonement for the killing of their friends. Only building the settlements destroyed by the Arabs, and erecting new ones, would be real payback for the killing of the thirty-five.[111]

For soldiers who continued to seek bloody revenge despite these warnings, Palmach offered some guidelines. Soldiers were reminded to be vigilant that their brutal behavior did not trickle down into day-to-day life.[112] In a letter by a father of a fallen soldier, printed in the Palmach bulletin, the father encouraged his son's comrades to be brutal, but to understand that brutality must cease at war's end:

> The claws the Hebrew avengers use to rip the bodies of the murderers are artificial, borrowed from the destructive world that spills our blood mercilessly. Our sons will shed the claws of blood when the murder and strangulation plot [against us] is removed. Our children will remain pure lambs in their souls even after the wolves made them pay back in their own coin . . . Blessed we be for raising a generation of fighters, that drink from the fountain of bravery, but not in order to be intoxicated.[113]

The observation of the bereaved father echoed that of Karkoubi. Both men were concerned, not by the violence inflicted on the men and women who were seen as the enemy, but rather with the implications of such violence on the character of the new nation.

If the Palmach was inconsistent about hatred and revenge, the education materials prepared for ultra-orthodox (*haredi*) soldiers were far more forceful in their dealing with violence, and repeatedly warned against adopting the gentile way of war: "We must remember to make our ways pure, correct our actions, and renounce once and for all the view of 'the House of Israel like all other nations [*ke-khol ha-goyim beit yiśrael*],' because this view is the reason we are in the diaspora close to two thousand years."[114] Instead of imitating the brutality of gentiles, the emphasis needed to be on Judaism's eternal message as a "light unto nations." The Jews were tasked with establishing "a glorious state which will set an example in its regime and morals."[115] Only if Israel's violence is checked would the reestablishment of the Jewish temple create "a light house for humanity, drowning in a sea of blood, yearning for salvation."[116]

The commander of the ultra-orthodox battalion offered soldiers a step-by-step process on how to overcome the "eye for an eye" urge. "Spilling the blood of he who killed your friend brings satisfaction," the battalion commander conceded. Nevertheless, the Bible clearly instructs: "Don't rejoice when your enemy falls" (Proverbs 24:17), and therefore "we must remember that a fellowman, even if he is our enemy, also desires to live. He too has a family who would grieve heavily if he died." In fact, when the battalion commander learned of a soldier who turned his gaze away when he was ordered to shoot an Arab, he became optimistic that there were still a few righteous men, unlike the majority of soldiers "who have true bloodlust, who rejoice and become excited when they have an opportunity to 'chop up' the enemy."[117] The Jews, the battalion commander insisted, may not rejoice in killing:

> If we need to kill an Arab, we must not do so out of desire, but out of compulsion. . . . If engrained bloodlust developed—and many are already afflicted with it—we would not be able to contain it.[118]

The battalion commander urged that the Jews in Palestine remember they were "the chosen people, impregnated with a noble spirit," and therefore "even if we must kill, we must never turn into murderers."[119]

Stricter enforcement against murder and brutality of the kind Kovner and others were advocating only came at the end of 1948. On the eve of the last offensive on the southern front, Operation Horev (which began on December 22, 1948), and shortly after the UN rejected Israel's first bid to be admitted as a member-state, the IDF launched a campaign against the murder of POWs and civilians.[120] Yigal Allon, who commanded the southern front, warned that any unjustified killing of civilians would be regarded as murder and that the soldiers would be prosecuted. He also cautioned against harassing the civilian population and against looting and expelling Palestinians without a direct order.[121] Another intervention came from Ben-Gurion: in March 1949, after the war was essentially over and just as the UN was reviewing Israel's second request to be admitted as a member-state, Ben-Gurion ordered the distribution among soldiers of a poem written by Nathan Alterman that criticized the murder of innocent civilians by soldiers. The poem, "On This" ('al zot), was originally published in Mapai's daily newspaper, *Davar* (Word) and described a young soldier "trying out" his machine gun on Arab civilians.[122] Alterman was concerned by the complacency of Israelis to atrocities.[123]

> Let us sing then also about "delicate incidents"
> For which the true name, incidentally, is murder
> And let songs be composed about conversations between sympathetic inter-
>   locutors
> Who with collusive chuckles make concessions and grant forgiveness.[124]

The publication of the poem included a short introduction by Ben-Gurion, who emphasized: "If this conscience is not at work and palpitates in our hearts during these days—we shall not be worthy of the greatness we were given thus far."[125]

As fighting subsided, education materials turned to discuss those Palestinians who remained in the newly conquered areas, and the hundreds of thousands who found themselves beyond the borders of the Jewish state. Soldiers were called to treat the population respectfully, while at the same time regarding every civilian as a potential enemy: "You must make them follow your instructions quickly (purposeful tardiness in following instructions is one of the techniques in which the masses help the enemy)."[126] The soldiers were also warned not to engage in conversation with civilians "and not to be

tricked by the pleas of elderly men and women and their crying." Finally, soldiers were ordered not to threaten civilians with weapons unnecessarily and
to avoid hitting or cursing them. "In short, one might say that you are asked
to treat the population with an iron fist inside silk gloves."[127]

It is noteworthy that the aforementioned silk gloves were not invoked when
discussing the Palestinian "exodus," i.e., the expulsion and flight of hundreds
of thousands of Palestinians, which became a pressing concern in the months
following the adoption of Plan D (*tokhnit dalet*) by the Haganah's general staff
in March 1948. The plan is the subject of intense scholarly debate. It includes
the following instruction: "Destruction of villages (setting fire to, blowing up,
and planting mines in the debris), especially those population centers which
are difficult to control continuously." Some historians argued that this was a
masterplan to expel Palestinians and destroy their villages; others maintained
this line only referred to villages where the Haganah encountered armed resistance.[128] While perhaps not the "smoking gun" scholars have been looking for
in order to prove there was a blueprint for the nakba, Plan D certainly shows
that expulsion was often planned and approved from above.

When discussing the Palestinian exodus, shortly after the Israeli cabinet
voted against the return of Palestinians in mid-June 1948, the education
officers sometimes employed verbal acrobatics. At times, they explained, it
was crucial to "cleanse/purify" (*le-ṭaher*) the villages that did not collaborate
with the Jews.[129] Other times, it was stated that the villages were "cleared"
(*punu*) or "emptied" (*hitroḵnu*), without specifying who was responsible. Yet
the most popular explanation for the exodus was "psychosis and general
fear," while the Dayr Yasin massacre was mentioned as a contributing factor.
Dayr Yasin was a village west of Jerusalem that had signed a nonbelligerence
agreement with the nearby Jewish settlement; nevertheless, the Irgun and
Stern Gang killed 125 Palestinian civilians upon occupying the village on
April 9, 1948, including women and children (for more on the aftermath of
the massacre, see chapter 4). IDF education officers, however, claimed that
it was not the massacre itself that caused the flight but Arab propaganda.
Rather than priming the Arabs to exact revenge, a pamphlet explained, the
propaganda's emphasis on the massacre caused the masses to flee. The education officers quoted a British sergeant who witnessed the flight in Jaffa:
"The Arabs were scared to death when they imagined to themselves that

the Jews would do to them half of what they would have done to the Jews if things were the other way around."[130]

To the soldiers taken aback by the stream of refugees leaving their villages and marching toward the borders, Menahem Talmi, a Givati soldier, explained in the pages of *Bamahane*:

> We do not do to them what they would have done to us if they were in our place. We do not massacre our one-time murderers, but we will not be caught up showing mercy! We rejoice in a jubilation of an army that won. We will not be weak at heart from seeing the thousands of refugees sprawling in the streets, bending over their few belongings, with their gloomy faces. They threw stones at us and shot lead at our skulls, ran wild and promised to throw us into the sea. Their fantasy was our downfall, our spilled blood pleasing to their eyes. This is their punishment.[131]

Much space was devoted to depicting what the Arabs would have done had they been victorious, including "fantasy killings" and "slaughters which gladden one's soul and satisfy the desire," and the soldiers were advised not to offer any help to the refugees but water and some food. The soldiers were told to remember the Jews killed on the roads at the beginning of the war and "feel the sweet revenge. Once again you do not feel any compassion or regret."[132] The IDF conquests, the education officers explained, put an end to the wandering of the Jews; their walking sticks were turned into weapons, and now another people became the wandering nation.[133] And to those Arabs who expressed their wish to return to their villages, another article stressed, the soldiers must say that there is no way to turn back the clock.[134]

Throughout this chapter, the voices of soldiers responding to propaganda have been difficult to discern. However, some indoctrination materials seem to suggest that soldiers did question the policy in regard to the Palestinian refugees. For example, on April 5, 1948, when the Palestinian exodus had just started, the education department published a pamphlet entitled "Answers to Questions Soldiers Frequently Ask." It opened with the question, "Why don't we agree to the return of Arab refugees during the lull [in fighting]?" If the presentation of this question represented a response to indoctrination efforts, the education officers took the opportunity to stifle any dreams of peace, explaining that the return of refugees during the war would pose a security risk. They emphasized that this was a pressing issue for the Arab states and that the Yishuv leadership did not want to make things any easier for them while the war was still going on. It was also stressed that the Arab states were not really concerned with the humanitarian aspect of the refugee problem and that it was merely a political maneuver.[135]

> No one understands better than us the pain of these refugees . . . but the one guilty of their situation cannot demand that *we* solve his problem. The enemy started the war that brought about a *Shoah* [the Hebrew word used for the Holocaust] on hundreds of Arab villages . . . and he must face the consequences.[136]

The volume of pamphlets discussing the Palestinian refugees suggests the issue was one in which soldiers were particularly interested. Again and again, education pamphlets emphasized that the Palestinian exodus was not Israel's fault. "The fact that hundreds of villages were destroyed, fields were trampled and much toil was lost is the direct fault of the rotten Feudalism of the East and its English allies. They need to pay the price for the spilled blood—we did not have a choice."[137] By the end of the war, the education pamphlets articulated the new Israeli narrative, clearly stating that "the Arabs of Israel left the country not under Jewish pressure" and more importantly that Israel would refuse to allow the return of the refugees.[138] Only when the Arab states recognized the permanence of Israel would there be time to address the refugee question, but never through their return. They would instead have to be resettled in the Arab states (which was their preference anyway, the narrative went).[139] The reason for the refusal to allow refugees to return was that they would form a fifth column in Israel and hinder the absorption of Jewish immigrants.[140] Commanders were advised to call on their soldiers to settle the conquered land as soon as possible so that the refugees would not have anywhere to return to.[141]

Another mechanism used to ease any qualms the soldiers may have had about the departure of Palestinians was by casting doubt on Palestinians' attachment to the land and on their existence as a nation, a theme also used by Ben-Gurion himself.[142] In fact, the soldiers were told that it was an Arab characteristic to flee during wartime. As proof, an "Arab proverb" was quoted: "Two thirds of bravery is fleeing."[143] One battalion pamphlet featured an account by a soldier walking inside emptied Palestinian homes, a very common practice.[144] One house caught his attention: "windowless rooms, dark, with a heavy aroma surrounding them. On the ground, wretched rags roll around, emitting stench."[145] Seeing the lice and other insects running around the house, the soldier had a hard time believing that "this house, with these pitiful objects, is being used as a place of residence for our cousins [the Palestinians] who fled the village in panic before we came here."[146] Looking around, the soldier could not help but ponder, "this house is indeed a house. Somewhere I too have a house, and my mother sits in it, and my father and sisters [too]." But upon further reflection, the soldier realized that his house was very different from that of the Palestinian in whose house he was now an uninvited guest: "if there was an enemy approaching my house, to which I so yearn right now, would I too abandon it in panic and run to save myself, while losing my honor, or . . ."[147] While the soldier did not provide his final thoughts on the conundrum, it appears that by contrasting his own honorable attachment to the home of his family to the supposed lack of attachment and loss of honor of the Palestinian, he could witness the Arab exodus without regret.[148]

ANGLOPHONE VOLUNTEERS CHECK THEIR LIBERALISM AT THE DOOR

As early as 1940, when the Yishuv leadership first considered the option of bringing American volunteers to fight in Palestine, concerns were raised that American youth would not be susceptible to political indoctrination and that many held antimilitaristic views. Indeed, pacifist views were common among American Jewish youth, at least on the eve of the Second World War.[149] In a special report, submitted to the chief staff of the IDF after the arrival of the Mahal volunteers, it was determined that most were not genuinely Zionist, even if they formally declared they were.[150] To instill militaristic views, and other themes deemed important, Mahal volunteers, while en route to Palestine/Israel and throughout their time in the IDF, were required to attend special hasbara talks on Zionism and Israel's war aims, and education materials were prepared for them in English and other languages.[151] The flagship publication, *Frontline*, explained in its first volume that it was intended "to help all of you who speak approximately the same language to understand each other and why you came here; to explain something of this country and the people you meet in it to you."[152] In other words, the volunteers' own interpretations for why they came could not be trusted; they had to be told why they came and who they would be fighting with. Even though publications stressed to volunteers that "you are home" and "your arrival to our aid is greatly appreciated," the underlying message in many of the propaganda materials created a subtly coercive atmosphere in which volunteers would feel reluctant to express any disapproval of the war conduct or of Israel itself.[153]

Frontline shared some themes with the Israeli military's Hebrew-language education materials, but its tone was more reserved. The war, one *Frontline* article stressed, proved the cowardice of the Arab. Mocking the commander of the ALA, Fawzi al-Qawuqji, it said, "Flight is an art, one in which Kaukji has become expert."[154] The Egyptian officers, another article remarked, did not fare any better: they left their soldiers dressed in pajamas and fled.[155] Comical portrayals of Palestinians were often printed next to articles about the Arab defeat, conveying the idea that the defeat could be explained at least in part by the supposed weak mental faculties of Arabs. One picture showed an old man in Arab garb extending both hands to the side, looking baffled. The caption under the picture reads "Maalesh!", colloquial Arabic for "never mind." Another picture showed soldiers posing next to the Ottoman mosque in Biʾr al-Sabʿ (Beersheba) and in front of them a young man trying to drag a donkey. The caption reads, "Stubborn resistance in Beersheba" (see fig. 5).[156]

One theme discussed in *Frontline* far more frequently than in the Hebrew-language propaganda was Israel's approach to peace with the Arabs. "There may by now be a glimmering suspicion that to destroy Israel's cities and settlements and to drive the Jews into the sea is not a task that is lightly undertaken," an article from December 1948 explained.[157] Israel wanted peace with the Arabs, the article stressed, but it demanded direct negotiations. The refusals of Arab states to sit at the table with Israel and to vacate Palestine "constitute a warlike threat and show evidence of warlike intent." Echoing the militaristic approach, the article stipulated that Israel would not allow "Arab dillydallying": "It is now business or nothing, serious armistice talks or the consequences of Arab refusal."[158] A month later, it was explained to the volunteers that Egypt was paying the price for its refusal to negotiate.[159]

The issue of the Palestinian refugees was rarely mentioned in *Frontline,* in stark contrast to the Hebrew education materials. One article stated briefly that "Arab villages along the road [to Jerusalem] were cleared,"[160] and another

FIGURE 5. "Stubborn resistance in Beersheba." October 1948. Source: Israel Defense Forces–Sherut Tarbut/Gahal, *Frontline*, 25 November 1948. Held at Klau Library, Cincinnati, Hebrew Union College–Jewish Institute of Religion. Courtesy of the IDFA.

repeated the claim that Arabs fled because of panic.[161] In any case, it was a well-deserved punishment:

> The Arabs on[c]e dreamed of throwing the Jews into the Mediterranean, but now it seems that the situation has been reversed. It is the Arabs who are begging that the return of hundreds of thousands of refugees to Palestine be permitted.[162]

Stating that "the situation has been reversed" might suggest that Israel had *intentionally* depopulated Palestine and expelled the Arab population. If this was the intention of the author, it was a singular proclamation. In fact, trigger-happy sentiments were almost completely absent from Mahal education materials, unlike their prevalence in the Hebrew-language pamphlets. In a column meant to be humorous about the characteristics of the Sabra, apparently written by a Mahal volunteer, the following was noted:

> The Sabra is usually quite peaceful unless someone carelessly mentions his legendary enemy, the Ayrab [meant to imitate the pronunciation of the word Arab by Ashkenazi Jews]. Then he chokes on his Mitz [Hebrew for juice], straps on his traditional weapon, the sten-gun . . . and makes noise like Joshua looking for Jericho. The Ayrab is very much afraid of the Sabra, and with good reason. If things keep going like they have in the past, there won't be any Arabs left in a short while.[163]

It appears that some Mahal volunteers noticed the Sabra had adopted brutality as one of his or her defining characteristics.

For those volunteers who were concerned with the way Israel was treating the Arab population, *Frontline* explained that "2,000 years of exile have given them [the Israelis] ample training in 'how to treat a minority.'"[164] Although war was barbarous, "our forefathers enjoyed the reputation of being more humane in the treatment of their captives than their contemporaries in neighbouring lands."[165] The Palestinian POWs in Israeli camps, another article explained, "live more comfortably than they did as civilians."[166] Volunteers were promised that "non-Jews" would not be discriminated against in the new state.[167]

Where there was similarity between the Mahal and the Hebrew-language education materials was in the comparison of current events to biblical times. The first issue of *Frontline* showcased a letter supposedly written by King

David in which the author drew parallels between the wars he waged and that of 1948.[168] Other articles in Mahal publications portrayed the story of the revolt led by Judas Maccabeus against the Seleucid Empire and the subsequent victory of the Maccabeans. The rebels fought against "authoritarianism" in the "defense of freedom of conscience" and their victory was "proof that the few who love what they are fighting for can beat the many who fight only for gain"—again, an attempt to draw parallels between the Zionist just cause and the supposed lack of ideology among Arabs.[169] Volunteers were also told that once fighting ceased, the Maccabeans were allowed to enjoy the loot, hinting that IDF soldiers would be allowed to do the same (which contradicted the message of other Hebrew pamphlets).[170]

Self-sacrifice, discussed extensively in Hebrew education materials, was also stressed in the English ones. The military leaders of the Israelites, one article pointed out, "knew how to die," like King Ahab who was stabbed during battle but kept standing upright until he died, so that his soldiers would not lose heart.[171] In fact, education materials often discussed the role models that volunteers were to follow, and there was very little room for volunteers to express their unique culture or values. They were repeatedly asked to "make an effort to understand and appreciate the mentality and makeup of your fellow Jews in Palestine."[172] To do this, volunteers needed to curb any criticism they might have:

> We came to fight, and thereby earned the right to criticise. But let us never forget that those who came before us came to build, and only incidentally to fight. When this war began they built less and less and fought more and more. Had they not built or fought as they did, there would be nothing for us to do here, nothing for us to fight for. They fought a good fight and more than held their own. We've come to help, not to rescue. Let's remember that, and we'll get along better with them, and with ourselves too.[173]

But as the next chapters suggest, Mahal volunteers were unwilling just "to help," and demanded their voices be heard on the conduct of the army and the future of Israel.

COMBAT DOCTRINE AND IDEOLOGICAL TRAINING IN THE ALA

The first stop for most of the Arab volunteers after leaving their countries of origin was the ALA training camp, next to Qatana, southwest of Damascus. Training there started as early as October 1947, with the vast majority of volunteers arriving after the partition plan was approved by the UN.[174] The structural problems faced by the ALA were already evident in Qatana. Volunteers who arrived at the camp were supposed to undergo a rigorous training program.[175] The curriculum included grenade throwing, marches, night combat, demolition, armored-vehicle operation, and anti-aircraft missile defense. Even commando fighting was purportedly in the program. In practice, however, very little training took place, and what training occurred was significantly substandard due to a dearth of funds and lack of qualified officers.[176] In fact, some volunteers were shipped out of Qatana after only two days of training and still in their civilian clothes. They were only issued uniforms and arms en route to Palestine.[177] Al-Qawuqji complained years later that "some of the men could not even load a rifle properly."[178]

From Qatana volunteers were driven to Bint Jbeil in southern Lebanon, which was a logistical center and transfer point for the ALA.[179] According to Haganah intelligence, upon arrival in town, clerks from the volunteers' bureau examined the papers of each group of arriving soldiers, gave them food and additional equipment, and then assigned them to guides who would take them to Salha, a village on the border of Mandate Palestine. From there, the volunteers boarded buses that would take them under cover of darkness to Acre or Haifa.[180]

The problems that plagued the ALA while in training did not improve much inside Palestine. In fact, the spread of dysentery and other diseases made even waiting for the battle to begin a difficult task.[181] Soldiers were also not paid regularly.[182] A junior officer in the Hittin battalion alerted his commander in February 1948 that they lacked provisions, gasoline, and clothing. "We are practically naked," he protested.[183] Securing rifles for all volunteers was also a major challenge, since most Arab countries failed to provide the quota of weapons to which they had committed.[184]

ALA administrative orders suggest that it was quite difficult to maintain discipline within the diverse group of volunteers who came from many different backgrounds. The documents also suggest an aim of molding soldiers into new kinds of humans, uplifting them from their purportedly primitive existences of the past. For example, one administrative order to company commanders warned that "the neglect of sergeants knows no limit. They do not feel themselves responsible for anything and live with their soldiers as if they were living tribal life."[185] Therefore, company commanders were instructed to order sergeants to sleep together with their men in barracks and supervise them closely, since "the soldier needs to feel that there is someone who gives him orders, and if not, we are doomed."[186]

What exactly unsupervised soldiers were engaged in is not entirely clear from the administrative orders. One order suggests that the most urgent challenge was soldiers deserting their units, and officers were instructed to locate these deserters and punish them severely.[187] The commander of the Second Yarmuk battalion, Adib al-Shishakli, wrote the chairman of the Palestinian national committee in Acre that if the city's inhabitants came across a deserting soldier, they were "to confiscate his weapon or even strip him of his uniforms and inform me immediately."[188] Even when soldiers were staying put, they were not always willing to carry out orders, likely due to the physical conditions in camps.[189] An order forbidding soldiers from drinking alcohol suggests that it was another favorite pastime.[190]

On March 6, 1948, al-Qawuqji himself crossed the border into Palestine and shortly after made his way to Jabaʿ, near Tubas (in the Jenin district), where he established his headquarters.[191] Sam Souki, an Egyptian writing for the American-based United Press (UP) who accompanied al-Qawuqji, reported that "thousands of cheering troops assembled in the Samarian hills" to greet him.[192] Al-Qawuqji addressed his soldiers, reminding those who accompanied him in the 1936–39 Arab Revolt that, unlike then, this was the ultimate battle: "We shall not leave Palestine before the Holy Land is relieved from the Zionists, or we shall die here, to be buried in the land we love." For those volunteers assembled in Jabaʿ who were not familiar with al-Qawuqji and his bombastic language, or for those fearful that the relatively small volunteer army would not be able to overcome the Yishuv, al-Qawuqji promised that "we are but the pioneers of the big armies which will pour continuously into Palestine to help keeping [sic] it for our grand-children."[193]

According to Hani al-Hindi, the foremost historian of the ALA, commanders did not take much interest in the ideological training of their soldiers.[194] This may not be entirely true. ʿAli Nasir al-Din, the Lebanese head of the ALA propaganda department, who arrived in Palestine several weeks before al-Qawuqji with the first ALA forces to cross from Lebanon, launched an indoctrination and propaganda campaign aimed at the Arab volunteers who were assembling in Palestine, and more broadly at Palestinians. A key tool

FIGURE 6. Commander of the Arab Liberation Army, Fawzi al-Qawuqji, talking to officers. 1 March 1948. Photo by John Phillips. Source: The LIFE Picture Collection via Getty Images.

in this campaign was the ALA radio station, which began broadcasting on April 11, 1948, "so that the entire world could hear . . . the sound of freedom and truth."[195] In line with his previous depiction of al-Qawuqji as a giant, Nasir al-Din referred to the ALA commander during the first broadcast as "the hero who gave away his genius and life for the sake of his nation." More than that, al-Qawuqji was presented as a holy figure "who was created [khuliqa] to carry out a holy mission [risala]," that is, to save Palestine from Zionism.[196]

Based in Jaba', the station featured four daily broadcasts in Arabic, each about fifteen minutes long. The Arabic broadcast was followed by an English-language version, followed by Hebrew.[197] The radio's chief announcer was Sa'di Basbus, who, like al-Qawuqji, was a native of Tripoli, Lebanon, and had also participated in the 1941 Rashid 'Ali al-Gaylani revolt in Iraq. During the Second World War, Basbus worked as an announcer in a Nazi-affiliated radio station, broadcasting from occupied Athens. He later moved to Berlin where he broadcasted Nazi propaganda to the Middle East, with a heavy dose of gory antisemitic themes (which were largely absent from his ALA broadcasts). During his time in Berlin, Basbus worked closely with Amin al-Husayni, Rashid 'Ali al-Gaylani, and with al-Qawuqji himself, which is likely why he was chosen as the announcer for ALA radio once it was established.[198]

The ALA propaganda style inside Palestine was very different from the themes used to mobilize the volunteers to begin with. The radical messages during mobilization had to be abandoned since the patrons of the ALA were fearful that the revolutionary zeal of volunteers might eventually be directed back at them. The Ba'th party's sharp criticism of Syrian president Shukri al-Quwwatli was replaced with radio accolades: Basbus wished the president longevity and added, "May God allow the Syrian President to save Palestine from the despotic enemy."[199] In fact, while in Palestine, Nasir al-Din abandoned his radical preaching about colonialism and the corruption of Arab regimes, and focused instead on the Zionists, described as disciples of the crusaders.[200] This was already evident in the first ALA radio broadcast, in the midst of the battle for Mishmar ha-'Emek (see chapter 4). Al-Qawuqji himself declared:

> With terror and fear the Zionists see through the windows of their demolished forts and houses the crumbling of their imaginary aspirations and the evaporation of their golden dreams. . . . I pledge that after preliminary and sporadic skirmishing, I shall give the Zionists a blow from which they will never recover.[201]

With the abandonment of his revolutionary posture, al-Qawuqji resorted to stories of Islamic glory and modern Arab heroism to galvanize his men: "Our martyrs' blood, shed in the various parts of the Holy Land, hardly vanishes in the earth before it meets that of their ancestors, these heroes who responded to Palestine's call throughout history."[202] Among those mentioned by al-Qawuqji were Sayf Allah Khalid ibn al-Walid, a companion of the prophet who was instrumental in capturing Syria (including Palestine) and Iraq in the seventh century; Salah al-Din, who conquered Jerusalem from the crusaders; and even 'Abd al-Qadir al-Husayni, the commander of the Army of the Holy Jihad, who was killed three days earlier in battle.[203] ALA fighters, al-Qawuqji pleaded, must take up these heroes' banner and strive to complete "their tasks of crushing Zionism and rescuing Palestine." If al-Qawuqji feared these might be difficult tasks to accomplish, he said nothing of it, and instead reassured his listeners that "I see no difficulty in achieving this."[204] To reinforce the message, ALA armored vehicles were decorated with an emblem of a dagger thrust into a Star of David.[205]

Around the same time that the radio speech was delivered, al-Qawuqji also gave a lengthy interview to the Palestinian daily *al-Difa'*, during which he explained his views on Jews and the war more broadly. In line with the pan-Arab tone of his earlier radio broadcasts—although careful not to incite any rebellious action—al-Qawuqji explained in the interview that he saw the Palestine problem as "a blessed issue" that brought together the Arabs and united them; in fact, "if there were not a problem, it would have been necessary for the Arabs to create an issue of the same magnitude so it could connect them to the point that the Palestine problem brought them to."[206] When discussing the ongoing fighting, al-Qawuqji stressed that "the Arabs are the most merciful people and the most compassionate ones"; however, they would not agree to share their lands with the Jews, and if the Jews persisted in their actions they would suffer.[207]

To explain the rationale behind Jewish behavior, al-Qawuqji invoked antisemitic tropes, but also made some effort to distinguish between good Jews and bad Jews. He stressed that the Jews were the "chosen people" only when it came to "commerce and money," and that in Palestine they had made a grave miscalculation. To explain the nature of that mistake, al-Qawuqji decided to compare the Zionist ideology to the Nazi one: the Germans wanted to rule the world, and to do so "relied on the principles of Nazism that they invented, the Aryan blood that flows in their veins and their love for control." Zionism, according to al-Qawuqji, tried to imitate these principles:

The Jews—while different—also want to follow the Germans and take on the principle of Zionism and the desire for sovereignty over Palestine and what came to them in their dreams, to create a Jewish state. The Jews know that [pursuing] these three principles carry a death sentence, and they will have neither sovereignty nor a state in Palestine.[208]

The origin of al-Qawuqji's assertion that these actions carried a death sentence is not immediately clear. It is possible that he was referring to the persistent view among some Arab elites that the Jews remained dhimmi subjects in Islamic lands, which conditioned protection on submission to Muslim rule, and as such did not tolerate any form of sovereignty. It was an outdated view. In his native Lebanon, modernization of the Alliance and colonial legacy had long made the dhimmi status obsolete.

In any case, al-Qawuqji blamed only some Jews of rebellion, namely "a great number of fantasizers . . . who served in the army in Poland or elsewhere and came to deceive those whom the Arabs treated well." And it was the duty of those dhimmi Jews who were well treated to "not deny the goodness of the Arabs' deeds toward them and . . . to avoid getting carried away behind these mercenaries." For those good Jews, al-Qawuqji even went so far as to suggest that they "live in Palestine like their brothers live in Iraq and other Arab states. They have the rights minorities have all over the world and are obligated by the duties of the ruling country."[209] A similar pledge was given on the ALA radio about the future Arab state in Palestine "in which Jews will live as ordinary citizens and will enjoy full rights of citizenship."[210] Thus, while al-Qawuqji invoked certain Western antisemitic tropes (not to mention death threats), he also was careful to stake out a position of moderation about the future of Jews in Arab lands.

If al-Qawuqji directed his propaganda efforts toward speaking about Jews and Zionists rather than Arab regimes, other materials produced by Nasir al-Din showed that extricating critiques of Zionism from the colonial reality which outlived formal colonialism in the Middle East was challenging. This dynamic was especially clear in an article prepared by Nasir al-Din, which purportedly included the views of ordinary ALA soldiers about the appointment of a Swedish diplomat and nobleman, Folke Bernadotte, as the UN Security Council's mediator in Palestine.[211] In the text from May 1948, published in several Arab newspapers and possibly also distributed within the ALA, Nasir al-Din exhibited some of the same antagonism to diplomacy apparent in his earlier writing, but without casting blame on Arab regimes.[212] According to Nasir al-Din, frontline soldiers were against any truce and also demanded that Bernadotte solve the Jewish problem through "the creation of a Jewish state in Sweden with its president being Count Bernadotte."[213] When Nasir al-Din explained to the soldiers that the Jews were insistent on creating their state in Palestine, where the Jewish temple once stood, the soldiers replied:

> No problem. Write [addressing Nasir al-Din] that soldiers of the ALA suggest that Count Bernadotte move the stones of the temple and the soil of its foundations from Jerusalem to Sweden, using American ships.[214]

Arab states, the soldiers suggested, would donate a golden calf to guard the temple in its new location, and Bernadotte's observers could protect it.[215] It seems that invoking the biblical golden calf story in Nasir al-Din's article was to further signal that the Jews were straying from the true path.

According to the soldiers' plan, presented by Nasir al-Din, all Jews who immigrated to Palestine after 1918 (a year after the Balfour Declaration) would have to leave for Sweden, while Jews who resided in Palestine before that date would be allowed to stay. Finally, the soldiers called for "the creation of an Arab state in Palestine and east Transjordan and Iraq, and leaving the door open for [other] parts of Greater Syria [al-sham] area to join that state."[216] If Bernadotte rejected these ideas, or if he influenced the Jews to reject them, "then the ALA will eliminate the source of evil and bring down the disturbances in Palestine, and spread confidence and peace."[217]

It is hard to make much of the suggestion to establish a Jewish state in Sweden. More than anything else it was likely aimed at conveying Nasir al-Din's view that the Jewish problem was essentially a European one to be solved inside Europe, and also to show scorn for Bernadotte's mediation and diplomacy more broadly. However, the few words devoted to the Arab state the soldiers were proposing, which were likely Nasir al-Din's own words, offer more promise when attempting to understand ALA propaganda. While the proposed state included Hashemite Transjordan and Iraq, it did not include Syria or Lebanon (al-sham), for which the soldiers were "leaving the door open ... to join that state." This is a surprising kind of precision, not least because Nasir al-Din's views on this topic dating to the 1930s were clear: as a founding member of the League of Nationalist Action, he was supportive of the inclusion of Syria and Lebanon in a unified Arab kingdom, and in fact, in his view, Syria was to be the center of such a kingdom.[218] What may explain his sudden decision to walk back from this position was fear of angering the Syrian president al-Quwwatli, who, of course, was the chief sponsor of the ALA, and possibly also the Lebanese prime minister, Riyad al-Sulh, both of whom were uninterested in any form of unification.[219] In other words, Nasir al-Din made sure ALA propaganda did not dispute the existing state system in the Levant. As for Hashemite-controlled Transjordan and Iraq, he was much less concerned about ruffling their feathers, perhaps because of an understanding reached between al-Qawuqji and King Abdullah.[220]

Battalion operational orders provide us with a glimpse into how the ALA central command articulated its strategic goals to officers deployed through-out Palestine. Unsurprisingly, these goals were rather different than those used in propaganda aimed at volunteers and the rest of the Arab world. Al-Quwwatli announced, both in private and in public, that the purpose of the ALA was to "destroy the Zionist threat altogether," and the military committee of the Arab League, nominally in charge of the ALA, publicly declared that the ALA was supposed to "thwart the division of Palestine."[221] In the Lebanese press, al-Qawuqji was quoted as saying: "The object of our mission in Palestine is to destroy Zionism, to kill the partition plan, and to implement Arab League decisions for safeguarding the Arabism of Palestine. . . . Thus, we will wage this war for a month, for a year, for a generation, and even for a century, until we finally realize our aspirations."[222]

Army orders portrayed more limited goals. An operational order for an ALA battalion stationed in the Haifa region from late March 1948 defined the ALA strategic goal as "preventing the partition of Palestine by performing military tasks with the aim of: 1. Convincing the Jews that their hostility to Arabs will result in a disaster for them; 2. Preventing Jewish attacks against Arabs, and causing casualties [among Jews]."[223] Even though the words "pre-venting partition" appeared in the order, the two aims following them were far more confined. The Second Yarmuk battalion under the command of Adib al-Shishakli had an even more limited *raison d'être*. The order for the battalion was "to strengthen the morale of the inhabitants of Palestine, to learn the

capabilities of the Zionist armed forces in Palestine and to examine the position of the British mandate authorities in regard to military actions taking
place between Jews and Arabs."[224]

It is noteworthy that ALA propaganda includes no mention of "extermination," pushing Jews into the sea,[225] or killing the Jewish inhabitants of
Palestine in an organized manner, which Israeli propaganda had claimed at
the time was the Arab war objective.[226] The claim is used, even to the present
day, in polemics aimed at drawing parallels between Islamism and fascism
(the so-called "Islamofascism" neologism).[227] In fact, Haganah intelligence
concluded just the opposite in 1948: "the ALA does not intend to massacre the
Jews if they surrender and raise a white flag," explained one internal memo.[228]
Attacks on Jewish settlements were to look quite differently: ALA soldiers
were ordered to collect intelligence before attacks and "use the vulnerabilities
discovered in the settlement's defense system to attack it and destroy it, or
at least damage its fields and orchards to the extent possible." Soldiers were
instructed to ambush Jewish transportation and blow up bridges and roads
connecting Jewish settlements.[229] While in battle, burning down or blowing up
houses in captured settlements was strongly encouraged because it "helps the
success of the operation."[230] Even inside Palestinian villages, during a retreat,
ALA soldiers were told to "burn the houses down and plant mines so that the
enemy does not enjoy one shred of land."[231] Taking plunder, ALA commands
stipulated, was not allowed unless special permission was given.[232]

Orders clearly specified who the soldiers were allowed to kill, and the ALA
attempted to ground these rules of engagement in a sense of civilizational
values shared among Arabs and non-Arabs alike. On the ALA radio, Jews were
censured for allegedly mutilating Arab bodies and kidnapping Arab doctors
and nurses.[233] But as the operational orders explained, ALA soldiers were required to act differently: according to Haganah intelligence, the ALA central
command forbade the abuse of corpses and instructed soldiers to move all
captives to POW camps.[234] "Religion and the Arab tradition which we inherited
from our forefathers necessitate that we spare women, children and the elderly.
This duty must be observed," an operational order explained.[235] Another order
from the General Headquarters in Damascus notified all units that the ALA
had committed to the Red Cross to follow the Geneva Conventions. All officers
were instructed to inform their soldiers of the requirement to give adequate

medical treatment to wounded enemy soldiers and civilians.[236] At least some ALA volunteers and their Palestinian affiliates sought to echo back these rules of engagement to the Yishuv. A Jewish woman captured in Haifa in February 1948 was released carrying a note to the Haganah:

> The lady carrying this letter was found in exclusively Arab territory and in accordance with Arab noble customs, we did not lay a hand on her. . . . We want you to understand that Arabs have a delicate soul and they do not prey on women and children like you do.[237]

Trying to assuage volunteers' fear of the Jewish forces, the ALA tried to distinguish between different types of Jewish fighters. One intelligence briefing explained that the residents of most Jewish settlements were ex-servicemen, along with some career officers with European training who were partisans during the Second World War. "From the operations carried out by the kibbutzim, we can learn that their aim is merely defensive and also to respond to hostilities with similar actions according to the 'eye for an eye' law," declared one intelligence report—rather accurately—as the Mishmar ha-'Emek battle demonstrated (see chapter 4).[238] The Jewish residents of the cities, on the other hand, "do not have the same militaristic inclination those of the kibbutzim have." Still, all Jews, according to the report, feared the Arab villages in their vicinity.[239]

But fear was apparently as prevalent among ALA volunteers: a company commander in the First Yarmuk battalion wrote his junior officers and sergeants after a failed attack on kibbutz Tirat Zvi in February 1948 that the battle revealed "who is a soldier with true military qualities and who shows disdain for the orders of his commander and his entire militancy is expressed only through wearing adorned uniforms."[240] Some soldiers, the company commander continued, viewed battle as merely a drill, while others "trembled from horror and fear thinking that death follows them in each step they take, and that each bullet fired by the enemy means certain death for them."[241] The company commander asked his junior officers to convey to their soldiers that "there is no escaping death. It is the lot of every man, and [can] reach him anywhere and anytime, that is why there is no room to fear it."[242] To encourage acts of bravery, commanders instituted a system of decorations for those who excelled in battle. Those soldiers were also gifted money that was taken as spoils from the Jews. Meanwhile, those who were guilty of misconduct were publicly reprimanded.[243]

BRINGING PALESTINE INTO THE FOLD

Upon entering Palestine, al-Qawuqji sought to convince Palestinians that preventing partition would not be a difficult task. To justify his authority in the eyes of the inhabitants, he recalled the time he spent in Palestine during the 1936–39 Arab Revolt, when he recruited and led bands of Iraqi and Syrian volunteers in fighting:

> From the village of Qabatiya, which I left twelve years ago after completing the last battle of the successful relief combats, I return to it today to begin from here the battle of the Arab nation. From this village I send you my greetings and devotion, while confidence in victory fills me, and great happiness that I was allowed the honor to participate in this battle. [244]

So confident was al-Qawuqji that he pledged to the Syrian president al-Quwwatli, "We will meet next in Tel Aviv."[245]

To the Palestinians gathered to hear him upon his entrance to Palestine, al-Qawuqji stressed the pan-Arab nature of the ALA and highlighted the fact that he had recruited people from all around the Arab and Muslim world to come to Palestine:

> We come to you today as a vanguard for the Arab armies that would follow one after another to the rescue. Hundreds of millions of Arabs and Muslims are standing behind us and they swore to keep the immortal Arabness of Palestine . . . We all come with one heart and one goal to annul the UN partition decision, to destroy the landmarks of Zionism and eliminate it altogether, to carry out the Arab League's decisions, and to reaffirm the Arabness of Palestine.[246]

Palestinians hearing these words were likely reassured. Furthermore, *al-Difa'* quoted an ALA officer as saying that the Arabs had more weapons than they needed to defeat the Jews, and a correspondent embedded with the ALA added that "Palestine's Arabs will only play a secondary, helping, role in the current war waged against Zionism."[247] To those Palestinians concerned that the ALA was secretly plotting to take over the country, perhaps at the behest of the

Transjordanian king, the ALA promised to stay away from internal matters. On March 29, 1948, it published a notice in *al-Difaʿ* stating that its goal was only to remove the Zionist threat in Palestine "and that it does not have any other political desire in the country."[248]

It appears this may have actually been al-Qawuqji's intention. As early as February 6, a month before entering the country, he wrote to the commander of the First Yarmuk battalion, Muhammad Safa, who was already deployed in Palestine, and requested that the latter stay clear of Palestine's civilian affairs:

> Do not enter into internal matters in the country except when you need to se-cure your needs through the channels of the national committees. We absolutely desire that there should be no stirring up of emotions, or exacerbating of differ-ences. It is our duty to work towards a mutual understanding with the citizens whatever their political outlook. They should have no relationship with us ex-cept when it comes to matters of security and fighting the Jewish forces.[249]

Initially, ALA units followed al-Qawuqji's directive and sought to assign li-aison officers to the Palestinian national committees in the various towns, strictly for coordination purposes. In Nablus, for example, an Iraqi officer was appointed on February 19, 1948, as the "commander of ordering the security of the city" (*'amr 'inḍibat al-'amn lil-madīna*). The letter of his appointment, sent by the ALA to the national committee, included a strong endorsement of the officer's "noble character, in addition to his devotion, reliability, love of the homeland and strong inclination toward the Palestine cause."[250]

Perhaps realizing that the shortcomings of the volunteer army would not allow the swift victory promised by the propagandists, however, many ALA officers chose to abandon al-Qawuqji's directive, and sought to have a say in every "internal matter" they could. The Hittin battalion, for example, worked to put an end to robberies of cattle and weapons in the Tulkarm area, which was under its control. Apparently, the battalion's military police was very active in working these cases, deposing witnesses and trying to solve disputes. The military police also investigated murders, threats, and delays in paying wages to day-laborers.[251] One of the most important tasks of the ALA battalions was to settle feuds among villagers, some of which could be traced back to the 1936–39 revolt. The Hittin battalion staff, one report stated, "is doing its best to make these forgotten and promote, as much as possible, solidarity and the idea of the great jihad and the main goal [i.e., preventing partition]."[252] The battalion credited itself with doing a good job in this matter.

In another region, near the village of Kafr Qasim, the local ALA commander ordered the national committee to hand over two men who were feuding. Apparently, one Abu Nimr from Kafr Qasim had insulted Dhib Faraj from Majdal. The local ALA commander instructed Abu Nimr to apologize and swear not to insult Dhib Faraj again in a signed affidavit. Meanwhile, Dhib Faraj was required to sign a document testifying to the fact he forgave Dhib Faraj.[253] Even al-Qawuqji tried to intervene in quarrels, forgetting his earlier pledge. When rival groups clashed or engaged in shootouts in areas under ALA control, he told the village heads and members of the national committees that he held them responsible for such incidents and demanded that they arrest transgressors and hand them over to the ALA.[254]

Other orders to civilians dealt with more mundane issues: for example, non-ALA fighters were forbidden from wearing military uniforms. Apparently, wearing military garb was a tactic used to frequent coffeehouses and restaurants without having to pay.[255] Orders also warned merchants, peddlers, and others to avoid price gouging.[256] Weapons in the hands of civilians were also a major concern for the ALA, and it appears that instances of civilian deaths from random shootings were common. Soldiers were warned that "some [Palestinians] bought weapons not for jihad, but for commerce and for making profit" and that these people were waiting for anarchy to prevail so that they could use the weapons for robberies.[257] In Nablus, the ALA regional commander published a notice regulating the use of arms: those without licenses were forbidden from carrying them, and those with licenses were forbidden from shooting them except in battle.[258] Battalion commanders were ordered "to prevent shooting by civilians . . . even if this necessitates using force."[259]

Although the national committees resisted the ALA's encroachment at first, they eventually learned to take advantage of the coercive powers of the ALA for their own means. In Nablus, the national committee approached the ALA, asking it to arrest cattle thieves from Beit Furik, explaining that attempts to put an end to their predations through customary means had been unsuccessful.[260] Adjudicating the cases of those arrested by the ALA was a newly established military court system under the leadership of a famous Syrian judge (*qadi*).[261] The actions taken by the ALA suggest that the volunteer army was creating new kinds of authority outside of the common modes of informal justice in Palestine, including customary law (*'urf*) and communal reconciliation (*sulh*).[262] These were rooted in local power dynamics to which the volunteer army was not privy.

The new military court system also distinguished the ALA from the British colonial legal framework and its heavy reliance on collective punishment. Unlike British law, the ALA military courts could claim to operate in the name of pan-Arabism, affording them, in theory, greater legitimacy.[263] Indeed, the court system allowed the ALA to entrench itself in Palestine and appear at least as able as the AHC led by Amin al-Husayni. A Palestinian informant for the Haganah noted that in Nablus, "the inhabitants need no other court."[264]

When it came to strictly military matters, the ALA quickly found itself having to rely heavily on the people it was supposed to be saving. After al-Qawuqji's unsuccessful attempts to recruit Palestinian fighters to the ALA, the commander of the volunteer army turned to solving the ALA's weapons and equipment deficiency, again by relying on the local population. Strapped for weapons, al-Qawuqji pleaded with Palestinians in pamphlets to bring forward their rifles, or at minimum allow for them to be registered in order to account for them.[265] The same went for "cars, radio receivers, medical supplies etc. which were taken as spoils from the Jews" or bought by civilians. Al-Qawuqji promised "a fair monetary price" to anyone who brought such equipment, but also resorted to threatening to court-martial those who hid such articles.[266] Evidence suggests that he kept his word, and those who did not "donate" their goods were prosecuted.[267]

Indeed, despite all the promises of brotherhood and companionship between the ALA and Palestinians, many ALA commanders did not trust those they came to save. Volunteers were instructed not to discuss military matters with civilians, and ALA officers were ordered to warn Palestinians that divulging army movements or military activity to anyone would constitute treason and would be severely punished.[268] Still, officers were concerned that civilians could be potential spies and required soldiers to acquaint themselves with the population in their region and closely follow those who still had commercial or other ties with Jews.[269] Special attention was given to the lucrative business of smuggling foodstuffs, and ALA officers were instructed to do all in their power to stop Palestinian smugglers who were helping to supply the Yishuv.[270] ALA volunteers were also warned not to be fooled by "Arab Jews and Yemenites who adorn themselves with Arab clothes" and may frequent coffeehouses in Arab cities.[271] These were reasonable concerns, given that the Haganah employed numerous Palestinian informants and many Mizrahi spies, some of whom were placed inside the ALA.[272]

Naturally, crossing into Jewish-controlled territory was strictly forbidden for Palestinians.[273] Nevertheless, it apparently happened frequently enough to merit special attention. A pamphlet targeting Palestinians who sought treatment by Jewish physicians explained that the Jewish doctor only "desires your money" and that the medication he prescribed would not heal their wounds.[274] "You, o Arabs, are demolishing your houses with your bare hands by turning to doctors who are not Arabs," the pamphlet warned.[275] Volunteers were also ordered to stop robberies of Jews by local Palestinians because it created a bad name for the ALA and allowed the Yishuv to claim that ALA soldiers were behind these thefts. It also swayed Western public opinion to think that the ALA could not keep order inside Palestine.[276]

But it was not just theft from Jews that was forbidden; even independent military action against Jews in areas controlled by the ALA was banned. The commander of the Druze battalion, the Syrian Druze Shakib Wahab, who was in charge of the region between Acre and the Jewish settlement of Hadera (including Haifa), notified the Arab inhabitants in the area: "Every man or group that takes an action of liberation without my permission, or an order from my headquarters, would constitute rebelling against the liberation and salvation leadership in Palestine [the ALA] and will be put on trial for this by me."[277] Other battalions issued similar warnings. In the Nablus, Jenin, and Tulkarm region officers were told to make sure no one outside of the ALA forces engaged in "destroying bridges and roads or attacking convoys and isolated cars or settlements" that were next to ALA bases. Anyone guilty of disobeying these orders "will be dealt with as if he were a Jewish renegade [mārik]."[278] When Palestinians approached ALA officers in their vicinity to get permission to launch joint attacks against Jewish targets, hoping that the ALA would help them with equipment and weapons, they were often turned away.[279]

TALE OF TWO PROPAGANDAS

Readers may be surprised by the significant discrepancy between the tones of the two propagandas. Compared to the IDF propaganda, the ALA propaganda was more measured, less violent, and placed a greater emphasis on universal values and international law. The material presented in this chapter, it is important to note, is representative of the overall tenor of the sources I collected. As for what accounts for the discrepancy, a number of explanations are possible. While it could be a matter of an incomplete source base, I believe that is unlikely, having looked at numerous IDF pamphlets and hundreds of ALA documents from a dozen archives and repositories. I maintain that these pamphlets and documents represent an accurate cross-section of IDF and ALA propaganda, and further, it is doubtful that there exists some trove of currently unlocated or inaccessible materials that would significantly depart from the general spirit of the sources discussed in this chapter.

Another possible explanation is the structural differences between the two armies: the IDF was a professional army of a nation-state, and as such was fiercely tribal and nativist, which may explain the use of hatred as an indoctrination technique for a (purportedly) clearly defined enemy—the Arabs. Meanwhile, the ALA was a makeshift force and far less cohesive. Although it branded itself with a pan-Arab ideology, it had many enemies: the volunteers themselves were seen as a potential enemy if their revolutionism became unleashed; the British were an enemy, albeit one that could not be engaged (at least in Palestine); Jews from Arab lands were considered less an enemy, and more a "stray child" because of the lingering influence of the dhimmi concept; and Ashkenazi Jews—who comprised the backbone of the Yishuv—were certainly considered an enemy but largely an unknown one. All of these aspects made ALA propaganda a more difficult venture compared to that of the IDF. Finally, the short time span in which the ALA operated—about ten months in total—may also provide a clue as to why its indoctrination was so vastly different. It simply did not have an opportunity to perfect a message in the same way the Haganah and IDF did.

Still, some parallels between the propagandas of the two armies can be found. To galvanize their men, both the IDF and ALA sought to draw on religious traditions they believed would be appealing to the largest number of Jews and Arabs coming from different places and motivated by different reasons. Despite its varied enemies, the ALA tried to present all Jews as dhimmis who overstepped their bounds, and therefore had to be defeated (whether this was convincing is discussed in the next chapter). Education officers in the IDF, meanwhile, believed that likening the Arabs to the arch-nemesis of the

Israelites, Amalek and the Seven Nations of Canaan, would be an effective "social cement." But more than a rallying cry to get soldiers to fight, the IDF was overseeing a revolutionary new way of educating soldiers, borrowed in large part from the Revisionist Right. It was an attempt to give a "Jewish justification" to a militaristic worldview, and explain why the "Jewish nature" condoned the physical eradication of the invading armies and indifference to the fate of Palestinians, be they combatants or civilians. IDF education officers advanced a view that had a long tradition in Zionist thought—that is, that Jews should become "a nation like all other nations" and adopt the gentile way of war. Dissenting views, be they of Mahal volunteers or ultra-orthodox officers, were sidelined.

Another characteristic unique to the IDF education apparatus was the belief that hate propaganda was beneficial because it made killing the enemy easier. Yehuda Wallach, a Givati battalion commander during the war and later the commander of the brigade, commented in 1950 that hatred was one of the most important motivating factors in 1948, something he realized only after he saw the impact Kovner's slogan "death to the invaders" had on his soldiers.[280] "You cannot be a good fighter without hatred," he explained to the general staff, adding:

> As cruel as it might seem . . . it is clear to me that the turning point in fighting
> in the southern front happened at the same moment when you could feel and
> show [soldiers] the first Egyptian dead soldier. Until that contact was made,
> our soldier was not imbued with a will to fight.[281]

Nonetheless, education officers needed to balance two conflicting ideas: on the one hand, a desire to create the best fighters possible by pushing them to be brutal and remorseless, and on the one hand, a larger concern about the kind of values they desired for the future Israeli society. Another concern was that private looting interfered with the need of the state to keep the spoils for itself.

These were not concerns of the ALA command. Much more pressing for them was taming the enthusiasm of Arab volunteers, and making sure their anticolonial fervor did not extend to fighting the Arab regimes that remained client states of the British and French. The striking difference between the fiery rhetoric used to mobilize volunteers around the Arab world and the somewhat watered-down language used for ideological indoctrination inside the ALA reconfirms that the volunteer army was ultimately co-opted as a tool of Arab regimes. The ALA's official patrons were fearful of the "monster" they created: groups of rebellious young men who would soon leave Palestine and possibly attempt the overthrow of the corrupt regimes in their home countries. Even pan-Arabism, in the sense of a call to unify all Arab states, which was a major theme for mobilization of volunteers around the Arab world, was almost completely abandoned as a tool for propaganda inside Palestine. Once in Palestine, only a much vaguer "cultural pan-Arabism," focused on Arab myths of bravery and not on revolution, was used to galvanize soldiers. Moreover, ALA propaganda was especially careful of anything hinting at criticism of Shukri al-Quwwatli, the Syrian president. Instead, propaganda was concerned with the good name of the ALA and with the personality cult of al-Qawuqji himself.[282]

Even more ironic than the ALA's propaganda directed at volunteers was the attempt of the ALA, which ostensibly came to free Palestine, to control Palestinians' daily lives. When the officers of the ALA realized that it would be extremely difficult, if not impossible, to deliver on their promise of preventing partition, they quickly abandoned their earlier pledge to stay out of the country's internal affairs. But controlling Palestine also proved difficult, and was often curtailed by the ALA's unwillingness to launch attacks in coordination with local Palestinian militias and by the volunteers' own unruly behavior, which could not be contained by the ALA command. It was at that point that the ALA changed its tune and stopped making promises of a swift victory. Instead, it sought to use its coercive powers to force Palestinians to stay put and not flee in the face of devastating attacks by Jewish forces.

Chapter 3

WELCOME TO PALESTINE

What Brings You Here?

AFTER EXAMINING THE MOBILIZATION AND INDOCTRINATION of Jewish and Arab recruits "from above," it is now time to delve into what the volunteers themselves, and their families, had to say. This correspondence illuminates not only how volunteers explained their reasons for coming to Palestine and what being there meant for them, but also how the experiences of volunteers became significant for their loved ones back home. Of course, not all Jews or Arabs in 1948 could read and write. According to IDF figures from 1949, of Jewish soldiers then serving 0.2 percent could not read or write at all, 50.8 percent had only a primary education, and only 36.4 percent had postprimary education.[1] There are no literacy figures for the ALA, but in the Arab states from which the Arab volunteers arrived, literacy rates varied greatly in the mid-twentieth century: 60 percent in Syria, 23 percent in Egypt, 15 percent in Transjordan, and 10 percent in Iraq.[2] The Palestinian literacy rate in 1948 is estimated at between 15 and 27 percent, with some 20 percent of Muslims and 75 percent of Christians being literate.[3] The relatively low literacy rates for Palestinians and Arab volunteers do not mean that they and the rest of the population that was not literate did not engage with the written word. As the works of several scholars have demonstrated, many illiterate people exchanged letters through the use of scribes to write them and confidants to read them.[4]

For those coming from afar, and for the families they left behind, participation in the 1948 war was driven by complex, and often surprising, interests and causes, not all of which can be tied back to the mobilization campaigns back home. Still, both Jews and Arabs subscribed to a certain collective logic that emphasized a "duty" to volunteer for their respective ethnic groups. Indeed, Ashkenazi Jews who came to Palestine from Western countries to volunteer in 1948 cited an obligation to help establish a Jewish state. Whether they intended on immigrating there permanently or not, volunteers thought they were performing a vital service for the survival of the Jewish people. A sense of shared destiny, and also fear of the anticolonial revolt back home, also brought Jews from Morocco to Palestine. Meanwhile, their families still in Morocco saw Jews taking arms in Palestine as marking an end to their dhimmi status in Islamic lands. Nevertheless, within months of the arrival of Moroccan volunteers, many discovered that Israel was neither the paradise they were promised nor the mythic homeland reuniting the Jewish tribes based on equal access to resources and recognition of the cultures created in the diaspora.[5] Similarly, ALA men from around the Arab world came to Palestine in solidarity with Palestinians, but also for other reasons: from a will to improve the volunteers' standing inside their immediate families, to financial constraints, to Islamic and anti-Fascist solidarity. Even when pan-Arabism was cited as the motivation for volunteering, it was never an ideology embraced in a vacuum. It was always locally inflected. For Iraqi volunteers and their friends, the momentum of fighting the British in Baghdad in January 1948 carried over to Palestine, in contrast to the cynical intentions of the Iraqi government, which wished for a continuation of British influence.

WHAT DOES IT MEAN TO BE A MUJAHID?

In the chronicles of the 1948 war, ALA volunteers are often presented as jihadists, as "unemployed workers" who came to Palestine "due to a desire for fame and material gains," or as criminals, busy frequenting bars and bordellos.[6] In reality, Arab and Muslim volunteers with the ALA were in many ways unexceptional, and their writing greatly resembled that of soldiers from other places and other times, even if they saw themselves, and were seen by others, as *mujahidin* (Arabic for those who struggle for the sake of God and Islam).[7] In fact, ALA men, as reflected through letters, were a far cry from the jihadi-obsessed radicals presented by some scholars.[8] True, Palestine, in the imagination of some, was a mystical and sacred place, which the majority had never visited before, but that was not the only impetus for their volunteering.[9] Lieutenant Zabun Husayn, whose place of origin is unclear, wrote to his friend how much "the breeze passing through the violet and jasmine flowers in Arab Palestine" made him happy.[10] "We are struggling against the vagrant [*sharida*] Zionism and guarding our honor and history will bear our witness and God is with us," he explained to a friend.[11] Labeling Zionism as "vagrant" was in line with Islamist rhetoric that suggested Jews were punished with eternal wandering because of their insubordination to God. Still other volunteers chose to frame the fight against Zionism as a civilizational one, perhaps echoing secular indoctrination like that of the Ba'th. One letter referred to Zionists as "the enemies of humanity."[12] A volunteer asked to make clear in his letter that "I volunteered not for my own personal gains but rather to fight for our Arab homeland together with the rest of my brave brothers."[13]

Other topics for discussion in letters were more mundane. Some wrote about their yearnings for their families ("even if our bodies are separated, our hearts and souls are connected"; "our sorrow is like a flame of fire from a stove"), while others sent requests to receive more letters, pictures, and greetings from the extended family.[14] The volunteers' families responded in kind, sometimes attaching short poems about the misery of being apart, or the anticipation of news from their loved ones.[15] Naturally, news of volunteers being injured or killed caused much grief back home where their families awaited their return.[16] One frequent request in letters of families to their loved ones in Palestine was to corroborate the reports in the local press celebrating victories on the battlefield against the Yishuv. "Inform me about the remarkable success you attained in Palestine and that we have read about in the newspapers in Baghdad," asked Jamil al-Hasan of his friend, Madlul, from the Hittin battalion.[17] Another Iraqi commented that "the news flows from all the radio stations about your immortal bravery."[18] It is possible that friends and families of volunteers viewed the reports in the press with some skepticism, and wanted to be informed by their loved ones about what was really going on in Palestine. Indeed, many of the reports in the Arab press—in Baghdad, Beirut, Damascus, and Cairo—were false. Journalists relied on Nasir al-Din's communiques or on statements of Arab leaders, often celebrating fabricated

ALA victories. It seems that at least in some cases, journalists on their own volition tried to bolster the morale by offering celebratory but false reporting.[19] Regardless of whether the relatives and friends of volunteers suspected this, or genuinely believed the celebratory news, the volunteers themselves in their accounts to their families often chose to echo these fictitious reports about victories rather than disclose the much more complex situation they found on the ground in Palestine upon arrival.[20]

Exaggerations in letters home were also not unique to the ALA. Soldiers writing to their families from war zones around the world have often chosen to boast about victories—real or invented—in order to placate or impress their loved ones.[21] An Iraqi volunteer writing his family on April 11, 1948, about the Battle of Mishmar ha-'Emek in which he participated, informed them that 200 Jews were killed and that his unit later "conquered Jerusalem," killing another 450–750 Jews.[22] All the towns he and his friends occupied, the volunteer explained, were delivered to "our brothers, the Arabs of Palestine." In fact, the Iraqi volunteer explained in his letter, al-Qawuqji himself was so impressed by his conduct that he reportedly asked to promote him—a promotion that was currently pending the approval of the Arab League.[23] "We are always winning," wrote another Iraqi volunteer, Jalal Ma'aruf, to his friend Akram Nashat al-Qarawi, who was a student in the military academy in Baghdad.[24] He added that they killed 200 Jews in one battle (apparently in Jaffa) in which a friend of theirs, Taha, was also killed.[25] Like their comrades in other parts of the world, ALA volunteers also wished to bolster the morale back home.

For an Alawite volunteer from Syria, who was part of the Alawite battalion and did not sign his name on the letter, volunteering was a rite of passage.[26] Writing to his brother, Abu Kamil, the volunteer apologized for not helping other family members enlist in the ALA as he had promised, reportedly because of the death of his contact inside the ALA. This, he felt, made his own volunteerism unique and a personal source of pride. In fact, he insisted that even if other family members were allowed to join, not everyone was cut out for army life. He provided his cousin, Rif'at, who initially enlisted with him in the ALA despite the fact that the writer had advised him against it, as an example. As he had expected, Rif'at deserted: "Jihad requires endurance of hunger, thirst and worn-out clothes [but] there is no hardship which is not

FIGURE 7. Lebanese volunteers with the Arab Liberation Army use 75mm trench mortars near Jerusalem. 13 May 1948. Source: Bettmann Collection via Getty Images.

followed by deliverance."[27] His own redemption, the volunteer felt, was also a source for personal growth:

> You cannot imagine how much I worry about all of you, and everyone who yearns to see me, and especially those who suffered [i.e., made efforts] until I reached this stage of devotion, seriousness and diligence. . . . Battle taught me about the strength of the heart, [so that] even if no one asks about me, or, God forbid, one of us dies, I will not be sad because death is a right.[28]

The elevated status of the writer, as a volunteer who stayed in Palestine despite the hardships and had learned to overcome fear, allowed him to make certain requests: "Send my regards to my dear mother. She is the mother of the entire world, not only my own. Therefore, I request your devotion to her, as you promised me before."[29] Hoping to secure Abu Kamil's devotion to their mother, the volunteer tried to leverage his newly earned status.[30]

Some letters hinted at family tensions regarding the decision to volunteer. "We never thought you would part from us," wrote parents to their child who left for Palestine. They also reported being in a state of "despair . . . your mother is [sick] in bed and your father is . . . in a very bad mood."[31] Families were perhaps proud of their sons for volunteering, but they were also pushing for their return shortly after their departure, likely after they received word of setbacks on the battlefield, or because they needed help to tend to the family's crops. "Your brother Abdullah has an idea to go to Palestine if he can, and leave us on our own, which will sabotage our entire work here," wrote parents to their volunteer son, Muhmmad S'aid. They asked that he pressure his brother not to follow him.[32] "My dear son, all your friends returned to their families, why are you not coming back?" a father from Baghdad asked his son stationed in Nablus in late April 1948.[33] Yet another relative of a volunteer tried a more direct approach: "I am tired of asking about you, and I was informed by Father that you returned to Palestine."[34] The author of the letter notified the volunteer that he had contacted the commander of Haifa, apparently in an attempt to secure the return of the volunteer home.[35] Even with the devotion to Palestine, some family matters could not wait.

WHEN IDEOLOGIES MIX

In most cases, the letters that randomly made it into the Israeli archives offer few clues as to what those family matters were. Yet a rare file in the archives that preserved four letters between one volunteer and his family and friends helps unearth some of those matters and with them a complex set of motivations and ideologies which brought Arabs from around the Middle East to support the Palestine cause. The letters of Maki Mahmud, a junior Iraqi officer with the ALA, and the people with whom he corresponded suggest that the most active supporters of the fight in Palestine were not only motivated by Islamic solidarity and pan-Arabism but also by Iraqi nationalism (*wataniyya*), a general pledge to fight colonialism wherever it may be, and, perhaps most interestingly, a commitment to combat fascism. Moreover, this assortment of letters reveals the way that some volunteers and their friends connected the fighting in Palestine to struggles back home.

Maki Mahmud was from Baghdad, and judging by the letters he sent and received, he likely belonged to a middle-class, Sunni family.[36] It is evident that the family was not of the upper classes because they were largely dependent on the small sum of money Mahmud earned as a volunteer in the ALA.[37] In the letter to his mother,[38] Mahmud mentioned he would be sending 15 Egyptian pounds, which was about 25–30 percent of his ALA monthly salary.[39] The need for extra funds was certainly not unique to the Mahmud family. In late 1947 and early 1948, Baghdad was suffering from an acute shortage of bread. Middle-class civil servants like Maki Mahmud were struggling almost as much as the lower classes. The salary of those civil servants had increased 54–140 percent above 1939 levels, while the cost of living had increased 600 percent during that same period. One of the reasons for the sharp increase in poverty was the closing down of workshops by the British military forces following the Second World War. These workshops had been a primary source of income for many families.[40]

It is likely that Mahmud was an active officer in the Iraqi army at the time of his enlistment in the ALA, since he indicated in the letter to his mother that after arriving in Palestine he was promoted to company commander (suggesting he had already been an officer).[41] Although a great number of officers were forced out of the Iraqi army following the Rashid 'Ali al-Gaylani revolt of 1941, it is unlikely Mahmud was one of the co-conspirators to be dismissed because of his junior rank.[42] As a second lieutenant (*mulāzim thāni*) or a lieutenant (*mulāzim awwal*) in the Iraqi army he would have earned 20–25 Iraqi dinars (which, according to the exchange rate at the time, would have equaled 20–25 Egyptian or British pounds) as his monthly base salary, with an additional 3 dinars as service allowance each month.[43] The salary figures for these ranks in the ALA suggest that switching over from the Iraqi army did not improve Mahmud's earnings by much.[44] In fact, there is also evidence that Iraqi volunteers in Palestine were not paid the full sums they were owed.[45]

After conscription and training Mahmud was placed in the Qadisiyya battalion, composed primarily of Iraqi volunteers. According to Haganah intelligence, the battalion entered Palestine sometime between mid-February to mid-March 1948, with 354 soldiers and six officers.[46] By late March or early April 1948 Mahmud was stationed in Nablus in the west bank of the Jordan River.[47] Writing to his mother in Baghdad shortly after the Mishmar ha-'Emek battle in which he took part, Mahmud explained what drove him to travel as far as Palestine: "My dear mother, the happiest life I spent and encountered, and the most honorable duty I carry out is in saving the pride and dignity of Arabism [*'Urūba*]."[48]

The commitment to pan-Arabism was even greater in the letters Mahmud's friends sent him. One of Mahmud's close friends, 'Abd al-Majid al-Salihi, a clerk at the Ministry of Labor and Social Affairs, stressed the connection between Iraq and Palestine, describing his message as being sent "from the fertile lands of Mesopotamia to the district of fighting and striving, Syria [*suriya*]."[49] The decision to point to Syria rather than Palestine as the destination for his message signified either lingering geographic ambiguity (large parts of what would become Palestine were seen as part of Syria during the Ottoman period) or pan-Arab visions (many presented Palestine as an indivisible part of Greater Syria). Al-Salihi was deeply moved by Mahmud's decision to go to Palestine. Mahmud, al-Salihi insisted, stood apart from most Iraqis because they only grieved for Palestine, while Mahmud would not have to "live in misery," seeing the disaster unfolding from afar. "The noble Iraqi people are proud of you and lift their heads up high among the Arab nations. You etched your pure, honorable name at the front of Arabism," al-Salihi flattered Mahmud.[50] Even if al-Salihi could not fight for Palestine himself, he and all Iraqis could still feel pride since Mahmud was fighting in their name too.

For al-Salihi, talk of pan-Arabism was not empty words. Indeed, he had a clear vision of how to rid the Arab world of colonialism, which, in his view, "burdened the people, depressed them, sucked their blood, and consumed their wealth."[51] Al-Salihi insisted that the fighters of pan-Arabism, like Mahmud, would address these injustices not only in Palestine but everywhere in the Arab world:

> There is no doubt that the brutal colonizer is not interested merely in looting and starving [but] to impose obedience on the peaceful population, and therefore the liberation of Arab countries is a vow and a charter from God and his prophet to us, which we must implement. God is with us and will enable us to prevail over the nation of non-believers [*qawm al-kāfirīn*].[52]

Al-Salihi was not alone in his reference to God's role in the fight for Palestine. Mahmud also quoted from the Qur'an to console his mother after delivering the news that a family friend had died in the battle of Mishmar ha-'Emek.[53] Yet for al-Salihi, references to Islam were intrinsically linked to pan-Arabism.

Only Arabs, he insisted, could "heal" Palestine and "dress her wounds," and this was not only a national duty but a religious one as well. The British and the Zionists were the "enemies of God" and fighting them was jihad, which opened "one of the doors to heaven."[54] For al-Salihi, to consider the struggle against Zionism as a war that was religiously mandated came naturally and was in line with the nationalist motivation to defend Arab soil.

In this fight, al-Salihi wrote, Mahmud must "cleanse Palestine from the detestable Zionism . . . by planting fear and horror in the souls of the Fascists."[55] The mention of "Fascists" by al-Salihi may seem perplexing because it is a reminiscent of the language of anti-Fascist organizations that were widespread in the Middle East during the Second World War and its aftermath. Al-Salihi's writing, meanwhile, is clearly situated in the pan-Arab and Islamist camps, which are often portrayed in Iraqi historiography as being pro-Fascist.[56] But as several scholars have shown, liberal and pro-democratic voices were more prevalent in Iraq by the late 1930s and early 1940s than previously accounted for.[57] In fact, despite the considerable influence of pro-Fascist and pro-Nazi tendencies, especially among pan-Arabists, there were also people of all stripes who fought these ideologies, namely Sherifians,[58] Shi'i and Sunni religious clerics, pan-Arabists, leftists and, unsurprisingly, Jews.[59] Al-Salihi's letter demonstrates the extent to which all of these convictions and sectarian identities intersected: not only did he display an anti-Fascist sentiment but also an ideological mix of Iraqi nationalism, pan-Arabism, anticolonialism, and Islamic solidarity. Of course, this degree of ideological mixing should not surprise us, given how ideologies mutate as they make their way from the minds of ideologues to the thoughts and conduct of ordinary people. The manner in which this process takes place is most clearly elucidated in personal letters, before an individual has the opportunity to polish the narrative in his or her memoir and remove what would seem to future readers as contradictory or inconsistent sentiments.

But the commitment to Palestine in Baghdad was even more complicated, because unlike in other Arab states, in Iraq the government was the one shouldering much of the Palestine propaganda in late 1947 and early 1948. Scholars have suggested that the Iraqi regime promoted pro-Palestinian sentiments as a way of distracting the public from British colonialism at home.[60] At no time was this more true than in late 1947, when Prime Minister Salih Jabr began negotiations to revise the Anglo-Iraqi agreement of 1930. Despite Britain's promises to fully withdraw its forces from Iraq (which was nominally independent since 1932), the draft treaty from January 1948 showed that Britain wanted to maintain two airbases in Iraq, keep its communication facilities in the country, and reserve the right of British forces to reenter Iraq in time of war or threat of war.[61] To provide a smokescreen to conceal the major concessions made to the British, various figures in the Iraqi regime—including the regent, 'Abd al-Ilah—called for military action in Palestine.[62]

Based on the letters of Maki Mahmud and his correspondents, I argue, the government's plan backfired spectacularly: instead of ignoring the domestic arena, Iraqis linked Palestine to their opposition to the government's ploy. They saw the battle in Palestine as another front in the pan-Arab struggle against colonialism throughout the region, including in Iraq.

This point is demonstrated most clearly in the letters that Maki Mahmud received in late March from a teacher at the Baghdadi al-Zawra' elementary school. Like al-Salihi's writings, the teacher's letters are full of references to the bonds among Arab nations: "The Iraqi is a brother of the Syrian and the Lebanese and the Egyptian and the Hijazi and the Najdi and the Palestinian. You are all fighting for one goal and for one glory: to expel colonialism and the colonizers, no matter who they are."[63] But stressing the anticolonial and pan-Arab nature of the fight for Palestine was even more concrete for the teacher than it was for al-Salihi. The teacher asked Mahmud "to inform us about our homeland [watanuna] Palestine in detail because we are all for Palestine's redemption."[64] It appears that for the teacher, Palestine was part of the homeland still occupied by foreigners:

> My dear brother, we are now in Baghdad, where there is complete serenity and confidence after the unrest that occurred against the unjust treaty in the era of the previous administration. We have few victims, much less than the numbers cited in the newspapers and the radio broadcasts. The country [would have not been] saved from disaster were it not for God's care and the wisdom of his highness, the Regent and the holy nation, and its faithful men who rejected the new treaty.[65]

The teacher was referring to al-Wathba (Arabic for "the great leap"), the wave of protest that began in Baghdad on January 5, 1948, against the signing of the revised Anglo-Iraqi agreement. A number of people were killed by police fire in the first few days of protest. As a result, on January 21, the Iraqi regent 'Abd al-Ilah capitulated, announcing that he would not ratify the treaty.[66] But protests did not stop, and in the following days dozens, perhaps even hundreds, were killed by the military and the police. Prime Minister Salih Jabr was forced to resign and flee the country to England, and a new government was formed.[67]

Although the protest in Baghdad was initially against the treaty, it quickly came to encompass a much wider range of demands: from calls to send Nuri al-Sai'd (the pro-British politician who dominated Iraqi politics for decades) and Prime Minister Salih Jabr to the gallows, to calls to distribute bread to the people (which was in short supply), to calls to free Palestine.[68] The Istiqlal party, the most outspoken in seeking complete independence for Iraq, explained as early as January 2 that the new treaty was intrinsically linked to the Palestine question, even though it was not sure whether the British were trying "to sway public opinion from the Palestine issue by preoccupying Iraqis with the treaty, or seize the opportunity when Iraq is preoccupied with the [Palestine] issue to complete amending the treaty."[69] In any case, Istiqlal insisted that Iraqis would vigorously fight for their rights.[70] Salih Jabr's government, before being dissolved, also tried to use the Palestine question one last time for its own purposes. On January 7, an official government notice explained that the protest movement was trying to distract Iraqis from the issue of Palestine and weaken the work of the negotiators who were seeking to secure Iraq's independence.[71] But the teacher—and likely Mahmud too—saw things very differently. They saw the war in Palestine as a continuation of al-Wathba, and perceived Zionism as an extension of British imperialism.

In fact, by the 1940s, many Iraqi nationalists insisted that Zionism was everywhere, not only in Palestine. Iraqi Jews were (falsely) accused of being Zionists, and therefore guilty of displacing Palestinians.[72] In his letter, the teacher not only conflated "Jews" and "Zionists," but referred to both as "the impure humans ['arjās al-bashar]" and "the wicked ['andhāl] ones." [73] It appears that these epithets were related to a supposed transgression by Jews:

> It is an irony that the Zionist Jews are fighting us, the sons of those who ruled the globe by our sword. We shall make them taste the punishment for their sin ['ithmuhum] . . . Hit the Zionists with consecutive fatal strikes until they throw down their weapons and surrender.[74]

This reasoning about a "sin" the Zionists had to pay for may be alluding to the abrogation of the status of Jews in Islamic lands as dhimmi subjects, which had conditioned protection with submission to Muslim rule, and as such did not tolerate any form of sovereignty.[75] The teacher's language was intended to make sure Mahmud realized that the ultimate solution would be a violent one: "Tie the hanging noose onto the Zionists [necks] until they are completely defeated and take them back to where they had come from."[76]

Of course not all Iraqi volunteers and their acquaintances used this kind of rhetoric in reference to the native Jews of the Middle East. Another Iraqi ALA officer writing home on April 4, 1948, relayed that the heads (*mukhtars*) of several Jewish settlements—'Afula, Tel-Yosef, Hadera and Binyamina—came to his base and asked that the ALA protect them against the Haganah that had come to their settlements and confiscated their belongings, and even took their daughters.[77] While this report may refer to Mizrahi resistance to the forced conscription in the Yishuv during the war, it remains highly opaque. Al-Qawuqji also mentioned this visit in his memoir, quoting an ALA intelligence report stating that the Jews who arrived at the ALA base were Jews indigenous to the Middle East, "farmers and industrialists who are resident in Palestine or who came from Arab countries for commercial reasons and without political motives."[78] They reportedly offered to surrender if the ALA would guarantee their families' safety, but the Haganah prevented them from doing so.[79] The Iraqi officer writing home did not share with his family how he and his friends responded to the unique request, but it nevertheless attests to the complicated battle lines in Palestine itself, where bonds between Jews from Arab lands and volunteers from those same Arab lands persisted even in the midst of a conflict that seemed to pit these groups against one another. Indeed, this anecdote captures a moment when identities were still in formation. Only a few years later, this incident would have been unimaginable.

THEY TREAT US LIKE SAVAGES

The behavior of those Jews from Arab lands who were encountered by al-Qawuqji and his officers certainly went against the intention of the IDF chief of staff Yadin. As we saw in chapter 2, Yadin called on his field commanders to convince their soldiers that killing Arabs on the battlefield in 1948 would constitute "payback" for the treatment of their parents who were still in Arab lands. But as he quickly discovered, not only did most North African Gahal soldiers not demonstrate a pathological hatred of Arabs, many showed hostility toward Ashkenazi Jews and their brand of Zionism. In fact, some of the very same people who fought for the establishment of Israel became deeply ambivalent about it.

The beginning of Moroccan immigration in late 1948, nevertheless, was harmonious, founded upon hopes for the future and fears of the past, in which Hitler loomed large. Those writing to their families in Morocco reported that "the country was a paradise," "conditions are great," and "we have never been better."[80] Indeed, hundreds of Moroccan volunteers in the IDF were, according to the censor who was reviewing their private letters, "full of excitement for the Zionist idea and the current war." In fact, the censor noted, most "tend to permanently settle down in Israel in a constructive manner. All of them, almost without exception, wrote their families and friends to follow them and immigrate."[81] In October 1948 Shem-Tov sent the following letter to his family in North Africa (the exact location was not specified by the censor):

> I am very concerned with your condition and the condition of Jews in Arab lands. The press here only brings occasional data on the conditions in the Arab states, but what we hear is enough to worry me terribly. . . . You are in great danger. The Arabs will annihilate you as Hitler had done in Europe. Come here! Craftsmen can make a decent living and earn their bread respectfully, and live among their brothers . . . When I fight here, I fight for you too.[82]

Likely still under the influence of the June 1948 killings of Moroccan Jews in Oujda and Jerada, which were extensively covered in the Israeli press, North African volunteers called their family to follow them and immigrate to Israel.[83] Shem-Tov himself repeated one of the most popular Zionist propaganda claims, suggesting that the Jews of Arab lands would be at risk of a second holocaust, perpetrated by the Arabs, if they did not flee.[84]

Even some of those who planned on staying in Morocco for the time being felt that the establishment of the State of Israel was a game-changer in the relationship between Jews and Arabs. In a letter Habiba sent to her relative, who was an IDF soldier in July 1949, she shared her excitement: "You know how happy I am every time I say the word 'state' because the Jews suffered for 2,000 years and in a split second God found them a country."[85] Beyond Israel being a refuge for Jews from all over the world, Habiba's joy was also related to the end of the dhimmi status. As Habiba narrated: "During the time of the Arabs, the Jews walked around with their heads lowered, and now we need to walk with our heads held high and they in humility."[86] Habiba felt that the Arab-Muslim superiority over Jews would now give room not to equality but to Jewish superiority, born of the Israeli victories in battle.

But the view of Israel by Moroccan Jews who came to fight in late 1948 was quickly changing. Five months after the reassuring commentary by the censor regarding the North African immigrants being "full of excitement for the Zionist idea," in the March 1949 *Soldier's Opinion* report, the censor painted a slightly different picture:

> North African immigrants are suffering from an inferiority complex (*regesh nehitut*) that might be caused by the way their Ashkenazi colleagues treat them. This phenomenon is serious and raises concern not just because of the mutual feelings inside the army, and the deplorable influence on the morale in "African" and mixed units, but also because of the information sent by the "offended" to their family and friends in their countries of origin.[87]

The censor's analysis requires decoding: portraying North Africans as suffering from "an inferiority complex" was the typical way Jews from the Middle East and North Africa were portrayed by Israeli sociologists at the time.[88] But the censor hinted at another supposedly essential Oriental disposition—whining (*bakhyanut*). By referring to "the offended" and deciding to include that word in quotation marks, the censor alluded to what various experts described as a propensity of Jews from the region to burst into tears or be intensely emotional.[89]

The signs of Moroccan disenchantment were clear for the censor to see, and they had much to do with race. This example—in the words of the censor, "not one of a kind"—was a letter in French sent by Na'im, a soldier in the IDF, to his family in North Africa:

> As I wrote you, the European Jews who suffered tremendously from the Hitleristic Nazism see themselves as a superior race [*geza' 'elyon*] and the Sephardi [Mizrahi] as belonging to an inferior one [*geza' nahut dargah*]. The poor African who came here from afar and was not required to leave his home because of racial discrimination is now humiliated at every turn. . . . Instead of

gratitude, they treat us like savages or unwelcomed elements. Bloodline rules here.[90]

Na'im broke away from the Zionist narrative in his writing. First, he used vocabulary from Nazi Germany (and, perhaps, from colonial North Africa) to describe the hegemonic Ashkenazi group. His suggestion that Ashkenazi Zionists created a racial hierarchy based on blood, with themselves at the top and Mizrahi Jews as racially inferior subjects, was a radical departure from Zionist tenets that, at least in theory, advanced equality among all Jews.[91] But Na'im did not stop there. He explicitly mentioned that unlike European Jews, who were forced out of Europe because of persecution, North Africans were not persecuted and did not suffer racial discrimination back home. Since North Africans came of their own volition, Na'im thought, racism and discrimination against them was even more galling. It also caused him to question himself: "When I see [North] African friends wandering the streets, one without a hand, the other without a leg, friends who spilled their blood in war, I ask myself, 'Is it worth it?'" Na'im came to Israel to fight in solidarity with his coreligionists, even though he was content in his homeland of Morocco. The racism and discrimination he suffered upon arrival made him rethink his initial decision.

By April 1949 the censor reported that as a result of discrimination, "most prefer to hide the fact they are Moroccan immigrants."[92] Nonetheless, many repeated their commitment to Zionism, such as in this letter by Hananiah to his friends or relatives in Morocco:

> A few weeks ago I was in a soldiers' club when a quarrel started between a Palestine-born soldier and a Moroccan one. The quarrel soon escalated into an all-out fight, which included the following slurs: "Down with the Moroccan," "Kill the Moroccan!" etc. I thought I was in Morocco hearing the famous call, "Down with the dirty Jew!" Believe me, I left the hall with tears in my eyes. But in any case, this won't change a thing in my belief. I came here as an idealist and I will remain one for the rest of my life. And as for my parents, I want them to come as soon as possible because it is better to hear "dirty Moroccan" than "dirty Jew."[93]

The slurs against immigrants from North Africa shocked Hananiah, who never expected to hear Jews using such "imported" language against fellow Jews. In his mind, however, this language was less dangerous than the persecution suffered in Morocco, where he feared for his physical well-being. Similar conclusions came occasionally from Morocco itself. In June 1949 Albert urged his relative in Israel to complain less:

> I understand all the difficulties you are facing in Israel, the hard life of a soldier, the loneliness in the desert . . . But you must explain to all the friends from Morocco who have given up hope, who are sick of life in Israel, that their lot is not as bad as they think, and that they must stop complaining. On the contrary, tens of thousands of Jews would gladly accept to live in these conditions, and even worse ones.[94]

Albert's observations from Morocco allow us to delve deeper into the main grievances of Moroccan immigrants in Israel. The living standards for some Moroccans who immigrated to Israel may very well have been better than their condition in Morocco, especially for those who used to live in the *mellah*s, the traditional Jewish quarters of the cities, or in the countryside. However, soldiers made it clear that the dire economic situation and the harsh conditions in the temporary transit camps (*ma'abarot*), where they were housed by the government for years before being transferred to newly constructed towns (many built on the remains of Palestinian villages), were just one factor behind their grievances. More emphasis was placed on the daily racism and discrimination they suffered.

For Nissim, living under Israel's rule did not signal an end to the dhimmi status. He wrote his family in Morocco that he was recently discharged from the army and "thrown out on the street like a dog, with no house and no work." He asked his relative, "How do you want me to be quiet and not speak badly [about Israel], if you are with Jews and they treat you like Arabs??"[95] Mazalto went a step further and explained to his family that "living conditions under the Arabs were better than under Jewish rule."[96] The difference in perception between the people who actually immigrated to Israel and those who remained in Morocco becomes clear in these letters. For Nissim and Mazalto, it was not just the material aspects that mattered, but the sense that they were treated the same way (or worse) as when living under Arab rule. In other words, immigration to the Jewish state did not mean an overhaul of the old power dynamics. Even among Jews, Moroccans continued to be treated as inferior.

ISRAEL MEANS THAT WE STOP RUNNING

Mahal volunteers—almost all of them Ashkenazi Jews who came from Western countries—did not go through the same experience as Moroccans. Being relatively well-received, many continued to feel immense pride in their volunteerism, and cited a sense of duty to the Jewish people and securing a place of refuge for themselves as reasons for coming. In their letters, volunteers often invoked a "pan-Judaic" sense of solidarity, in the hope it would convince their relatives back home to do more for the Jewish state.

For some volunteers from Western countries, being able to touch the soil of the Land of Israel held special significance. Writing to the United States, Zalman explained:

> The second I saw the Land of Israel from the airplane, tears started flowing from my eyes. . . . As I got off the plane, I kissed the land I was standing on. Can you imagine to yourself what it means to be in our own country, free to go and do whatever it is that you feel like?[97]

Most newcomers did not focus on the sacredness of the land; rather, they emphasized that a Jewish state meant a new start, a place devoid of the bad memories of the Jewish past, where no one "shouts 'dirty Jew' when you pass in the street."[98] In fact, Akiva from England noted that in Israel, "no one . . . tell[s] you to go back to your own country, [because] this is your country!"[99] The new state, Roland explained, meant that Jews were again in charge of their affairs: "We fought . . . to build a homeland for every Jew around the world, a homeland where we all have equal rights, and we are not inferior citizens, subject to the wrath or benevolence of gentiles."[100] Harley too was enchanted with the feeling of freedom: "What was the essence of our lives thus far? Running. We ran and fled from one place to another. The State of Israel means an end to running."[101] Although they were coming from affluent countries where Jews were ostensibly equal citizens, those volunteers felt that the freedom they could exercise in Israel, and the sense of belonging they experienced there, could not be attained anywhere else.

Besides seeing Israel as a possible refuge in times of need, Ashkenazi volunteers coming from Western countries described their volunteerism as a duty to the Jewish people. Many insisted that "every Jew must come here" and fight for a Jewish homeland. Some expressed their willingness to die to achieve it.[102] Stephen explained that he did not intend to stay in Israel when the war was over, but he felt he must fight for the Jewish state "so that I can have a clear conscience" and that people back home "could not scold me for being faint-hearted."[103] Other volunteers felt that the people back home ought to share more of the burden of war, even if they did not offer themselves as volunteers. Nathan reprimanded his relatives, and the entire American Jewish community by extension, for not doing enough for Israel:

> We are fighting for our lives, for the pride and honor of the Jewish people. Don't [Jewish] Americans understand that it is not enough to donate 18 dollars, or 100 dollars, or a 1,000 dollars, and say "I did my share" ... Our war here is not simply for this state [Israel], but for the existence of Jews everywhere, and if we lose it would be the fault of American Jews.[104]

Not unlike Iraqis who wished to join the pan-Arab fight for Palestine, Nathan felt himself part of a "pan-Judaic" fight for the same land. Like in Iraq, the family and friends back home had a role to play, and he urged them to write the US president and their congressmen and ask them to support the Jewish state. And for those back home who were not yet converted to the Zionist cause, Nathan offered an alluring comparison, drawing on the parallels between the Yishuv fight against the British for Israeli independence to the first American pioneers who fought the British king to gain their independence.[105] At least in Nathan's imagination, a common struggle against a British enemy could bring all Jews together, just as it had brought together all Arabs.

DUTY-BOUND

Decades after their participation in the 1948 war, a poll conducted among Mahal volunteers listed "the Holocaust" as the most prominent justification for the decision to go to Palestine.[106] The term "the Holocaust" was only popularized in English between the 1960s and 1980s, and therefore its absence from letters is not necessarily surprising.[107] In fact, we may consider the references to "a duty" as connected to the feeling of guilt in the aftermath of the extermination of most of Europe's Jews.

This "duty" to come fight for the Jewish state was in many ways a "pan-Judaic" collective logic that bears resemblance to the pan-Arab sentiment cited by ALA volunteers. Indeed, both Ashkenazi Mahal volunteers from

Western countries and Moroccan Gahal volunteers saw the fight for Israel as an obligation, and felt that the new state would be a place of refuge for all Jews, and thus constituted a revolution in Jewish history. This was especially the case in Morocco where the establishment of Israel purportedly signaled an end to the dhimmi status. Yet there was one crucial difference between Moroccan volunteers and those coming from Western countries: while most of the latter were grateful to the state because of their warm welcome (with the exceptions discussed in chapter 5), for Moroccans, the racism they experienced at the hand of Ashkenazi Jews made many rethink their decision to go to Israel. Ultimately, it also made them doubt their initial belief that the dhimmi status—and the marks of interiority which came with it—had really come to an end.

In the ALA, the reasons for volunteering and supporting the Palestine cause were far more extensive. Not unlike what drew young men to enlist in armies all around the world in the twentieth century, ALA volunteers also exhibited diverse, and sometimes conflicting, motivations and ideologies. For some volunteers, religion played a role. For others a major consideration was the hope that enlisting in the ALA would elevate their status within their families. Many volunteers and the families behind them also cited a pan-Arab duty to defend Palestinians and win back the entire country for them, yet few mentioned that fighting in Palestine would be a first step, like Ba'ath propaganda had suggested, in the liberation of all Arab lands from the yoke of colonialism. In fact, only a handful of Iraqis hinted at the idea that all Arab lands should be unified in one kingdom in their letters. Even pan-Arabism in the correspondence of Iraqis was not a standalone ideological conviction, but part of an amalgam of beliefs, which included Iraqi nationalism, anticolonialism, antifascism, and Islamic solidarity. These convictions may seem conflicting, but the letters demonstrate that some saw them as complementary, and perhaps especially so in Iraq.

Chapter 4

THE VIOLENCE OF VICTORY AND THE VIOLENCE OF DEFEAT

THIS CHAPTER EXAMINES VIGNETTES OF BATTLE FROM PERSONAL letters written throughout the twenty months of the war. These vignettes are not meant to be exhaustive and they do not tell "what really happened"; rather, they were chosen because, together, they add up to a very different narrative than the one commonly found in histories of the 1948 war. Central to the story are the reflections of ordinary men and women on violence. Violence caused both perpetrators and victims to reflect upon the meaning of community in their lives. Among Jewish soldiers, it was the violence of victory that determined the course of reflection. Being successful in depopulating Palestine of most of its Arab inhabitants led soldiers to wonder what it meant to be Jewish in the age of nation-states. Some wondered how violence and atrocities fit with their vision of a civilized Israel and Judaism. Others, perhaps influenced by IDF indoctrination, had fewer scruples, deeming violence an essential and, indeed, constitutive part of membership in the community of Western nations.

Among Palestinians and their allies, optimism that the ALA would defeat Zionism was increasingly called into question as the failure to stem the depopulation campaign became apparent. These were concerns about community of a different kind. While there was little challenge to the principle of pan-Arabism, its practice in Palestine by the ALA was often questioned and doubted. The rank-and-file of the volunteer army certainly doubted it, and then—I argue—tried to distance themselves from the failure by creating local alliances with Palestinians, often against direct orders from the ALA. Palestinians came to doubt the promise of pan-Arabism too, but for them the stakes were much higher: many had to make the fateful decision of whether to believe ALA propaganda that the volunteer army was in control, and stay put despite the deadly attacks at their doorsteps, or leave their homes in the hope that the pan-Arab pledge to save Palestine would soon be realized. Many oral histories of the nakba focus on this moment, but it is told here differently—the way it was narrated in real time in personal letters. These reflections spoke less to the questions of self-definition that were at stake in IDF letters, and were perhaps a testament to the differences between the violence of victory and the violence of defeat—i.e., the violence suffered by Palestinians but also forms of violence perpetrated by the Arab armed forces as defeat became imminent. It is in these fractured, uneven accounts from the lives of ordinary people—accounts of mutilated corpses as well as post-bellum thank you notes—that the parameters of the conflict as we know it today become visible.

VOLUNTEERS DISCOVER THE TRUE ALA

As they made their way to the country, the Arab volunteers who had answered the call of Palestine were greeted as heroes, at least at first. In early March 1948 Khalid Arslan, a Syrian volunteer likely of Druze origin, was part of a seventy-car convoy headed by Fawzi al-Qawuqji making its way to Palestine, with tacit British approval.[1] While passing through Zarqa in Transjordan, Arslan wrote his uncle: "The inhabitants, old and young, greeted us, shouting 'Long live Arab states' and 'Long live Arab Palestine.' This welcome excited the men of the convoy, who shouted in reply, "We are hurrying to Palestine to save it from the infidel Jews."[2] Soldiers of the Transjordanian Arab Legion apparently helped the convoy cross into Palestine via the Allenby Bridge, and spirits were high. "We are ready to enter the first battle, no matter how dangerous," Arslan wrote to his uncle.[3] The volunteers were further heartened by the festivities that greeted their arrival. Marʻi Hasan Hindawi, a Syrian volunteer from Dayr al-Zur, reported in his diary that the inhabitants of Tubas (near Nablus) and Jenin cheered them and fired celebratory shots in the air.[4]

The Arab volunteers were also encouraged by what appeared to be structures that the ALA had built. Writing to his family, Arslan reported that despite some hardships such as having to sleep on the floor ("don't be surprised because we are volunteers and do not care what conditions we're in"), he was content with the arrangements: "Everything is organized, and I must note that this guerrilla war is arranged by a regular army," he wrote to his uncle.[5] Arslan was also pleased with at least some of those who came to the aid of the Arab volunteers, such as the two defectors from the British army ("one from England, one from Scotland") who earned his accolades:

> I asked them why they were fighting the Jews. I told them we were fighting the Jews in the name of religion and God, and they answered me they were a hundred percent certain that the Arabs would win this war, and that after the Arab victory they would obtain al-Qawuqji's help in acquiring citizenship.[6]

These were evidently not the only British servicemen who enlisted in the ALA. Whatever pan-Arab community these Arab volunteers were a part of, it was sufficiently attractive to appeal to outsiders.[7]

Yet Arslan had reservations about some of the people the ALA had come to rescue. On one hand, he was impressed with the local women volunteering in hospitals: "Believe it or not, the female nurses in the hospitals in Nablus are of the highest social class," he noted.[8] But Arslan was less impressed by the men he encountered, complaining how shameful it was that so few Palestinians had joined the volunteers, leaving outsiders to do the heavy lifting while Jewish women were fighting in battles with their own rifles.[9]

Arslan's perception of the absence of Palestinian men on the battlefield contained a measure of truth. Ironically, this was in part the result of the confidence promoted by the arrival of the ALA itself. The sight of hundreds of volunteers from around the Arab world descending on various villages in Palestine understandably generated real excitement among Palestinians, and many believed that this volunteer army alone would be sufficient to defeat the Yishuv.[10] In Nablus in mid-February 1948, Hani Abu Jawala conveyed to a friend in Tiberias the excitement engendered by the volunteers:

> The streets here are as full [of ALA soldiers] as the streets of Tiberias on a Saturday. I must tell you that the volunteers eat for free, sleep in hotels for free, and go to the cinema for free, and therefore you see them everywhere you

go. There are in Nablus in great numbers, in full military garb, and with many modern weapons. It is truly uplifting.[11]

Abu Jawala felt a sense of pride in seeing an independent Arab fighting force, probably for the first time in his life. He also commented that many Palestinians in the areas under ALA control felt that with the arrival of these troops, the fight to save Palestine would be easy and swift. There was no need to enlist, he concluded, either in the ALA or (its oft-rival) the Army of the Holy Jihad, led by 'Abd al-Qadir al-Husayni.[12]

> I want to tell you that the company that 'Abd al-Qadir put together was disbanded. He assembled this company before he was called to Syria. The reason it was dissolved is that the people of Nablus greeted him with disparagement while they welcomed the volunteers from Arab states kindly.[13]

Many Palestinians saw the ALA as the epitome of the Arab promise to save Palestine, a promise that became crucial after the brutal suppression of the 1936–39 revolt by the British, which left the Palestinian society in a state of exhaustion. They subscribed to ALA propaganda, believing—in the words of one Palestinian—that "fifteen thousand" volunteers had arrived in Palestine, and that "weapons are flowing to them from the sister countries which scared up whatever needed to be scared up to purchase them"—in the words of another Palestinian.[14] Marches of volunteers in the streets of Palestine's towns "with full heavy and light weapons, including heavy artillery, tanks, ambulances and mobile hospitals" helped solidify these feelings.[15]

But the celebrations did not last long. Volunteers who spent any time in Palestine quickly realized that the stories of glorious victories and abundant weapons may have been grandstanding. In an attack on Tirat Zvi, a settlement west of the Jordan River, already in mid-February 1948, dozens of Palestinian and ALA fighters were killed (and one Jewish man). With the attack botched, a British armored column arrived at the scene and demanded that ALA forces retreat immediately. The commander of the First Yarmuk battalion, Muhammad Safa, agreed but reportedly asked that the British fire at his forces so he could later claim that he withdrew under British duress. The British agreed. "Much of the ALA," one ALA volunteer wrote his friend after the incident, "fled to Transjordan and Syria."[16]

The letters of ALA volunteers, as well as reports written by the volunteers' superior officers, reveal some of the underlying reasons for the Arab army's defeat. That the ALA was losing ground to the Jewish forces had more to do with poor supplies, and lack of weapons and training, than with the will of the volunteers to fight. Letters by volunteers report shortage of food, uniforms, and even underwear. Salaries were also irregular and medical treatment insufficient.[17] The dire extent of the shortage of weapons can be gleaned from correspondence between 'Uthman al-Hurani, the ALA mobilizer from Hama, and the volunteers he recruited in his hometown, stationed in Jaffa. Throughout the war, volunteers wrote him, pleading to make sure the ALA supplied them with weapons because they had none.[18] But al-Hurani's appeals on behalf of the volunteers to the ALA command went unanswered.[19] To compensate for the failure to send weapons, al-Hurani reassured volunteers that the families they had left behind would be taken care of, presumably upon the death of volunteers in battle.[20]

To try to help ALA units and simultaneously prevent soldiers from stealing from them, Palestinians established special support committees. These committees were successful in collecting donations and provisioning the forces in their vicinity. From a report of the Tulkarm committee in charge of providing for the Hittin battalion, we learn that in March 1948 all battalion soldiers were allowed to shower in bathhouses in Nablus (where they were greeted with sweets) or in special showers constructed in their camps. Barbers were also made available to them, and shoe-shiners were sent to their barracks. The soldiers' clothes were mended, washed, and ironed, and each soldier received undergarments and socks. Their barracks were fumigated with DDT, and so were their beds and clothes. Hospitalized soldiers received cigarettes, and the battalion was given extra clothes, soap, wheat, gasoline, and a complete set of an Arab flag and flagpole.[21]

Nevertheless, despite hospitality in many areas, the needs of volunteers far exceeded what Palestinians could provide. It seems that confiscation of Palestinian property (including houses), borrowing money without returning it, and theft from Palestinians may have been frequent, since orders to soldiers continued to warn against such acts. Letters of complaint from Palestinians also mentioned physical violence against them, and a Haganah informant reported of an ALA officer raping a Palestinian woman and her son.[22] For those reasons, ALA directives stipulated that while on the move, units must camp at least five kilometers from cities "in order to keep the army's good name."[23] Put differently, the army was to stay away from the very people it was supposed to save.

Al-Qawuqji himself was required to address his soldiers' unruly behavior, notifying his officers that "the complaints came to the attention of the highest authorities, which stains the reputation of the ALA."[24] Ghasan Jadid, the commander of the Alawite battalion in charge of the Safad area, reminded his soldiers of "the need to maintain the reputation of your battalion and the ALA and its good conduct with people so that they feel you are coming to free them and help them and not be a burden on them."[25] Apparently these supplications had only minimal effect, even when ALA soldiers were punished for misbehaving.[26] In some areas the soldiers' disorderly conduct reached such an extent that the commanders asked Palestinians to report any soldier they saw walking about in the city.[27] Palestinians were cautioned against showing hospitality to soldiers who defected, lest they themselves be tried in a military court.[28] To say the least, such directives stood in striking contrast to the images of hospitality and optimism that opened this chapter.

But the lack of food, clothing, and shelter was not the most urgent problem facing the ALA: volunteers being killed or injured by their comrades due to poor training and dysfunctional weapons was probably more acute. Letters and diaries of volunteers frequently reported the death or injury of comrades as a result of "friendly fire" or malfunctioning weapons, many of which were provided by Arab states.[29] Mar'i Hasan Hindawi, a Syrian volunteer from Dayr al-Zur, narrated in his diary the story of his comrade being killed by hand grenades that blew up while he was carrying them. Apparently, the man had come to see Hindawi before he was killed and told him, "In God, with each grenade I will kill 20 Jews."[30] Hindawi, knowing that these grenades were easily triggered when carried on the body, urged him to use caution, but the man ignored his warnings and was killed shortly afterward, taking another villager from Zir'in with him.[31] Another of Hindawi's friends was later killed when the army vehicle carrying him was involved in an accident, and Hindawi himself was injured after being accidentally shot at by his friends who mistook him for an enemy soldier.[32] Other soldiers reported similar incidents of the wrongful death of their friends. The Syrian volunteer Khalid Arslan wrote to his uncle of an incident where six ALA volunteers, including two officers, were killed when two British volunteers with the ALA accidentally triggered explosives as they were trying to disarm them. Arslan was devastated by their death, and kept imagining he saw the two British soldiers alive.[33]

When the incompetence of the army in which they were enlisted became evident, some deserted, but others did not abandon their resolve to save Palestinians.[34] It was outside of the battlefield that the volunteers' commitment to pan-Arabism came across most clearly. Volunteers often acted of their own volition to relieve Palestinians from Jewish attacks or harassment. These "partisan" operations were not sanctioned by the ALA command, and in fact sometimes resulted in punishment for disobedience.[35] Volunteers' letters suggest that Palestinian peasants and Bedouins were the most vulnerable to Jewish attacks during the first few months of war. Muhammad Salih Saʿid, a Syrian volunteer stationed in the village of Shafa-ʿAmr, east of Haifa, wrote to his parents how he and his friends rescued the peasants of the nearby village of Ras ʿAli. Apparently, the peasants were being harassed by Jews from nearby settlements who were trying to chase the peasants away from their fields. Saʿid and his friends decided to retaliate: they ambushed the Jews and drove them away from the fields.[36] Similarly, in early April 1948, an Iraqi officer named Muhi al-Din al-Tayar wrote to his father in Baghdad about how upset he was to see that Jews had carried out "a treacherous attack" against Bedouins camping next to their base on the outskirts of Baysan, southeast of Nazareth.[37] Apparently, Jews had killed four men and three women "while in their tents" and also put landmines on the roads leading to the Jewish settlements, presumably where the Bedouins camped. "We managed to rescue the tribe but we were a bit late," al-Tayar informed his father. The Iraqi officer and his men also blew up the landmines left by the Jews and set up new positions to guard the Bedouins. "We will avenge the blood of the innocent people who fell prey to the treachery of the criminals," al-Tayar promised his father.[38]

Despite this strong sense of devotion, it was also apparent that Arab volunteers thought Palestinians should be doing more to defend themselves. Marʿi Hasan Hindawi, the Syrian volunteer from Dayr al-Zur, recalled in his diary that he and his friends became angry at the Palestinians of Zirʿin, north of Jenin, where the ALA had a small base, for failing to push back an attack by Jewish forces, probably in mid-March.[39] "We were angry at the people of Zirʿin, as if they were our people [i.e., soldiers]," Hindawi commented in his diary.[40] But the reason that the village was left to fend for itself had to do with Hindawi and his friends being sent for rest and recuperation (R&R) by the commander of the First Yarmuk battalion, Muhammad Safa, after failing to prevent an earlier Jewish attack on Zir'in.[41] "As the saying goes, if the government [meaning the battalion commander] is angry at the company, it shall send it on vacation," Hindawi jested in his diary.[42] He too realized, it appears, that the anger at Palestinians was unwarranted.

Faced with the failure of the ALA to deliver victories in the battlefield, but still wishing to appease Palestinians, Hindawi and his friends decided to appeal to the basest of human instincts. After another Jewish attempt to capture Zir'in, likely on March 19, Hindawi reported in his diary that his unit managed to kill 63 Jewish soldiers.[43] Although the actual number was seven, the importance of this story lies in what ensued:

> We took seven corpses to the village and showed them to the inhabitants, that is the village of Zir'in, and afterward we took them [the corpses] to Jenin [and they were] in a monstrous state, one whose head was cut off, one whose ear or leg was dismembered. After their celebration [*hafla*] we took the corpses to the English, and they put them in their armored vehicles and afterwards brought them to the Jews.[44]

Hindawi does not explain in his diary why he and his men decided to deliver the corpses to the villagers so they could be defiled, in violation of ALA orders.[45] Other volunteers chose instead to deliver Jewish captives to the AHC, rather than to the ALA command, perhaps thinking that the ultimate decision of affairs in Palestine should rest with Palestinians, not Arab officers from elsewhere. Indeed, orders aside, the choice of what to do with Jewish civilians captured by Arab forces differed from one place to another, and from unit to unit.[46]

In a dramatically different way, some volunteers were able to develop an independent relationship with Palestinians by sending "thank you" notes to those who had hosted them in different parts of the country. Six Syrian volunteers stationed in the Tiberias jail (in an unclear capacity) sent the correspondent of *al-Difa'* newspaper in the city a request to publish a "thank you" note in his newspaper. The note expressed gratitude to the chairman and members of the city's national committee, the commander of the police, and the wardens for "their assistance and for making it easier [for us] and for the good attitude shown us . . . during our stay."[47] Other rank-and-file soldiers displayed similar gratitude. Upon his return home in March 1948, Shamil al-Samra'i, a volunteer from Damascus, felt a strong urge to thank Salman Salih Abu Hashim, a Palestinian from Tubas, for hosting him while he was fighting for the ALA. Al-Samra'i wrote that he arrived home safely, adding, "My brother and I [will] always remember your beautiful hospitality which you honored us with during the days we spent with you."[48] Al-Samra'i offered to return the favor of hospitality "if things got worse" in Palestine.[49]

THE BATTLE OF MISHMAR HA-'EMEK AND THE SECOND LOSS OF AL-ANDALUS

For a moment in late March 1948, the expectation of Palestinians that the ALA would turn the tide did not seem unreasonable. A successful attack on a convoy heading to the besieged Kibbutz Yehiam near al-Kabri in the Western Galilee on March 27 resulted in forty-seven Jews killed.[50] It was the single most lethal ambush against Jewish forces in the 1948 war. Days later, the attack on the Jewish settlement of Mishmar ha-'Emek was supposed to be the sequel to Yehiam, but it was ultimately bungled and marked a turning point regarding Palestinian confidence in the volunteer army. Now, everyone in Palestine, not just the volunteers, could see the chasm between the bold claims of the ALA's propaganda machine and its actual conduct on the battlefield.

Kibbutz Mishmar ha-'Emek was established in 1926 on land purchased by the Jewish National Fund in the area known as Marj Ibn 'Amir, or the Jezreel Valley. It had strategic importance because of its location on the Jenin-Haifa road.[51] Although the kibbutz had spent weeks preparing for an attack, and the Haganah intercepted phone calls indicating that the operation was about to start, the settlement was nevertheless taken by surprise when it began.[52] At 4:50 p.m. on April 4, while the 600 residents of the settlement were going about their normal day, ALA forces commenced heavy shelling of the kibbutz.[53] Witnessing the shelling, one of the Palestinian volunteers with the ALA wrote to a colleague:

> Here a fire, there a cabin collapsing on what's inside, and mines exploding as a result of the mujahidins' shells. The believers answered [the firing of] every shell with *"Allahu Akbar* [God is great], glory and victory" and, if given the opportunity, the youth of Jenin would have charged the settlement until the last

of them [was martyred], but the wisdom of the [high] command prevented them from doing so.[54]

The author of this letter was Burhan al-Din al-'Abbushi, a poet and a member of one of Jenin's most notable families. Born in 1911, al-'Abbushi was what one might call a revolutionary poet. In his day job he worked in the Arab Bank in Nazareth, but from early on, al-'Abbushi also participated as a fighter in anticolonial rebellions throughout the Arab world while writing poetry.[55] During the 1936–39 Arab Revolt in Palestine he was captured by the British and spent ten months in jail. Fearing for his life, al-'Abbushi fled to Beirut and eventually found himself in Iraq, taking a teaching position in the city of 'Amara, southeast of Baghdad.[56] In 1941 he participated in the Rashid 'Ali al-Gaylani revolt, and was wounded in a battle with the British.[57] From Iraq, al-'Abbushi fled to Damascus where he took refuge for six years, eventually making his way back to Palestine in 1947. Upon returning, he resumed his position at the Arab Bank. In April 1948 he joined the Iraqi volunteers of the ALA, fighting alongside them in the Battle of Mishmar ha-'Emek.[58]

For al-'Abbushi, like for many Palestinians of his generation, to consider the fate of Palestine as separate from that of other Arab lands would have seemed strange indeed. Many of his poems took on political themes and implored the Arabs to resist the colonial forces in their home countries. This, he believed, would eventually enable Arabs to come to the rescue of Palestine, which was struggling against both the British and the Zionists.[59] Al-'Abbushi was famous for his poignant language, which he often used to lash out at those who sold lands to Jews. In 1947 he censured the Lebanese Greek-Orthodox family and large absentee landlord, the Sursuqs, for selling the lands of Marj Ibn 'Amir (the Jezreel Valley) to the Zionist movement thirty years earlier, wishing that "their name be lost" and lamenting: "My sorrow for the Marj, how great is its disaster, and no son of the homeland is found to avenge it."[60] His harshest critique was reserved for the Palestinian and Arab leadership, calling them in the 1940s "the wicked ones" and declaring that they "had sold my homeland for a whore," likely referring to reported incidents where Jewish brokers provided Palestinian landowners with sex workers to convince them to sell.[61] But whatever critique he had of the leadership, in those days of April 1948 he was still confident in the "wisdom of the [high] command," and promised, "we will not stand silent until we defeat imperialism, imperialists, and the Jews."[62]

As a result of the shelling of Mishmar ha-'Emek, which al-'Abbushi described in his letter, the kibbutz suffered heavy damage and several casualties, yet ultimately avoided being overrun by the ALA advance.[63] Subsequently, about a thousand ALA soldiers advanced toward the settlement, shooting at it, but stopped short of passing its barbed wire. One of the reasons later given for the debacle was that the forces did not have proper wire cutters.[64] The lull in fighting allowed the Haganah to reinforce Mishmar ha-'Emek from nearby settlements, and when the battle ensued the following day, on April 5, the kibbutz was better prepared.[65]

For al-Qawuqji, the battle of Mishmar ha-'Emek was to be a major spectacle, and his headquarters even sent invitations to journalists to come view it on April 6, 1948. Carter Davidson, head of the Associated Press Jerusalem bureau, informed the Haganah intelligence that he and several other journalists were approached and invited to come to the village of al-Mansi, the staging ground for the ALA forces attacking the kibbutz. When they arrived, they were greeted by the Iraqi commander of the Qadisiyya battalion, Mahadi Salih al-'Ani, who told them: "I am happy you are here. You may choose from where you wish to witness the conquest of the Jewish settlement. But you must hurry because in a few moments we will start the final shelling. In 20 minutes I will be inside Mishmar ha-'Emek."[66] The journalists witnessed another episode of shelling, as planned, and were waiting for the settlement to be stormed. It never happened. After the journalists reminded the Iraqi officer of his earlier promise to meet them in Mishmar ha-'Emek in twenty minutes, the officer replied that there was no intention to conquer the Jewish settlement, just to frighten it. However, the officer also admitted that "at the last minute there was an order from al-Qawuqji to stop the operation and retreat," apparently for fear of the British.[67] Still nominally in control of Palestine, the British may have turned a blind eye to ALA activity in the country, but were apparently unwilling to have a Jewish settlement overrun on their watch.

On April 7, under British auspices, ALA officers and representatives of the kibbutz met in the village of al-Mansi to negotiate a permanent truce, with each side claiming that the other side was requesting mediation.[68] The British offered a compromise whereby the ALA attack on the kibbutz would permanently cease if, in exchange, the Haganah committed itself to allow the ALA to retreat peacefully and not to retaliate against the villages surrounding

Mishmar ha-ʿEmek. The British also offered that the women and children would be evacuated from Mishmar ha-ʿEmek during the twenty-four-hour temporary truce, without stipulating any conditions for that proposal. The kibbutz replied that they would welcome the evacuation of women and children but needed the consent of the Haganah for the other conditions. Reluctantly, the British agreed to wait until the kibbutz contacted the Haganah in Tel Aviv.[69]

Al-Qawuqji's version of the meeting was quite different. *Al-Difaʿ* stressed that al-Qawuqji's delegate presented the kibbutz with a set of conditions and allowed them twenty-four hours to respond.[70] According to the conditions, apparently drafted by al-Qawuqji himself, the residents of Mishmar ha-ʿEmek had to surrender their weapons and submit to ALA rule:

> I demand that you stop the attacks your men carry out against the civilian cars passing on the main road, and I demand that you not provoke the nearby Arab villages. I warn you that any aggressive acts done by the settlement will expose it to total destruction this time, and the annihilation [*fanāʾ*] of its residents. On the day of the punitive attack, my people avoided entering the settlement . . . only because they spared the lives of the women and children.[71]

This was one of a few instances where the ALA threatened to murder civilians. Even so, al-Qawuqji apparently believed there was a real chance that the residents of the kibbutz would surrender to the ALA. His conditions were not only published in the Arab press but also broadcasted in Hebrew on the ALA radio, where the residents were called "to abandon the Zionist aspirations for a Jewish state and the criminals of the Haganah" in return for protection.[72] Another Arabic radio broadcast stated that Mishmar ha-ʿEmek residents were assured by al-Qawuqji that "non-fighting citizens will be treated according to the honorable military code and the Arabs will not take their revenge for the slaughtered people of Deir Yassin [*sic*]" (a massacre that took place only a week before the radio broadcast).[73]

At the time negotiations were held, a propaganda campaign, led by ʿAli Nasir al-Din, the director of the ALA propaganda department, attempted to guarantee that the Arab and Palestinian press portray Mishmar ha-ʿEmek as a success story. The ALA radio reported that its forces "destroyed nine transport cars" of the Haganah and killed 180 Jews, wounding another 210. "This Mishmar battle was a severe lesson for the Hagana [*sic*] forces," the radio announcer notified listeners.[74] Newspapers echoed these reports and then embellished them: one reported that a senior Haganah commander was captured together with several of his men, and another that the road from Jenin to ʻAfula was now open and safe for passage.[75] Haganah officers, who were monitoring phone lines coming from al-Qawuqji's headquarters in Jabaʻ, heard even more fantastic accounts about "the Arab flag waved over Mishmar ha-ʻEmek," likely when the information was being conveyed to reporters.[76]

But Mishmar ha-ʻEmek had no intention of surrendering or honoring a truce. The negotiations were merely a ploy to buy enough time for reinforcements to arrive and for women and children to be evacuated.[77] On April 8, once the evacuation was completed and sufficient Haganah forces had congregated in the kibbutz, Mishmar ha-ʻEmek notified the British that they rejected the proposal for a permanent truce.[78] In Tel Aviv, the Zionist leadership decided to retaliate harshly, drive the ALA out of the Jezreel Valley, and level the villages around Mishmar ha-ʻEmek—Ghubayya al-Fawqa, Ghubayya al-Tahta, al-Naghnaghiyya, Abu Shuhsa, al-Kafrayn, al-Mansi, and Abu Zurayq.[79]

When the battle ensued on the night of April 8, it became clear the ALA could not defend the Palestinians in those villages. In fact, much of the ALA forces retreated from Marj Ibn ʻAmir and were dispatched to Jerusalem to relieve the forces there after the death of ʻAbd al-Qadir al-Husayni in battle that day. Although ALA forces occasionally managed to recapture a few of the villages singled out by the Haganah for retaliation in the six days after the resumption of fighting, they were unable to hold on to them. The 700 Haganah men easily defeated the remaining ALA forces and local Palestinian fighters, expelled or drove away the villagers, and quickly blew up their houses. In several cases, the residents of Mishmar ha-ʻEmek or nearby kibbutzim supervised the razing of the villages and their subsequent pillage.[80] One IDF soldier described the retaliation in a soldiers' magazine: "With dawn we arrived [back] in Mishmar ha-ʻEmek, with a slogan [in our head], 'once upon a time there was a village.' Indeed, when we came to Ghubayya al-Fawqa a village was standing there, but when we left, a pile of rubble remained."[81] On April 13, after his plea for a second ceasefire was rejected by the Haganah, al-Qawuqji sent a desperate request for large amounts of ammunition from Damascus, which was quickly denied with a statement that Mishmar ha-ʻEmek had become "a battle of attrition" and that he should consider withdrawing his forces (which he was already in the midst of doing).[82]

Just as things turned badly for the ALA on the battlefield, its propaganda machine sprung into action again to prevent Palestinians from becoming aware of the grim situation. On April 11, *al-Difaʿ* quoted Nasir al-Din threatening that the ALA "will destroy the settlement on the heads of its inhabitants and its reinforcement forces, and we will teach them a lesson they will never forget."[83] The ALA radio also reassured Palestinians that "a large number of Jews are secretly leaving Palestine" and "taking their fortunes with them."[84] Still, for those Palestinians who might have caught wind of the lies surrounding Mishmar ha-ʿEmek, Nasir al-Din explained that the ALA had to dispatch forces to the Jerusalem area after the Dayr Yasin massacre and the killing of ʿAbd al-Qadir al-Husayni. The ALA chief propagandist also called on Palestinians "not to make light of things, not let the severe events distract them from protecting the towns and villages, and not leave a chance for the enemy to benefit from them."[85] The force, which so many Palestinians had hoped would save them from displacement and obliteration, was now telling them to fend for themselves.

At the same time the ALA was calling on Palestinians to stand guard, representatives of thousands of displaced refugees from the villages that the Haganah had expelled sent a note to al-Qawuqji, pleading with him to come to their rescue: "We are now displaced and scattered in the area of Jenin with nothing except what the sky can give us, and only our blankets as protectors. So we have come to you in desperation to ask you to look at this situation with compassion and help us get our fields back."[86] It appears that al-Qawuqji did not respond to the villagers, prompting Jenin's prominent families to intervene by going over his head to appeal directly to the Arab League and the AHC.[87] On April 19, 1948, the Haganah intelligence intercepted the families' telegram claiming that "the Jews destroyed the villagers' houses and killed their babies and elderly" (something for which there is no evidence).[88] Swift action was required: the notables requested in the name of "your honor" and Arabism "to send reinforcements to avenge what happened to these villages."[89] The urgent plea by Jenin's prominent families revealed that they held the Arab states responsible for what had taken place.

Al-ʿAbbushi, too, witnessed the assault on the villages of Abu-Zurayq, north of Mishmar ha-ʿEmek. The village had 550 residents in 1945, but by the time the Haganah launched their attack on the night of April 11, only a few adult men and some 200 women and children remained.[90] In the initial stages of the attack, the remaining inhabitants were taken as captives, and the Haganah forces began blowing up Abu-Zurayq's houses. Shortly after, the women and children were released and expelled.[91] Al-'Abbushi was devastated:

> The Jews took revenge by launching an attack on the Arab village of Abu Zu-rayq and drove away all the women and children. They hurt some of the men, and all of them [the village's inhabitants] are crowded in the roads and alleys of Jenin. This painful sight crushes one's soul.[[92]] I joined those who went to face the danger of the settlement and rescue the women and children who wander in the fields after the Jews released them. . . . The exodus of these people . . . and the people of al-Mansi is just like the exodus of the sons of al-Andalus.[93]

This was not the first time al-'Abbushi resorted to the forced exile of Muslims from Spain (al-Andalus) to tell the story of Palestine. As early as 1945, al-'Abbushi warned Palestinians that if their complacency continued, they would lose their homeland:

> You, native of the country and the master of its land!
> Listen to the raven's crow [i.e., the voice of the raven], foretelling the day of exile.
> What happened to al-Andalus could happen to you. Sacrifice [for the sake of your country] before it is too late![94]

Although not the first to adopt the expulsion of Muslims from al-Andalus as a rhetorical tool to warn Palestinians, al-'Abbushi would come to perfect this analogy.[95] In late 1949, a year and a half after his prophecy materialized, al-'Abbushi would choose *The Ghost of al-Andalus (shabah al-andalus)* as the title for a play he wrote that portrays the events of those days in Palestine, from the attack on Mishmar ha-'Emek to the depopulation of the Palestinian villages of Marj Ibn 'Amir.[96] In the play, the women of Abu-Zurayq reproach the Arab fighters for allowing their expulsion. One girl says:

> Have the lions of my nation turned into dogs? They have cursed my honor and the honor of the girls of my nation and they did not leave for your sons any buxom women. We defended [our land] and cried out *ya shabab* [o young men], and how can those who inhabit the dust reply?[97]

As the cry from the women of Abu Zurayq emphasized, not only did the Arabs fail to defend Palestine's villages, they also failed to defend the honor of Palestine's women.[98] The reason for their failure, according to al-'Abbushi, was the factionalism among Palestinians and the infighting between Arab leaders. Just as the internal confrontations among the Muslim rulers of al-Andalus led to the exodus there, the same factionalism had caused many other losses in Arab history, culminating with that of Palestine.[99] In other words, the disintegration of pan-Arabism brought about the second loss of al-Andalus.

Al-'Abbushi decided to call his play *The Ghost of al-Andalus* to convey that the ghost of that fateful event would continue to haunt the Arabs until pan-Arabism fulfilled its promise to save Palestine. Only when victory over colonialism was achieved, he explained in the prelude, would Arabs be allowed to change the ending of the play:

> This title "The Ghost of al-Andalus" returns to Arab memory the narrative of the Arab exodus from al-Andalus. How long have we acted this drama out in order for people to learn a lesson from it?! And even now we are acting out the story of the Arab exodus from Palestine. When will the Arabs act out the story of the Arab entrance into Palestine and its liberation? But of course this narrative will be acted out in the day when the influence of every foreigner vanishes from our land.[100]

Thus, while decrying the failures of the Arab world on behalf of Palestine, al-'Abbushi was at the same time invoking a renewed commitment to pan-Arab anticolonialism as the remedy. Many Palestinians may well have ultimately agreed with al-'Abbushi's assessment, but in the wake of the defeat at Mishmar ha-'Emek, it would become increasingly difficult for them to view the ALA as their savior.

HEBREW HEART AND JEWISH SENTIMENT

If defeat left Palestinians asking who they could count on, victory left Jewish forces wondering who they were. Scholars of Zionism tend to conflate the worldview of the Zionist leadership with that of ordinary Jewish men and women in Palestine. According to Oz Almog, "expressions of nonconformism and anti-establishment discontent [among soldiers in 1948] are almost completely absent, and there is certainly no challenge to principles of Zionism such as doubts about the duty to serve in the army, the moral right to the country, or the confiscation of home and land from the Arabs."[101] But in fact the violence that accompanied the conquest of the Negev (*al-Naqab* in Arabic) and Galilee made some IDF soldiers question aspects of the officially sanctioned understanding of Zionism, as was conveyed to them by education officers. Indeed, those soldiers were uncertain about what form Judaism should take in the national era. Their letters demonstrate that Israeli-Jewish national identity was neither monolithic nor uniform, even among Zionism's most prized subjects: the soldiers who fought to create the state in the first place.

The vignettes of battle that tell this unknown story are available to us starting in September 1948, with the publication of the first *Soldier's Opinion* report by the censorship bureau. In the showcased letters, we meet IDF soldiers stationed in the Negev in the midst of a long ceasefire with the Egyptian army. This was the second truce, when the military superiority of the IDF was already established.[102] "This long lull is getting on my nerves, and I wish we'd already start wrestling again," wrote Dov to his family.[103] Like other soldiers at the Negev front, Dov wanted action: "I want to confront our Arab friends and feel the joy of conquest, although there aren't many conquests left to do. I have the impression that if hostilities start, we will finish off the enemy in the shortest time possible," predicted Dov.[104]

The prediction quickly became a reality in mid-October, when Operation Yoav to drive the Egyptians out of Palestine began.[105] "The Egyptians are dropping like flies. We are conquering all the important spots, and as a result they are facing either certain death or captivity," wrote Avshalom to his family.[106] The war was important for him to prove another point: "Our enemies must know … that even though we haven't fought for hundreds of years, we Jews are first-class warriors."[107] Avshalom's writing echoed exactly what the education officers had tried to instill in their soldiers: Although for two millennia Jews may have shied away from the use of force, now it was time to restore a glorious past. For Avshalom's friend, Lev, being like other nations, especially when it came to using organized violence, was the essence of national liberation. "Our soldiers demonstrated combat readiness, self-sacrifice, valor and national consciousness that could [easily] be compared with those of other armies around the world," he wrote. Lev was thrilled that the Jews had attained their place alongside other nations that exercised organized violence: "The Jewish soldier proved he could blow up a tank with a hand-grenade, and bring explosives to detonation even if he knows that he'd be blown up with them."[108] To Lev, the fact that Jews managed to claim agency through such acts was of great importance. It meant that the Jews escaped what he saw as their passive nature and managed to "return to history."

But overcoming passivity came at a huge price in Arab casualties. In November 1948, in a short prologue to the IDF soldiers' letters from the newly occupied areas in the Galilee and the Negev, the censor noted,

> The victories of the Israeli army . . . and the conquests that followed were accompanied by *acts of pillage, looting and murder* [emphasis in original], and many [letter] writers have expressed shock, resentment and disappointment at this behavior. . . . It should be noted that in many units there were no reactions, most likely because of censorship inside the units or fear of it. Despite the fact that some writers tried to excuse these outbursts as "intoxication with victory," it turns out that those who did not take part in these acts on moral grounds were deeply upset by what they saw.[109]

Soldiers' letters from the Negev and the Galilee demonstrate that the soldiers were divided in regard to the appropriate relationship between Judaism and the use of force. While some soldiers thought that "victory intoxication" or being "a nation like all other nations" condoned murder and looting, others, believing that the mainstream Jewish exegesis detested violence, were, at least initially, appalled by these acts.

The quick advance in Operation Yoav brought the soldiers to the outskirts of the Palestinian town of Bi'r al-Sabʿ (Beersheba) on October 21, 1948. Before the war, Bi'r al-Sabʿ had been a small town with 3,000 inhabitants, famous for the large mosque the Ottomans had built in 1902. By the time the IDF soldiers reached the town, most of its Arab residents had already fled to Hebron, but 350 remained. The IDF conquered the city from the Egyptian soldiers and Palestinian militia forces in a swift and brutal raid. Shortly thereafter, Israeli soldiers who wished to avenge their fallen comrades threw a grenade into a small mosque where the army was holding POWs. A few perished and the others were quickly sent to a POW camp elsewhere. Palmach poet Hayim Guri would later depict what he saw in Beersheba as the "eruption of the black wolf of hatred."[110]

Nor were the civilians who remained in Bi'r al-Sabʿ spared. Looting soldiers stripped some of the inhabitants of their valuables and then executed them.[111] They then assembled the civilians in the courtyard of the local police station and continued pillaging their homes.[112] It was the kibbutzim and moshavim around Bi'r al-Sabʿ that were the most industrious in looting, and later enjoyed much of the rural land expropriated from Palestinians (in fact, 350 out of 370 new settlements established in Israel between 1948 and 1953 were built on that land).[113] "This was no socialism, brotherhood of nations or morality, but Grab and Go!" wrote David to his family.[114] He lamented the fact that his kibbutz did not have any cars or people to send over on the day of the occupation, and that by the time they got there, the military police was already on site. While not alluding to Judaism, David was nevertheless concerned about how the ideals he was brought up on should play a part in the battlefield. At first he seemed to have difficulty reconciling the socialist principles he had learned on the kibbutz with the looting he witnessed in Bi'r al-Sabʿ, but on further thought he decided that he too wanted to take part in the orgy. In fact, it appears families back home sometimes pressured their loved ones to bring back with them part of the loot.[115] David's comrade was happy to oblige. He wrote to his family about the nice reading room he set up for his unit thanks to looted armchairs, "luxurious rugs," two big radio receivers, and an electrical gramophone. "Everyone brought something back," he noted in his letter and listed his own gains.[116]

But contrary to the soldier's assertion, not everyone partook in the pillage of the town. Even if the people of the kibbutzim could easily forget their socialist principles, for Mordechai the Jewish tradition called for something better: "The city looks like after an earthquake. I did not imagine that the army of the Israelites could be so horrid in plundering Arab property. They crossed the line. I am sure Arab soldiers are no more righteous, but still, where is the Jewish morality? To me this is a badge of shame."[117] Mordechai's words echoed IDF propaganda, which insisted that the Arabs would act more brutally toward the Jews had they been victorious. Still, he thought that pillage was contrary to what he perceived to be the essential Jewish disposition.[118]

Operation Yoav quickly drew to an end, but atrocities continued. On October 29, in the village of Dawayima, south of Hebron, IDF soldiers found the belongings of the thirty-five comrades who had been killed a few months earlier while on their way to reinforce the besieged kibbutzim of Gush Etzion near Bethlehem.[119] Writing to his family, Ezra recalled that he and his friends "took an oath to avenge the death of our 35 friends."[120] When they found the dining tables that belonged to Gush Etzion in Dawayima, they "became furious beyond recognition." In response, Ezra noted, "We routed the Egyptian soldiers who were there, blew up all the houses and retreated."[121] What Ezra did not disclose in his letter was that the soldiers' fury quickly turned into bloodlust. They executed 80–100 (100–200 according to different estimates) of Dawayima's inhabitants, including women and children. The soldiers believed that the villagers had participated in the killing of their friends.[122]

The massacre in Dawayima was not a singular incident. Writing from another village on the southern front that week, Yitzhak told his friends back home: "My staff sergeant, a great friend, was shot and killed. But we avenged his blood the way we do for all our fallen. . . . . We choose a place as a target, and all the Arabs there have no choice but to flee or be killed."[123] Although encouraging revenge in the beginning of the war was a norm, by the end of 1948 the IDF high command felt that it was losing control over the soldiers. In December, Southern Front Commander Yigal Allon issued new orders to stop killing POWs, looting, and expelling Palestinians without a direct order.[124]

Shortly before entering the Palestinian villages of Majdal and Isdud, the commanders of the Givati brigade warned their soldiers through the pages of the combat bulletins, "No one is to defile his hands in robbery and plunder. . . . Don't open any door without a direct order. . . . Everyone who defies this command is to be treated as a traitor."[125] What soldiers made of these policy changes is not entirely clear. When Givati soldiers eventually marched into Majdal in late October, Egyptian forces were pulling back, and only a few hundred out of the original 10,000 inhabitants were still there, the rest having fled to nearby villages or to Gaza.[126] Photographs of Majdal from the first days after occupation show that the town was in a state of chaos, and the interaction between the occupying forces and the local Palestinians tense. One photograph, taken by the IDF, appears emblematic of the new relationship between occupier and occupied (see fig. 8). It shows a Palestinian villager in a *dishdasha* (an ankle-length robe worn by men) and a *kufiya* trying to explain something to an Israeli soldier who was wearing shorts. The villager was on the verge of tears, while the soldier looked at him suspiciously. Standing around were a few dozen men watching to see whether the soldier would budge.[127] Somewhere nearby, Shaul was writing to his family:

> Strange is the feeling of an occupying soldier. It is hard to put into words.... How feelings arise in you when you see those that till yesterday were among your enemies, those who supported, certainly also admired, the invading armies ... now they are groveling in front of every soldier, willing to serve you, and in their eyes—cold fear. Sometimes, you think, what if, God forbid, things were different, and they were to enter our place. Would they, too, allow us to wander around with some freedom? And do these elderly women, who introduced hatred through their breast milk, who educated their sons to kill ... deserve compassion and humane treatment? These doubts run around in your mind, but your hands are tied by your Hebrew heart, by your Jewish sentiment. And thus you wander the streets intoxicated, not with wine, but with victory.[128]

IDF indoctrination stressed that if things had been the other way around and the Arabs had had the upper hand, they would have annihilated the Jews. Shaul was clearly influenced by such reasoning. In fact, he became convinced that Arab mothers introduced hatred of Jews through their breast milk, meaning that Arab opposition to Zionism stemmed from biologically ingrained enmity toward Jews rather than legitimate grievances. However, Shaul's cultural background and the experience he had in Majdal also made him contest the army's indoctrination, which forbade showing mercy to the enemy. Shaul found himself in a position that was completely new for Jews in the twentieth century: occupying another people as a sovereign Jewish nation and controlling every aspect of their lives.[129] Having the IDF indoctrination in mind, he still felt "tied" by his "Hebrew heart" and "Jewish sentiment." In that sense, he was not completely convinced that Jews should revel in the use of violence, something he likely associated with the gentile way of war. We do not know what path Shaul chose and whether he decided to help the Palestinians left behind, stand aloof, or expel or even kill them. In any case, Shaul's personal choice did not matter much, since in 1950 the Israeli government decided to expel the remaining Palestinians in Majdal to Gaza and destroy the village. Ashkelon, a Jewish-only city, was erected in its place.[130]

FIGURE 8. The occupation of Majdal in southern Palestine. 30 October 1948.
Courtesy of the IDFA.

TO STAY OR TO LEAVE

For Palestinians, the series of calamities in the first two weeks of April
1948—including Mishmar ha-ʿEmek, Dayr Yasin, and the death of ʿAbd al-
Qadir al-Husayni—marked a turning point. It was also then that the ALA
tried to walk back some of its earlier promises, and especially al-Qawuqji's
pledge to "destroy the landmarks of Zionism and eliminate it altogether." On
April 29, 1948, Nasir al-Din himself addressed Palestinians on the ALA radio
with a very different message:

> The Arab leaders heading the Arab Governments and the Arab League real-
> ize far better than you or me the best way to safeguard Arab interests. These
> meetings being held on behalf of Palestine, which is on the edge of a volcano,
> are surely quite useful, otherwise they would not have been held so often. Ev-
> ery meeting helps avoid a repetition of Haifa [i.e., the loss of the city to the

Haganah]. Some of you may be inclined to compare the amount of assistance offered by each Arab State to Palestine. You may say that some have offered more than others and that the sons of some Arab states have shed more of their blood for Palestine than others. In fact, if it were not for the strong nerves of Fawzi al-Kawukji and the bravery of the al-Inqaz forces [the ALA] and their firm decision to fight to the last man, all the Arab countries would have offered far more men and equipment than they are doing now. It is known that such delay is intentional in the interests of the cause.[131]

If what appeared to be major setbacks was in fact "intentional," then Palestinians had no reason for concern. But of course, Nasir al-Din's admonition had a very different purpose: the ALA was not only trying to nip discontent in the bud, but also to make sure Palestinians remained loyal to the ALA and supportive of Arab leaders. But in the aftermath of this catastrophic month, many Palestinians were forced into a fateful decision: to stay in the face of hostilities taking place at their doorsteps, or leave their homes in the hope of returning soon. Without actual help from the ALA or local forces, these Palestinians had to weigh the volunteer army's propaganda, warning them against leaving their homes, against the news coming from Dayr Yasin, and the rumors that a similar fate may be waiting for their own villages too.

For a few Palestinians, the events of April 1948 served as a wake-up call. They were adamant to try a last-ditch effort to force the Arab world to fulfill its promise to save Palestine.[132] Indeed, for Wasif, a young Palestinian, Dayr Yasin was a watershed moment that made him decide to join the ALA and leave immediately for training in Qatana.[133] Eleven days after the massacre he promised his sister:

> I'll come back from Syria with hundreds of Syrian, Egyptian and Iraqi fighters and they will be the ones to determine the fate of this country. I solemnly promise you that I will never forget the Dayr Yasin affair. I will publish it in the Syrian newspapers, and in the different clubs, and I will spread anti-Zionist propaganda all over Syria. I will induce a spirit of revenge in the hearts of the Syrian youth, and they will all come to Palestine full of rage and wrath against the Jews.[134]

Wasif continued to believe that mobilization of young Arab men through propaganda and "a spirit of revenge" would be sufficient to turn the tide. He made no mention of the systemic problems plaguing the volunteer army. Still, he

made a final request to his sister that many of his generation would see as a
radical change in gender roles:

> I ask that you always help the wounded fighters as much as you can, because
> the attacks may intensify, and things could get much worse than they are
> now. . . . The murder of the nurse in the al-Qastal should serve as a lesson for all
> Arab girls in this country. She was killed in the line of duty.[135]

Wasif not only commemorated the sacrifice of the nurse apparently killed in
the al-Qastal battle (in which 'Abd al-Qadir al-Husayni died) but urged his
sister to volunteer and help the fighters herself.[136] Arslan, the Syrian volunteer, had already reported on the participation of Palestinian women in the
struggle as nurses, including women from the middle and upper classes. In
fact, Palestinian women established a special unit during the war, Zaharat al-
'Uqhuwan ("the chrysanthemum flower"), which accompanied armed fighters
and treated the wounded.[137] Even al-Qawuqji's daughter, the Palestinian press
reported at the time, volunteered as a nurse helping wounded ALA soldiers.[138]
Still, according to Haganah intelligence—quoting the Arabic press—female
members of the unit wrote Amin al-Husayni to complain that Jaffa's military
commanders (presumably from the ALA) only used them "for propaganda
purposes at postings with British officers," but refused to let them take part
in military action.[139]

Not only Wasif's view that his sister should take part in the armed struggle but also his optimism were an exception.[140] In the aftermath of the Mishmar ha-'Emek blunder and the Dayr Yassin massacre, some Palestinians
concluded that neither the ALA nor the Army of the Holy Jihad would save
Palestine.[141] It was at that point that the ALA initiated a propaganda campaign aimed at stopping Palestinian flight. In contrast to the oft-repeated
myth that most Palestinians left their homes at the urging of Arab leaders
(thereby exculpating Jewish forces), commanders of the ALA in different
regions in fact warned Palestinians against deserting their homes and fields
as a result of Jewish attacks or the fear thereof.[142] In fact, al-Qawuqji himself
was very concerned by the great number of people fleeing their villages. It
is estimated that 230,000 Palestinians had fled by the end of April 1948 due
to attacks by Jewish forces, fear of future attacks, or the result of Haganah
psychological warfare. Jewish forces had forcibly expelled an additional

10,000 by that point.[143] On April 24 al-Qawuqji issued a public notice blaming "cowards [who] evacuated their houses in the villages and cities because of . . . false propaganda or fear which took over their weak hearts."[144] Those cowards, al-Qawuqji insisted, "instilled anxiety in the hearts of the remaining inhabitants," who also started to flee. He threatened to settle the score with those spreading the idea of departure and sentence them to death.[145] His printed notice was read aloud on the ALA radio and apparently distributed in villages on the same day it was issued.[146] Junior ALA commanders also took heed: the commander of the Hittin Battalion, in charge of the Tulkarm area, Madlul 'Abbas, warned that "houses and villages emptied by their inhabitants in violation of these orders would be subject to demolition and destruction."[147] Alawite battalion commander Ghassan Jadid took an even harsher stance, threatening the inhabitants of the villages around Safad that "whoever tries to leave his village will be fired upon and his possessions and livelihood confiscated."[148]

Palestinians were promised that the ALA would establish mechanisms to help protect their lands, although it appears that such mechanisms were never put in place.[149] There are, however, a few scattered reports of instances when the ALA retaliated against fleeing Palestinians.[150] Still, the shock surrounding the execution by Jewish forces of so many civilians in Dayr Yasin, including women and children, made much more of an impression on Palestinians than the pleadings by ALA commanders and al-Qawuqji himself to stay put.[151] Letters by Palestinians demonstrate how the news about the massacre traveled in real time among ordinary people: Muhsin Fawaz, who was a clerk at the British detainee camp at 'Atlit, wrote his family on April 18 about "the barbaric massacre of innocents" by "the Jewish criminals" in Dayr Yasin.[152] Citing the inflated numbers of casualties circulating in the Arab press, Fawaz told his family that "those killed were put in a deep well, and they are 25 pregnant women, 50 breastfeeding women, and 60 women or girls who were slaughtered like sheep." The survivors—Fawaz noted accurately—were paraded by Jewish forces in the streets of Jerusalem.[153] A monk by the name of Jordan Fortwangler, writing from the 'Ayn Karim convent next to Jerusalem to a friend in Germany, tried to describe the sense of urgency felt by the women and children who fled their houses in Jerusalem and ended up in his convent in May 1948:

These poor people live in constant fear and they do not yet know how far from their houses they'll need to flee. What the Jews have been doing recently redefines [the meaning of the word] barbaric. Things are getting worse by the day. Right after the British left, a major slaughter began. These crazy politicians are sitting in America and pushing the nations [here] to a disaster.[154]

Not only Jerusalem was in a panic. In Haifa, a city ostensibly under the protection of the ALA, at least 10,000 people left the country as early as December 1947, shortly after the civil war began. Those departing belonged mostly to affluent families who held foreign citizenship and members of the Christian elite, but also poor day laborers from nearby villages. According to Haganah intelligence, by late January 1948 another 10,000 had fled, relying on visas issued to them by the Syrian and Lebanese consulates.[155] The narrative of the Palestinian departure from Haifa—especially that of Christians—told in virtually all histories of the war, ignores the sentiments of some Palestinians who witnessed the departure of their brethren and tried to stop it: "The hearts of the Arabs break when seeing that the departure of Arab families from Haifa continues," wrote a certain Abu Qasim from the village of Kawkab Abu al-Hija to Nimr al-Khatib, a senior member of Haifa's national committee and the AHC.[156] It is unclear if Abu Qasim himself was in a leadership position, or if he was just a concerned citizen: "Publish a written warning in the streets of Haifa [threatening] to punish this activity by burning the trucks carrying the belongings of any family that is leaving." He also suggested punishing the trucks' drivers and owners of garages where the well-to-do stored their belongings.[157] It is unknown if Nimir al-Khatib ever got Abu Qasim's letter, or if he replied. The Haifa national committee, in any case, chose a less forceful approach in early 1948, and tried to convince the elite not to leave the city by publishing appeals in the press.[158]

Other letters suggest that some members of the elite in Haifa considered alternatives to fleeing the city when it turned into a battlefield in early 1948. Edward, a Christian Palestinian, wrote his friend that "for three consecutive days no one in Haifa could leave his home."[159] Apparently, Jews living next to his neighborhood "used to hunt the Arabs [passing by]." Fearing for his family's life, he decided to leave the house and move his family to a rented one far from the Jewish neighborhoods, but still in Haifa. The family intended to wait there until the hostilities ended.[160] But finding new housing that would keep them out of harm's way was not the only problem facing Haifa's Palestinians. Those who had already left the city or who were in safer parts of the country often exerted pressure on their family members in Haifa. Nur wrote his relative:

> My brother, our thoughts are always with you, how are you, and what is going on with you. I listen to the news [on the radio], and when they mention there was an incident in Haifa, I become like a madman.[161]

Urging the recipient to leave Haifa, Nur explained that the road to Nazareth was still open and that the recipient should make use of it. "If your intention is to come to us, let us know so we can hurry up . . . and send you a truck so you could come to our side immediately."[162]

Nevertheless, some Palestinians who had already relocated to safer places outside Palestine chose to return to Haifa during the peak of the civil war in March–April 1948. As Hisham explained in a letter from Haifa to Beirut from March 8:

> When I left Beirut I was missing my dear country, Palestine, but when I got to the city of Haifa, I saw the fire burning in our midst in the main street and I remembered when we were all in Beirut, and I became sad for the separation from you . . . I pray that God brings us all together to one house . . . while achieving complete independence.[163]

In any case, none of these calculations made much of a difference, at least not in Haifa. On April 21, 1948, the British redeployed their forces in the city, withdrawing their troops from most neighborhoods, while maintaining presence only in several strategic locations deemed essential for the final withdrawal in May. That same day, the Haganah, which (unlike the local Palestinian national committee) was privy to the British plan of redeployment, launched a military operation and swiftly occupied much of the city, including the Arab neighborhoods. The marketplace, where many Arabs congregated, and likely some of the Arab neighborhoods, were shelled with mortars to frighten the civilian population.[164] The Palestinian national committee of Haifa decided not to sign a capitulation treaty and instead called on Palestinians to leave the city en masse on April 23.[165] In three weeks' time, over 30,000 of Haifa's Arabs had left the city, leaving behind only about 6,000 Palestinians by the time the regular Arab armies entered Palestine.[166]

The news from Haifa quickly traveled to other parts of the country, further creating panic. From Kafr Yasif, Ahmad Muhammad 'Abdalla 'Afifi wrote his parents in Acre that "in Haifa, the [British] army removed all the [Arab] inhabitants before giving the city over to the Jews."[167] 'Afifi was concerned that his father may have already been arrested and urged his mother to promptly leave with the remaining family members. Fearing that trying to arrange for their belongings to be moved would be too dangerous, he urged his family to leave empty-handed, "and God will provide."[168] Indeed, many were preparing to leave as the Jewish forces started shelling the city. A father wrote his son, Munir Effendi Nur, from Acre:

> The enemy's shells fell inside the city. The attack had caused panic among the inhabitants. Many left or are about the leave. We may go to Beirut. The preparation to leave Acre includes all social classes: the rich-, middle- and poor classes. They are all getting ready to leave, and they are selling everything they can ... you won't believe how expensive it is to rent a car."[169]

FIGURE 9. The Departure of Palestinians from Iraq al-Manshiyya, in southern Palestine, to Transjordan. 31 March 1949. Photo by Beno Rothenberg. Courtesy of the Israel State Archives.

Even though Acre was defended by various Palestinian youth movements—in addition to ALA forces—they could not withstand the Jewish attack, which began in full swing on May 16.[170] One of the primary reasons for the city's collapse was the influx of refugees from Haifa. Thousands of them escaped to the fortress town, depleting its food and water reserves. After the Jewish forces disconnected the city's utilities, it stood no chance. An outbreak of typhus led those who remained in Acre on May 18 to raise a white flag.[171]

BEING LIKE ALL OTHER NATIONS

Some Jewish soldiers did not regard the accusation of the ʿAyn Karim monk—that their actions had redefined the meaning of "barbaric"—as slander. In fact, they rejoiced in being brutal, as instances from Operation Hiram demonstrate. The campaign was supposed to finalize the occupation of the Western and Upper Galilee (designated for the Arab state by the UN, but reallocated to the Jewish state in the plan published by Bernadotte), and deal a final blow to the ALA.[172] For months the IDF had been waiting for a pretext to break the ceasefire resolution brokered by the UN Security Council and wage an offensive in the north, and the opportunity finally presented itself on October 22, 1948, in the form of an ALA attack on the IDF hilltop position on Shaykh ʿAbd. The attack by the Arab forces was in defiance of the ceasefire, and in response the IDF launched Operation Hiram, which lasted from October 28 until October 31.[173]

The propaganda campaign aimed at soldiers prior to the operation was again ambiguous. The Golani brigade—one of the four brigades participating—warned soldiers in a special bulletin about misconduct, especially looting and damaging sacred places.[174] But other commands conveyed a different message altogether. A few days into the fighting, Moshe Carmel, the officer in charge of the campaign, ordered his soldiers to "do all in your power to clear quickly and immediately from the areas conquered all hostile elements in accordance with the order issued. The inhabitants should be assisted to leave."[175] Perhaps there was no explicit order to act brutally, but the ambiguity made Operation Hiram and the occupation of the Galilee one of the most violent chapters in the 1948 war. IDF troops executed at least 200 Arab civilians and POWs in 12 instances alone. Looting was also widespread. Based on Israeli estimates, 50,000 Palestinians became refugees during the operation, which reached into Lebanon.[176] All in all, 23 villages and towns inside Palestine were conquered (in addition to a dozen villages across the Lebanese border) during Operation Hiram.[177]

In fact, there was not much fighting in Operation Hiram. As we will see, forces from the ALA, reinforced by the Syrian army, fled almost immediately.[178] But the Israeli soldiers were not merely interested in forcing the ALA to surrender. They had another score to settle: a month before the operation, two IDF soldiers had been killed after stumbling onto ALA soldiers near the village of 'Ailabun. Not unlike the gory "celebration" in Zir'in, in this instance too, the IDF soldiers were decapitated, their heads put on sticks and paraded around the village of 'Ailabun. During Operation Hiram, the heads were discovered in one of the houses. In retaliation, the soldiers executed fifteen Palestinians and looted the village.[179] Close by, other IDF forces crossed the international border into Lebanon. They were trying to block a reinforcement battalion from coming to the rescue of the ALA forces besieged in the Galilee.[180] On October 31, in the Lebanese village of Hula, officers executed several dozen Lebanese civilians with machine guns and then buried them under a house.[181]

Nearby, Rivkah was visiting the battlefields right after the occupation was completed.[182] As a scout, she had likely been on other battlefields before November 1948—a rather late stage of the war. But she was still shocked by what she saw during Operation Hiram:

> Howls and rampage of soldiers, intoxicated with victory, vibrate here from every corner. I want to share with you our shouts of triumph. I think that such an occupation is the work of the devil. Right after the conquest of the large villages, I visited these places as a frontline scout. Our way was paved with Arab casualties. The commander said on the wireless that the corpses reached up to the knees. Entire families were shattered and only a few were left as remnants. In the houses, everything was scattered. They found a lot of food, jewelry, money and other spoils. Corpses were still lying around in the houses. Soldiers made a fortune of the plunder.[183]

It was not the plunder that bothered Rivkah; the spoils, she wrote, rightfully belonged to the kibbutzim that "deserve it."[184] However, seeing her friends go on a rampage and wallow in the blood of combatants and civilians made her feel that the victory was not a gift bestowed by God to the Israelis but the work of the devil. Although she was deeply troubled by what she saw, she kept it to herself and did not intervene. When she witnessed the pleas of a Syrian soldier, locked in the battalion prison, she felt sorry for him. The soldier kept insisting he had not done anything, asking incessantly if they were going to kill him. "Living like this without knowing your destiny is dreadful," Rivkah wrote to her family.[185] At some point she felt she must speak up:

> I saw how they loaded two jeeps with German officers, a Yugoslavian and two Syrians, all blindfolded. They were tortured and interrogated for hours. Today, an artillery officer told me that they were burned alive. A few days ago, when I saw one of our soldiers cracking the skull of a young Syrian by hitting him over the head with a steel helmet, I preached to him and the officer in charge about fair treatment of the captives. Of course, everyone knew what made me talk like this. Eliezer is always right in front of me.[186]

It seems that Rivkah intervened to stop the Israeli soldier who was cracking the skull of the Syrian soldier because she felt that Eliezer also would have intervened. We do not know who Eliezer was, but it is clear that his memory held special significance for Rivkah. If she indeed stepped in due to the memory of a loved one who died in battle, then she did not react as most soldiers did after the death of a comrade. As already noted, often the death of a fellow soldier was used to justify brutal killing as "payback." In any case, Rivkah indicated that everyone understood what made her talk the way she did, suggesting that she knew that her behavior was not in keeping with the norm.

But what was the norm that Rivkah betrayed when speaking out? It was not a gender norm.[187] Other female soldiers in the IDF acted as brutally as their male counterparts. In fact, some went above and beyond to prove they were not soft.[188] What Rivkah had a hard time accepting (at least initially) was the idea of "muscular Judaism" and its followers relishing violence:

> Our boys are acting with dreadful brutality in the villages of Lebanon. But there is no wonder; we, and the first boys in the Galilee, have suffered so much. I think that if the Jewish guys are expected to fight and murder legitimately, like the soldiers of other nations, they too should be allowed to erupt and kill just like that, out of revenge and pleasure. At first, it was hard for me to believe and get used to the idea that a Jewish soldier from a good kosher home can abuse people in such a horrific way. The last battles taught me a lot and opened my eyes.[189]

Rivkah referred explicitly to the Zionist ethos of being "a nation like all other nations," which emphasized a Jewish "return to history" through, among other things, normalizing the use of force and taking pleasure in it. If Jewish boys were expected to fight for their independence, she believed, then they too should be allowed to act on bestial instincts and draw pleasure from the blood of their enemy, just like soldiers of other nations. Rivkah's writing suggests that this transformation of her thought was not done without hesitation. She was quick to invoke the idea that there was something unique in Jewish morality, and she had trouble reconciling the fact that "a Jewish soldier from a good kosher home can abuse people in such a horrific way." Still, her last words about the battles opening her eyes imply that she eventually came around and learned to accept the marriage between Judaism and violence. Indeed, atrocities were seen by some as a vital part of the violence of victory because they symbolized Jewish sovereignty after two millennia.

WHO IS TO BLAME?

Atrocities were also important to the violence of defeat on the Palestinian side—as demonstrated by the abuse of Jewish corpses—because they apparently allowed some distraction from the unfolding catastrophe. However, the distraction was ultimately fleeting. Palestinians who watched as their country was depopulated had more pressing concerns. On June 26, the Arab youth club in al-Tira village near Haifa wrote to the ALA headquarters that the British had evacuated the area, and that the Jewish forces were closing in on them while UN observers stood idly by:

> We call on you and any other interested parties to quickly come to our rescue in the name of Arabism. The road is open for you [to do so] if you wish. If this complaint and plea for help does not result in your immediate consent, then God will determine our destiny.[190]

Apparently, no response arrived from ALA headquarters. Twenty days after, on July 16, 1948, the IDF occupied the village and expelled its inhabitants.[191]

By July 1948 most ALA forces were busy defending themselves rather than launching attacks on the IDF. Another favorite pastime was the blame game, which started after the failed attack on Mishmaek ha-'Emek. Al-Qawuqji was quick to scapegoat those he felt were responsible for the fiasco. A certain second lieutenant, al-Qawuqji insisted, had neglected to make sure his men carried wire cutters and explosives, thus preventing them from entering the kibbutz. Al-Qawuqji announced that the officer would be court-martialed and "subject to the harshest punishment for his shameful and despicable act."[192] But at least some of al-Qawuqji's officers pointed upward when looking for the responsible parties.[193] A company commander from the Hittin battalion, writing to the battalion commander, blamed the ALA leadership for not having a detailed operation plan for the attack, failing to coordinate among the different forces, and not providing sufficient food, ammunition, and explosives to soldiers. But his most potent critique was directed at local Palestinians, who, he said, did not trust the ability of ALA volunteers to fight the Jews. These Palestinians only "join the mujahidin in collecting plunder, but resist the mujahidin's attempt to stop [battle] or retreat, thinking that the mujahidin were there only to make a profit."[194] The young officer was deeply hurt by this behavior: "If the mujahidin secure [plunder] then the people are overcome [with joy], but if they fail, woe to them from the resentment of the people and the mockery of the women and children."[195]

But did Palestinians really mistrust ALA volunteers at the time? Letters by Palestinians and rank-and-file volunteers suggest otherwise.[196] In fact, it is possible that the real issue at stake was who should lead the fight. Palestinians may have asked the greater Arab community to come to their rescue, but they still wished to be the ones with the last word on how that rescue mission should unfold, including the decision about when to stop a given battle or retreat. At least in the view of the ALA officer, Palestinians could not be trusted with such matters since they were "extremely frightened of the Jews, to the degree that if they hear one shot directed at them from the Jews they imagine that the Jews are surrounding the village and that it's in need of saving."[197] But when the rescue mission of the ALA stalled, the officer claimed, Palestinians were quick to abandon their villages.[198] Indeed, the view that Palestinians themselves were to blame for the failure of the ALA to save Palestine's villages was apparently popular among ALA officers. Some officers saw Palestinians as ungrateful and even disruptive of the operations carried out in their defense.[199]

The blame game continued alongside the disintegration of the ALA.[200] By the time the regular Arab armies invaded Palestine on May 15, 1948, major towns under the auspices of the ALA—like Haifa, Tiberias, and Safad—had already been occupied by Jewish forces. Even after the arrival of the regular Arab armies, the ALA remained the principal force defending the Galilee. From May to October, the volunteer army was involved in several more key battles with the IDF, sometimes with the help of the Syrian and Lebanese armies. Even though in two key battles—in Malkiya (in June) and Sejera (in July)—the ALA showed military competence, the balance sheet clearly tilted in favor of the IDF, especially after the loss of Nazareth in July 1948.[201] The final blow came in late October 1948, when the IDF launched Operation Hiram to drive out what remained of the ALA from Palestine. Although the Galilee was an area where the ALA was deeply entrenched, the IDF attack caught the troops by surprise, and they were unable to regroup to defend what was left of northern Palestine.[202]

As the end drew near, ALA commanders became more abusive toward their own men. An administrative command from October 28, 1948—the day Operation Hiram started—instructed a deputy commander of an ALA unit to "kill whoever disobeys your order."[203] The deputy commander was also instructed "not to retreat no matter what the order says," promising him that a Syrian battalion was on its way.[204] But the Syrian forces were unable to turn the tide. Within sixty hours of the start of Operation Hiram, most of the ALA forces had retreated to Lebanon, but only after suffering heavy casualties. Dozens had also been taken captive by the IDF. That was effectively the end of the ALA, at least in Palestine.[205]

After al-Qawuqji was relieved of his command, the ALA forces that had retreated into Lebanon were integrated into the Lebanese army and instructed to defend Lebanese soil from IDF encroachments. Some of the volunteers were later transferred to the Syrian army and integrated there. In March 29, 1949, the commander of the Syrian army, Husni al-Zaʿim, overthrew President Shukri al-Quwwatli and appointed himself president of Syria. Six weeks later, al-Zaʿim disbanded the ALA, or what was left of it, and officers and soldiers alike were sent home. Budgetary constraints were one reason for al-Zaʿim's decision, but a more pressing consideration was his fear for the stability of his regime. Al-Zaʿim apparently had good reasons to be concerned: the revolutionary officers of the ALA, led by Wasfi al-Tal who later rose to prominence in Jordanian politics, were unwilling to let the pan-Arab dream evaporate. They wanted to launch a new attack on Israel, bringing together the ALA volunteers who were still in Syria, Palestinian volunteers in the ALA, and the Syrian and Lebanese regular armies.[206] That was something in which the new Syrian president, who was secretly negotiating with Israel, had no interest.

WHAT BRINGS US TOGETHER

The regular Arab armies—and especially the Egyptian army—continued to fight for several months after the ALA was pushed out of Palestine in late October 1948. However, each Arab army fought on its own, with little to no coordination. In that sense, the collapse of the ALA signaled the end of the pan-Arab endeavor to save Palestine, at least until 1967. This defeat brought to the surface an unspoken question: What good was pan-Arabism if it had failed to save Palestine? Or put differently: What did it mean to be Arab, if this national/ethnic/linguistic affiliation, shared by some 80 million people in 1948, could not do something as simple as overcoming 628,000 Jews trying to seize Palestine?

The question of who was to blame for this failure haunted Arabs as soon as the true nature of the volunteer army was revealed in the midst of fighting. Few Palestinians blamed the ALA volunteers themselves (at least initially), even though volunteers, who were not regularly trained, paid, or fed, often stole from Palestinians or otherwise mistreated them. Other Palestinians, like al-'Abbushi and the residents of Marj Ibn 'Amir, placed most of the blame on Arab leaders. Those Palestinians had bought into the ALA's propaganda, and were waiting for Arab leaders to make good on their promise to save their country. Instead, they were left to fend for themselves, and many were ultimately forcibly expelled in what al-'Abbushi described as the second loss of al-Andalus. When the scale of the nakba became apparent, al-'Abbushi and other ALA volunteers expected that a revolution would shake the region and enable the Arabs to deliver on their commitment.

Some of the non-Palestinian veterans also worked to force reluctant Arab leaders to act, or vacate their seats. They were targeted by Arab governments for that reason.[207] But even the volunteers who held Arab leaders responsible for the failure of pan-Arabism to save Palestine sometimes saw Palestinians as partially at fault for the loss of their homeland. Volunteers were willing to act on an individual basis outside the ALA's purview in order to show their commitment to Palestinians and to pan-Arabism more broadly, but some believed that Palestinian men were unwilling to fight with them shoulder to shoulder until it was too late. Other ALA officers felt that Palestinians, even when they came forward to fight, could not be trusted.

The violence of victory had made the bonds of the Jewish community that formed in Palestine in 1948 much clearer. In a post-Holocaust world, most soldiers of Ashkenazi background became convinced that the marriage between Jews and the use of force was a necessity, and they celebrated the emergence of "muscular Judaism." They did not shy away from drawing pleasure from violence, and sought to adopt the chauvinistic nationalism exhibited by other nations. In fact, they saw violence as a constitutive part of membership in the community of Western nations. Some dissent did emerge, however, and as the next chapter demonstrates, at the war's end, a few Jews were unwilling to remain part of a new community that established itself with Jewish bayonets.

Chapter 5

DIFFERENT KINDS OF RETURN

WHEN THE DUST SETTLED, BOTH JEWS AND ARABS TOOK TIME TO reflect on the results of the 1948 war—the loss of a homeland for Palestinians and a new homeland for at least some Jews. Letters show that a preoccupation with "return" became the cornerstone of these reflections. Yet return meant very different things to different groups, and to the various classes and ethnicities within these groups. Perhaps the most straightforward embrace of return occurred among Jewish Ashkenazi soldiers, for whom the creation of the State of Israel was precisely the "return to history" promised by the Zionist movement for decades. But not everyone felt the same: some volunteers from Western countries argued that what they had witnessed during the war violated what they saw as Judaism's essence, and, exposing a rift among Zionists, they pointed to Ashkenazi Jews and their allegedly aggressive, corrupt ways as the culprit. Those disenchanted volunteers subsequently used their privileged status to return to America, South Africa, or elsewhere, grateful to have Israel as a refuge in times of need but relieved, too, to leave it and its complexities behind. Many Moroccan Jews also expressed a desire to leave Israel shortly after the war had ended. In fact, over 70 percent of Moroccan soldiers, according to statistics secretly collected by the postal censorship bureau, wanted to return to Morocco because of Ashkenazi racism. But their departure was far more difficult, not least because their passports were confiscated by Israel, and because the Moroccan government was reluctant to take them back. Finally, a return in the opposite direction—to Palestine—became the raison d'être of Palestinians after the onset of the nakba. Their condition was far more precarious than that of Moroccan soldiers or Ashkenazi volunteers. They had lost not only their homeland but also, in many cases, their loved ones, as families found themselves on opposite sides of borders.

The crises brought about by 1948 played out very differently among elites, as letters demonstrate. A small part of the Palestinian elite was preoccupied with its own role in the disaster, while others were focused on preserving their monetary wealth by selling their lands in what had become Israel. This was often not the first choice of these men, but something they were forced to do in an attempt to support their families and maintain their class status.[1] Moroccan Jewish elites also acted in different ways compared to the majority, choosing to stay in Israel and "become Ashkenazi." Finally, the Israeli state did not stand idly as attempts were made to undo the results of the 1948 war. In fact, it did all in its power to thwart the return of the two groups, Palestinians to Palestine and Moroccan Jews to Morocco.

WHEN A STATE HAS GOT YOUR BACK

For many Jews, the sense of euphoria about national liberation after hundreds of years of Jewish suffering overshadowed any harsh reality that accompanied the war. It was the Jewish "return to history" that excited many of the new immigrants. Alan, a Mahal volunteer, explained to his family in America:

> We are making history, on a grandiose scale, in an astonishingly short time. A short guy with a gray quiff [likely referring to Ben-Gurion], a group of devoted daydreamers full of belief, and an army which started as a group of partisans ... succeeded in generating a revolution, one bigger than what 2,000 years of misery, prayers, bribery, quips, and humiliation have managed to do.[2]

Like many Jews, Alan saw the creation of Israel as the most important event in Jewish life in two millennia. In this "return," misery and humiliation, which were seen as outside of history, were replaced by national pride, that is, agency that placed the Jews inside Western history.[3] But it was not merely the "return to history" that Alan was celebrating. He was equally as excited by the trappings of a modern nation: "We have a government, a workers' government, and we were recognized by the nations of the world. We have our own stamps, our own money, the badge on our hats is ours, and we are full of recognition and pride."[4] This pride served as a screen, concealing the less positive aspects of war.

Other Anglophone Jews saw the creation of Israel as a miracle and therefore a sign for Jews and non-Jews alike: "Who thought that such a small country . . . could win over so many armies?" wrote Alfred to his family in England, and insisted that a unique Jewish spirit was responsible for the victories.[5] This spirit, he thought, would serve "as a torch, illuminating the righteous way for the world."[6] Alfred felt Israel was a "light unto nations" because it symbolized the triumph of good over evil and reaffirmed Jewish moral superiority. This moral superiority, however, would not replace the desire to be "a nation like all other nations." Jeffrey, another Anglophone soldier, explained, "I don't want the war to end before we conquer the entire land [of Israel]. That's the only way that will truly allow us to be a nation like all others."[7] The sentiments expressed by Alfred and Jeffrey were not, in fact, contrasting views. In the worldview of Alfred, Jeffery, and some of their friends, Israel managed to fuse the ideas of being a "light unto nations" and being "a nation like all other nations." It managed to do so through the use of force. The violence that Israel inflicted during the war allowed it to join the community of nations through imitation, but it also placed Israel in a unique position to serve as "a torch" for other nations, setting the standards as to which acts were morally justifiable and which were not.

Palestinians, on the other hand, were not a "a nation like all other nations." In fact, in the immediate aftermath of the nakba, as their Arab comrades were being released in prisoner exchanges, the 10,000 Palestinian POWs in Israeli captivity were realizing that a nation-state by their side was absolutely imperative for survival.[8] What made the release of non-Palestinian POWs possible were the direct negotiations between Israel and the defeated Arab states.[9] But without a nation-state to intercede on their behalf, Palestinian POWs had a problem. Hundreds started sending letters requesting their release to Arab newspapers and Arab statesmen. Most letters were not addressed to Palestinian leaders but to people associated with the Hashemites, who were seen as the only ones who still held some sway over the Palestine question at the time.[10] "The style of the letters is almost always identical," the censor noted,[11] and included an example:

> We want to express our faithful gratitude to His Majesty, the venerated Hash-
> emite king . . . We hope that His Majesty would be willing, with his good grace,
> to pity us and work for our release.[12]

It was a mark of the Palestinian predicament that they were left pleading for help from Transjordan's King Abdullah, who made no secret of his plans to thwart the establishment of an independent Arab state by incorporating parts of Palestine into his kingdom (and as Palestinians later learned, also secretly negotiated with Zionist movement during the course of the war).[13] Indeed, Abdullah's ambitions would ultimately serve to further divide Palestinians even as the war was coming to an end, as he worked to have himself declared "King of Palestine" at the Jericho Conference on December 1, 1948. For this maneuver, Abdullah relied on the support of handpicked Palestinian notables, such as Hebron mayor 'Ali Ja'abari.[14] Such plans drew the ire of other Palestinian notables, like Amin al-Husayni.[15] But ordinary Palestinians were far removed from such proceedings, and arguing over who ought to speak for the Palestinian people meant little for those lingering in POW camps. As one POW wrote from inside an Israeli camp to Ja'abari in February 1949:

> Sir! Did you pay attention during the days of the Jericho conference to the pris-
> oners [in Israel's hands]? Did you even think what you should do for them
> and their families, who are scattered under the skies in all four corners of the
> earth?[16]

It is unclear if Ja'abari ever received the letter. There is no evidence to suggest that Transjordan, or the participants of the Jericho Conference, worked for the release of the remaining Palestinian POWs.[17]

Other Palestinian POWs chose to praise the nation-state in which they found themselves. "My dear mother, I feel well. Our treatment in the camp is very good. I hope to live under Israel's rule as long as I live," wrote one POW in December 1948.[18] Another conveyed in February 1949 to a relative in Acre that "we pray that God strengthens this government in the holy land because it is a government of justice and integrity."[19] Palestinians knew their letters were being read by the Israeli authorities.[20] Their rosy remarks about Israel could have been sarcastic. Or they could have been aimed at currying favor with the authorities in the hopes of avoiding expulsion, as most Palestinian POWs were trucked to the nearest border and promptly expelled upon release.[21] In any case, these Palestinians realized that a nation-state, even that of the enemy, was crucial for remaining in their homeland. While not celebratory of a "return to history" like the Ashkenazi volunteers, they nevertheless realized that history was determined by those who had a state to rely on.

IDEALISTS, PHILANTHROPISTS, AND SABRAS

Frightened POWs may have resorted to praise to avoid being expelled, but Jewish volunteers from Western countries, known as Mahal, could afford to tell a more complicated story about the new state, knowing that no one would retaliate against them. In fact, the IDF command knew that quite a few Mahal volunteers did not view Israel favorably, although Israeli authorities were unable to do much about it.[22] Polling by the IDF Center for Research of Public Opinion conducted in March 1949 among 387 Mahal volunteers showed that 55 percent of the volunteers had negative views of Israel and its citizens. "Vitamin P," or cronyism, was given as the primary reason for the animosity.[23] "It's not what you know but who you know [here]," was a frequent answer in the poll. Other reasons for resentment were chutzpah, egoism, hypocrisy, and lack of respect.[24]

Mahal volunteers were often warned to keep the purpose of their arrival a secret, and "weigh your words very carefully when writing home."[25] Still, the responses in the poll correspond to a large extent with the volunteers' personal letters to their families. It is, however, unclear whether these critical letters were stopped at the censor's desk and prevented from reaching their destination, or if they were allowed to pass as written.[26] In any case, copies of the letters ended up in the *Soldier's Opinion* reports. Examining them, the censor noted that many Mahal volunteers felt that the Sabra Jews lacked "real idealism."[27] Writing to his family in England, Arnold explained, "It is enough if I say that when the Anglo-Saxons [first] came here, 95 percent were interested in . . . settling. Today, you can't even find 5 percent. On the contrary, many don't want to see this country again." Arnold cited lack of hospitality as one reason for disenchantment.[28] Sydney tried to explain to his family in America what a lack of idealism meant in his eyes: "In this army, the boys try not to die for their country but try, and with success, to have others (foreigners) die for their country."[29] Indeed, the censor reported intercepting several telegrams by Mahal volunteers asking their families to send emergency notices to the IDF requesting that their sons be released from military service and sent back to their home countries.[30] Commenting in his diary about Mahal in November 1948, Ben-Gurion wrote, "Their leaving before the war ended is a moral defeat for American Jewry and for us."[31]

As the poll showed, however, even volunteers who had a strong resentment toward Israel still saw it as a place of refuge, in case they ever needed one.[32] Martin, an American Jew, also had mixed feelings. "We are coming back to America. The Palestine-born Jews in our unit managed to drive me away with their intrigues and all sorts of lies."[33] Martin (and whoever else he was alluding to) wished to hold the Israeli government to their promise to facilitate his return home.[34] His long harangue reveals that he suffered a great deal, which made him conclude that the Sabra Jews were "terrible people." It is unclear what brought about this sentiment. What is clear, however, is that he still thought that the establishment of a Jewish state, not necessarily in its current form, was a just cause:

> But despite the fact that these are cheaters and irresponsible people . . . despite the reprehensible behavior towards those who traveled thousands of kilometers to help—Israel would win the war. It should win and it would win, because this is a just cause, although the people representing it are not worthy to play this historical role. . . . When I come back home, I'll tell you how the people here falsify all the ideals that you work so hard for, and that for the sake of their realization I came here.[35]

It is not entirely clear what made Martin think that the Sabra Jews were not worthy of playing their historical role, and what ideals they were falsifying. However, the last part of his letter suggests that the reason had to do with the admiration of physical power:

> A golem is being formed here, and no one knows how it would turn out when it grows. And we, American Jews, help to create this golem, [but] without having any say about its moves. At any rate, the Jews of Israel traded [heḥlifu] their religion for a revolver, in every respect.[36]

Martin maintained that the view that Jews can be "a nation like all other nations" when it came to exercising violence was heretical.[37] But a close reading of his letter demonstrates that the revolver was not entirely outside the Jewish framework. In addition to the metaphor of the use of force, the revolver also stood for the *golem*. According to Jewish legend, a golem was a mythical creature created to protect Jews in times of need. The golem was believed to be extremely powerful but not intelligent. The most famous golem story is connected with Rabbi Judah Loew ben Bezalel of Prague, known as the Maharal, who in 1580 created a golem to protect his community from nearby Christian villagers. The golem in fact defended the Jews; however, it then started to run wild, attacking innocent bystanders.[38] The golem myth was widely known among Jews from European origin, and the golem became the symbol for the potentially destructive power of man if he is unrestrained.[39] To Martin, Israel was a golem, one whose behavior he could not predict. Moreover, to Martin, this golem partially owed its creation to American Jews who funded the war with their donations, helped smuggle weapons to Palestine, and even volunteered to fight.[40] But they—just like the Maharal—had little, if any, control over Israel's behavior in the war. It seems he was implying that Israel, like the golem in the Maharal's story, turned wild and violent, perhaps against Palestinians, or Arabs more generally.

Another way to read Martin's mention of the golem myth is by turning to what some scholars have termed "the defensive ethos." In this reading of the letter, one could argue that Martin rejected Israel's resort to militarism, but he did not reject *all* violence. Perhaps he viewed the use of force as justified only in response to attacks. If that was the case, Martin's views did not diverge much from those of most American Jewish leaders who maintained an uneasy relationship with the claim that Zionism allowed a "return to history." Even if there was such a return, many leaders argued, its essence should not be military might, but creating a just society in Palestine that could serve as the moral conscience for the entire world as a "light unto nations."[41]

Other letters display similar resentment toward the excessive use of force. Writing to his family in South Africa in October 1948, months before the war ended, Richard insisted that "the war is, in fact, over, and the Bernadotte Plan secures independent living for the Jews of the Land of Israel."[42] According to the Bernadotte Plan, Israel was supposed to yield the Negev to Transjordan, and in return would have been allowed to keep the Galilee. Therefore, Richard felt that any further aggression on the part of Israel would be unjust:

> I do not want to fight for the territorial and imperialist ambitions of the Zionist *effendis*, even if they call themselves socialists. The Zionist leadership is

instigating war in order to expand the borders of Israel. They create the war-like atmosphere on purpose, tension and jumpiness.

Richard did not reject the use of force altogether, but he opposed militarism as a tool for creating "facts on the ground" and conquering territory beyond that allocated to the Jewish state. He also mocked the attempt of Zionist think-ers such as Tabenkin of the kibbutz movement to argue that militarism and socialism went hand in hand. In fact, he rejected the self-portrayal of Zionist leaders as "socialists," calling them instead "effendis," a Turkish/Arabic word, used in Hebrew for large landowners. The implication was clear: all that Israeli leaders cared about was territorial expansion. Richard's disenchantment with what Israel had become caused him to express his desire to leave it "as soon as possible":

> I don't want to take part in this game anymore. I want to come home as soon as possible because I feel that we have paid our dues. What we fought for until now—that was essential, it was defending the existence of the people. War, if it resumes, will be for political goals.[43]

Like Richard, Marcel of Wadi Salib in Haifa, who was likely from North Africa,[44] wrote to a friend in Paris in February 1949 that violence had destroyed the utopian idea of the revival of the Jews in the Land of Israel:

> It's necessary to keep in mind that all of the Zionists are gangsters and even criminals. It is the country of antisemitism, without any exaggeration. All of the Jews of Europe have imported the totalitarian spirit of Nazism. There it is, my dear Ellie, the beautiful life of Erez [Israel]. It's too bad. The country doesn't lack attractions, but because of these Hitlerites everything is under a shadow.[45]

Both Richard and Marcel used damning words against Zionist leaders, and accused them of imitating all that was corrupt with Europe, including impe-rialism, totalitarianism, and Nazism. However, even with this harsh critique of the Zionist admiration of force, Richard was unwilling to completely forego his connections with the Jewish state. His mention of paying dues to the Jewish people suggested he still saw Israel as a place of refuge.

Critical views by Mahal volunteers about the resort to force were some-times mocked by soldiers of the Sabra generation.[46] Tikva Honig-Parnass, a female soldier in the Palmach, wrote her parents about two Mahal American volunteers she encountered:

> Nice fellows. But yesterday, when they saw all the Arabs, the women and chil-
> dren returning to their villages starving for bread, they became "soft-hearted
> and had pity on them," and in the evening, they began to shout that if the Jew-
> ish state lacked the means to take responsibility for the economy in the terri-
> tories it had occupied, it should never have gotten involved in a war. And that
> there was no reason just to kill Arabs without any justification.[47]

Responding to the Mahal men's protest, Honig-Parnass wrote her parents, "this America, with its idealistic Zionists, gets on one's nerves sometimes. Their entire philanthropic approach toward life and the world is also expressed in their attitude to Zionism."[48] Honig-Parnass's letter accurately depicts what was then the sentiment of some American volunteers.[49] Pacifism had a long tradition in American Judaism, in both its Conservative and Reform denomi-nations.[50] Until the 1967 war, the majority of American Jewish leaders repeat-edly expressed fear that Israel would adopt chauvinistic nationalism and an overreliance on military might.[51]

But the reliance on force to solve the problems facing the Jews of Palestine was exactly the prospect that many IDF soldiers sought to celebrate. "First we want another period of battles so we could expel the rest of the Arabs from here. Then we could go home," wrote one soldier to his family in March 1949.[52] Around the same time, a South African volunteer observed that "the Govern-ment did not want to let the Arabs return, so that every Arab village has been systematically blown up."[53] Indeed, for some, turning more Palestinians into refugees, and making sure those who left or were expelled could not return, was directly linked to national liberation. In May 1949, when the issue of repa-triation was raised at the UN, Menahem briefly summed up the Israeli view:

> The Arabs . . . demand that we return the Arab refugees, who till yesterday
> fought us and helped the foreign invaders. Our government knows what the
> public thinks. No Arab shall return to the State of Israel. We did not expel them
> and we shall not return them.[54]

In line with what the army education officers were advocating, Mena-hem did not think it was the moral obligation of the Jews to solve the refugee problem. He also repeated the army's propaganda that "the Arabs left of their own free will."[55]

Menahem was right in concluding that the public was against the return of the refugees. Polling by the IDF Center for Research of Public Opinion conducted among Tel Aviv residents in 1949 concluded that 73 percent opposed allowing Palestinian refugees to return to their villages, while only 27 percent were inclined to allow such return.[56] Place of origin reportedly factored into the response: according to the reported findings, while only 55 percent of German Jews rejected the return of refugees, 100 percent of Yemenites favored rejection.[57] The pollsters concluded that the issue of returning refugees was not a central or acute problem for most people.[58] They were apparently unaware of the views of the disenchanted volunteers who had already left Israel before the poll was conducted. In that sense, the pollsters were right: the majority of Israeli Jews were content with the violent depopulation of Palestine, and had no interest in undoing the results of the war.

WHERE ARE THOSE BEAUTIFUL DAYS?

Return was a central and acute issue not only for Palestinians forced from their homeland but also for Moroccan Jews who became disenchanted with Israel and wished to return to their former homeland. For Palestinians in the aftermath of the nakba, the struggle for survival and return was literally a matter of life or death. Moroccan Jews in Israel faced different but related challenges, including extreme poverty and Ashkenazi racism.

In the aftermath of the nakba, whatever did not involve immediate subsistence or the prospects for return had to wait. Palestinian refugees were scattered in hundreds of makeshift refugee compounds in Syria, Lebanon, Transjordan, Egypt, and Iraq. The Israeli intelligence apparatus invested substantial resources in following the lives and sentiments of Palestinian refugees in their new diaspora.[59] The refugees' letters were used to track the exact place of residence for each group of Palestinians, and their activities in their host countries—making sure they could not return.[60] It appears that refugees in Lebanon were in especially dire straits. "We have 60 more Palestinian liras and 70 Lebanese liras. After that there would be no other option but to starve to death," announced 'Adil from Lebanon in September 1948 in a letter to his family in Israel.[61] "I often work so we can keep on living," wrote Marwa in an effort to explain the reversal of traditional gender roles that had caused her to seek employment.[62] "There is no way to live but [taking on temporary] daily work," she added.[63] But temporary work did not make much of a difference. Letters indicated that most refugees were denied permanent job permits or Lebanese ID cards that would allow them to secure higher-paying positions and move around freely.[64] The Lebanese government saw Muslim refugees in particular as a threat to Lebanon's delicate demographic balance. Banning them from much of the job market and from renting apartments was in line with its overall policy of restricting their activities and encouraging their departure. Christian refugees, meanwhile, fared better. Many of them received Lebanese citizenship and were allowed to rent apartments in the larger cities and open businesses.[65]

Refugees in Transjordan were better off than those in Syria and Lebanon, and they also received better treatment from the government, though poverty was still widespread.[66] The snow in Amman in January of 1949 was one source of hardship, and the Hashemite government moved the refugees from one place to another, fearing they would freeze to death.[67] Although renting apartments in Amman was allowed, rent was beyond the reach of most refugees. "Because of the high rent we live in the mountains. Most people live in tents and caves," explained Amjad in February 1949.[68] Work in Transjordan, though not formally banned, was also hard to come by. From Salt, Fuad wrote to a relative, "Your brother was unable to find any job. He goes from one house to the other and sells za'atar [an herb that is a staple of the Palestinian diet]."[69]

The nakba not only brought material losses and displacement but also depression and grief. Refugees missed Palestine's beloved landscapes, and especially its celebrated oranges, as Iskandar from Amman wrote to a POW inside Israel in February 1949: "How are you and how are your oranges? We don't get to see them here. One orange here is worth a camel's head [i.e., very expensive]."[70] Life in a POW camp would seem unenviable. But it appeared differently from Iskandar's vantage in Amman, where he was deprived of the citrus so evocative of home. From this perspective, being a POW meant maintaining a connection to these mundane aspects of life that for refugees had altogether disappeared. With the exception of pleas for monetary support, many Palestinians in their new diaspora chose not to write. Mona, a

FIGURE 10. Palestinians in a refugee camp in Lebanon. Circa 1948. Courtesy of the United Nations Photo Library.

Christian Palestinian refugee in Transjordan, explained in February 1949 to her cousin who was a POW in Israel:

> You ask me why I don't write. The heart is heavy and is not free to write. There is nothing beautiful in this world . . . Where are those beautiful days? The laughter had stopped and there is no trace of humor . . . The entire life is a burden on us.[71]

Besides the burden of displacement, letters indicated that many refugees also suffered the loss of family members, presumably in battle or due to the harsh conditions.[72] Having to bury their loved ones outside of Palestine deepened the grief of parting. When in June 1948 a Palestinian by the name of Abdullah Ya'qub died of a heart attack in Transjordan, a family friend, in a condolence letter to the family of the deceased, explained, "I was beside myself [*ṭāra 'aqlī*] because of his death far away from home."[73] It appears that already in 1948, Palestinians saw their forced displacement from Palestine as exile in its most profound sense. The yearning to the land, to its fruits, and to the "beautiful days" in Palestine united many Palestinians.

Alongside despair, however, was also optimism, especially on the west bank of the Jordan River, the part of historic Palestine now under Transjordanian rule.[74] Being so close to their former dwellings stoked the flame of hope: "Everyone is waiting for the imminent solution. With the help of God this will end soon with an agreement between the two rival sides, and then we can all go back to al-Ramla, and life will return to what it used to be," wrote Jalal in December 1948.[75] Munir added in January 1949, "May God make Transjordan and Israel into sisters."[76] The optimistic view expressed by the refugees that they would soon return to their villages persisted throughout the armistice negotiations in Rhodes in 1949.[77] Even as the talks were concluded without the return of Palestinians, the hope in the refugees' letters did not diminish.[78]

While waiting to return, Palestinians were concerned with the status of their property left behind (as early as May 1948, Ben-Gurion issued an order to move new Jewish immigrants into houses emptied of their Arab inhabitants).[79] Letters of refugees from Jaffa who ended up in Transjordan were especially imbued with such anxiety over the Jews looting their belongings: "Please inform me," wrote Maha to an acquaintance still in Jaffa in October 1948, "if the house was completely ransacked or only partially, because there is a lot of news about stealing and robbery in Jaffa, and I am very concerned."[80] 'Azzam too wrote to a relative in Jaffa asking him to check on his house, and if it was indeed ransacked, to bring a carpenter to fix the door so that it could be locked again. He also instructed the relative to hire a guard for which 'Azzam would pay.[81] In answering such queries, Habib from Acre wrote to his family abroad in July 1949 that "most buildings were taken by Jews and the gardens and vegetables [fields] were transferred into their hands in full. All this is the result of Arab men sitting in coffeehouses, speaking empty words."[82] Although Habib did not explain what these empty words were exactly, it is likely he was referring to Palestinians echoing the propaganda of Arab leaders that the battle for Palestine would be an easy one.

Even when confronted with the intentions of the Israeli state to expropriate their possessions, Palestinians were not willing to give in. "One can learn that the owners [of orchards] assume they will be able to return in a short while, and do not want their orchards to go fallow in the meantime because of temporary lack of care. They hope to enjoy them soon," commented the censor, perhaps cynically.[83] The censor was of course aware of the October 1948 Cultivation of Fallow Land Act (and later, the March 1950 Absentee Property Law), which allowed for the transfer of hundreds of thousands of dunams from Palestinians into the state's hands under the pretext that those lands were abandoned and therefore uncultivated.[84] Hoping to prevent their lands from being expropriated, some of Jaffa's grove-owners who had become refugees tried to reach agreements with their old neighbors who remained in Jaffa, whereby the neighbor would tend to the grove for a fixed sum.[85] These sorts of arrangements between refugees and Palestinians who remained in Israel were apparently very common in the years following the nakba. One such contract from November 1948, which was located in the possession of a Palestinian who tried to sneak across the border into Israel, stipulated that a certain Muhammad al-Rashid Sharida, who was likely the refugee, contracted with a man by the name of Ahmad Thahir to till Sharida's land in the Haifa district.[86] Israel, through the postal censorship bureau, was monitoring these arrangements closely, likely to make it easier to determine which lands could be expropriated. Israel was also monitoring the payouts to Palestinians who had homeowners' insurance with British firms, and tried to claim the money to support themselves in exile. Letters reveal that claims for compensation were often denied. Insurance companies tended to "reject any claims for abandoned property in the case that the owner of the property did not take precautionary steps before abandoning that property."[87] In other words, Palestinians had to prove they tried to protect the property before fleeing or being expelled if they were to stand any chance of having the insurance company compensate them.

When faced with the alternative of starvation, some Palestinian refugees opted to sell their property in Israel. Although most letters related to this were redacted by the archives, apparently refugees contacted friends and family still in Israel and asked them to obtain the deeds to their lands in preparation for their sale. A refugee from Acre now in Lebanon asked his friend back home to try to till his lands for him, sell the crops, and then send him the money or sell the land altogether. Another refugee from Haifa whose mortgage was owned by a Jew tried to sell his assets in the city and have the money transferred to him.[88] The sale of Palestinian land to Jews has long been a sensitive topic, particularly with respect to absentee landholders, who, in the view of many, betrayed the national cause in pursuit of profit. But these stories of land sales are different, as they concerned refugees coerced by the desperation of poverty and displacement into selling their property now included within Israel's borders.[89]

By 1949 many Palestinians realized that a return to Palestine at that point could only be facilitated by their families still in Israel.[90] The letters intercepted by the censorship bureau extensively discuss the arrangements made with the state authorities for the return of relatives, even though most of the details of these arrangements had been redacted by the archives.[91] For the majority of Palestinians who were unable to obtain the government's permission for the return of their loved ones, calling on their families to sneak across the border into Israel was the only way of reuniting their families. But as a letter from Iman in Haifa to her family in Lebanon from February 1949 indicated, not all Palestinians were easily convinced to let smugglers bring them back home:

> How is our dear father, and why doesn't he listen to what I say and take my advice? After all, this is a once in a lifetime opportunity. Read him my words . . . As long as the movement [of people] continues [between Arab states and Israel] . . . and others are paying thousands of liras to do it, why did your feelings die and your right mind disappear?[92]

Iman was trying to get her family to cross the border into Israel despite the dangers. She realized that what was possible at that time would not be possible soon. But most Palestinians, even in late 1949, continued to hold onto the hope that the refugees would be allowed to return legally. According to the censor, Palestinians chose to believe "the rumors on the willingness of the government to return hundreds of thousands of refugees."[93] A typical line in letters from July 1949 was that "the compassionate government of Israel will not agree to the splitting of the families of its citizens."[94] Much like the laudatory portrayal of Israel in the letters of POWs, such messages were likely sarcastic or intended for the censor.

As Palestinians were trying to make their way back into Israel, Moroccan Jews in Israel were attempting to take the opposite route, out of Israel. With the end of the war and the discharging of most soldiers, many Moroccans found themselves out on the street, beaten by police officers and arrested for loitering.[95] The letters from June 1949 onward depict a steep process of disenchantment among North Africans volunteers in the IDF. Soldiers started telling their families to stay where they were. In the words of Ya'qub, writing to his family in Morocco:

> We came to Israel and thought we'd find a paradise here, but regrettably it was the opposite, we saw Jews with hearts like Germans. All the refugees who come to Israel are thrown into the army, with no home and no job. If you want my advice—stay in North Africa; it is better than the Land of Israel.[96]

Once again, we see Moroccan immigrants comparing Ashkenazi Jews to Germans, who were, at the time, a symbol of evil. This time the soldier took a step further and advised his family not to come.

The army command was very concerned about this new trend. In July 1949 the censor noted:

> North African immigrants are the most problematic group [among soldiers]. Most of those people are filled with bitterness for the government and show special sensitivity to "racial discrimination" that they are subject to here. . . . Many want to return [to North Africa] and most advise their relatives not to immigrate.[97]

In a special report from August 1949 the censorship bureau examined 950 letters by North African soldiers sent between July 16 and July 31. The censor was surprised to find out that "although these people are of low education and culture, they exhibit a strong sense of criticism and reflection."[98] In 200 letters the soldiers discussed the question of their family's immigration to Israel, and the results were shocking: The majority of North African soldiers were against their families coming to Israel.

> About 26 percent advise [their family] to postpone their immigration for a period of time until the economic situation becomes clear. About 24 percent advise their relatives to immigrate to Israel immediately. About 50 percent advise their relatives not to immigrate at all.[99]

All in all, 76 percent of soldiers called on their families either not to come to Israel at all, or at least not to come at the present time. Another 250 letters discussed the individual soldier's desire concerning whether or not to remain in Israel after the end of the war. The numbers were almost the same, with 55 percent of soldiers wanting to permanently return to North Africa, and 14 percent wanting to return to North Africa at present, but leaving open the option of going back to Israel in the future.[100] The censor mentioned that the numbers might even be higher because an additional 138 soldiers asked their family to provide them with birth certificates, which were needed in order to obtain return visas to North Africa. Taking these people into account raises the percentage of soldiers who wanted to return to North Africa to over 70 percent.[101] The civilian censorship bureau, reading the mail of North Africans in Israel that for one reason or another was not sent through the army post, cited 60 percent of North Africans actively trying to return to their countries of birth, and 90 percent telling their families not to follow them to Israel.[102] "What unites them all is 'hatred' of 'Poles' (that is how they call the Ashkenazi)," the censor noted.[103] Indeed, the Israeli leadership was worried about this tendency to leave the country, and even Ben-Gurion commented on this trend in his diary with concern.[104]

Writing in April 1949 to his family, Nahum explained why he wished to return to Morocco:

> The Poles here control everything. Ninety-five percent of our guys are unhappy and their only desire is to go back to where they came from. Palestine may be good for those who suffered in the camps in Germany, but not for us, the French, who love freedom.[105]

It was the love of freedom that the Haganah cited in the first place to convince North African Jews to volunteer for fighting in Israel. Now, the same love of freedom prompted Nahum to desire leaving Israel. But it was not only Francophile Jews who felt this way; letters by other Moroccan immigrants suggest that those from modest backgrounds wanted to return as well. Ya'ish, from Casablanca, tried to explain to his parents why staying in Israel was out of the question:

> How do you want me to stay [when] my wife is pregnant and I can't even give her a glass of water when she's tired? I'm certain we'll be happier in Casablanca. What do I have here? Not even a bed for two. . . . Instead of collecting

money to rent a room, in which I don't have anything to put, it's better to use this money to pay for our return journey.[106]

Trying to explain his decision to leave Israel, Ya'ish further alluded to the country's Polish Jews who "think Moroccans are savages and thieves. When we pass by, they look at us like [we are] brutes."[107] Ya'ish was certain this was not a temporary condition, and that "there is no getting used to life here." Until the time when he would be able to collect the necessary money for the return ticket to Morocco, Ya'ish, by his own admission, was "sitting and weeping . . . thinking about life in Casablanca."[108] Other letters were even more forceful. Mas'ud wrote to his relatives about his intentions to return to Morocco as soon as possible, cautioning them: "If you immigrate to Israel, I will disown you, and chances are that I will kill you if I see you in Israel."[109] To be sure, people like Ya'ish and Mas'ud suffered in considerably different ways than Palestinian refugees did, but they all wanted to return home.

As indicated by the letters, soldiers often mentioned the dire economic situation as an incentive to leave, suggesting they did not have the means to support themselves.[110] However, the economic situation was far from a burden that everyone bore equally. It was closely linked to the actions of the hegemonic Ashkenazi group, as Matityahu explained:

I can't stand this country which is worse than the strictest jail. The Ashkenazi exploit us in everything and give the best and easiest jobs to Poles. The wages are worth nothing. For his easy labor the Pole gets 2.5 Liras, while the maximum we Moroccans can earn for our arduous and strenuous work is only 1.5 Liras.[111]

As conveyed by Matityahu, poverty was a direct consequence of discrimination against North Africans, and it compelled the majority of soldiers to express their desire to leave.[112]

Nevertheless, the letters show that poverty—even when caused by discrimination—was not the only factor pushing North Africans to leave. As 'Aziz explained to his family:

Don't trust the Zionist office [in Morocco]. It spreads propaganda, lies and falsehoods, and don't dare to set foot in this office because here they call you dirty Moroccans and publish in the newspapers that the Moroccans can't dress, can't eat with a fork, only with their hands. They think only Poles are human beings here.[113]

'Aziz was referring to the series of articles published in 1949 in the Israeli daily *Haaretz* (The Country) by Arye Gelblum. Gelblum visited the transit camps and described North African immigrants as being "only slightly better than the general level of the Arabs, Negroes, and Berbers in the same regions."[114] Moreover, since they suffer from "chronic laziness and hatred for work," they were of little use to the Zionist movement.[115] Gelblum was the first to air the views of the Ashkenazi leadership in public.[116] The leadership feared that North African immigration would invert the demographic balance of the new state, and make Israel into an Arab country by causing "Levantinization." Another major concern was that North Africans would help bring the Revisionist Right to power, ending the hegemony of Mapai.[117]

It did not take Moroccan immigrants in Israel long to realize that Gelblum's views were in fact those of the Israeli leadership, and were by no means fringe views.[118] Hanun explained to his family that antisemitism in Israel was much worse than in Poland "and discrimination is so widespread that one can certainly compare it with the racial discrimination between blacks and whites in America."[119] Olivier, whom the censor noted was an "educated" North African, wrote to his family in Paris: "All the Orientals are treated here something like negroes in the South of the U.S. There is a great hate between the Orientals and the Westerners who are the Government."[120] Even those who were mistakably identified as "Oriental" suffered, like Isidore from France: "I only know French but my skin is tan and I resemble a North African. What should I do? No one believes me I'm not North African. I don't have a job, and even 'white' girls don't want to dance with me."[121] Indeed, more and more immigrants started seeing Israel as a segregationist state, akin to the Unites States, and like in America, some started to contemplate organized action, or even rebellion.

The daily newspaper *Davar* reported on June 24, 1949, that fifty North African immigrants "representing the immigrants in [transit] camps" met in Tel Aviv to protest the articles in *Haaretz* and voice their opposition to the "scorn they meet everywhere they go" from the Ashkenazi. Government officials who arrived at the meeting to speak with the delegates asked them "to shake off the inferiority complex (*regesh neḥitut*) and share the burden with the rest of the ethnicities in the country."[122] But even Israeli officials realized that statements like this would not change the course of collision. The censor was extremely alarmed by a Moroccan Jewish underground he believed was forming. One letter the censorship bureau intercepted related how "several young men went to Israel to take revenge for the sons of Morocco and crack the skulls of 'Poles'—without caring who they are."[123] Although the full report of this underground is kept classified by the Israel archives, the mention which was not redacted (likely by mistake) suggests that the threat was taken very seriously.

Racism not only drove North African immigrants to express their will to leave Israel en masse and avenge the treatment of their families but also engendered a new identity that emphasized an emotional connection to another homeland and to other people: "I want to finish my service in the IDF and return to you, to my hometown Morocco that I loved. This makes me very happy," reminisced Atias.[124] Maimun emphasized who were his true brothers:

> It is not the right time now to immigrate to Israel. It is better to eat dry bread in Morocco than chickens here. You must know that the Arabs are our brothers, unlike the Ashkenazi Jews who make our lives miserable. For all the money in the world I will not stay here.[125]

These letters are significant in that they challenge several key Zionist tenets. Atias's statement about Morocco being a homeland, one to which he must also "return," is a clear breach of the Zionist narrative that only recognizes return to the Land of Israel. Maimun's reference to Moroccan Muslims as "Arabs" and "brothers" and the letter's suggestion that Moroccan Arabs are better than Israel's Ashkenazi Jews are even more subversive: they challenge the leadership's narrative that "the Arab" is a one-size-fits-all label for "enemy." It also inverts the concept of "the ingathering of the exiles" by stating that Arabs—and not Ashkenazi Jews—were the real family of North African Jews. Both soldiers sought to heal the rupture that was created by their dislocation in Israel: the spatial one by returning to Morocco, and the cultural one by reasserting Moroccan identity and stressing its connection to Arabness.[126]

THE PREOCCUPATIONS OF THE ELITES

Members of the Palestinian elite, as well as some with higher socioeconomic standing among the Moroccan immigrants in Israel, elected to deal with the crises caused by the 1948 war in different ways compared to the majority. While some members of Palestine's prominent Arab families were coming to terms with their own culpability for the nakba, well-to-do Moroccan Jews were often able to integrate into Israel, and rejected the idea of returning to Morocco. In fact, some of them developed strong enmity toward Morocco and its Muslim population.

Even if Israel and Zionism were seen as the main culprit behind the nakba, the letters intercepted by Israel demonstrated that the Palestinian elite cast some of the blame on Arab states, but also blamed themselves. While it is not surprising that crises invite introspection, the fact that some Palestinians were discussing their role in the defeat is noteworthy because it stands in contrast to the Israeli claim that Palestinians never accepted any responsibility for the nakba. A son of a prominent Palestinian leader, the representative to the UN, Jamal al-Husayni,[127] expressed certainty that Palestine could still be salvaged in February 1949:

> It appears we had lost. I don't mean in the battle against the enemy, but [in the battle] for ourselves, for our hopes, and for our unity. We became the laughingstock at the exact time when we were close to succeeding. . . . But do not despair! We will start anew and get ready for a long battle. The mistakes of the past will serve as a lesson for the future.[128]

Although he was part of the Palestinian leadership of 1948 (and a relative of Amin al-Husayni), the author implied that some of the responsibility for the defeat fell on Palestinians; however, he did not explain exactly how. Interestingly, the author remained convinced that the defeat did not mean that he and his family would lose their status as notables: "In the spring, the UN assembly will meet, and there will most certainly be a Palestinian delegation there, under the presidency of my father. I want my father to arrange a job for me in that delegation," he wrote.[129] The author could not have been more wrong: not only did the Husaynis lose much of their prestige in the aftermath of the nakba, a Palestinian delegation to the UN would not be seated until 1974, and even then, only accorded observer status.

Much harsher critique of the Palestinian leadership, and especially the notables, was part of a pamphlet distributed by Antoine Francis Albina, a prominent Palestinian Christian leader from Qatamon in Jerusalem. Albina was forced to flee to East Jerusalem under Transjordan's control in February 1949.[130] His pamphlet was apparently secretly circulated among Palestinians.

The Israeli censor noted with surprise that it had passed both the Transjordanian and the Egyptian postal censors before arriving in Israel. Explaining the Palestinian defeat, Albina wrote:

> We should not condemn anyone but ourselves because we talk but do not do anything. Because we do not know what sacrifice and martyrdom is. Because we trust the publications of different [propaganda] offices and ignore the facts. Because we let fear take over our hearts. Because we did not have the courage to put on trial those who made themselves the nation's leaders. Because we did not fight the profit-makers and those who exploit . . . Because we relied on Arab governments who are themselves in need of an iron fist which will rescue them from this enslavement.[131]

Like Burhan al-Din al-'Abbushi, Albina argued that until Arab governments were freed from the yoke of colonialism, they would not be able to fulfill their promise of saving Palestine. But Albina also felt that much of the responsibility for the defeat fell on Palestinians, and he cited unwillingness to sacrifice on behalf of the homeland and fear as reasons for the failure.[132] Although several prominent Palestinians published their perspectives in the immediate aftermath of the nakba in an effort to explain the defeat, Albina's pamphlet was especially harsh.[133] Suggesting (if obliquely) that the AHC or Amin al-Husayni was responsible for the defeat and calling for the nation's leaders to be put on trial was a bold act in February 1949. However, taking into account the fact Albina was writing from Transjordanian-controlled East Jerusalem suggests that his criticism of Palestinian leaders may have been related to the rivalry between the Hashemites and al-Husayni in the aftermath of the Jericho Conference, and the continued effort of Amin al-Husayni and his allies to prevent the Hashemites from controlling Palestine.

Not all members of the elite were getting ready to resume the fight for Palestine. Some of the Palestinian upper classes who ended up in Arab or European capitals were trying to sell their assets inside Israel and begin a new life. One Palestinian who was apparently helping Israel to acquire property wrote in a letter from England to Jerusalem in February 1949 that "many here are eager to sell the property they have in Israel. . . . I got in touch with . . . owners of homes in Jerusalem, orchards and lands in the Baysan valley. They all want to sell."[134] 'Issa, who in his words was the "heir to much property in Jerusalem," wrote a senior Israeli official in early March 1949 from Cyprus, demanding that the Israeli government promptly reach an agreement with his family and pay them monthly rent for the use of their lands (the exact location of which was redacted by the archives). "It's a travesty to keep in squalor a family in whose veins the blood of Turkish governors flow," wrote 'Issa from Cyprus to the Israeli official.[135] In deciding to sell their lands, maintaining their elite status was likely important to these men. But seventy years later, it is difficult to assess the importance of such an impetus compared to desperation, financial ruin, or a sense of helplessness.[136]

Many of the well-to-do among the Moroccan immigrants to Israel also displayed different sentiments compared to the majority of Moroccan Jews who wanted to leave Israel. As mentioned, 30 percent of North Africans in the IDF wanted to stay in Israel and also called their families in Morocco to come join them.[137] Explaining their desire to stay, some adopted an Orientalist discourse themselves and internalized their alleged inferiority. Others feared the Muslims in Morocco and believed Israel was the only safe haven for North African Jews, and a minority held Zionist views that outweighed any oppression at the hands of Ashkenazi Jews.

It is common for westernized elites in colonial settings to adopt the Orientalist gaze and come to see themselves or nonwesternized compatriots as inferior.[138] While not entirely equivalent, it is not implausible to describe Moroccans in Israel at the time as colonized people.[139] Ezra, a soldier writing in August 1949, contended that "those who are leaving are the lazy ones. They are those who don't want to work and think that money falls from the skies."[140] Leon used even harsher language, explaining that it was no wonder so many wanted to leave "since those who came were the animals and rabble of the ghetto."[141] Viewing Orientals as lazy people who shy away from hard work, and as animals, was standard colonial discourse.[142] The only chance at reform, some soldiers believed, was through mimicry.[143] 'Amram's letter is a case in point:

> In the camp where I am, most soldiers are Jews who were born in Palestine and they are well educated. They treat me exceptionally well. I think that it is better to live with soldiers who are Palestine-born since you can learn something from them. But if I live with North African soldiers, I will only learn bad things, like how to use a knife for stabbing and how to steal . . . They are bastards and can't tell left from right.[144]

'Amram repeated the Orientalist idea that Moroccan immigrants were hot-tempered and prone to violence.[145] He came to see his own people as criminals, and he sought to distance himself from them and instead imitate the behavior of Ashkenazi soldiers.[146]

Indeed, only when Moroccans "became Ashkenazi" would they be useful members of society. The kibbutz, Prosper believed, was the ultimate test for those Moroccans:

> We want to make Moroccan Jews immigrate so that we will be like the others and build our home and our kibbutz. That is why we established a Moroccan core group [gar'in]. We will be the first to have a Moroccan kibbutz. . . . In the Land of Israel, we are all partners in building the land.[147]

The kibbutz, the quintessential Ashkenazi institution in Israel, was a crucial element to imitate for those interested in assimilation. It is evident that Prosper thought this was his ticket into the dominant group in society: after a Moroccan kibbutz would be established, "we will be like the others," meaning like the Ashkenazi. Only the kibbutz education, another soldier explained, would make Moroccan children "healthy people in heart and soul."[148]

Some of the letters coming from Morocco also expressed a sense of urgency as the coexistence between Jews and Muslims was disintegrating in the aftermath of the Israeli victory. "I am telling you explicitly, you can't live together with the Arabs, and that is why I want to leave them. I don't need to tell you what they did to us. You know what they do to Jews," explained one relative to a soldier in Israel.[149] Another letter exemplified how the creation of a Jewish state changed the power dynamics between Jews and Muslims. From Morocco, André wrote in July 1949:

> My dear friend, you are lucky that you are in Israel and can't hear the curses that the Arabs use against us. These are the same ones they used against you when you worked in the store. I ask that you send me a submachine gun with 800 bullets so I can kill them before I come to Israel. We live in misery with these bastard Arab Moroccans. And in their eyes, we are dirty and they call us "dirty Jews" all the time. [150]

This letter shows that for some Jews, the persecution they suffered in Morocco after 1948 instilled in them a growing sense of enmity for the Muslim community. The access to arms that Jews now had in the new Jewish state excited André as he fantasized about revenge. He was not the only one. As Chief of Staff Yadin had hoped, some Moroccan soldiers in the IDF—the censor noted in March 1949—had taken immense pride in "killing dozens of Muslims," while fighting for the Jewish state. They described these killings in detail in the letters to their families in Morocco. Apparently, the letters were also read by the Moroccan postal censorship bureau, which made the families back in Morocco fear revenge by Moroccan Muslims or the authorities.[151]

For André, it was hard to believe any Jew would be willing to give up the trappings of a modern nation-state: "Tell me a bit about the families that return from Israel and let me know if they are crazy. Perhaps those returning are not Jews, and they don't deserve to be called Jews . . . I am telling you—be courageous and stay in Israel."[152] André wanted to make sure his friends and relatives in Israel were not contemplating a return to Morocco, and to do so he went as far as questioning the Jewishness of those who returned. Another soldier, Levy, thought the returnees should be dealt with violently:

> There are people who tell nonsense and lies. I think these people deserve hanging.
> I am telling you this without being bashful even one bit, because they are liars and
> robbers. Let me tell you what really goes on in here: There is no government in
> the world that after being through a big war provides food like our government.[153]

Levy thought Israel was a "light unto nations" for providing food to the needy shortly after the end of the war. For him, the slander of Zionism was unacceptable and he saw those who left Israel as traitors.

Some well-to-do also offered advice to those who recently immigrated from Morocco to Israel. A veteran immigrant, who had "made it" in Israel, came up with the suggestion that new North African immigrants to Israel actively try to forget "the delicatessens and comfort (if there was any) left behind in their [former] countries. They must understand that here they have freedom and the confidence of a nation, something they could not even dream of anywhere else."[154] Another added that "we didn't come here to take advantage of the country, but to devote ourselves to it . . . Unfortunately many Moroccans failed to understand it, and that's why they returned."[155] These voices, nevertheless, were a minority in 1948–49. The majority pointed to racism as the main reason for their desire to return to Morocco.

THE STATE STRIKES BACK

The surveillance of letters from Palestinians and Moroccan Jews was done primarily to control those who would remain inside Israel (Moroccan Jews) and those who would remain outside it (Palestinians). Israeli officials used the intelligence gathered from letters to implement new policies aimed at securing the two goals. Against Palestinians, these policies were often violent ones, and included expulsions, arrests, and sometimes killings. Against Moroccan Jews, Israel often elected to use propaganda and deception to attract immigrants to Israel and convince them to stay. Confiscation of passports was another useful tool to prevent the departure of Moroccans already in Israel.

While concerned about Moroccan Jews, the Israeli government directed most of its attention toward preventing Palestinian refugees from returning. The censor reassured the Israeli decision-makers reading his reports in July 1949 that at least a minority among Palestinians in Israel realized that this wishful thinking of the majority, hoping for the return of their families, would never materialize. The censor was especially exhilarated to find one Palestinian explaining this to his friend in a letter: "Things are going to be different from now on. Those who fled from fear of death and destruction will never get to see their homes [again]."[156] But for those who were not willing to accept this—the majority of Palestinians—Israel planned to use coercion to force them into submission.

It did not take long for Palestinians to realize that their personal letters were used against them, and were sometimes even manipulated.[157] In the aftermath of war, to facilitate the exchange of letters between refugees and their families who remained in Israel—ostensibly not under Israel's watchful eye—Palestinians contracted the services of smugglers. Those who regularly crossed the borders from the neighboring Arab countries into Israel to sell commodities (especially meat, which was in short supply in Israel) now added letters to their daily route.[158] They would pick up letters from Palestinians inside Israel, cross the border into Syria, Lebanon, Jordan, or Egypt, and mail them there from the nearest village. The opposite would happen when refugees wanted to contact their families in Israel: They would give the smuggler the letter, he would cross into Israel, and mail it from the nearest Arab village using the Israeli post.[159]

To the detriment of Palestinians, the Israeli postal censorship bureau closely monitored these smuggled letters, not only to gather intelligence on the refugees and their whereabouts but mainly to block the return of refugees ("infiltration" in Israeli jargon) into Israel.[160] Although the archives redacted most of the details on how these intercepted letters aided the "war on return," as aptly termed by one scholar, the censorship bureau's reports tell at least part of the story.[161] Apparently, letters exposed smuggling networks and specific routes used by refugees to cross back into Israel. The routes discovered by the censor were reported to the border police, which would then ambush the refugees.[162] According to one letter showcased by the censor in September 1949, a young female, her father, and her aunt crossed from Lebanon, and walked into the village of Shafa-ʿAmr, apparently intending to proceed to their old village from there, but upon arrival the father was arrested and expelled.[163] Many other violent methods were employed concurrently to stop "infiltration," including a "free-fire" policy along the borders with the neighboring Arab countries, which led to the killing of thousands of Palestinians after the war had ended.[164]

Although Israel estimated that as many as 25,000 Palestinian refugees managed to return to Israel by the end of 1949, the army apparently believed that the tactics used to deter Palestinians in Israel from housing "infiltrators" and the ambushing of those trying to enter Israel had yielded results.[165] These results became apparent through correspondence via mail. "In several cases," the censor noted in September 1949, "we got our hands on letters where relatives in Israel answer their family members in Arab countries 'Don't come in secret. The way is extremely dangerous. Wait until we get you an official entry permit.'"[166]

Meanwhile, the sight of Moroccan Jews leaving Israel to return to their old homeland alarmed the Israeli authorities a great deal, even if it was not as immediate a threat as Palestinian return. But what concerned the officials most was not the individuals leaving, but rather that their return to Morocco would influence those who were still considering immigration to Israel. As one Jewish Agency report stated: "Those who hate Zion could effectively make use of this: if those who fought and suffered in Israel for over a year could not . . . make a life and a future for themselves there, surely others would not be able to do so either."[167] This was no small concern. In the aftermath of the Holocaust and the destruction of most European Jews, the number of potential Jewish immigrants was severely depleted. The Jewish Agency and Israeli authorities could hardly ignore the threat that the majority of Morocco's 250,000 Jews may choose to stay put. Letters from Morocco indeed indicated that people there took the returnees' warnings seriously, and reconsidered their plans to immigrate to Israel.[168] An open letter by a Zionist leader in Morocco published in the Israeli-Sephardi newspaper *Hed Hamizrah* (Echo from the East) in July 1949 reported that Jews in Morocco were horrified by the reports of discrimination. The author lamented the fact that hundreds of young Moroccans fought for Israel's independence but were now suffering in the hands of their fellow citizens. "Why is their blood different from the blood of their Western brothers?" the author wondered.[169] Local Jewish leaders who were formerly Zionists started calling their communities to stay in Morocco, or to stop donating money for Zionist goals. [170]

To counter these negative portrayals of Israel in Morocco, the Israeli authorities attempted to influence the tone in letters coming from Israel. First and foremost, criticism of Israel was redacted from letters sent to Morocco.[171] Far more ambitious was another scheme, where immigrants from Morocco were approached by Jewish Agency officials, or by activists associated with pro-government organizations, and were asked to write their relatives in Morocco letters that echoed the official Israeli narrative. It is not clear whether the idea for this bold move came from the Jewish Agency itself or from established immigrants from Morocco who formed a pro-government organization under the name "the forum for veteran North Africans," later named *Ahi-'Azar* ("helping my brother"). In any case, the Jewish Agency funded the organization, hosted its meetings, and its senior members sat on its board. Much of the forum's activity was aimed at countering radical voices among North African immigrants and especially blocking the return to Morocco.[172]

The draft letter that exists in the Jewish Agency archives was addressed to a generic "My Dear Uncle" and emphasized the religious ties that linked all Jews to the Land of Israel. It also stressed the need to work hard in developing the country before one could reap the rewards, and the importance of sacrifices in the present in order to make the country bloom for the next generations. "We may be on the verge of a third [world] war, and just as we had lost the six millions in Europe, we could, God forbid, lose the survivors, and among them Moroccan Jews," the unidentified author warned.[173] More controversial was the manner in which those who decided to leave Israel and return to North Africa were depicted: "They thought they were immigrating to a country that has palaces and houses of entertainment, and did not imagine to themselves that hard work awaits them." These returnees were unable to integrate into the new Israeli society that emphasized collective work because they did not agree to work in agriculture or construction.[174] "Suddenly the people of Morocco became delicate in body and spirit," the author mocked them. The slander of Israel by those returning to North Africa was also easily explained away: "It is no wonder that he who returned [to Morocco] comes up with excuses so that you do not put him to shame."[175] In other words, in order to save face, the returnees had made up stories about racism. In fact, the fabricated letter argued, there was no racism against North Africans in Israel:

> You must often speak about the difference between the ethnicities ['adot] and so forth. I'll write about it in detail another time and tell you the truths, lies, and exaggerations in this whole story. In the meantime, you'll have to do with me hinting at the major difficulties that exist when the different tribes of Judaism, which parted in ways and customs for two thousand years, meet [again]. We, native Israelis, Moroccans and Poles, feel ourselves brothers and equal and we hope that the day is not far when all immigrants from different countries feel the same way.[176]

At the instruction of the Israeli elite, Moroccan Jews were to refute the stories of their countrymen who returned to Morocco and reaffirm Israel's supposed commitment to equality among all Jews.

Those Moroccan Jews who, despite immense pressure, considered the option of leaving Israel and returning to Morocco found that it was very difficult to do. Upon their arrival to Israel, the Israeli government confiscated the immigrants' passports and travel documents, and denied the requests for the documents' return.[177] Moreover, the cost of the return ticket was hard to muster. The Makhzan did not see it as its duty to fund the return of those who chose to leave, and while the French government wanted to assist these Jews, it did not consider them French citizens but rather protected Moroccan subjects of the sultan. Nevertheless, the French consulate in Israel did take some steps to help those wishing to return to Morocco.[178] This position often put the French at odds with the Israeli government.[179]

But even those who managed to secure the necessary funds often found themselves having to negotiate their return with reluctant Moroccan authorities. On the one hand, the sultan feared that the return of Jews, whom many Muslims saw as traitors, would further exacerbate tensions in Morocco.[180] On the other hand, the return of Jews was good for public relations because it portrayed Morocco as tolerant to minorities (just as it was fighting to obtain independence from France). Indeed, the returnees were ultimately greeted by the sultan with the following words:

> The Moroccan Jews are my sons as is the case with Moroccan Muslims . . . and I value my responsibilities towards them. I am very sorry for those who chose to leave, and on the other hand, I feel content when I learn that there are Jews returning to the homeland, and to them I say: you are welcome again in your homeland. I treat them like a father treats his sons who lost their way for some time, then returned home a second time.[181]

After lengthy negotiations between the sultan and the French colonial authorities, it was decided that Jews would be allowed to return, as long as they used French travel permits and not Israeli passports. The entire process of return was done secretly. According to French data, from 1949 to 1953, about 6 percent of Moroccan immigrants in Israel made the journey back to Morocco (2,466 out of the 40,000 Moroccans who resided in Israel at the time).[182]

THOSE WHO RETURNED AND THOSE STILL WAITING

In the aftermath of the 1948 war, many Palestinians refused to accept the loss of their homeland, and started looking for a way back to Palestine, even if it meant living under Israeli rule. Although not yet canonized as "the right of return" (*haqq al-ʿawda*), as it would come to be known in later years, this right was sanctified already in late 1948.[183] It was also at that point that many Palestinians started searching for new leaders who could make return a reality, while the old class of notables began pondering their role in the defeat. Meanwhile, on the Israeli side, "the war on return" became one of the primary endeavors of the Israeli bureaucracy, not without the support of the country's Jewish population. Blocking the return of refugees at all costs would continue to drive the actions of the Israeli government for decades. Indeed, it has not ended.

Moroccan Jews in Israel wanted their own "right of return" in the aftermath of the 1948 war. Disillusioned by Ashkenazi racism, they wanted to leave Israel and go back to Morocco, and were even willing to renounce some of the key tenets of Zionism in order to do so. Here too, Israel had done its outmost to block the return of these people to Morocco and reduce their influence on family members still in Morocco (who were reconsidering their plans to immigrate to Israel). Ultimately, the laudatory letters dictated by the Zionist leadership were unnecessary. By 1954 the return of Jews to Morocco had practically ceased with the intensification of the anticolonial revolt there against the French. Most Moroccan Jews became convinced that Israel, even racist, was better than the uncertainty of Morocco. The one to limit Moroccan immigration to Israel in the 1950s was the Israeli government itself, which feared the "Levantinization" of the country and the loss of Ashkenazi hegemony.[184]

The only group who could effortlessly perform a return to their old homeland in the aftermath of the 1948 war was the group of disenchanted Mahal volunteers, however small their numbers. They refused to accept the marriage between Judaism and violence and saw Israel's resort to militarism as un-Jewish or immoral. But even they did not sever their ties with the Jewish state altogether: their privileged position allowed them to return to their place of birth, but still keep Israel as a possible place of refuge. Conversely, most Ashkenazi soldiers in the aftermath of the 1948 war were either born in Palestine or were Holocaust survivors and did not see Israel's resort to militarism as un-Jewish, nor were they interested in an alternative homeland (possibly because one was not available for them in the aftermath of the Second World War). In fact, some strongly felt they could fuse the desire to be "a nation like all other nations" with the commandment to be a "light unto nations." The former was achieved through the celebration of the use of force, while the latter would be achieved in the future by making Israel the world's conscience on what was just and what was unjust.[185] In that sense, these soldiers indeed felt they achieved a "return to history."

Conclusion

THE VIEW FROM THE GROUND

OVER A DECADE AFTER THE 1948 WAR, THE ISRAELI CENSOR CON-
tinued to read soldiers' letters, and soldiers continued to express opinions at
odds with the officially sanctioned understanding of Zionism:

> The surroundings here are full of ruined Arab villages. We were always taught
> that we won over the Arabs because we loved the land more, and that it's ours.
> But when I walk around, and see all these mountains covered with terraces, I
> can see it's a lie. Hundreds of years of work were put into every site here. It's
> unbelievable. There aren't even 50 meters without a terrace and there are a lot
> of carob trees. It's hard to grasp this change. People used to live in these ruins.
> Maybe they loved and hated like we do, and now—who knows where they are.
>
> Letter from December 1, 1960[1]

For the longest time, this soldier was convinced of the Jewish entitlement to
Palestine, and the lack of Arab attachment to it, and he was clearly willing to
fight because of this inculcated view. But more than that, his letter offers us the
kind of honesty that we typically do not see from politicians, generals, or the
various historians who have used their words as scaffolding. Seeing the ruined
villages and fields made this soldier go against what "we were always taught";
he recognized the indigenous Arab attachment to Palestine, and perhaps even
regretted turning Palestinians into the "wandering nation."

Indeed, the view from the ground among both Jews and Arabs—dissenting or not—paints a rather different picture than the one craftily spun by political elites and their propagandists. This was certainly true for the motivations of those who came from around the world to fight in Palestine in 1948 as part of the IDF or ALA. Still, in line with the appeals of mobilizers, "pan-Judaic" and pan-Arab logics were pull factors for thousands of Jews and Arabs, and these ideas were supplemented with local appeals: love of freedom for Moroccan Jews; ending the reign of those collaborating with colonialism, but masquerading as nationalists, in Syria; replacing diplomacy with military action in Lebanon; among others. The largest number of recruits came from European DP camps. Those Holocaust survivors who enlisted in the IDF while still in the camps may have feared a second holocaust, like Zionist propaganda had warned, but they were also desperate to leave the continent that had become a mass grave for their loved ones. The claims on them by Zionist emissaries were far more effective than elsewhere because of this desperation. Moreover, the state institutions and extensive funding available to the Zionist movement made mobilization for the IDF more effective than that of the ALA, which relied on disparate societies, parties, and tribes with little state backing.

Once Jews and Arabs from around the world made it to Palestine and joined the Jews and Arabs already there, propaganda shifted dramatically: from the diverse stories told in the countries of mobilization to a univocal message. In the IDF, this message was aimed at dispelling the idea that Jews had an uneasy relationship with the use of force. Taking a page from the propaganda playbook of the Revisionist Right, IDF education officers advocated that Jews become "a nation like all other nations" and adopt the gentile way of war. Arabs (including Palestinians) were presented as the disciples of the Seven Nations of Canaan and Amalek—ancient nations that the Bible commands the Israelites to annihilate as part of the conquest of Canaan or, in modern interpretation, Palestine. This, education officers hoped, would condone the physical eradication of the invading armies and indifference to the fate of Palestinians, be they combatants or civilians. In the ALA there was also an attempt to liken the Jews to an ancient enemy or submissive rival, and Jews were sometimes presented as dhimmis who were no longer entitled to protection because they had tried to seize power and refused to acknowledge the superiority of Islam. But far more important to the ALA's patrons was a different message altogether, one not entirely related to the fighting in Palestine: an attempt to guarantee that the anticolonial zeal of volunteers did not turn against Arab leaders upon the return of the volunteers to their home countries.

What ALA soldiers made of this indoctrination was not always in accord with what the propagandists had in mind. Some Iraqi volunteers and their friends back home saw the fight in Palestine as an extension of the struggle against the collaboration of the elites with colonialism at home. They connected the uprising known as al-Wathba against the Hashemite government to combating Zionist colonization and the British in Palestine. Other ALA volunteers also tried to overthrow corrupt Arab regimes, which colluded with colonial forces, upon their return.

Even if some ALA volunteers and their families alluded to the supposed dhimmi status of Jews, thus echoing ALA propaganda, it was actually Moroccan Jews who considered the transformation of this classical Islamic principle far more seriously. (This should not surprise us, given that the dhimmi status was largely defunct in most of the Middle East by the mid-twentieth century.) Some Jews in Morocco saw the Israeli victory over the Arab states as an opportunity to break away from this inferior status and "walk with our heads held high" while Morocco's Muslims walk "in humility," in the words of a female relative of a soldier. But those Jews who actually came from Morocco to Israel and joined the fighting quickly changed their perspective: Ashkenazi racism made them rethink their relationship with Zionism and yearn for their old lives in Morocco. They were no longer certain that the dhimmi status had come to an end.

Meanwhile, most Ashkenazi soldiers, Sabras and Holocaust survivors alike, became convinced that violence was a constitutive part of membership in a community of Western nations, and not at all contradictory to the "Jewish nature." Some even believed that Jews should take pleasure in such violence like the soldiers of other nations. This marked a resounding success for Zionist political and military elites who pushed for this view. In the case of these soldiers, complex identities gave way to more reduced binary identities, as dictated from above.

By early 1949, as the negotiations for an armistice started on the island of Rhodes, it was necessary for IDF propagandists to explain why fighting had to give way to diplomacy. The soldiers were told that the diplomatic factor would provide cover for the great achievements that were realized through "the military factor," i.e., the use of force. Diplomacy would ensure that the heroic victories would not be squandered.[2] However, education officers re-assured soldiers—echoing Chief of Staff Yadin's principle—that the Rhodes talks would not be the end of the story, because "in the current psychosis of the eve of war, 'peace' is but a local and temporary concept."[3] Soldiers were promised that "we would not sacrifice the security of the state on the altar of peace with the Arab states. Too numerous were the efforts and sacrifices to acquire these achievements ... for them to be left aside in the way of diplomatic concessions."[4] IDF propagandists prophesied that the use of force would be reintroduced in a "second round," because the Arabs could not accept their defeat. It was not that Israel wanted to fight, but rather, IDF propaganda insisted, "there is no alternative" (Hebrew: *'eyn brerah*).[5]

Only a minority of soldiers contested the axiom of "no alternative" in response to the atrocities they witnessed during the war. This minority detested the violence that accompanied war and believed that it violated what they saw as Judaism's essence. Most of those soldiers were Mahal volunteers who came from affluent countries and could effortlessly return there, while keeping Israel as a safe haven in case they ever needed one. They—an education pamphlet from the end of the war stated—"came because the great war unsettled them and they could not remain quietly in civvy [civilian] life. . . . Many of these adventurers continued unsettled (and unsettling [others]) here, and have already gone from us."[6] In other words, these Jews were beyond repair, and their dissent could not be undone. Since they were "unsettling" others, perhaps by helping change their mind about Israel and Zionism, it was better that they had left.

Dissent among Palestinians took a very different route. As this book has demonstrated, many Palestinians had great confidence in the ALA early on in the war, and even when the volunteer army was proven to be ineffective, they still held out hope that Arab leaders would make good on their promise to save Palestine. With the onset of the nakba, some Palestinians like Burhan al-Din al-'Abbushi became disappointed with pan-Arabism, and were waiting for a revolution to shake the Arab world so that it could keep its promise of saving Palestine. Other members of the elite began pondering their own role in the defeat, and also that of the old class of notables.

The entrance of the Arab armies into Palestine on May 15, 1948, did not slow down the Palestinian exodus, and even provided further justification for the Jewish forces to continue expelling the inhabitants of villages in the Negev and the Galilee, while defeating the Arab armies, one after the other. By war's end, a mere 156,000 Palestinians remained within the three-quarters of Palestine that had become Israel, forced to rebuild their lives under military rule. Meanwhile, the 750,000 Palestinian refugees kept hope alive of an imminent return. They mourned the disappearance of Palestine's beloved citrus from their lives, and made arrangements to guarantee that the fields and orchards they were forced to leave behind did not go fallow. They also seized on any rumor suggesting Israel would eventually allow their return. That hope continues to persist, now more than seventy years after the official end to the 1948 war.

Notes

INTRODUCTION

1. "The Battle over Malkiya" [Hebrew translation], July 1948, *al-Jundi* (Lebanon), in Kibbutz Meuhad Archives [KMA] 15/1/3.

2. A *kibbutz* is a form of communal settlement that was popular in the first decades of Zionist colonization. Most kibbutzim (pl. of *kibbutz*) professed a socialist ideology.

3. Sarah Leibovitz-Dar, "Ten Bullets and One in the Barrel," *'Al ha-Mishmar*, 14 September 1990.

4. According to his son, Dawud regretted coming to Israel. After spending six years in a transit camp (*ma'abara*) in complete destitution, he longed to return to Iraq. When he, his wife, and their seven children were finally provided a small house in the city of 'Afula, he refused to follow social norms and separate himself from his Arab past. Not only did he continue speaking Arabic almost exclusively, he mostly fraternized with Palestinians, leaving every Sunday on a donkey to visit nearby Palestinian villages, selling and shining copper. Phone interview with Shimshon B., 28 June 2017.

5. Frederick Cooper, *Colonialism in Question: Theory, Knowledge, History*) Berkeley: University of California Press, 2009), 99.

6. The term "religious internationalism" refers to an identity rooted in religious conviction that transcends the political boundaries of nation-states.

7. Abigail Green, "Nationalism and the 'Jewish International': Religious Internationalism in Europe and the Middle East c. 1840–c. 1880," *Comparative Studies in Society and History* 50, no. 2 (2008): 535–58.

8. For a survey of Zionism, see David Engel, *Zionism* (Harlow: Pearson/Longman, 2009); Michael Brenner, *In Search of Israel: The History of an Idea* (Princeton, NJ: Princeton University Press, 2018), 18–87.

9. Scott M. Eddie, "Ethno-nationality, Property Rights in Land and Territorial Sovereignty in Prussian Poland, 1886–1918: Buying the Land from under the Poles' Feet?" in *Land Rights, Ethno-Nationality, and Sovereignty in History*, ed. Stanley L. Engerman and Jacob Metzer (London: Routledge, 2004), 56–86; Shalom Reichman and Shlomo Hasson, "A Cross-Cultural Diffusion of Colonization: From Posen to Palestine," *Annals of the Association of American Geographers* 74, no. 1 (March 1984): 57–70; Gershon Shafir, "Theorizing Zionist Settler Colonialism in Palestine," in *Routledge Handbook of the History of Settler Colonialism*, ed. Edward Cavanah and Lorenzo Veracini (New York: Routledge, 2016), 339–51.

10. For the complex tapestry that makes up the Arab *nahda*, see Albert Hourani, *Arabic Thought in the Liberal Age: 1798–1939* (Cambridge: Cambridge University Press, 1962); Ilham Khuri-Makdisi, *The Eastern Mediterranean and the Making of Global Radicalism, 1860–1914* (Berkeley: University of California Press, 2013); Dyala Hamzah, ed., *The Making of the Arab Intellectual (1880–1960): Empire, Public Sphere and the Colonial Coordinates of Selfhood* (London: Routledge, 2013); Jens Hanssen and Max Weiss, *Arabic Thought beyond the Liberal Age: Towards an Intellectual History of the Nahda* (Cambridge: Cambridge University Press, 2016).

11. Ehud Luz, *Wrestling with an Angel: Power, Morality, and Jewish Identity* (New Haven, CT: Yale University Press, 2003), 44, 179; Anita Shapira, *Land and Power: The Zionist Resort to Force, 1881–1948* (New York: Oxford University Press, 1992), 11. For a different view, see Gideon Reuveni, "Sports and the Militarization of Jewish Society," in *Emancipation through Muscles: Jews and Sports in Europe*, ed. Michael Brenner and Gideon Reuveni, 44–61 (Lincoln: University of Nebraska Press, 2006).

12. Shapira, *Land and Power*, 21–29; George Lachmann Mosse, *Confronting the Nation: Jewish and Western Nationalism* (Hanover, MA: published for Brandeis University Press by University Press of New England, 1993), 1, 17, 26–27.

13. Robert Eisen, *The Peace and Violence of Judaism: From the Bible to Modern Zionism* (New York: Oxford University Press, 2011), 198–99; Shapira, *Land and Power*, 10, 52; Daniel Boyarin, "The Colonial Drag: Zionism, Gender, and Mimicry," in *The Pre-Occupation of Postcolonial Studies*, ed. Fawzia Afzal-Khan and Kalpana Seshadri-Crooks (Durham, NC: Duke University Press, 2000), 237.

14. Shapira, *Land and Power*, 14, 23, 30; Derek J. Penslar, *Jews and the Military: A History* (Princeton, NJ: Princeton University Press, 2013), 69, 78, 152, 203.

15. Eisen, *Peace and Violence of Judaism*, 173; Luz, *Wrestling with an Angel*, 25–26.

16. Mosse, *Confronting the Nation*, 163–67; Reuveni, "Sports and the Militarization," 47–48.

17. Quoted in Paul Mendes-Flohr and Jehuda Reinharz, *The Jew in the Modern World: A Documentary History* (New York: Oxford University Press, 1995), 547.

18. Deborah S. Bernstein, ed., *Pioneers and Homemakers: Jewish Women in Pre-State Israel* (Albany: State University of New York Press, 1992); Reuveni, "Sports and the Militarization," 46–53.

19. Luz, *Wrestling with an Angel*, 249–50.

20. Shmuel N. Eisenstadt, "Ha-Omnam Hehezirah ha-Tsiyonut et ha-Yehudim la-Historiyah?," in *Ha-Tsyonut ve-ha-Hazara la-Historiyah: Diyun me-Hadash*, ed. Shmuel N. Eisenstadt and Moshe Lissak (Jerusalem: Yad Yizhak Ben-Zvi, 1999), 9.

21. Eisenstadt, "Ha-Omnam Hehezirah ha-Tsiyonut," 11; Uri Ben-Eliezer, *The Making of Israeli Militarism* (Bloomington: Indiana University Press, 1998), 96–99.

22. Eisen, *Peace and Violence of Judaism*, 186–87.

23. Steven J. Zipperstein, *Elusive Prophet: Ahad Ha'am and the Origins of Zionism* (Berkeley: University of California Press, 1993), 204–8, 319–21; Shapira, *Land and Power*, 17–29; Eisen, *Peace and Violence of Judaism*, 199; Luz, *Wrestling with an Angel*, 53, 199, 218–19. Ahad Ha'am did not oppose all forms of violence. He supported the formation of self-defense groups in Europe.

24. Alan Dowty, "Much Ado about Little: Ahad Ha'am, 'Truth from Eretz Israel,' Zionism and the Arabs," *Israel Studies* 5, no. 2 (2000): 154–81. On rare occasions, local Ottoman officials who originated from Palestine tried to restrict Zionist land purchases. See Michelle Campos, *Ottoman Brothers: Muslims, Christians, and Jews in Early Twentieth-Century Palestine* (Stanford, CA: Stanford University Press, 2010).

25. The commoditization of land in the Ottoman domains predated the 1858 Land Code. Moreover, the code was not only supposed to simplify tax collection but also protect small landownership. Yet the unwillingness of peasants to register land under their name, for fear of conscription, made it easier for urban notables to lay claim to those lands. See Beshara Doumani, *Rediscovering Palestine: Merchants and Peasants in Jabal Nablus, 1700–1900* (Berkeley: University of California Press, 1995), 159; Samuel Dolbee and Shay Hazkani, "'Impossible Is Not Ottoman': Menashe Meirovitch, 'Isa

al-'Isa, and Imperial Citizenship in Palestine," *International Journal of Middle East Studies* [*IJMES*] 47, no. 2 (2015): 241–62.

26. Shafır, "Theorizing Zionist Settler Colonialism."

27. Rashid Khalidi, *Palestinian Identity: The Construction of Modern National Consciousness* (New York: Columbia University Press, 1997), 89–144.

28. Campos, *Ottoman Brothers*; Salim Tamari, *Year of the Locust: A Soldier's Diary and the Erasure of Palestine's Ottoman Past* (Berkeley: University of California Press, 2011); Melanie S. Tanielian, *The Charity of War: Famine, Humanitarian Aid, and World War I in the Middle East* (Stanford, CA: Stanford University Press, 2017); Hasan Kayalı, *Arabs and Young Turks: Ottomanism, Arabism, and Islamism in the Ottoman Empire, 1908–1918* (Berkeley: University of California Press, 1997), 174–206.

29. Jacques Kornberg, *Theodor Herzl: From Assimilation to Zionism* (Bloomington: Indiana University Press, 1993), 159–89; Engel, *Zionism*, 53–76; Khalidi, *Palestinian Identity*.

30. Quoted in Engel, *Zionism*, 78.

31. Quoted in William R. Louis, *Ends of British Imperialism: The Scramble for Empire, Suez and Decolonization: Collected Essays* (London: I. B. Tauris, 2006), 269. For demographics, see Laura Robson, *States of Separation: Transfer, Partition, and the Making of the Modern Middle East* (Berkeley: University of California Press, 2018), 105–6.

32. Susan Pedersen, "The Meaning of the Mandates System: An Argument," *Geschichte und Gesellschaft* 32, no. 4 (October–December 2006): 560–82.

33. Under the Ottoman system, Jerusalem and Mount Lebanon had a special administrative status. See Michael Provence, *The Great Syrian Revolt and the Rise of Arab Nationalism* (Austin: University of Texas Press, 2005), 5, 22.

34. Michael Provence, *The Last Ottoman Generation and the Making of the Modern Middle East* (Cambridge: Cambridge University, 2018), xx–xxii, 112–46. During the 1925–27 Syrian revolt, Druze notables were prominent in leadership positions, as were former Ottoman officers. Some of these tribal leaders were educated in new Ottoman tribal schools and as such should also be seen as a product of Ottoman modernization. See Provence, *Great Syrian Revolt*, 40–42, 58.

35. Provence, *Last Ottoman Generation*, 147–226.

36. Jennifer M. Dueck, "A Muslim Jamboree: Scouting and Youth Culture in Lebanon under the French Mandate," *French Historical Studies* 30, no. 3 (2007): 492–96; Arnon Degani, "They Were Prepared: The Palestinian Arab Scout Movement 1920–1948," *British Journal of Middle Eastern Studies* 41, no. 2 (2014): 202–11; Peter Wien, *Arab*

Nationalism: The Politics of History and Culture in the Modern Middle East (New York: Routledge, 2017), 92–93.

37. Quoted in Wilson Chacko Jacob, *Working Out Egypt: Effendi Masculinity and Subject Formation in Colonial Modernity, 1870–1940* (Durham, NC: Duke University Press, 2010), 122. Colonial officials often complained that Arab scouting organizations did not truly adhere to Baden-Powell's principles. See Dueck, "Muslim Jamboree," 496, 508–9; Degani, "They Were Prepared," 202.

38. Dueck, "Muslim Jamboree," 507–9; Jacobs, *Working Out Egypt*, 114; Keith D. Watenpaugh, *Being Modern in the Middle East: Revolution, Nationalism, Colonialism, and the Arab Middle Class* (Princeton, NJ: Princeton University Press, 2006), 256–78.

39. Wien, *Arab Nationalism*, 93, 113–14, 195–96. For a polemic counterview, see Barry M. Rubin and Wolfgang G. Schwanitz, *Nazis, Islamists, and the Making of the Modern Middle East* (New Haven, CT: Yale University Press, 2014).

40. Jacob, *Working Out Egypt*, 3–4; Wien, *Arab Nationalism*, 92–93, 101.

41. Wien, *Arab Nationalism*, 79, 90.

42. Watenpaugh, *Being Modern*, 256.

43. Shapira, *Land and Power*, 129.

44. Shapira, *Land and Power*, 124; Meir Chazan, *Metinut: Ha-Gishah ha-Metunah be-ha-Po'el ha-Tsa'ir uve-Mapai, 1905–1945* (Tel Aviv: 'Am 'Oved, 2009).

45. Anita Shapira, *Herev ha-Yonah: Ha-Tsiyonut ve-ha-Koah, 1881–1948* (Tel Aviv: 'Am 'Oved, 1992), 175, 320; Luz, *Wrestling with an Angel*, 202, 204. Shapira argued that the defensive ethos was crucial in veiling the national aspect of the struggle between the Zionist movement and Palestinians. One may go a step further to suggest that Zionism—hailing from European settler colonialism—was predisposed to violence. Actual military preparations did not begin in earnest until the 1930s, because up to that point Zionism could rely on the British. Nonetheless, the Sabra generation, as explored below, was crucial in tilting the balance from a British to a Zionist use of force.

46. Ben-Eliezer, *Making of Israeli Militarism*, 2–4; Joel Peters, *The Routledge Handbook on the Israeli-Palestinian Conflict* (New York: Routledge, 2015), 175.

47. Rashid Khalidi, "The Palestinians and 1948: The Underlying Causes of Failure," in *The War for Palestine: Rewriting the History of 1948*, ed. Eugene Rogan and Avi Shlaim, 17–21 (New York: Cambridge University Press, 2nd ed., 2007); Sherene Seikaly, *Men of Capital: Scarcity and Economy in Mandate Palestine* (Stanford, CA: Stanford University Press, 2016); Jacob Norris, *Land of Progress: Palestine in the Age of Colonial Development*

(Oxford: Oxford University Press, 2013); Fredrik Meiton, *Electrical Palestine: Capital and Technology from Empire to Nation* (Berkeley: University of California Press, 2018).

48. Khalidi, "Palestinians and 1948," 21–24; Weldon Matthews, *Confronting an Empire, Constructing a Nation: Arab Nationalists and Popular Politics in Mandate Palestine* (London: I. B. Tauris, 2014), 30–34.

49. Walid Khalidi, "Appendix IV: Note on Arab Casualties in the 1936–39 Rebellion," in *From Haven to Conquest: Readings in Zionism and the Palestine Problem until 1948*, ed. Walid Khalidi, 846–49 (Beirut: Institute for Palestine Studies, 1971); Khalidi, "Palestinians and 1948," 26; Matthews, *Confronting an Empire*, 25; Matthew Hughes, "From Law and Order to Pacification: Britain's Suppression of the Arab Revolt in Palestine, 1936–39," *Journal of Palestine Studies* 39, no. 2 (Winter 2010): 6–22.

50. Hillel Cohen, *Year Zero of the Arab-Israeli Conflict 1929* (Waltham, MA: Brandeis University Press, 2015).

51. Laila Parsons, *The Commander: Fawzi Al-Qawuqji and the Fight for Arab Independence 1914–1948* (New York: Hill & Wang, 2017), 3–106.

52. Parsons, *The Commander*, 111–12; Ghada H. Talhami, *Syria and the Palestinians: The Clash of Nationalisms* (Gainesville: University Press of Florida, 2001), 27.

53. Parsons, *The Commander*, 115–22.

54. Ibid. This word-of-mouth mobilization stood in stark contrast to the relatively organized manner in which Arab volunteers were mobilized in 1948, many of whom did not know al-Qawuqji at all.

55. Shapira, *Land and Power*, 234–35, 264–77; Ben-Eliezer, *Making of Israeli Militarism,* 8–9, 19–21. For a counterview—that militarism in Zionism was primarily the heritage of Polish Jews, not the Sabra—see Daniel K. Heller, *Jabotinsky's Children: Polish Jews and the Rise of Right-Wing Zionism* (Princeton, NJ: Princeton University Press, 2017).

56. Shapira, *Herev ha-Yonah*, 342–44; Ben-Eliezer, *Making of Israeli Militarism,* 21–28.

57. Shapira, *Land and Power*, 255; Ben-Eliezer, *Making of Israeli Militarism,* 24.

58. Luz, *Wrestling with an Angel*, 181; Shapira, *Land and Power*, 97; Heller, *Jabotinsky's Children*. A small faction of the Revisionist movement espoused an explicit Fascist ideology. Led by such figures as Abraham Stern and Abba Ahimeir, the faction sought to align itself with Fascist Italy and even with Nazi Germany (before it made antisemitism its staple policy). Jabotinsky himself, according to one study, should not be seen as supporting Fascism. See Dan Tamir, *Hebrew Fascism in Palestine, 1922–1942* (Cham, Switz.: Palgrave Macmillan, 2018).

59. For the argument that a class struggle and antagonism to elites was a major element in the 1936–39 Arab Revolt in Palestine, see Ted Swedenburg, *Memories of Revolt: The 1936–1939 Rebellion and the Palestinian National Past* (Minneapolis: University of Minnesota Press, 1995). In any case, the Zionist Left in Palestine played little role in "helping" Palestinians in such a struggle.

60. Ben-Eliezer, *Making of Israeli Militarism,* 58–63; Shapira, *Land and Power,* 298–310.

61. Shapira, *Land and Power,* 352, 366.

62. Michael J. Cohen, *Britain's Moment in Palestine: Retrospect and Perspectives, 1917–48* (London: Routledge, 2015), 289–304.

63. Shapira, *Land and Power,* 283–86; Rashid Khalidi, *The Iron Cage* (Oneworld, 2015), 105–27. The use of "commonwealth" rather than "state" in the declaration published in New York's Biltmore Hotel in 1942 was done primarily to appeal to American Jewish sentiment. However, at least some in the Yishuv's leadership did not rule out the option of being incorporated into the British Commonwealth of Nations, as Canada and Australia had done. See Derek Penslar, "Declarations of (In)Dependence: Tensions within Zionist Statecraft, 1896–1948," *Journal of Levantine Studies* 8, no. 1 (Summer 2018): 24–26.

64. During the 1936–39 Arab Revolt, the British revoked the license of several scouting troops, and only reversed this decision after the end of the Second World War. See Dueck, "Muslim Jamboree," 495–99, 504–6; Degani, "They Were Prepared," 201.

65. Issa Khalaf, *Politics in Palestine: Arab Factionalism and Social Disintegration, 1939–1948* (Albany: State University of New York Press, 1991), 288; Haim Levenberg, *Military Preparations of the Arab Community in Palestine, 1945–1948* (London: Frank Cass, 1993), 126–30.

66. Bayan N. al-Hut, *Al-Qiyadat wa-al-Mu'assasat al-Siyasiya fi Filastin, 1917–1948* (Beirut: Mu'assasat al-Dirasat al-Filastiniya, 1981), 508–11; Levenberg, *Military Preparations,* 130–38; Khalaf, *Politics in Palestine,* 143–45; Eliezer Tauber, "The Army of Sacred Jihad: An Army or Bands?," *Israel Affairs* 14, no. 3 (2008): 420–27.

67. Al-Hut, *Al-Qiyadat wa-al-Mu'assasat,* 511–14; Levenberg, *Military Preparations,* 139–53. The number of recruits in both organizations is a matter of debate. Based on British and Haganah intelligence, Levenberg estimated that al-Najjada had upward of 11,000–12,000 men in June 1947, and al-Futuwwa about 8,000 men. Khalaf, meanwhile, estimated the number of recruits in al-Najjada at 8,000 and those of al-Futuwwa at 5,000, but concluded that the number of fighters who belonged to both organizations

during the 1948 war did not surpass "a few hundred." See Levenberg, *Military Prepa-rations*, 144, 148–49; Khalaf, *Politics in Palestine*, 143, 208.

68. Cohen, *Britain's Moment in Palestine*, 442–58.

69. Cited in UN Document A/364 Add. 1, September 3, 1947, Annex 5, "Transmission by the Secretary-General of Cable Dated 13 June 1947 from the Arab Higher Com-mittee," accessed 16 May 2020, https://uniteapps.un.org/DPA/DPR/UNISPAL.NSF/c17b3a9d4bfb04c985257b28006e4ea6/fb6dd3f0e9535815852572ddoo6cc607?Open-Document.

70. Robson, *States of Separation*, 132–35; Rabinovich and Reinharz, *Israel in the Middle East*, 571.

71. Ben-Eliezer argued that Ben-Gurion did not adopt militarism as an official policy until after the war was in full swing. He suggested that the reason for the change of heart was Ben-Gurion's fear that if he resisted the demands of the Sabras, they might try to seize power. I was unable to verify these claims. See Ben-Eliezer, *Making of Israeli Militarism,* 155–62, 165–68.

72. David Ben-Gurion, *Yoman ha-Milhamah: Milhemet ha-'Atsma'ut, Tashah-Tashat*, ed. Gershon Rivlin and Elhanan Oren, vol. 1 (Tel Aviv: ha-Hevrah le-Hafatsat Mishnato shel David Ben-Gurion; Misrad ha-Bitahon, 1982), 58, 77, 101.

73. Ben-Gurion, *Yoman ha-Milhamah*, vol. 1, 97; Tom Segev, *A State at Any Cost: The Life of David Ben-Gurion* (New York: Farrar, Straus and Giroux, 2019), 411–12.

74. Joel Beinin, "Forgetfulness for Memory: The Limits of the New Israeli History," *Journal of Palestine Studies* 134 (Winter 2005): 6–20; Ben-Eliezer, *Making of Israeli Militarism,* 173–90.

75. Ben-Gurion, *Yoman ha-Milhamah*, vol. 1, 211.

76. Ben-Eliezer, *Making of Israeli Militarism,* 173–90; Ben-Gurion, *Yoman ha-Milhamah*, vol. 2, 440, 477, 523, 525, 572, 652–54, 683; Ben-Gurion, *Yoman ha-Milhamah*, vol. 3, 721–22, 776, 888, 919, 926.

77. Philip Shukry Khoury, *Syria and the French Mandate: The Politics of Arab Na-tionalism, 1920–1945* (Princeton, NJ: Princeton University Press, 1987), 415; Abdullah al-Khani, *Jihad Shukri al-Quwwatli fi Sabeel al-Istiklal wa al-Wihda* (Beirut: Dar al-Nafa'is, 2003), 70–71; Avraham Sela, "Tsava ha-Hatsala ba-Galil be-Milhemet 1948," in *Milhemet ha-'Atsma'ut, Tashah-Tashat: Diyun Mehudash*, ed. Alon Kadish (Israel: ha-'Amutah le-Heker Koah ha-Magen 'al-shem Yisra'el Gelili, 2004), 212–13.

78. Khoury, *Syria and the French Mandate*, 23, 235–36, 401–2, 416, 545–46, 569–70, 590–91.

79. Watenpaugh, *Being Modern,* 275–76.

80. Khoury, *Syria and the French Mandate,* 400–406, 415–16; Watenpaugh, *Being Modern,* 278.

81. Khoury, *Syria and the French Mandate,* 626–30. Zaki al-Arsuzi, a prominent member of the league, later became one of the founders of the Baʿth party.

82. Joshua Landis, "Syria and the Palestine War: Fighting King ʿAbdullah's 'Greater Syria Plan,'" in Rogan and Shlaim, *War for Palestine,* 189; Hizb al-Baʿth al-ʿArabi al-Ishtiraki, *Al-Baʿth wa-Qadiyat Filastin, 1944–1948* (Beirut: Dar al-Taliʿah lil-Tibaʿah wa-al-Nashr, 1973), 3–5; Michel ʿAflaq, "The Tragedy of Palestine and Amending the Syrian Constitution," al-Baʿth, vol. 212, 16 November 1947, in *Al-Baʿth wa-Qadiyat Filastin,* 41.

83. "Syrian Youth Told 'Be Ready to Fight'," 30 November 1947, Radio Damascus, in *Summary of World Broadcasts-BBC* [SWB], Part III (Caversham Park, Eng.: Monitoring Service of the British Broadcasting Corporation, 1947–1949), no. 28, 4 December 1947, 54–55; Al-Khani, *Jihad Shukri al-Quwwatli,* 70–71.

84. "Syrian Youth Told 'Be Ready to Fight.'"

85. Ibid.

86. Untitled report, 1 December 1947, Damascus Radio, in SWB, no. 28, 4 December 1947, 55.

87. Landis, "Syria and the Palestine War," 178–84.

88. Charles Tripp, "Iraq and the 1948 War: Mirror of Iraq's Disorder," in Rogan and Shlaim, *War for Palestine,* 132.

89. Landis, "Syria and the Palestine War," 178–82.

90. Sela, "Tsava ha-Hatsala ba-Galil," 210.

91. Landis, "Syria and the Palestine War," 189–91; "Syrian Volunteers Arrested in Northern Palestine," 9 February 1948, Sharq al-Adna Radio, in SWB, no. 37, 12 February 1948, 65.

92. Sela, "Tsava ha-Hatsala ba-Galil," 210; Landis, "Syria and the Palestine," 191, 210–11; Hani al-Hindi, "Jaysh al-Inqadh (1948–1949), Part I," in *Shuʾun Filastiniya,* no. 23, July 1973, 32–33. Another Arabic name for the army is *jaysh al-tahrir* ("the army of liberation").

93. Ronen Yitzhak, "Fauzi al-Qawuqji and the Arab Liberation Army in the 1948 War toward the Attainment of King ʿAbdallah's Political Ambitions in Palestine," *Comparative Studies of South Asia Africa and the Middle East* 28 (2008): 459–66; Talhami, *Syria and the Palestinians,* 27–28.

94. Al-Qawuqji's level of affiliation with Nazi Germany is a matter of debate. The foremost biographer of al-Qawuqji, Laila Parsons, suggested that he was not drawn to Nazi ideology, and Gilbert Achcar contended that al-Qawuqji was reluctant to declare his alliance to Hitler. Other scholars suggested a closer affiliation of al-Qawuqji with Nazi officials in charge of propaganda directed at the Middle East. See Parsons, *The Commander*, 141–80; Gilbert Achcar, *The Arabs and the Holocaust: The Arab-Israeli War of Narratives* (New York: Metropolitan Books, 2010), 92; Klaus-Michael Mallmann and Martin Cüppers, *Nazi Palestine: The Plans for the Extermination of the Jews in Palestine*, transl. Krista Smith (New York: Enigma Books, 2010), 83–85, 126–27.

95. Untitled report dated 1 March 1947, in KMA 15/2/7.

96. Ibid.

97. Amin al-Husayni was closely aligned with Nazi officials and extensively helped the German war effort. He was involved in producing antisemitic propaganda and likely supported the Nazi extermination campaign against the Jews. On the other hand, al-Qawuqji helped the German war effort to a degree—and possibly was involved in Nazi propaganda—but his role was not as significant as that of the mufti. In 1943 Amin al-Husayni accused al-Qawuqji of being a British agent, a claim he vehemently denied. See Parsons, *The Commander*, 141–80; Achcar, *Arabs and the Holocaust*, 104–76.

98. Landis, "Syria and the Palestine War," 191; Parsons, *The Commander*, 209–11.

99. Sela, "Tsava ha-Hatsala ba-Galil," 210.

100. 'Arif al'Arif, *Nakbat Filastin wa-al-Firdaws al-Mafqud*, Part I (Beirut: Dar al-Huda, 1980), 102.

101. Benny Morris, *1948: A History of the First Arab-Israeli War* (New Haven, CT: Yale University Press, 2008), 90; Sela, "Tsava ha-Hatsala ba-Galil," 207; Landis, "Syria and the Palestine War," 193.

102. Landis, "Syria and the Palestine War," 191; Parsons, *The Commander*, 209–11.

103. "Intelligence Report for the Period between 1–5 February 1948," submitted to HQ by the Hittin Battalion, 3, in KMA 15/2/2; Parsons, *The Commander*, 209–11, 218–20. For instances where the British interfered with ALA activity, see Sela, "Tsava ha-Hatsala ba-Galil," 211, 217–18.

104. Morris, *1948*, 205, 406; Al-'Arif, *Nakbat Filastin*, part VI, 7–8; Khalidi, "Palestinians and 1948," 13–14, 29. Updated village figures taken from Salman H. Abu Sitta, *Atlas of Palestine 1917–1966* (London: Palestine Land Society, 2010), 91, 106–7, 116–17.

According to Abu Sitta, with respect to villages: in 54.4 percent, Palestinians fled as a result of Jewish military assaults; in 24.6 percent, Jewish forces forcibly expelled Palestinians; in 9.9 percent, Palestinians fled because of the influence of the fall of nearby localities; in 7.7 percent, a general fear of Jewish attacks was the underlying cause for departure; in 2.4 percent, psychological warfare by Jewish forces spurred the exodus; and in only 1 percent, Palestinians left because they were ordered to do so by Arab political and military leaders.

105. Zachary Lockman, *Comrades and Enemies: Arab and Jewish Workers in Palestine, 1906–1948* (Berkeley: University of California Press, 1996), 366–67.

106. The ALA collection in the IDF archives includes propaganda materials as well as thousands of documents pertaining to strategy, combat tactics, maintenance, and soldiers' conduct. The record group for ALA documents in the IDF archives was created in 1953, after the Israeli security service, the Shin Bet, deposited materials it had received from the army itself during the war. According to data in the archives, the documents were largely collected by the IDF in 1948–49 from the police building in Nazareth, from an ALA compound in Safad, and from the villages of al-Jaysh, Tarshiha, and other locations in the Galilee. In 1957 the documents were sorted by the IDF history department and the IDF archives according to the hierarchy of the ALA units that created them (central command, brigades, battalions, etc.). Most of the materials are in their original Arabic; however, some documents were apparently lost and only exist in Hebrew translation. These translations were made for the IDF's internal history of the ALA, written by Gershon Gilad in the late 1950s. See Ministry of Defense / IDF Archives, "The ALA during the War of Independence (1948): Documents Catalogue 1962," 17–18, in Israel Defense Forces and Defense Establishment Archives [IDFA] 651/922/1975; "Letters Found in the Headquarters in Safad," March 1948, in Haganah Archives [HA] 105/216A; "Translation of the Tarshiha File," in KMA 15/2/5; Mordechai Bar-On, *Zikaron ba-Sefer: Reshita shel ha-Historyografyah ha-Yisre'elit shel Milhemet ha-'Atsm'aut, 1948–1958* (Tel Aviv: Misrad ha-Bitahon, 2001), 172–74. To my knowledge, these materials are still available to researchers.

107. Rona Sela, "The Genealogy of Colonial Plunder and Erasure: Israel's Control over Palestinian Archives," *Social Semiotics* 28, no. 2 (2018): 201–29; Shay Hazkani, "Israel's Vanishing Files, Archival Deception and Paper Trails," *Middle East Report* 291 (Summer 2019): 10–15; *Point of Access: Barriers for Public Access to Israeli Government Archives* (Tel Aviv: Akevot Institute for Israeli-Palestinian Conflict Research,

April 2016), accessed 25 April 2020, http://akevot.org.il/wp-content/uploads/2016/05/Point-ofAccess-English.pdf.

108. The irony of citing the privacy of Palestinians as the reason for blocking access to sources on 1948 is best captured by Tomer Gardi in *Even, Niyar* (Tel-Aviv: Kibbutz Meuchad, 2011), based on his experience at the Haganah archives. Gardi was forbidden, due to "privacy concerns," from viewing a protocol of a meeting of senior Israeli officials pertaining to the July 1948 rape and murder of four Palestinian women from the village of Hunin, in the Upper Galilee, by Israeli soldiers. He commented: "It became clear to me that those whose privacy the archive employee was attempting to protect were not the women who were raped and murdered but the rapist-soldiers. And now as I write these words I realize that it is not privacy that is at stake here, but the protection of a certain order. The protection of a certain male order, and the attempt to conceal, to silence the rape, in the name of a patriarchal order against women" (114).

109. Prime Minister's Office, Israel State Archives, "A Report by the Chief Archivist on Archival Declassification," 15 January 2018, 16–17, accessed 16 May 2020, www.archives.gov.il/archives/#/Archive/0b07170685341 1a1/File/0b0717068631567f.

110. Before the establishment of the postal censorship bureau in Palestine, mail was sporadically examined by the Criminal Investigation Department (CID) of the Palestine Police.

111. *History of the Postal and Telegraph Censorship Department*, vol. I (1952), 550, in the National Archives of the United Kingdom [TNA] DEFE 1/333; Willbourn, "Palestine Censorship," 30 April 1945, 1; "Palestine Censorship: Language Read," in TNA DEFE 1/259. Many of the letters examined in the Palestine censorship bureau were transit letters, going through Palestine to other destinations.

112. Chief Censor, "Instructions to Assistant Censors (Postal)," 5, 52, 22 November 1939, in TNA DEFE 1/222.

113. These reports appear to have been lost. See Willbourn, "Palestine Censorship," 30 April 1945, 8; Chief Censor (Palestine) to the Controller, Postal and Telegraph Censorship (London), 19 October 1939, in TNA DEFE 1/222; "Palestine Imperial Censorship," in "Middle East Censorships: Note," ca. 1942, in TNA DEFA 1/235.

114. MI12, Major Campbell Johnston, 27 January 1944, in TNA WO 208/5203.

115. See such reports in TNA WO 169/15644.

116. Willbourn, "Palestine Censorship," 30 April 1945, 1, in TNA DEFE 1/259.

117. E. S. Herbert, "Note by Director General on His Visit to Palestine Censorship," 7 December 1943, in TNA DEFE 1/256.

118. "List of People from Haifa Whose Letters Are under the Censorship Bureau Inspection," 20 March 1946, in HA 8/12; "Letters Examined in the Censorship Department Next to the Haifa CID," 6 August 1948, in HA 8/12; "Letters and Telegraph Censorship by the Haifa CID," 14 July 1947, in HA 115/25.

119. Dror's high position in the censorship bureau was unusual for a Jewish resident of Palestine. Apparently, this was overlooked because Dror was considered "an able administrator," and was also married to a British woman whose brother was a senior British official in Palestine. See Edwin Samuel, "Israeli's Probable Attitude towards Great Britain in the Event of War," 21 December[?] 1950, 4, in TNA DEFE 1/354; Jewish Agency for Palestine / Recruitment Office-Haifa to the Yishuv Recruitment Center, Jerusalem, "Attn: Gershon Schwalbe: Your Letter from 2 March This Year," 10 March 1943, in Central Zionist Archives [CZA] S25/32669.

120. Ministry of Defense, David Ben-Gurion to Gershon Dror, 12 July 1948, in Ben-Gurion Archives, Document no. 176606.

121. Avner Bar-On, *Ha-Sipurim she-Lo Supru: Yomano shel ha-Tsenzor ha-Rrashi* (Jerusalem: Sifere Yedi'ot Aharonot; Hotsa'at 'Idanim, 1981), 24–26.

122. Samuel visited the Israeli censorship bureau in order to determine whether Great Britain would be able to count on Israel to share materials obtained through postal censorship in the event of war against the Soviet Union. See Samuel, "Israeli's Probable Attitude towards Great Britain in the Event of War," 4; Southern Censor (Tel Aviv) to Chief Censor, "A Report for October 1949," 3 November 1949, 2, in IDFA 13/621/1985.

123. Samuel, "Israeli's Probable Attitude towards Great Britain in the Event of War."

124. Southern Censor (Tel Aviv) to Chief Censor, "Attn: Report for the Period 15 September to 30 September," 14 October 1948, 1, in IDFA 13/621/1985; Southern Censor, "A Report for the Month of November," 31 November 1948, in IDFA 13/621/1985; Southern Censor (Tel Aviv) to Chief Censor, "A Report for the Month of June 1949," 5 July 1949, 1, in IDFA 13/621/1985.

125. See, for example, Internal Department, Southern Censor to Chief Censor, "Special Report No. 39: The Mood among New Immigrants," in IDFA 18/621/1985; Intelligence Service [hereafter IS] HQ, "Report No. 9," 21 December 1948, 3, in IDFA 286/600137/1951; Operations Branch / Intelligence Department, "Censorship Report No. 9 for the Day of 12 May 1949," 5, 16 May 1949, in IDFA 875/1109/2005.

126. G. Dror, Commander of Intelligence 4 [censorship bureau] to Head of Intelligence Department, "'The Soldier's Opinion' Report," 18 August 1949, in IDFA

536/1109/2005; "Auditing of the Arrival of the Censor [staff] in the Central Mail Office in Tel Aviv on 3–4 of September 1952," 5 September 1952, in IDFA 18/316/1954.

127. Intelligence Corps Base / HQ of Intelligence 4, "Memorandum of the HQ Monthly Meeting from 11.4.51," 20 April 1951, 3, in IDFA 2427/1433/2002.

128. Interview with "Moshe" (pseudonym), 10 March 2011. Moshe served in the military censorship bureau during the 1950s and 1960s.

129. IS, "Attn: A Report on the Soldier's Opinion," 26 September 1948, in IDFA 353/535/2004.

130. Compare the warning in the British version in TNA WO 169/19519 to the one in Israeli reports in IDFA 353/535/2004.

131. David E. Omissi, Indian *Voices of the Great War: Soldiers' Letters, 1914–18* (London: Palgrave Macmillan, 1999), 9; Ann Pfau, "Postal Censorship and Military Intelligence during World War II," in *The Winton M. Blount Postal History Symposia: Select Papers, 2006–2009*, ed. Thomas M. Lera (Washington, DC: Smithsonian Institution Scholarly Press, 2010); Lionel Lemarchand, *Lettres censurées des tranchées, 1917: Une place dans la littérature et l'histoire* (Paris: Harmattan, 2001); William G. Rosenberg, "Reading Soldiers' Moods: Russian Military Censorship and the Configuration of Feeling in World War I," *American Historical Review* 119, no. 3 (2014): 738–39.

132. Intelligence Base / Intelligence 4, Commander of Intelligence 4 to Head of Intelligence Department, "Attn: 'Soldier's Opinion' Report," 5 June 1950, in IDFA 670/1109/2005.

133. Ibid. For other documents pertaining to the incident, see IDFA 670/1109/2005; 2423/1433/2002; 670/1109/2005.

134. General Staff / Operations Branch / Intelligence Department [ID], untitled [questionnaire to IDF commanders in regard to the Soldier's Opinion report], 15 September 1949, in IDFA 536/1109/2005.

135. Center for Applied Social Research, Dr. Guttman to Chief Censor, "Evaluation of the Method of Examining Letters to Determine the 'Soldier's Opinion,'" 11 June 1950, in IDFA 670/1109/2005.

136. Ibid.

137. Binyamin Gibli, Acting Head of Intelligence Department to Deputy Chief of the General Staff, "Attn: The Soldier's Opinion," 6 July 1950, in IDFA 670/1109/2005.

138. Raziel Vardi [?], in the Name of the Deputy Chief of Staff to Head of Intelligence Department, "Attn: The Soldier's Opinion Report," 11 July 1950, in IDFA 670/1109/2005.

139. Intelligence Base / Intelligence 4, Commander of Intelligence 4 to Base Censor for Military Mail, "Attn: 'Soldier's Opinion' Report," 4 July 1950, in IDFA 670/1109/2005.

140. Chief Censor to Dear Soldier, undated, in IDFA 49/637/1956.

141. Interview with "Moshe"; interview with "Nirit" (pseudonym), 17 August 2010 (Nirit served in the military censorship bureau during the 1970s and 1980s).

142. Nahla Abdo and Nur Masalha, "Introduction," in *An Oral History of the Palestinian Nakba* (London: Zed Books, 2018), 6–39, 21. In fact, the fundamental interest of this book—how elites manipulate collective memories by imposing top-down nationalist approaches—stems to a large degree from studies based on oral accounts.

143. Ahmad H. Sa'di, "After the Catastrophe: A Reading of Manna's Nakba and Survival," *American Historical Review* 125, no. 2 (April 2020): 571–78.

144. For Israeli soldiers, when the letter was originally written in a language other than Hebrew or sent abroad (which is sometimes indicated in the reports), I used common names for immigrants from those countries.

145. A major player in the war—for which primary sources do exist—is the Egyptian Muslim Brotherhood. As early as October 1947, the brotherhood opened up recruitment centers in Egypt, and thousands reportedly enlisted in special volunteer units within the first few days. In fact, the brotherhood played a crucial role in pushing the Egyptian government to send its army to fight in Palestine in May 1948. Since these volunteers largely did not fight in the ranks of the ALA, they are not included in this study. The role played by the brotherhood in 1948 awaits additional scholarly attention. See Abd al-Fattah el-Awaisi, *The Muslim Brothers and the Palestine Question: 1928–1947* (London: I. B. Tauris, 1997), 196–207; Thomas Mayer, "The Military Force of Islam: The Society of the Muslim Brethren and the Palestine Question, 1945–48," in *Zionism and Arabism in Palestine and Israel*, ed. Elie Kedourie and Sylvia G. Haim (London: Frank Cass, 1982), 100–117.

146. See, for example, Rogan and Shlaim, *War for Palestine*; Morris, *1948*; Yoav Gelber, *Palestine, 1948: War, Escape and the Emergence of the Palestinian Refugee Problem* (Brighton: Sussex Academic Press, 2006); Itamar Radai, *Palestinians in Jerusalem and Jaffa, 1948: A Tale of Two Cities* (New York: Routledge, 2016); Khalidi, *Iron Cage*; David Tal, *War in Palestine, 1948: Strategy and Diplomacy* (New York: Routledge, 2014).

147. Benny Morris, "1948 as Jihad," paper delivered at the Antisemitism in Comparative Perspective Seminar Series, Yale Initiative for the Interdisciplinary Study of Antisemitism, 3 February 2009, 3, accessed 16 May 2020, www.isgap.org/wp-content/uploads/2011/10/paper-1948-as-jihad.pdf.

CHAPTER 1

1. Muster Center for Service to the Nation, Proclamation No. 2, in IDF Archives Poster Collection, accessed 3 May 2020, www.archives.mod.gov.il/Exhib/tzavgiyus/Pages/ExhibitionsDocs.aspx?ExhbId=84.

2. Proclamation of Agudat Yisrael (*agudas yiśroel* in Yiddish), an ultra-orthodox party established in Poland in 1912, in IDF Archives Poster Collection.

3. See IDF Archives Poster Collection.

4. About 20 percent of the total 3,977 female soldiers in early 1948 were "females with combat fitness." However, after a female combat soldier was killed and her body mutilated in December 1947, most Palmach female soldiers were removed from the frontlines. See Yonit Efron, "Ahayot, Lohamot ve-'Imahot: Etos ve-Metsi'ut be-Mivhan Bnot Dor 1948," *'Iyunim Be-Tkumat Yisra'el* 10 (2000): 362, 364–65.

5. Moshe Naor, *Social Mobilization in the Arab/Israeli War of 1948: On the Israeli Home Front* (London: Routledge, 2013), 17–20, 44–47. By August 1948 the IDF laid siege to Tel Aviv and launched Operation Betser to capture draft evaders. The yield of the operation was somewhat disappointing: about 3,000 people were arrested, but only 652 men and 352 women of those were sent to active military service.

6. The High Command for the Holy Jihad, "The Battle for Palestine and Its Goals," undated, in Israel State Archives [ISA] MFA 4/2568; Danny Rubinstein, *Zeh Anahnu O Hem: 24 ha-Sha'ot she-Hikhri'u et ha-Ma'arakhah: Ha-Kastel vi-Yerushalayim, April 1948* (Rishon le-Zion: Yedi'ot aharonot: Sifre Hemed, 2017), 150–52; Al-Hut, *Al-Qiyadat wa-al-Mu'assasat*, 615–16.

7. The *faz'a* method was traditionally used to launch peasant uprisings against taxes or conscription, or to pit residents of one village or tribe against another. See Rosemary Sayigh, *The Palestinians: From Peasants to Revolutionaries* (London: Zed Books, 2013), 9; Swedenburg, *Memories of Revolt*, 127–28.

8. Rubinstein, *Zeh Anahnu*, 193–94; Haganah Intelligence, "Attn: Birzeit (Survey)," 23 March 1948, in IDFA 29/140/1991.

9. The High Command for the Holy Jihad, "O Arab Clerk," Notice no. 3, undated, in ISA P 26/358.

10. Report from *al-Sha'b*, 6–7 January 1948; report from *al-Sarih*, 27 January 1948, inside Haganah intelligence report, undated, in ISA P 16/1055.

11. The national committees were established by urban notables starting in late November 1947, similar to such committees established during the 1936–39 Arab

Revolt. However, while the 1936–39 committees were a grassroots creation, in 1948 the AHC was instrumental in setting them up. See Tauber, "The Army of Sacred Jihad," 427; Khalaf, *Politics in Palestine*, 146; Tal, *War in Palestine 1948*, 50–51, 64.

12. See, for example, "Message from the National Committee in Jerusalem," *al-Difaʿ*, 19 March 1948; "New Course in Officers' School in Damascus," *al-Difaʿ*, 22 March 1948; "Officers Course in Damascus," *al-Difaʿ*, 25 March 1948. Unless otherwise noted, historical Arabic press accounts were obtained from the Arabic Newspaper Archive of Ottoman and Mandatory Palestine at the National Library of Israel, accessed May 25, 2020, https://web.nli.org.il/sites/nlis/en/jrayed.

13. Radai, *Palestinians in Jerusalem and Jaffa*, 42. See letters of interest and replies in ISA P 41/349 and ISA P 44/351.

14. Committee for Arab Jihad, "al-Jihad—the Fourth Fatwa," undated, in ISA P 36/351.

15. Chairman of the Arab Youth Organization–Tiberias, "To All Arab Youth in the City of Tiberias," 22 February 1948, in ISA P 44/351; "A Large Meeting in the General Headquarters of the Northern Region," *al-Difaʿ*, 12 March 1948.

16. National Arab Committee in Tiberias and Its Jurisdiction, letter by President of Committee, 31 March 1948, in ISA P 44/351.

17. Security Council of Jaffa, "Proclamation No. 1: To the Dear People of Jaffa," 18 December 1947, in IDFA 677/922/1975.

18. Radai, *Palestinians in Jerusalem and Jaffa*, 24, 154–58. Hasan Salama, who was appointed commander of Jaffa in December 1947 after the ousting of Nimr al-Hawari, established his own militia force, the al-Aqsa Defenders Army (*jaysh humat al-aqsa*), ostensibly also under the command of ʿAbd al-Qadir al-Husayni. Nevertheless, even Salama cautioned against independent action. See Hasan Salama, "To the Dear People of Jaffa," ca. January 1948, in CZA S25/4015.

19. ALA / First Yarmuk Battalion, Muhammad Safa, "Daily News" [Hebrew translation], 28 January 1948, in KMA 15/2/2; Parsons, *The Commander*, 207, 221–22; Tauber, "The Army of Sacred Jihad," 437; Sela, "Tsava ha-Hatsala ba-Galil," 212; Talhami, *Syria and the Palestinians*, 31. ʿAbd al-Qadir al-Husayni denied publishing such pamphlets. See ALA / First Yarmuk Battalion, Muhammad Safa, "Daily News," 5 February 1948, in KMA 15/2/2.

20. Fawzi al-Qawuqji, "Instructions about Recruitment among Palestinians in the ALA," 13 March 1948, in IDFA 375/100001/1957.

21. Ibid.

22. Fawzi al-Qawuqji to Heads of Towns, National Committees and Municipal Councils in the Jenin, Nablus, and Tulkarm, "Notice 556" [Hebrew translation], 24 April 1948, in KMA 15/2/2.

23. General Command for the al-Inqadh Forces in the Northern and Central Front, Commander Fawzi al-Qawuqji to Mayor of Nablus, "No. 613," 30 April 1948, in Nablus Municipal Archives [NMA] S/65.

24. Parsons, *The Commander*, 212; "Jonny Says [A report by a Palestinian informant for the Haganah]," 25 March 1948, in ISA MFA 4/2568.

25. A major oppositional force to al-Husayni and his clan was the Nashashibi family. Led by Raghib al-Nashashibi, mayor of Jerusalem from 1920 to 1934, the family aligned itself with the British authorities. In fact, Khalidi suggested that the British (and Zionists) were active in fueling tensions between the Husaynis and Nashashibis. Another significant opposition to the mufti evolved as early as 1932 as part of the Istiqlal pan-Arab party. The party often criticized the mufti for his lack of action against British colonialism. See Khalidi, *Iron Cage*, 65–75; Matthews, *Confronting an Empire*, 33–34, 131, 161, 179–85, 224–27; Hillel Cohen, *Good Arabs: The Israeli Security Agencies and the Israeli Arabs, 1948–1967* (Berkeley: University of California Press, 2010), 230–58; Khalidi, "Palestinians and 1948," 24–28; Swedenburg, *Memories of Revolt*, 107–37.

26. "An Essay for Publication from Hanna Badr Salim, Istanbul Hotel, Haifa to the Editor of *al-Difaʿ*" [Hebrew translation], 29 February 1948, in HA 105/215A.

27. "Essay for Publication from Hanna Badr Salim."

28. Haganah Intelligence, "A Report from a Man Who Trained in the Qatana Training Camp in Syria," 20 February 1948, in HA 105/358.

29. Ibid. On the strained relationship between Amin al-Husayni and al-Qawuqji, including rumors the mufti himself tried to arrange al-Qawuqji's assassination, see Parsons, *The Commander*, 141–80, 213.

30. Tauber, "The Army of Sacred Jihad," 437; "Zamir [A report by a Palestinian informant for the Haganah]," 23 March 1948 in ISA MFA 4/2568.

31. As to the influence of rivalries from 1936–39 on the conduct of villages in 1948, see Elias Shoufani, "The Fall of a Village," *Journal of Palestine Studies* 1, no. 4 (Summer 1972): 108–21.

32. Commander of the First Company to Commander of Hittin Battalion, "Re: Your Letter from 12 February 1948," 13 February 1948, in IDFA 162/100001/1975.

33. "Intelligence Report for the Period between 1–5 February 1948."

34. Ibid., 6.

35. Ibid. Sela, "Tsava ha-Hatsala ba-Galil," 251. Some Palestinian recruits refused to be led by Palestinian officers because of disputes between families. See Parsons, *The Commander,* 212.

36. In late stages of the war, Palestinians also fought as part of the regular Arab armies. See "Arabs Active Recruiting Palestinians," 7 July 1948, in *Foreign Broadcast Information Service* [FBIS], Daily Report, no. 348, 8 July 1948, 112. The Foreign Broadcast Information Service was a CIA subsidiary. Retrieved via Readex Online Database.

37. Ismail Safwat reported that 2,500 Palestinian fighters had enlisted by March 1948. See Ismail Safwat to Jamil Mardam Bey, "A Brief Report on the Situation in Palestine . . . ," 23 March 1948, in Walid Khalidi, "Selected Documents on the 1948 Palestine War," *Journal of Palestine Studies* 27, no. 3 (Spring 1998): 65. For the controversy surrounding the numbers, see Tauber, "The Army of Sacred Jihad," 434–35.

38. "Where Is the Arab Youth Movement Now?" *al-Sarih,* 6 January 1948; Khalaf, *Politics in Palestine,* 145, 207–8; Tauber, "Army of Sacred Jihad," 426. See also Haganah Intelligence, untitled, 18 March 1948, in ISA MFA 4/2568.

39. For figures of drafted Holocaust survivors, see Hanna Yablonka, *Survivors of the Holocaust: Israel after the War* (New York: Palgrave Macmillan, 2014), 82.

40. These were groups of men and women who formed collective groups in DP camps and intended to establish kibbutzim upon immigration to Palestine.

41. Avinoam J. Patt, *Finding Home and Homeland: Jewish Youth and Zionism in the Aftermath of the Holocaust* (Detroit: Wayne State University Press, 2009), 201–13, 229.

42. Ibid., 213.

43. Ibid., 235–37.

44. Yablonka, *Survivors of the Holocaust,* 84–85; Yosef Grodzinsky, *In the Shadow of the Holocaust: The Struggle between Jews and Zionists in the Aftermath of World War II* (Monroe, ME: Common Courage Press, 2004), 170–71.

45. Yablonka, *Survivors of the Holocaust,* 87–93; Grodzinsky, *In the Shadow of the Holocaust,* 187–90.

46. Yablonka, *Survivors of the Holocaust,* 97.

47. The youth movements operating in DP camps were Nocham (Noham), Dror, Hashomer Hatzair (Hashomer Hatz'air), Hanoar Hatzioni (Hano'ar Hatsioni), and Bnei Akiva (Bnei 'Akiva). The movements were operating under an umbrella organization, the Executive Committee for Security for the People and the Homeland (*Exekutive Far Bitachon Le-'Am U-Moledet*). See Patt, *Finding Home and Homeland,* 239, 242.

48. Ibid., 243.

49. Pamphlet starting with "Youth to the Service of the People," signed by six youth movements, in Yiddish Scientific Institute Archives [YIVO], MK 483, reel 97. See also Patt, *Finding Home and Homeland*, 243–49.

50. Ibid.

51. Quoted in Grodzinsky, *In the Shadow of the Holocaust*, 180.

52. Patt, *Finding Home and Homeland*, 238–39.

53. Quoted in Grodzinsky, *In the Shadow of the Holocaust*, 168.

54. "A Plan for a Party: Self-Defense in Exile," published by *Anu ha-Homa*, Germany, in HA 36/11. For similar themes: "Bulletin on the Occasion of the Shavuoth Holiday," published by Ha-Haluts and the Haganah in Marseille, in HA 36/11; *Anu ha-Homa* 19, published by the Haganah in the German Exile, ca. 1949, 7, in YIVO; Patt, *Finding Home and Homeland*, 245–46.

55. *Ha-Haganah: Mahutah ve-Tafkidehah*) Berlin: Hotsa'ah "Anu ha-Homah," Germany, 1948), 15, in YIVO. Redeeming Jewish honor was a common theme in mobilization propaganda. See *Anu ha-Homa* 3 (published by the Free Pioneers Fighting in Germany), ca. 1948, 14, in YIVO.

56. *Anu ha-Homa* 18, published by the Haganah in the German Exile, ca. 1949, 4, in YIVO.

57. The responses in DP camps to the initiative to recruit survivors to the Jewish armed forces are a matter of debate. See Yablonka, *Survivors of the Holocaust*, 99–101; Patt, *Finding Home and Homeland*, 240–41; Yaakov Markovitzki, *Gahelet Lohemet: Giyus Huts la-Arets be-Milhemet ha-'Atsma'ut* (Tel Aviv: ha-Merkaz le-Toldot Koah ha-Magen ha-Haganah, 1995), 36; Grodzinsky, *In the Shadow of the Holocaust*, 190–94; Menahem Weinstein, *Peduyim le-Tsiyon be-Rinah: Tenu'at "Mizrahi Torah va-'Avodah" be-Mahanot ha-'Akurim be-Germanyah, 1945–1949* (Nir Galim: Bet ha-'Edut la-Moreshet ha-Tsiyonit ha-Datit, 2008), 194–99.

58. Patt, *Finding Home and Homeland*, 251.

59. "Circular No. 1," by the youth movements in the Munich DP camps, 18 February 1948 in YIVO, MK 483, reel 96.

60. Quoted in Yablonka, *Survivors of the Holocaust*, 93–94.

61. "Demand," signed by the Drafting Committee in Steyr (Austria) and the State of Israel, in YIVO, Bund Archives ME18–172 .

62. Patt, *Finding Home and Homeland*, 242.

63. Grodzinsky, *In the Shadow of the Holocaust*, 179–81.

64. "A Trial of a Dodger," published by Nocham in Germany, in HA 36/11.

65. Ibid. There is only limited discussion of Arabs in propaganda materials distributed in DP camps. One informative pamphlet from the eve of Israeli independence reported: "It is not just the case that the Haganah does not expel Arabs. In fact, it does not want them to flee." Another text stipulated that the Yishuv would forgive the Arabs (but not the British) for their behavior because they would be future partners in peace. See "A Plan for a Party: Self-Defense in Exile"; "Information," published by the Jewish Agency in Munich, 11 June 1948, in YIVO, MK 483, reel 96; *Anu ha-Homa* 18, published by the Haganah in the German Exile, ca. 1949, 4 in YIVO.

66. "A Trial of a Dodger."

67. Ibid.

68. Quoted in Patt, *Finding Home and Homeland*, 248.

69. For such lists, see YIVO, MK 483, reel 39; Grodzinsky, *In the Shadow of the Holocaust*, 198–208; Patt, *Finding Home and Homeland*, 247–53.

70. Grodzinsky, *In the Shadow of the Holocaust*, 207–8.

71. Yablonka, *Survivors of the Holocaust*, 103.

72. Yehudah Ben-David, *Ha-"Haganah" be-Eropah* (Tel Aviv: Tag, 1995), 105–31; Yablonka, *Survivors of the Holocaust*, 104–13, 125; Markovitzki, *Gahelet Lohemet*, 53–83, 118.

73. Pamphlet distributed to immigrant draftees, signed by Yehuda, Commander of Immigration Base, in HA 36/53.

74. Yablonka, *Survivors of the Holocaust*, 118–19; Markovitzki, *Gahelet Lohemet*, 116, 121.

75. Binyamin Gshur, "Mitnadvey Huts la-Arets (Mahal) me-Amerika ha-Tsfonit be-Milhemet ha-'Atsma'aut" (PhD diss., Hebrew University, Jerusalem, 2008), 126–31, 345.

76. Yaacov Markovitzky, *MACHAL—Overseas Volunteers in Israel's War of Independence* (Jerusalem: Ministry of Education, 2003), 5–9, 41. According to an estimate by Gshur, the number of volunteers from Western countries was 3,250, among them a handful of non-Jews. See Gshur, "Mitnadvey Huts la-Arets," 366.

77. The overwhelming majority of volunteers came from the United States, Latin America, Canada, South Africa, Britain, France, and the Scandinavian countries; however, the complete list of countries also included Holland, Belgium, Switzerland, and Italy among others. See Brigade Seven, "HAMITNADEV-A Newsletter for the Volunteer," no. 55, 4 April 1949, 5, in IDFA 48/1147/2002; Markovitzky, *MACHAL*, 4.

78. FA to IA, "FBI Agent in Possession of Monument and Rector Numbers," 4 November 1947, in ISA MFA 65/25; Amy Weiss, "1948's Forgotten Soldiers?: The Shifting

Reception of American Volunteers in Israel's War of Independence," *Israel Studies* 25, no. 1 (Spring 2020): 149–73.

79. Gshur, "Mitnadvey Huts la-Arets," 76; Penslar, *Jews and the Military*, 248.

80. Weiss, "1948's Forgotten Soldiers?"

81. Gshur argued that the magazine called for volunteering. I was unable to locate such calls. See Gshur, "Mitnadvey Huts la-Arets," 113–14.

82. "Get the Facts Straight," *Haganah Speaks*, 30 January 1948, 1.

83. "Act Now," *Haganah Speaks*, 30 January 1948, 4.

84. "A Million Hostages Look to Palestine," *Americans for Haganah*, 15 December 1947, 4.

85. "Haganah Defense Needs Urgent," *Haganah Speaks*, 16 February 1948, 1.

86. See cartoon in *Haganah Speaks*, 30 January 1948, 4, and "They Mutilate the Dead," *Haganah Speaks*, 16 February 1948, 3.

87. "Get the Facts Straight."

88. See "Profiles: Dov Seligman—Moshe Pearlstein," *Haganah Speaks*, 30 January 1948, 4; note on Ari Lashner and featured story on Noam Grossman, 16 March 1948.

89. "American Hero's Genius Shaped New Israel Army," *Haganah Speaks*, 16 June 1948, 1.

90. "Colonel David Marcus," in ibid., 6.

91. This ad appeared in every volume starting February 16, 1948. For portraits of some of the speakers, see "You Must Know Why You Fight," *Haganah Speaks*, 17 September 1948, 6.

92. For an ad to the film see *Haganah Speaks*, 2 July 1948, 8. For the story of the film's production, see Liat Steir-Livny, "Sipur Hafakato shel 'The Illegals'—ha-Seret ha-Rishon be-'Oreh Male she-Ti'ed 'Aliya Bilti Ligalit," *'Iyunim Be-Tkumat Yisra'el* 15 (2005): 393–412.

93. Gshur, "Mitnadvey Huts la-Arets," 117–18; Nir Arielli, "When Are Foreign Volunteers Useful? Israel's Transnational Soldiers in the War of 1948 Re-Examined," *Journal of Military History* 78, no. 2 (2014): 706–7. Approximately 80–85 percent of the volunteers had previous military experience. See Gshur, "Mitnadvey Huts la-Arets," 161, 370; Markovitzky, *MACHAL*, 5–9, 41.

94. Gshur, "Mitnadvey Huts la-Arets," 117–18.

95. The Jewish Agency was established in 1929 as the executive branch of the Zionist organization.

96. FA to IH, "Security Rules in Re 'Land and Labor for Palestine,'" 5 March 1948, in ISA MFA 65/25.

97. Gshur, "Mitnadvey Huts la-Arets," 83–84, 116–17; Weiss, "1948's Forgotten Soldiers?"

98. Thirteen percent of volunteers had one parent born outside North America, and the families of 11 percent of volunteers had lived in North America for three or more generations. See Gshur, "Mitnadvey Huts la-Arets," 369.

99. Gshur, "Mitnadvey Huts la-Arets," 158, 369.

100. Yaron Tsur, *Kehilah Keru'ah: Yehude Maroko ve-ha-Le'umiyut, 1943–1954* (Tel Aviv: 'Am 'Oved, 2001), 145; Michael M. Laskier, *Yisra'el ve-ha-'Aliyah mi-Tsefon Afrikah: 1948–1970* (Sedeh Boker: Mekhon Ben-Gurion, 2006), 198; Sikron, "Personal Drafting in the 1948 War," 95, in IDFA 159/1046/1970. According to Sikron, sixty of the North African Gahal recruits were women.

101. Muhammad Hatimi, "Al-Jama'at al-Yahudiya al-Maghribiya wa-l-Khiyar al-Sa'b bayna Nida' al-Sahyuniya wa-Rihan al-Maghrib al-Mustaqil, 1947–1961" (PhD diss., Faculty of Letters, Université Mohammed V-Agdal, Sais-Fès, 2007), 225–27.

102. Ibid., 221–22.

103. Quoted in Hatimi, "Al-Jama'at al-Yahudiya," 231n1.

104. Quoted in Hatimi, "Al-Jama'at al-Yahudiya," 221. Also in Tsur, *Kehilah Keru'ah*, 84.

105. Quoted in Hatimi, 222n1.

106. Ibid.

107. Ibid., 235–40.

108. Quoted in Mohammed Kenbib, *Juifs et musulmans au Maroc, 1859–1948* (Rabat: Faculté des lettres et des sciences humaines-Rabat, 1994), 671.

109. Hatimi, "Al-Jama'at al-Yahudiya," 236.

110. Quoted in Robert Assaraf, *Yehude Maroko: Tekufat ha-Melekh Muhamad ha-5* (Tel Aviv: Yedi'ot Aharonot, 1997) , 238–39.

111. Hatimi, "Al-Jama'at al-Yahudiya," 237; "Arab Youth Threatens Vengeance on Jews," 8 May 1948, Sawt al-Falestin, in FBIS, Daily Report, no. 308, 11 May 1948, II7.

112. According to the traditional Muslim belief, the first direction of prayer (*qibla*) set by Prophet Muhammad was toward Jerusalem. It was later changed to Mecca.

113. Quoted in Hatimi, "Al-Jama'at al-Yahudiya," 238.

114. Tsur, *Kehilah Keru'ah*, 19–21, 34–45, 179. Especially in the rural areas, Jews

were sometimes subject to cultural symbols of inferiority aimed at signaling Islam's superiority over all other religions.

115. Quoted in Hatimi, "Al-Jama'at al-Yahudiya," 238.

116. Ibid.

117. See Alma Rachel Heckman, "Jewish Radicals of Morocco: Case Study for a New Historiography," *Jewish Social Studies* 23, no. 30 (Spring/Summer 2018): 67–100; Kenbib, *Juifs et musulmans*.

118. A number of Muslim residents, together with a few police officers, managed to shield Jews who congregated in Jerada's Jewish-French school, and some of the old Jewish neighborhoods were also spared. Hatimi, "Al-Jama'at al-Yahudiya," 244–46.

119. Jamaâ Baïda, "The Emigration of Moroccan Jews, 1948–1956" (trans. Allan MacVicar), in *Jewish Culture and Society in North Africa*, ed. Emily Gottreich and Daniel J. Schroeter (Bloomington: Indiana University Press, 2011), 324; Tsur, *Kehilah Keru'ah*, 87–91; Hatimi, "Al-Jama'at al-Yahudiya," 247–48.

120. Hatimi, "Al-Jama'at al-Yahudiya," 242, 263.

121. Ibid., 242–43.

122. Ibid., 251–52.

123. Quoted in Assaraf, *Yehude Maroko*, 243.

124. Hatimi, "Al-Jama'at al-Yahudiya," 248–49; Tsur, *Kehilah Keru'ah*, 255–56.

125. Even before the Oujda and Jerada massacre, small groups of North African Jewish youth were being trained in self-defense by the Haganah. See Markovitzki, *Gahelet Lohemet*, 178–86.

126. Ishai Arnon, *Tsiyonut Datit be-Erets Mevo ha-Shemesh: Me-Ahavat Tsiyon bi-Tsefon Afrikah la-Etos shel Torah va-'Avodah be-Yisra'el (1943–1956)* (Bene Berak: ha-Kibuts ha-Me'uhad, 2016), 178.

127. Morocco's Directorate of Public Security Services (Casablanca), "Zionism," 1 July 1948, in Archives du Ministère des Affaires Étrangères–La Courneuve [AMAE] Palestine 401. Charles Netter was not necessarily the most Zionist of the youth movements; however, it was the only one licensed to operate legally by the French. The French saw the movement as nonpolitical and a useful tool for spreading French education and culture. See Ishai, *Tsiyonut Datit*, 104–5.

128. Residency General of the French Republic in Morocco to Foreign Minister, "The Jewish Communities of Morocco and the Land of Israel," 9 September 1948," in AMAE Palestine 401. Alliance schools, which were established in Morocco as early as 1862, attempted to foster better integration of the Jews in Morocco—not to Morocco's

predominant Muslim culture but rather to French culture. While the organization was non-Zionist until the Second World War, after the Holocaust some officials adopted a pro-Zionist position. See Tsur, *Kehilah Keru'ah,* 24–25, 37–39, 49–51; Aron Rodrigue, *Jews and Muslims: Images of Sephardi and Eastern Jewries in Modern Times* (Seattle: University of Washington Press, 2015), 14–15.

129. Residency General of the French Republic in Morocco to Robert Schuman, Ministry of Foreign Affairs, "Zionist Propaganda in Morocco," 23 September 1948, in AMAE Palestine 401.

130. Ibid.

131. "Annex I to Dispatch No. 1247 from 9 September 1948 of the Residency General of the French Republic in Morocco . . . ," in AMAE Palestine 401.

132. Annex III to Dispatch No. 1247 from 9 September 1948 of the General Residency General of the French Republic in Morocco: "Chief Manuals (For the Use of Moroccan Jewish Fighters Volunteering for Israel)," in AMAE Palestine 401.

133. "Jewish Communities of Morocco and the Land of Israel."

134. Ibid.

135. Annex II to Dispatch No. 1247 from 9 September 1948 of the Residency General of the French Republic in Morocco: "Application Form for Immigration Registration," in AMAE Palestine 401.

136. Baïda, "Emigration of Moroccan Jews," 324; Hatimi, "Al-Jama'at al-Yahudiya," 249–50, 258; Maud Mandel, "Transnationalism and Its Discontents during the 1948 Arab-Israeli War," *Diaspora: A Journal of Transnational Studies* 12, no. 3 (Winter 2003): 345. It seems that not all of these immigrants ultimately arrived in Israel.

137. Hatimi, "Al-Jama'at al-Yahudiya," 263–64, 269–77.

138. "Annex I to Dispatch No. 1247."

139. Ben-David, *Ha-"Haganah" be-Eropah,* 101, 106; Hatimi, "Al-Jama'at al-Yahudiya," 263–64, 269–77; Ben Maurice Ben-Shushan and Ilan Shtayer, *Mi-Maroco le-'Ako u-Ma she-Beyneyhen* (Jerusalem: 'Osim Historiya, 2010), 33–37. See also a journalistic account starting with "In Our Diaspora Country of Morocco," undated, in CZA S20/550/I.

140. "Report on a Visit to Syria 6–9 December, 1947" [Hebrew translation], in KMA 15/2/3.

141. "Recruiting in Syria," Sharq al-Adna Radio, 15 February 1948, in SWB, no. 38, 19 February 1948, 66–67.

142. Al'Arif, *Nakbat Filastin,* Part I, 102.

143. The Arab al-Fadl tribe resided for centuries in the Biqa' valley, but travelogues

indicate that by the early nineteenth century much of the tribe transferred to the Golan Heights. "Amir" was an honorary title for the head of the tribe. See Dawn Chatty, "Leaders, Land, and Limousines: Emir versus Sheikh," *Ethnology* 16, no. 4 (October 1977): 392.

144. "Report on a Visit to Syria 6–9 December, 1947"; "Attn: Amir F'aur and His People," 22 December 1947, in CZA S25/4018.

145. See Yosef Weitz, *Yomani ve-Igrotai la-Banim 1945–1948* (Tel Aviv: Masada, 1965), 121; Josef Nahmani and Joseph Weitz, *Yosef Nahmani: Ish ha-Galil* (Ramat Gan: Mishpahat Nahamni Le-yad Hotsa'at Masadah, 1969), 153–210; Chatty, "Leaders, Land, and Limousines," 394.

146. Chatty, "Leaders, Land, and Limousines," 389; "Attn: Amir F'aur and His People."

147. Simon Schama, *Two Rothschilds and the Land of Israel* (New York: Knopf, 1978), 289.

148. Sela, "Tsava ha-Hatsala ba-Galil," 215.

149. Although there is significant evidence of contacts between Zionist officials and Druze in Jabal Druze throughout the 1930s and 1940, the degree to which the leader of the Druze, Sultan al-Atrash, sanctioned these contacts is unclear. See Laila Parsons, *The Druze between Palestine and Israel, 1947–49* (New York: St. Martin's Press, 2000), 32–49.

150. Quoted in Parsons, *The Druze*, 57; Al-Khani, *Jihad Shukri al-Quwwatli*, 71.

151. Parsons, *The Druze*, 57. For a different account of al-Qawuqji's visit, see Kais Firro, *The Druzes in the Jewish State: A Brief History* (Leiden: Brill, 1999), 43–44. According to Firro, Sultan al-Atrash was excited to help with recruiting Druze volunteers.

152. Parsons, *The Druze*, 62–63; Randall S. Geller, *Minorities in the Israeli Military, 1948–58* (Lanham, MD: Lexington Books, 2017), 22–25.

153. Joshua Landis, "Shishakli and the Druzes: Integration and Intransigence," in *The Syrian Land: Processes of Integration and Fragmentation: Bilad Al-Sham from the 18th to the 20th Century*, ed. Philipp Thomas and Birgit Schäbler (Stuttgart: F. Steiner, 1998), 375–81; "Arab Military Preparations According to the Arab Press," 29 January 1948, in CZA S25/8996.

154. Itamar Rabinovich, "The Compact Minorities and the Syrian State, 1918–45," special issue, "A Century of Conservatism, Part 2," *Journal of Contemporary History* 14, no. 4 (October 1979): 693–712.

155. Samy S. Swayd, *Historical Dictionary of the Druzes* (Lanham, MD: Scarecrow

Press, 2006), 137; Parsons, *The Druze,* 62–63, 99; Rabinovich, "Compact Minorities," 707; Geller, *Minorities in the Israeli Military,* 22–25.

156. "Order of the Day" [Hebrew translation], 9 March 1948 and 5 April 1948 (documents found in Shakib Wahab HQ), in HA 105/132. The defection of a large number of Druze soldiers from the ALA to the IDF in late 1948 caused major tension between Druze and non-Druze in Jabal Druze and the Syrian army. See Geller, *Minorities in the Israeli Military,* 30–32.

157. "Arab Military Preparations According to the Arab Press"; Sela, "Tsava ha-Hatsala ba-Galil," 214.

158. Akram Hurani, *Mudhakkirat Akram al-Hurani,* Part I (Cairo: Maktabat Madbuli, 2000), 62–63, 71–74, 165–66, 220–21; Muhamad Abu 'Izza, "The Mujahid Hasan al-Qatan of Hama, of Jaffa," Palestinian Institute of Culture, 27 September 2006, accessed 13 January 2020, www.thaqafa.org/site/pages/details.aspx?itemid=2149#. VaMk1PmsWD8.

159. Hurani, *Mudhakkirat,* 220–22, 695; Elizabeth Thompson, *Justice Interrupted: The Struggle for Constitutional Government in the Middle East* (Boston: Harvard University Press, 2013), 207–35; Jonathan P. Owen, "Akram al-Hourani: A Study of Syrian Politics, 1943–1954" (PhD diss., Johns Hopkins University, 1992), 59; Sela, "Tsava ha-Hatsala ba-Galil," 212; "Arab Military Preparations According to the Arab Press"; Hanna Batatu, *Syria's Peasantry, the Descendants of Its Lesser Rural Notables, and Their Politics* (Princeton, NJ: Princeton University Press, 1999), 127.

160. See, for example, Association for the Liberation of Palestine-Hama, letter from 'Uthman al-Hurani (Hama) to Volunteers (Jaffa), 7 May 1948, in Abu 'Izza, "Mujahid Hasan al-Qatan."

161. Owen, "Akram al-Hourani," 58; Sela, "Tsava ha-Hatsala ba-Galil," 212.

162. Hani al-Hindi, "Jaysh al-Inqadh (1948–1949), Part I," 35–36.

163. Quoted in Owen, "Akram al-Hourani," 58.

164. "Arab Military Preparations According to the Arab Press." A third unit from Aleppo, "Lions of Shukri al-Quwwatli," sought to remind the inhabitants of the role of the president in saving Palestine.

165. Article from 26 March 1948 [Hebrew translation] in *Insha* (Aleppo), quoted in "Arab Military Preparations According to the Arab Press."

166. Ibid.

167. The decision was reached on November 5, 1947. See Hizb al-Ba'th al-'Arabi al-Ishtiraki, *Al-Ba'th wa-Qadiyat Filastin,* 3.

168. "A Proclamation of the Arab al-Ba'th Party," *al-Ba'th*, vol. 212, 16 November 1948, in Hizb al-Ba'th al-'Arabi al-Ishtiraki, *Al-Ba'th wa-Qadiyat Filastin*, 42–43.

169. Ibid.

170. John F Devlin, *The Ba'th Party: A History from the Origins to 1966* (Stanford, CA: Hoover Institution Press, 1976), 14, 39, 49–51; Hizb al-Ba'th al-'Arabi al-Ishtiraki, *Nidal al-Ba'th fi Sabil al-Wahda, al-Hurriya, al-Ishtirakiya* I (*Watha'iq Hizb al-Ba'th al-'Arabi al-Ishtiraki*) (Beirut: Dar al-Tali'ah, 1963), 225, 239; *Al-Ba'th wa-Qadiyat Filastin*, 4; 'Abd al-'Aziz Amin Musa, *Hizb al-Ba'th al-'Arabi al-Ishtiraki fi Filastin wa-Dawrihi fi al-Harka al-Wataniya al-Filastiniya: 1948–1982* (Jerusalem: al-Markaz al-Qawmi lil-Dirasat wa-al-I'lam, 2008), 33–35. I was unable to locate a record of how many volunteers the Ba'th actually sent to Palestine.

171. *Nidal al-Ba'th I*, 234; Al-Hindi, "Jaysh al-Inqadh (1948–1949), Part I," 35–36. In Lebanon, as of April 25, 1948, the Permanent Palestine Office collected a total of 1,700,038.40 Lebanese liras. See *Bayrut*, 30 April 1948, in American Legation–Beirut, *Review of the Local Arabic Press*, 30 April 1948, in Hoover Institution Library and Archives [HILA].

172. Devlin, *Ba'th Party*, 49; Thompson, *Justice Interrupted*, 216–17.

173. Michel Aflak, "The Tragedy of Palestine and Amending the Syrian Constitution," *al-Ba'th*, vol. 212, 16 November 1947, in *Al-Ba'th wa-Qadiyat Filastin*, 41.

174. Devlin, *Ba'th Party*, 49; *Nidal al-Ba'th I*, 225.

175. Hizb al-Ba'th al-'Arabi al-Ishtiraki, *Al-Ba'th wa-Qadiyat Filastin*, 4–5.

176. Like the leftist Ba'th, the Muslim Brotherhood in Egypt, for example, also blamed the Egyptian government for collaborating with colonialism. See Thompson, *Justice Interrupted*, 150–77.

177. Pamphlet from 2 December 1947 in *Nidal al-Ba'th I*, 227; pamphlet from 15 February 1948 in *Nidal al-Ba'th I*, 243–44.

178. Pamphlet from 21 December 1947 in *Nidal al-Ba'th I*, 229; Salah al-Din al-Bitar, "Saving Palestine and Collective Mobilization," 21 December 1948, in *Nidal al-Ba'th I*, 232; pamphlet from 23 January 1948 in *Nidal al-Ba'th I*, 235; pamphlet from 15 February 1948 in *Nidal al-Ba'th I*, 243.

179. Pamphlet from 23 January 1948 in *Nidal al-Ba'th I*, 238.

180. Al-Bitar, "Saving Palestine," 232.

181. Pamphlet from 23 January 1948 in *Nidal al-Ba'th I*, 238.

182. Al-Bitar, "Saving Palestine," 232.

183. Pamphlet from 2 December 1947 in *Nidal al-Ba'th I*, 228.

184. Shakir al-'As, "Sentiments, Sayings, and Deeds of the Partition Decision which Occurred," *al-Ba'thi,* vol. 210, 3 January 1948, in *Al-Ba'th wa-Qadiyat Filastin,* 64.

185. Ibid., 64–65.

186. Ibid., 65–66.

187. H. J., "The Palestine Problem and the Beginning of the Arab Resurrection," *al-Ba'thi,* vol. 216, 10 January 1948, in *Al-Ba'th wa-Qadiyat Filastin,* 67.

188. Ibid., 68.

189. Ibid., 69.

190. Ibid., 69.

191. 'A 'A, "Victory in Palestine Is Inseparable and if It Is Separable then It Is a Total Loss," 9 February 1948, *al-Ba'thi,* in *Al-Ba'th wa-Qadiyat Filastin,* 80–81.

192. Pamphlet from 2 December 1947 in *Nidal al-Ba'th I,* I, 227; pamphlet from 15 February 1948 in *Nidal al-Ba'th I,* I, 244.

193. Al-Bitar, "Saving Palestine," 230.

194. Ibid., 231. See Stefan Wild, "National Socialism in the Arab near East between 1933 and 1939," *Die Welt des Islams* 25, no. 1/4 (1985): 126–73; Achcar, *Arabs and the Holocaust,* 67; Israel Gershoni, "Introduction: An Analysis of Arab Responses to Fascism and Nazism in Middle Eastern Studies," in *Arab Responses to Fascism and Nazism: Attraction and Repulsion,* ed. Israel Gershoni (Austin: University of Texas Press, 2014), 22–23.

195. The word jihad in its meaning as "struggle" occasionally appears in Ba'th publications.

196. Sela, "Tsava ha-Hatsala ba-Galil," 210; article from *Zaman,* 11 March 1948, quoted in an intelligence report from 14 March 1948, in CZA S25/8996.

197. Al-'Arif, *Nakbat Filastin,* Part I, 102. The Arab press reported that a third of the Lebanese volunteers were Christians. The Haganah received reports about a Maronite Lebanese unit named after the Lebanese president Bashara al-Khuri. See report dated 7 April 1948 in HA 105/216G; Haganah intelligence report from 7 April 1948 in HA 105/216G; "Volunteers Detachment on Way to Palestine," 9 March 1948, Sharq al-Adna Radio, in SWB, no. 42, 18 March 1948, 58.

198. The journal was edited by Ja'afr Sharf al-Din, son of a prominent Shi'i cleric. Nonetheless, the publication was nonsectarian, and in fact purported to unite the different segments of Lebanese society and Arabs more broadly. See Majid Hamid 'Abas al-Hadrawi, "The Lebanese *al-Ma'ad* Journal, 1945–1948: A Historical Study," in *Dirasat Tarikhiya* ("Semi-annual journal issued by Department of Historical Studies in Bayt al-Hikma-Baghdad"), 131–62.

199. ʿAli Nasir al-Din, "Oh Arabs," *al-Maʿad*, December 1947. From the collection at the American University in Beirut. The translation is based on the version found in ALA compounds, in IDFA 4/100001/1957.

200. Ibid.

201. "Oh Arabs," in IDFA 4/100001/1957.

202. "Beirut Summary for the Month of December 1947, No. 16," 2, in TNA 371/68489. According to Haganah intelligence the bulk of volunteers were from Beirut (about 1,700 men), and another 350 men came from the northern province. See "Arab Military Preparations According to the Arab Press."

203. Ahmad Badran, *Al-Ittijah al-Wahdawi fi Fikr ʿAli Nasir al-Din* (Beirut: al-Markaz al-ʿArabi lil-Abhath wa-al-Tawthiq, 1996), 37.

204. Muhammad Shayyaa, *ʿAli Nasir al-Din: Safahat min al-Fikr al-Qawmi al-ʿArabi* (Beirut: Dar Sadir, 1993), 18–20.

205. Shayyaa, *ʿAli Nasir al-Din*, 20–25; Albert Hourani, *Syria and Lebanon: A Political Essay* (London: Oxford University Press, 1946), 197–98; Khoury, *Syria and the French Mandate*, 400–401, 417. Khoury does not list Nasir al-Din as one of the founders of the league.

206. Nasir al-Din's approach echoed that of Ottoman reformers before the First World War. After the Balkan Wars in 1913–14, members of the Committee of Union and Progress (CUP) who deposed Sultan Abdulhamid II in 1908 argued that diplomacy had to give way to defending the rights of the empire in the battlefield. See Mustafa Aksakal, *The Ottoman Road to War in 1914: The Ottoman Empire and the First World War* (Cambridge: Cambridge University Press, 2010), 19–41

207. Nasir al-Din, "Diplomacy and the Work of the Resolved Nations," *al-Maʿad*, January 1948. From the collection at the American University in Beirut.

208. Ibid.

209. Originally from al-Tayyibah village in Lebanon, the al-Asʿad family were part of the Banu ʿAli al-Saghir tribe (also known as Banu Bishara) and until the nineteenth century held only limited political power. At some point the family managed to increase its landholdings, thus also broadening the size of its rural client base. By the early 1950s, the family owned 3,700 acres in Jabal ʿAmil. See Rodger Shanahan, *Shiʿa of Lebanon: Clans, Parties and Clerics* (London: Tauris Academic Studies, 2005), 41; ʿAdnan Muhsin Dahir, Riyad Ghannam, *Al-Muʿjam al-Niyabi al-Lubnani: Sirat wa-Tarajim Aʿdaʾ al-Majalis al-Niyabiyah wa-ʿAdaʾ Majalis al-Idarah fi Mutasarrifiyat Jabal Lubnan, 1861–2006* (Beirut: ʿA. Dahir & R. Ghannam, 2007), 42–45.

210. Reuven Erlich, *Bi-Sevakh ha-Levanon: Mediniyutan shel ha-Tenu'ah ha-Tsiyonit ve-shel Medinat Yisra'el Kelape Levanon, 1918–1958* (Tel-Aviv: Tsahal, Hotsa'at Ma'arakhot, 2000), 48.

211. Yael Zerubavel, *Recovered Roots: Collective Memory and the Making of Israeli National Tradition* (Chicago: University of Chicago Press, 1995), 39–47.

212. Erlich, *Bi-Sevakh ha-Levanon*, 51–52; Nahmani and Weitz, *Yosef Nahmani*, 291; Nakdimon Rogel, *Parashat Tel-Hai: Te'udot la-Haganat ha-Galil ha-'Elyon be-Taraf (1919–1920)* (Jerusalem: ha-Sifriyah ha-Tsiyonit, 1994), 261.

213. Erlich, *Bi-Sevakh ha-Levanon*, 55–56.

214. Ibid., 57–58; Nahmani and Weitz, *Yosef Nahmani*, 202, 208, 224.

215. Erlich, *Bi-Sevakh ha-Levanon*, 58; Nahmani and Weitz, *Yosef Nahmani*, 228.

216. Erlich, *Bi-Sevakh ha-Levanon*, 272.

217. Quoted in Erlich, *Bi-Sevakh ha-Levanon*, 273.

218. Kayalı, *Arabs and Young Turks*, 185–92.

219. Ahmad al-As'ad pamphlet, January 3, 1948 [Hebrew translation], in IDFA 1/1058/1952.

220. Ibid.

221. According to several traditions, during the crusaders' conquest of the village in 1153 the head was transferred to Fustat (Cairo) for safekeeping. See Moshe Gil, *A History of Palestine, 634–1099* (Cambridge: Cambridge University Press, 1992), 193–94; R. Hartmann and B. Lewis, "'Āskalān," *Encyclopaedia of Islam*, 2nd ed., ed. P. Bearman, Th. Bianquis, C. E. Bosworth, E. van Donzel, and W. P. Heinrichs (Leiden: Brill, 1960–2004).

222. Prominent religious figures in Jabal 'Amil, like the cleric 'Abd al-Husayn Sharaf al-Din, who was based out of Sour, also participated in the mobilization attempts. See Muhammad Kurani, *Al-Judhur al-Tarikhiya lil-Muqawama al-Islamiya fi Jabal 'Amil* (Beirut: Dar al-Wasilah, 1993), 294–95.

223. Shanahan, *Shi'a of Lebanon*, 23–25; Stefan Winter, *The Shiites of Lebanon under Ottoman Rule, 1516–1788* (Cambridge: Cambridge University Press, 2010), 140–43.

224. "Ahmad al-As'ad pamphlet."

225. Ibid.

226. "Ahmad Bek al-As'ad," Haganah intelligence report, in HA 105/215.

227. Erlich, *Bi-Sevakh ha-Levanon*, 272–73.

228. On May 22, an IDF unit demolished al-As'ad's grand house in al-Tayyibah, across the Lebanese border. Apparently, some of al-As'ad's Jewish acquaintances opposed this action and argued that he had been forced to adopt an anti-Zionist position.

See Erlich, *Bi-Sevakh ha-Levanon*, 272–74; *Al-Hadith*, 24–25 May 1948, in American Legation–Beirut, *Review of the Local Arabic Press*, 25 May 1948, in HILA. Al-As'ad's opponents claimed that the destruction of his house was done with his consent in order to erase the shame of selling lands to the Zionist movement, and that the Jews intended to build him an even grander house to compensate him. See Haganah intelligence from May 1948, in HA 105/31.

229. 'Amir Hasik, *Min Ma'sat Filastin* (Baghdad: Matba'at al-Ma'arif, 1960), 15, 193. Copy from the collection at the Institute for Palestine Studies, Beirut.

230. "More Volunteers to Be Trained in Syria," in SWB, no. 32, 8 January 1948, 55.

231. Hasik, *Min Ma'sat Filastin*, 15–16.

232. "'Entire Division' Trained in Iraq," 22 December 1947, Sharq al-Adna Radio, in SWB, no. 31, 1 January 1948, 72.

233. British Consulate, Mosul to J. C. B. Richmond, Esq., Oriental Counsellor, British Embassy, Baghdad, "Palestine Policy . . . ," 10 September 1947, in TNA FO 624/124.

234. Ibid.

235. Jam'iyat Inqadh Filastin, *A'mal Jam'iyat Inqadh Filastin Khilal Sana 1948* (Baghdad: 1949), 3, in the Iraqi National Library and Archives; Muhammad M. Sawwaf, *Ma'rakat al-Islam: Aw Waqa'i'una fi Filastin Bayna al-Ams wa al-Yawm* (Mecca: 1969), 163; Ibrahim al-Marashi and Sammy Salama, *Iraq's Armed Forces: An Analytical History* (London: Routledge, 2008), 54.

236. Sawwaf, *Ma'rakat al-Islam*, 163; Muhammad M. Sawwaf, *Min Sijill Dhikrayati* (Cairo: Dar al-I'tisam, 1987), 169; *A'mal Jam'iyat Inqadh Filastin*, 3, 20.

237. *A'mal Jam'iyat Inqadh Filastin*, 20.

238. Ibid., 28.

239. Ibid., 7, 10–11, 20.

240. Al-Sawwaf was a student of one of Iraq's most prominent Sunni leaders, Sheikh Amjad al-Zahawi, who was also affiliated with the Association for Saving Palestine.

241. Sawwaf, *Min Sijill Dhikrayati*, 113, 176.

242. Muslim ibn al-Hajjaj al-Qushayri and Muhammad Mahdi Sharif, *Sahih Muslim: The Authentic Hadiths of Muslim* (Beirut: Dar al-Kutub al-'Ilmiyah, 2012), 722.

243. Salman Shina, *Mi-Bavel le-Tsiyon: Zikhronot ve-Hashkafot* (Tel Aviv: 1955), 134.

244. Ibid.

245. *A'mal Jam'iyat Inqadh Filastin*, 7, 10–11; Al'Arif, *Nakbat Filastin*, Part I, 49.

246. Sawwaf, *Ma'rakat al-Islam*, 164–65; Sawwaf, *Min Sijill Dhikrayati*, 176–77.

247. *A'mal Jam'iyat Inqadh Filastin*, 7–8, 19; Sawwaf, *Ma'rakat al-Islam*, 74–175; Al-'Arif, *Nakbat Filastin*, Part I, 51.

248. Cypher/OTP—Departmental, "From Bagdad to Foreign Office," 27 January 1948, in TNA FO 371/68365.

249. Cypher/OTP—Departmental, "From Bagdad to Foreign Office," 16 January 1948, in TNA FO 371/68365.

250. Sawwaf, *Min Sijill Dhikrayati*, 178; Al-'Arif, *Nakbat Filastin*, Part I, 49–50.

251. British Embassy Bagdad, "No. 69: Note Verbale," 31 January 1948, in TNA FO 371/68367.

252. "Iraqi Premier's Statement," 8 December 1947, Arab News Agency, in SWB, no. 29, 11 December 1947, 46.

253. Ibid.

254. For more on the theme of Palestine mobilization in Iraq as a strategy to curb anticolonial protest, see chapter 3.

255. Al-'Arif, *Nakbat Filastin*, Part I, 50.

CHAPTER 2

1. For the Egyptian sociopolitical education of soldiers in the nineteenth century, see Khaled Fahmy, *All the Pasha's Men: Mehmed Ali, His Army, and the Making of Modern Egypt* (Cambridge: Cambridge University Press, 1997). For the Transjordanian army, see Joseph Massad, *Colonial Effects: The Making of National Identity in Jordan* (New York: Columbia University Press, 2001). For the Yishuv armed forces, see Ben-Eliezer, *Making of Israeli Militarism*.

2. See, for example, Morris, *1948*, 98, 405.

3. Parts of this chapter were originally published by Berghahn Books in *Israel Studies Review* 30, no. 1 (2015).

4. Some scholars have argued that Labor Zionism and the Revisionist Movement were more similar than has been generally accepted. Moreover, they argued that Ben-Gurion's ideology was not altogether different than that of Jabotinsky's. This is a plausible assertion, but one for which evidence is lacking. Here, I argue that on the *discursive* level, Labor Zionist propaganda—which was vastly different than Revisionist propaganda before 1948—came to imitate Revisionist propaganda in 1948–49. For similarities between the movements, see Avi Shlaim, *The Iron Wall: Israel and the Arab World* (New York: W. W. Norton, 2001), 11–22; Segev, *State at Any Cost*, 211–73.

5. Tom Segev, *One Palestine, Complete: Jews and Arabs under the Mandate* (New York: Metropolitan Books, 2000), 382–87, 471–72; Shapira, *Herev ha-Yonah,* 339–41; Shapira, *Land and Power,* 170–71, 298–310; Meir Chazan, "The Dispute in Mapai over 'Self-Restraint' and 'Purity of Arms' during the Arab Revolt," *Jewish Social Studies* 15, no. 3 (2009): 98–107; *Anu ha-Homa* 3, published by the Free Pioneers Fighting in Germany, ca. 1948, 9–10, in YIVO.

6. Tom Pessah argued that while Zionism as a settler-colonial ideology may have been predisposed to expulsion, ideology on its own is insufficient to explain the nakba. Explicit orders to expel Arabs were rare in 1948; nevertheless, Pessah suggested that battle orders used purposely vague language on how to treat civilians. This, in turn, "allowed soldiers to leave 'on the outskirts of cognition' . . . the meaning of their actions—violence which engendered the flight of civilians and created a new ethnic reality, and not only military achievements" (155–56). In this chapter I argue that in addition to vague battle orders and the general contours of the Zionist ideology, direct political indoctrination was instrumental in soldiers' conduct. See Tom Pessah, "'Kravot Lo Kashim': Eykh Higdiru Hayalim Yisra'elim et Girush ha-Falastinim be-1948," in *Mifgashim: Historyah ve-Antropologyah shel ha-Merhav ha-Yisra'eli-Falastini,* ed. Daphna Hirsch (Tel Aviv: Van Leer Institute; Hakibbutz Hamechuad, 2019), 147–75.

7. The claim that Nazi and antisemitic propaganda was widespread in the Middle East during (and following) the Second World War is advanced by several scholars, primarily relying on the collaboration of Amin al-Husayni and several other Arab nationalists, with the Nazis as proof. Nevertheless, the evidence they present about the actual *dissemination* of such propaganda in the Middle East is scant at best. A better case could be made that antisemitism only became prevalent in the Arab world after the 1948 war. See Jeffrey Herf, *Nazi Propaganda for the Arab World* (New Haven, CT: Yale University Press, 2009); Morris, *1948,* 8, 393–94. For the counterclaim, see Wien, *Arab Nationalism,* 172–97; Achcar, *Arabs and the Holocaust;* René Wildangel, "The Invention of 'Islamofascism': Nazi Propaganda to the Arab World and Perceptions from Palestine," *Die Welt des Islams* 52 (2012): 526–43; Alexander Flores, "The Arabs as Nazis? Some Reflections on 'Islamofascism' and Arab Anti-Semitism," *Die Welt des Islams* 52 (2012): 450–70; Israel Gershoni and James Jankowski, *Confronting Fascism in Egypt: Dictatorship Versus Democracy in the 1930s* (Stanford, CA: Stanford University Press, 2010); Orit Bashkin, "Iraqi Shadows, Iraqi Lights: Anti-Fascist and Anti-Nazi Voices in Monarchic Iraq, 1932–1941," in Gershoni, *Arab Responses to Fascism and Nazism,* 145–50.

8. See pamphlets included in the Library of Congress's Eltaher Collection: Munir Sharif, *Al-Yahud wa-Tarikhuhum wa-al-Tariqa al-Daruriya lil-Takhallus Minhum* (Jerusalem: al-Matba'at al-Iqtisadiya, 1947); *Khatar al-Yahud 'ala Filastin al-Muqaddasa wa-al-Aqtar al-'Arabiya: Nida' wa-Bayan min Filastin al-'Arabiya al-Islamiya al-Mujahida ila Kull Muslim wa-ila Kull 'Arabi fi Mashariq al-Ard wa-Magharibiha* (undated); *Taqsim Filastin wa-Insha' Dawla fiha: Qada' 'ala Mustaqbal al-'Arab: Marami al-Yahud wa-Ahdafuhum* (al-Matba'at al-Salfiya, 1947). For a radio broadcast with anti-Jewish themes: "Arab Youth Threatens Vengeance on Jews," 8 May 1948.

9. See 1947–48 issues of *Majallat al-Ikhwan al-Muslimun* (Cairo); Gershoni and Jankowski, *Confronting Fascism*, 234–66.

10. Yehuda Slutsky and Shaul Avigur, *Sefer Toldot ha-Haganah*, vol. 3, part II (Jerusalem: ha-Sifriyah ha-Tsiyonit, 1954), 1267–70; Ehud Gross, "Military, Democracy, and Education," in *The Military in the Service of Society and Democracy: The Challenge of the Dual-Role Military*, ed. Daniella Ashkenazy (Westport, CT: Greenwood Press, 1994), 56, 62.

11. While scholarship on sociopolitical training in armies tends to differentiate between "education" and "indoctrination," I contend that such a division is unuseful. Political themes were sometimes disguised as educational ones and vice versa. See Stephen D. Westbrook, "Sociopolitical Training in the Military: A Framework for Analysis," in *The Political Education of Soldiers*, ed. Morris Janowitz and Stephen D. Westbrook (Beverly Hills: Sage, 1983), 16.

12. Restraint was also justified on moral grounds. See Shapira, *Land and Power*, 234–57; Meir Chazan, "Dispute in Mapai."

13. Zehava Ostfeld, *Tsava Nolad: Shelavim 'Ikariyim bi-Veniyat ha-Tsava be-Hanhagato shel David Ben-Gurion* (Tel Aviv: Misrad ha-Bitahon, 1994), 437; Slutsky and Avigur, *Sefer Toldot ha-Haganah*, 1267–70. The main endeavor of the new branch was the publication of the journal *Ma'arakhot* (Campaigns), which focused on military thought.

14. The term "Palestinians" was not used in official IDF publications until at least the late 1970s.

15. Ze'ev Drori, *Utopyah be-Madim: Terumat Tsahal le-Hityashvut, li-Kelitat ha-'Aliyah ule-Hinukh be-Reshit Yeme ha-Medinah* (Sedeh-Boker: ha-Merkaz le-Moreshet Ben-Gurion, 2000), 135.

16. Palmachai, "Our Education Officers," *Bamahane*, 5 August 1948. The Soviets were the first to incorporate permanent political officers, *politruks*, into their army.

Those officers indoctrinated soldiers with officially sanctioned political views and also monitored the soldiers' behavior and the state of morale in units. See Roger R. Reese, *Why Stalin's Soldiers Fought: The Red Army's Military Effectiveness in World War II* (Lawrence: University Press of Kansas, 2011), 190–98.

17. A few months after the April restructuring, the unit changed its name again to Education Service (*shirut tarbut*), but both names were used interchangeably. The literal translation of *mahleket tarbut* is "culture department," but "education department" seems to better capture the purpose of the unit. Ostfeld, *Tsava Nolad,* 437; Drori, *Utopyah be-Madim*, 137.

18. Ostfeld, *Tsava Nolad*, 438; Drori, *Utopyah be-Madim,* 139.

19. Ibid.

20. I compiled this biographical information based on untitled minutes from a 1949 meeting of education officers in IDFA 137/1042/1949; Zafrira Din, "Heker ha-Moral ba-Haganah," *'Iyunim Be-Tkumat Yisra'el* 9 (1999): 70–86; David Tidhar, *Entsiklopedyah le-Halutse ha-Yishuv u-Vonav: Demuyot u-Temunot,* accessed 3 May 2016, www.tidhar. tourolib.org/.

21. Drori, *Utopyah be-Madim*, 144. Yisrael Rozenson, *Kotvim 'ba-Mivtsa", 'ba-Mishlat', 'ba-Mivtsar': 'al Bit'one Yehidot be-Tsahal be-Tashah-Tashat* (Jerusalem: Karmel, 2016), 21–23.

22. Education Department / Hasbra, Dov Berger, Chief Hasbara Officer to Education Officers, "Attn: Carrying Out Hasbara Actions," 14 August 1948, in IDFA 10/284/1949.

23. Sh. Farber, "Culture and Hasbara," *ha-Sherut ha-Klali* (Brigade 4 / Education), in HA 80/774/3.

24. For the Palmach definition of activism, see Palmach Pamphlet no. 37 (December 1945), 45, in Palmach Archives [PA].

25. Education Department, Chapter Headings for Hasbara, "Bravery Map," 24 February 1949, in Israel National Library [INL]; Education Department, Chapter Headings for Hasbara, "The Israelite Exodus from Egypt and the Conquering of the Country," 30 March 1949, in INL; Education Service, "Kabalat Shabbat [Trumpeldor]," 13 March 1949, in KMA 15/12/3. Self-sacrifice was a recurrent theme in education materials, often embodied in the story of Joseph Trumpeldor. Killed by Arabs in 1920 while defending the settlement of Tel Hai, he was commemorated for his alleged last words, "Never mind, it is good to die for our country."

26. Education Service, "Kabalat Shabbat [the Jewish Legion]," 4 March 1949, in

KMA 15/12/3. See also Moshe Belinson, "The Purpose of the Battle," in *Ba-Mivtsaʿ: Ha-Hayal, Gedud 4., Hefah* (Carmeli Brigade pamphlet, early 1948), no. 1, 1, in Stanford University Libraries; A. Rits, "Seminar for Mahal Personnel," *Ba-Galil* (Bulletin of Brigade Seven), April 1949, 27, in IDFA 48/1147/2002. The view that the establishment of the legion constituted a major shift in Jewish history was one borrowed directly from Jabotinsky. The view was mocked by Labor Zionism in Palestine for decades before its leaders eventually adopted it during the 1948 war. See Luz, *Wrestling with an Angel*, 181; Shapira, *Land and Power*, 97.

27. Morris, *1948*, 102–3.

28. Tsadok Eshel and Zvi Sinai, *Hativat Karmeli Be-Milhemet Ha-Komemiyut* (Tel Aviv: Maʿarakhot, 1973), 55–57.

29. Morris, *1948*, 103.

30. Bet-He, "Conversaion B," 16, *Ba-Mivtsaʿ: Ha-Hayal, Gedud 4., Hefah*.

31. See Yoram Kaniuk, *Tashah* (Tel Aviv: Yedioth Ahronoth, 2010), 46. *Volokolamsk Highway* was published as *Anshey Panfilov* (Panfilov's Men) in Hebrew in 1946. It was also used in Palmach and Golani education materials. See Palmach Pamphlet nos. 12–13 (November–December 1943), 30, in PA; HQ Brigade 1 [Golani], "Field Bulletin No. 13," 8 January 1949, in KMA 15/2/1.

32. Ibid. In another story conveyed in the same pamphlet, a soldier afraid to shoot at the enemy is coached by his comrades, who explain to him that the enemy would not hesitate to shoot and kill him. See also Patrolman H. L., "Seriously and Jokingly," *Ba-Mivtsaʿ: Ha-Hayal, Gedud 4., Hefah*, 19–20, in IDFA 43/1147/2002.

33. Untitled article, *Mahats* (Bulletin of the Staff Company, Battalion A, Combat Corps Jerusalem), March 1948, 6, in IDFA 63/1147/2002.

34. Paul Fussell, *Wartime: Understanding and Behavior in the Second World War* (New York: Oxford University Press. 1989), 119. For the Israeli soldiers' reaction to Arabs mutilating bodies, see Kaniuk, *Tashah*, 57, 109.

35. Education Service, "Kabalat Shabbat [Convoy of 35]," 4 February 1949, in KMA 15/12/3.

36. Another possible translation: "The Morality in the Israelite Army."

37. "Morality in Israel's Army" [31 May 1948–8 October 1948], in IDFA 259/1003/1950.

38. Ibid.

39. Ibid.

40. "Morality in Israel's Army." The depiction of Amalek in the pamphlet is in line with the *Peshat* (literal) commentary of the biblical story. See Shalom Carmy, "Origin

of Nations and the Shadow of Violence," in *War and Peace in the Jewish Tradition*, ed. Lawrence H. Schiffman and Joel B. Wolowelsky (New York: Michael Scharf Publication Trust of the Yeshiva University Press, 2007), 181–82, 186–87.

41. The biblical story differs from the one laid out in the pamphlet. According to Samuel 1:15–34, Saul defied God's order and allowed his men to enjoy the Amalekite spoils. He also refrained from killing the Amalekite king until reproved by God for not doing so.

42. The biblical text indeed mentions this prohibition, and so does Midrash and medieval exegeses. See Moshe Sokolow, "What Is This Bleeting [sic] of Sheep in My Ears," in Schiffman and Wolowelsky, *War and Peace in the Jewish Tradition*, 134–38, 141–42.

43. It is noteworthy that scholars of war in biblical times usually have distinguished only between discretionary war (*milḥemet reshut*) and war by commandment (*milḥemet mitsvah*). War of complete extermination (*milḥemet ḥerem*) was not considered a type of its own, and it was typically associated with war by commandment. See David Shatz, "Introduction," in Schiffman and Wolowelsky, *War and Peace in the Jewish Tradition*, xv.

44. It is unclear from where this biblical commentary is taken. A different view is presented in the *Bamahane* article below.

45. It is possible there are pages missing from this pamphlet. I could not locate any additional pages in the IDF Archives.

46. "Morality in Israel's Army." This also seems in line with *Peshat* and other biblical exegeses. See Sokolow, "What Is This Bleeting [sic] of Sheep in My Ears," 135, 141–42, 150–51.

47. An article from the education department's weekly *Bamahane* stressed: "A war by commandment is a war in which Israel is ordered by the Torah to fight the 'Seven Nations' of Canaan and Amalek, and also *war against an enemy who plots against the nation and the country*" (emphasis in original). The article also stressed that in a war by commandment, the leader must first make a peace offer to the enemy, albeit stipulating the right to levy taxes and asserting that the enemy must completely submit to the conquering force. If the enemy refuses the offer and its attendant conditions, then it is permissible to go on the offensive. See Ri-Sh, "The Laws of War in Israel," *Bamahane*, 24 June 1948. Ben-Gurion also compared the Arab armies to the enemies of the Israelites, including Amalek. See David Ben-Gurion, *Be-Hilahem Yisra'el* (Tel Aviv: Mifleget Po'ale Erets-Yisra'el, 1950), 184, 294, 340.

48. "A Message by the Palestine's Chief Rabbi, Rabbi Y. A. HaLevi Herzog to the Defenders," *Ba-'Igud* (A Religious Sports Association *'Eli-Tsur*), 6 February 1948, vol. 9, 6, in IDFA 22/1147/2002. For educational materials produced for religious Zionists that present the 1948 war as a war by commandment, see "I Saved Myself," *Ba-'Igud*, April–May 1948, vol. 11, 19, in IDFA 22/1147/2002; "Folklore: We Left for the Base," *Ba-'Igud*, March–April 1948, vol. 10, 11, in IDFA 22/1147/2002.

49. "Message by the Palestine's Chief Rabbi."

50. This is a biblical reference to Lamentations 4:3. According to most interpretations, the verse is a reference to the supposed behavior of the ostrich, which does not protect its offspring in a time of danger but chooses to save itself.

51. Boaz P., "Giving Our Thoughts on Pillage," *Ba-'Igud*, July–August 1948, vol. 14, 18, in IDFA 22/1147/2002.

52. Ibid., 19–20. According to Israeli sources, IDF soldiers perpetrated at least a dozen rapes during the war. Amos Kenan, an Israeli war veteran who became a famous writer, wrote in 1989 that while his unit was camped inside the Lydda airfield, "those of us who couldn't restrain ourselves would go into the prison compounds to fuck Arab women." Palestinian sources are often silent on the matter, but it is clear that fear of rape was a major factor in the flight of Palestinians. See Morris, *1948*, 405–6; Haganah Intelligence, "Attn: Abuse of Arab Women," 19 May 1948, in HA 105/358; Frances S. Hasso, "Modernity and Gender in Arab Accounts of the 1948 and 1967 Defeats," *IJMES* 32, no. 4 (November 2000): 491–510; Amos Kenan, "The Legacy of Lydda: Four Decades of Blood Vengeance," *The Nation*, 6 February 1989.

53. M. B., "Remember What Was Done to You . . . ," *Ba-'Igud*, December 1948–January 1949, vol. 19, 11, in IDFA 22/1147/2002.

54. Ibid.

55. Ibid.

56. The familiarity of the authors with both the biblical text and medieval exegeses is apparent in that the texts echoed debates among Bible commentators about the meaning of Maimonides's silence when it came to Amalek. Some saw this silence as a concession that Amalek still existed (unlike the Seven Nations of Canaan), and hence war by commandment could still be sanctioned. A few scholars have gone as far as to suggest that any enemy of the Jewish people can be considered Amalek. See Carmy, "Origin of Nations," 173–77; Norman Lamm, "Amalek and the Seven Nations," in Schiffman and Wolowelsky, *War and Peace in the Jewish Tradition*, 214–20.

57. Luz, *Wrestling with an Angel,* 22; Schiffman and Wolowelsky, "Introduction," in *War and Peace in the Jewish Tradition,* xxi; Carmy, "Origin of Nations," 168–69, 172–73; Lamm, "Amalek and the Seven Nations," 213–20.

58. It seems "Amalek" was sometimes used as a generic name for an enemy by Jewish communities in the nineteenth and early twentieth centuries. It was also occasionally invoked to convince Jews, in certain conflicts, that to fight for the European nation in which they resided was to fight against an enemy of the Jewish people. See Penslar, *Jews and the Military,* 59, 153, 207, 252; Marsha L. Rozenblit, *Reconstructing a National Identity: The Jews of Habsburg Austria during World War I* (New York: Oxford University Press, 2001), 43–54.

59. Luz, *Wrestling with an Angel,* 203–4.

60. Segev, *One Palestine Complete,* 382–84; Shapira, *Land and Power,* 170–71, 298–310; Shapira, *Herev ha-Yonah,* 322, 340.

61. Uri Avnery, who was a soldier in the Givati brigade, narrated in his memoir how he and his friends were deeply moved when they listened to the combat bulletins read aloud by their commanders. See Uri Avnery, *1948: A Soldier's Tale—The Bloody Road to Jerusalem* (Oxford: Oneworld, 2008), 113, 181; N'eima Barzel, *'Ad Kelot umi-Neged: Ha-Mifgash ben Manhige Mered ha-Geta'ot le-Ven ha-Hevrah ha-Yisre'elit* (Jerusalem: Ha-Sifriyah ha-Tsiyonit, 1998), 106, 109; Dina Porat, *The Fall of a Sparrow: The Life and Times of Abba Kovner* (Stanford, CA: Stanford University Press, 2010), 243, 246.

62. Porat, *Fall of a Sparrow,* 244–45, 247. Because of the high level of trust between the commander of the Givati brigade, Shimon Avidan, and Kovner, the bulletins were usually not preapproved by the former.

63. Barzel, *'Ad Kelot,* 104.

64. Ibid., 63, 108.

65. Ibid., 106, 111. Porat argued that "it is an oversimplification to say that World War II directly influenced Kovner." She maintained that "worry and anxiety" better explain his style in the bulletins. See Porat, *Fall of a Sparrow,* 246.

66. Porat, *Fall of a Sparrow,* 250–56; Barzel, *'Ad Kelot,* 105.

67. Givati Brigade, *Daf Kravi* (Tel Aviv: Ofakim, 1962), no. 5.

68. This phrase refers to King Farouk, ruling monarch of Egypt at the time. Given the strong British influence in the country, it was widely believed in Israel that the British were assisting the Egyptian army during the war (a claim shown to be false).

69. Egyptian forces repeatedly attempted to occupy Kibbutz Negba, established

in 1939. Several of the settlement's residents were killed before IDF forces managed to push the Egyptian army out of the area. See Morris, *1948*, 277.

70. Bayt Daras was a Palestinian village twenty miles north of Gaza where fierce fighting between Israeli forces and Egyptian soldiers took place. See Morris, *1948*, 275.

71. In Hebrew, the command "to run over" (*va-yidros*) sounds similar to the pronunciation of the village Bayt Daras.

72. *Daf Kravi*, no. 6.

73. Ibid., no. 9.

74. Ibid., no. 6.

75. In a famous speech from 1942, Stalin himself endorsed hatred, saying that Soviet troops "realize that one cannot defeat the enemy without learning to hate him with every fiber in one's soul." Ilya Ehrenburg, the foremost Soviet wartime propagandist, made the same connection between hatred and love that Kovner would make six years later: "Hatred, as love, is inherent to pure and warm hearts. We hate fascism because we . . . love life. The stronger the love of life is within us, the firmer is our hatred." See Reese, *Why Stalin's Soldiers Fought*, 178.

76. The reception of S. Yizhar's short stories "The Prisoner" and "The Story of Hirbet Hizah" in Israel suggests that in the immediate aftermath of the war, few denied IDF soldiers' brutality, even if they justified it. This changed within a few decades following the war. In fact, Dina Porat, Kovner's biographer, argued that his horror propaganda was not understood literally by most soldiers, and that Kovner saw a strong need for a "humane Jewish military force." Avidan's deputy, Meir Davidson, argued that the soldiers never took Kovner's bulletins as literal instructions on how to deal with the enemy. See Anita Shapira, "Hirbet Hizah: Between Remembrance and Forgetting," *Jewish Social Studies* 7, no. 1 (Autumn 2000): 1–62; Porat, *Fall of a Sparrow*, 239, 248–49.

77. In addition to debates inside the IDF, Kovner's writing was also extensively discussed within his own movement, Hashomer Hatza'ir. See *Yad-Mordekhai ba-Ma'arakhah* (Tel Aviv: Mahleket ha-Tarbut shel Tseva Haganah le-Yisra'el, 1948); Aba Kovner to Party Secretary, Meir Ya'ari et al., undated, in IDFA 905/922/1975; Porat, *Fall of a Sparrow*, 248; Barzel, *'Ad Kelot*, 110.

78. It is unclear whether this was the same education officer from the Carmeli brigade who authored the pamphlet discussed earlier.

79. In other instances as well, the Golani education officer cautioned his soldiers against being excessively cruel. Such "abusive cruelty," he warned, would be "a

disaster" for the IDF. See Golani Brigade, "Fighter's Bulletin," vol. 4, 24 August 1948, in IDFA 14/1147/2002.

80. Education Department, "Hasbara Methods about the Enemy," 4 August 1948, in IDFA 102/6127/1949.

81. This unit was composed of a militarized work force that was deemed essential for the economy and the war effort. Aside from their daily public works tasks, the brigade's men were also deployed to the battlefields. The brigade was responsible for conquering the village al-Tira, next to Haifa. See Yizhak Grinberg, "Hativat 'Avoda Tsva'ait: Ha-Nisayon le-Militerizatsya shel Koh ha-'Avoda be-Milhemet ha-'Atsma'ut," *'Iyunim Be-Tkumat Yisra'el* 8 (1998): 375–97.

82. "Hasbara Methods about the Enemy."

83. Ibid.

84. Penslar, *Jews and the Military*, 125, 134, 156–59.

85. Several Iraqi Jews fought in the Iraqi brigade of the ALA. See Introduction, note 3.

86. Unit for Psychological Research / Center for Research of Public Opinion, "The Lessons the Soldiers Learned in Battle Learned in Battle," April 1950, 8–9, in the Guttman Center Surveys at the Israeli Democracy Institute.

87. "Major-General Y. Yadin," in General Staff / Chief Education Officer-Hasbara, *Education and Morale in the IDF (Debates, Lectures and Methodic Material)*, 21, in IDFA 206/385/1963. I could only locate one report on letters by Iraqi soldiers, which does not allow me to draw any conclusions about this group of soldiers.

88. ID, "The Soldier's Opinion [TSO] Report No. 41A," May 1951, 1, in IDFA 355/535/2004.

89. "Major-General Y. Yadin."

90. Ben-Eliezer, *Making of Israeli Militarism*, 211–12.

91. See chapter 5.

92. Ibid. Yadin presented an opposing view to the Israeli cabinet on April 26, 1950, explaining: "In regard to North African immigrants, they were oppressed by the Arabs in their countries [of birth] to such an extent that their hatred of Arabs is innate, and when we take them to deal with [Palestinian] infiltrators down south etc., they do so gladly." See Israel Ben Dor, "Dimuy ha-Oyev ha-'Arvi ba-Yishv ha-Yehudi uve-Medinat Yisra'el ba-Shanim 1947–1956" (PhD diss., Haifa University, 2003), 171.

93. Z. H., "From the Diary of Nazareth," *Ba-Galil* (Bulletin of Brigade Seven), 12 August 1948, 11, in IDFA 48/1147/2002.

94. D. Ahi-Eliahu, "The Esprit de Corps," *Bamahane*, 12 August 1948.

95. See the header for each bulletin in Givati Brigade, *Daf Kravi.*

96. *Daf Kravi*, no. 18.

97. Front C / Education, "The Battlefield Journal," 19 October 1948, in IDFA 7/1147/2002. Barzel identified the author of this pamphlet as Kovner. See Barzel, *'Ad Kelot*, 109.

98. "Battlefield Journal."

99. Eliezer Libenstein, "The Abomination of Robbery," *Bamahane*, 29 July 1948.

100. For a warning against looting in the Golani, Carmel, and Alexandroni brigades, see Golani Brigade, "Fighter's Bulletin," vol. 4, 24 August 1948, in IDFA 14/1147/2002; "From the Talk of the Day," "A Bit of Truth about Pillage," *Ba-Mivtsaʻ: Ha-Hayal, Gedud 4., Hefah*, vol. 5, June 1948, 9–12, in IDFA 43/1147/2002; Sh. Aminadav, "Pillage," *Ba-Mishlat* (Bulletin of Battalion 33), August 1948, 12–13, in IDFA 55/1147/2002.

101. Palmach Pamphlet no. 60 (April 1948), 30; no. 65 (23 June 1948), 3; no. 62 (18 May 1948), 40–41; no. 67 (19 July 1948), 61–62; no. 68 (30 July 1948), 5, 27–32; no. 69 (11 August 1948), 18–19; no. 70 (23 August 1948), 35, in PA.

102. Rebecca L. Stein, "Israeli Routes through Nakba Landscapes: An Ethnographic Meditation," *Jerusalem Quarterly* 43 (2010): 6–17; Sherene Seikaly, "How I Met My Great-Grandfather: Archives and the Writing of History," *Comparative Studies of South Asia, Africa and the Middle East* 38, no. 1 (2018): 6–20.

103. Dr. Shmuel Landa, "Read and Learn: The Rights of POWs," *Bamahane*, 22 July 1948.

104. Mordechai Tabib, "In Enemy Lines behind Bars," *Bamahane*, 15 July 1948.

105. HQ of Brigade 1 [Golani], "Field Bulletin No. 1," 2 January 1949, in KMA 15/2/1.

106. See Dolbee and Hazkani, "'Impossible Is Not Ottoman.'"

107. Dissenting voices of soldiers, though rare, did appear in unit bulletins at times. After the murder of an Arab young man by soldiers from the Carmeli brigade, one soldier voiced his opposition to the murder in the unit's journal: "The Arab fighter is a barbaric man, unrestrained and cruel. All that is true, but at the end of the day, he is a soldier like us . . . and murderers all around the world are put to the wall [to be executed]." See Rozenson, *Kotvim 'ba-Mivtsaʻ*, 98.

108. Palmach Pamphlet no. 37 (December 1945), 4–10, 46; no. 55 (August 1947), 5; no. 56 (September–October 1947), 8, in PA.

109. Quoted in Zvi Inbar, *Moznayim ve-Herev: Yesodot ha-Mishpat ha-Tsevaʾi*

be-Yisra'el (Tel-Aviv: Ma'arakhot, 2005), 929. See also Palmach Pamphlet no. 68 (30 July 1948), 6, in PA.

110. More commonly, the story of the thirty-five Haganah men was reproduced in education materials to encourage self-sacrifice. One pamphlet stated, "[These men] had fallen while loving. Love is their last whisper, and when they ascend to the altar with the joy of youthfulness, they intend to be a sacrifice of salvation, from which there is no escape." See Education Service, "Kabalat Shabbat [Convoy of 35]." For more on the theme of sacrifice, see Zerubavel, *Recovered Roots*; Kaniuk, *Tashah*, 41–43.

111. Palmach Pamphlet no. 76 (3 November 1948), 46, in PA.

112. Palmach Pamphlet no. 60 (April 1948), 30, in PA.

113. Y. Ben-David letter in Palmach Pamphlet no. 57–28 (January–February 1948), 11, in PA.

114. M. Halevi, "We Are All in Charge," *ha-Mivtsar* (a Monthly Magazine Published by the Tuvia Yeshiva Students Battalion, Jerusalem), vol. 2, September 1948, 8, in IDFA 63/1147/2002. The ultra-orthodox soldiers were yeshiva students conscripted with the consent of the rabbinical leadership. Most were assigned to fortification work while continuing their religious education. See Rozenson, *Kotvim 'ba-Mivtsa'*, 149–51.

115. M. Halevi, "Christianity and Islam—versus Judaism," *ha-Mivtsar*, vol. 2, September 1948, 17.

116. Ibid. See also Herev A-Z-N, "To Learn and Teach," *ha-Mivtsar*, vol. 1, August–September 1948, 10, in IDFA 63/1147/2002.

117. Tuvia Bir, "War and Murder," *ha-Mivtsar*, vol. 2, September 1948, 9

118. Ibid.

119. Ibid. See also M. Meiri, "From the Tree of Thought—I Picked Flowers," *ha-Mivtsar*, vol. 2, September 1948, 10.

120. For Israel's first bid for UN membership, see Shira Robinson, *Citizen Strangers: Palestinians and the Birth of Israel's Liberal Settler State* (Stanford, CA: Stanford University Press, 2013), 36, 74.

121. HQ of Front D, "A Special Annex to Operation Order Horev," December 1948, in IDFA 187/121/1950. Some of these orders had made it to the bulletins of units earlier than December. See Ben-Yemin, "Do Not Lay a Hand on the Loot," *The Battalion: Bulletin of Battalion 54 Southern Brigade*, September 1948, 8, in IDFA 13/1147/2002.

122. *Davar* was the daily newspaper of the Histadrut, but was regarded as the mouthpiece of the ruling party, Mapai.

123. Benny Morris, *The Birth of the Palestinian Refugee Problem Revisited* (Cambridge: Cambridge University Press, 2004), 489.

124. Quoted in Stuart Cohen, *Israel and Its Army: From Cohesion to Confusion* (New York: Routledge, 2007), 153.

125. *'Al zot* pamphlet, in HA 80/P18/4.

126. Palmach Pamphlet no. 69 (11 August 1948), 36, in PA.

127. Ibid.

128. See Walid Khalidi, "Plan Dalet: Master Plan for the Conquest of Palestine," *Journal of Palestine Studies* 18, no. 1 (1988): 4–33; Morris, *1948*, 116–21; Ilan Pappé, *The Ethnic Cleansing of Palestine* (Oxford: Oneworld, 2006): 86–126.

129. Yizhak Avrahami, "The Bells of Nazareth Are Ringing in Hebrew," *Bamahane*, 22 July 1948; Morris, *The Birth*, 309–40.

130. Education Department, Chapter Headings for Hasbara, "Facts and Figures about the Arab Fleeing," 18 July 1948, in IDFA 7/794/1950; Y. Tsalaf, "Behind the Enemy Lines," *Bamahane*, 22 July 1948; Golani Brigade, "Fighter's Bulletin," vol. 4, 24 August 1948, in IDFA 14/1147/2002.

131. Menahem Talmi, "In the Areas of the Beaten Enemy," *Bamahane*, 22 July 1948.

132. Ibid.

133. Ibid.

134. "The Last Bisani," *Bamahane*, 6 October 1949.

135. Education Department, "Straight to the Point: Questions and Answers (Answers to Questions Soldiers Frequently Ask)," 5 April 1948, 1, in IDFA 156/710/1950.

136. Ibid.

137. "In Our World," *Ba-Mivtsa': Ha-Hayal, Gedud 4., Hefah,* vol. 5, June 1948, 4, in IDFA 43/1147/2002. See also Rozenson, *Kotvim 'ba-Mivtsa'*, 94.

138. Education Department, Chapter Headings for Hasbara, "Army Day," 26 June 1949, in IDFA 156/710/1950.

139. "Straight to the Point"; Education Department, Chapter Headings for Hasbara, "The Survey Group: Its Functions and Prospects," 28 September 1949, in INL.

140. Education Department, Chapter Headings for Hasbara, "The Political Assassination in Israel," 26 June 1949, in IDFA 156/710/1950.

141. AB. N. Polack, "The Arab Refugees," in Education Department, *Browsing Pamphlet for the Commander 2*, September 1949, in IDFA 491/721/1972, 24.

142. *'Idud-Support Company of Battalion 53 in the Alexandroni Brigade,* vol. 1, quoted in Rozenson, *Kotvim 'ba-Mivtsa'*, 102. For Ben-Gurion's adoption of the idea,

see David Ben-Gurion, *Be-Hilahem Yisra'el* (Tel Aviv: Mifleget Po'ale Erets-Yisra'el, 1950), 100.

143. "Arab Proverbs on Bravery and War," *Bamahane*, 6 October 1949.

144. Stein, "Israeli Routes through Nakba Landscapes," 9.

145. "Pontifications with the Occupation," *The Battalion: The Journal of Battalion 54*, vol. 9, 21 May 1948, in IDFA 13/1147/2002.

146. Ibid.

147. Ibid. Mockery of Palestinians for supposedly being quick to flee their villages, even if there was no real danger, was a popular theme in education materials. See Bobo, "A Tale of an Arab Village and Its Conqueror," *Niv* (Battalion 23–Brigade 2), vol. 3, November 1948, 10, in IDFA 32/1147/2002.

148. "Pontifications with the Occupation." For a different interpretation, see Rozenson, *Kotvim 'ba-Mivtsa'*, 102–3.

149. Gshur, "Mitnadvey Huts la-Arets," 64–65; Penslar, *Jews and the Military*, 209; see also chapter 5.

150. Gshur, "Mitnadvey Huts la-Arets," 139. Polling from the early 2000s among North American volunteers suggests that almost half were members in Zionist organizations.

151. Gshur, "Mitnadvey Huts la-Arets," 171, 179, 247, 250, 269, 368. For hasbara talks, see "Seminar for Mahal on January 2," in *Frontline* 3, 26 December 1948, 9, in Klau Library [KL], Cincinnati, Hebrew Union College–Jewish Institute of Religion. There were also short-lived publications in French, Spanish, and even Swedish.

152. "Frontline Forum," *Frontline* 1, 25 November 1948, 2, in KL. See also Gshur, "Mitnadvey Huts la-Arets," 367–68.

153. "Instructions for Volunteers from Overseas," in IDFA 19/1042/1949.

154. "Army Negev, Galilee Drives Guarantee Israeli Borders," *Frontline* 1, 25 November 1948, 4, in KL.

155. "Pyjama Party Down South," *Frontline* 1, 25 November 1948, 5, in KL.

156. Ibid.

157. Moshe Pearlman, "U.N., Israel and Arab States," *Frontline* 3, 26 December 1948, 3, in KL.

158. Ibid.

159. Moshe Pearlman, "Egypt's Choice," *Frontline* 4, 9 January 1949, 3, in KL.

160. "The Road of Valour," *Frontline* 3, 26 December 1948, 7, in KL. Penslar demonstrated how, in a semiofficial publication of the Haganah in the United States, the

expulsion of Palestinians was mentioned rather matter-of-factly. See Penslar, *Jews and the Military*, 248–51.

161. David Courtney, "Worth Being Part Of," *Frontline* 2, 12 December 1948, 7, in KL.

162. "From the Arab Press and Radio," *Frontline* 4, 9 January 1949, 7, in KL.

163. Yehuda Lev, "Frontline Falafel," *Frontline* 8, 24 March 1949, 7, in American Jewish Historical Society [AJHS].

164. "Minorities in Israel," *Frontline*, 23 January 1949, 6, in MACHAL and Aliyah Bet Records, I-501, box 8, folder 3, in AJHS.

165. ". . . And Joshua Smote Them with the Edge of the Sword," *Frontline* 4, 9 January 1949, 7, in KL.

166. "Arab POWs," *Frontline* 4, 9 January 1949, 16, in KL.

167. "What Makes an Israeli Citizen," *Frontline* 1, 25 November 1948, 11. Reality on the ground, as chapter 5 demonstrates, was different.

168. H. R. H. King David Makes a Point," *Frontline* 1, 25 November 1948, 5, in KL.

169. Brigade Seven, "HAMITNADEV-A Newsletter for the Volunteer" [English], no. 42, 27 December 1948, 5, in IDFA 48/1147/2002.

170. "Frontline—2114 Years Ago," *Frontline* 3, 26 December 1948, 2, in KL.

171. ". . . And Joshua Smote Them with the Edge of the Sword." Another Jewish war hero commemorated on the pages of *Frontline* was Trumpeldor. See Leo Rissin, "Haganah Day: From Tel Hai to the Kastel," *Frontline* 8, 24 March 1949, 9, in AJHS.

172. "Instructions for Volunteers from Overseas."

173. "Frontline Forum," *Frontline* 2, 12 December 1948, 2, in KL.

174. Sela, "Tsava ha-Hatsala ba-Galil," 210.

175. Al-Hindi, "Jaysh al-Inqadh (1948–1949), Part I," 48–49.

176. Al-Hindi, "Jaysh al-Inqadh (1948–1949), Part I," 48–49; Wasfi al-Tall and Nahid Hatr, *Fi Mujabahat al-Ghazw al-Sahyuni* (Amman: Amanat 'Amman al-Kubra, 1997), 37.

177. Al-Tall and Hatr, *Fi Mujabahat al-Ghazw al-Sihyuni*, 38. A report by a Palestinian informant working for the Haganah who trained in Qatana suggests that at least some trainees received rigorous training in the initial period after the camp was opened. See "Report from a Man Who Trained in the Qatana training Camp in Syria."

178. Fauzi al-Qawuqji, "Memoirs, 1948—Part II," *Journal of Palestine Studies* 2, no. 1 (Autumn 1972): 48; Josh, "Interrogation of a Prisoner Who Was Captured in the Yehiam Battle on 21 January 1948," in HA 105/215A.

179. Gershon Gilad, "History of the ALA," 72, 110, in IDFA 648/922/1975.

180. Haganah intelligence report from January 1948, in HA 105/215. While some

(continued)

British officials intervened to stop the crossing of ALA forces into Palestine, others turned a blind eye. See Parsons, *The Commander*, 210–11.

181. Parsons, *The Commander*, 221, 225; "Special Administrative Order to Platoon Commanders," undated, in IDFA 948/100001/1957.

182. Al-Qawuqji, "Memoirs, 1948—Part II," 4–5.

183. Commander of the First Company to Commander of Hittin Battalion, "Re: Your Letter from 12 February 1948," 13 February 1948, in IDFA 162/100001/1975.

184. Sela, "Tsava ha-Hatsala ba-Galil," 210–11, 249.

185. "Administrative Order No. 4/Sh" [Hebrew translation], in KMA 15/2/4.

186. Ibid.

187. "Document No. 86: Order of the Day No. 1 by Taha al-Hashimi," 24 February 1948, in IDFA 648/922/1975; "Document No. 10: Taha al-Hashimi to the Army Chief of Staff," 21 March 1948, in IDFA 648/922/1975. See also reports about searches for runaway soldiers and lists of deserting soldiers in KMA 15/2/3 and KMA 15/2/2.

188. "Adib al-Shishkali to the Chairman of Acre National Committee" [Hebrew translation], undated, in KMA 15/2/6.

189. Al-Hindi, "Jaysh al-Inqadh (1948–1949), Part II," in *Shu'un Filastiniyah*, no. 24, 116.

190. ALA / Nablus, Jenin and Tulkarm Area / First Yarmuk Battalion, Muhammad Safa, "Daily News" [Hebrew translation], 31 January 1948, in KMA 15/2/2.

191. Parsons, *The Commander*, 221; Al-Hindi, "Jaysh al-Inqadh (1948–1949), Part I," 54; "Fawzi Bek al-Qawuqji Enters Palestine," *al-Difa'*, 10 March 1948.

192. S. Souki, "With the Arab Army Somewhere in Palestine," [English] undated, in HA 105/216B.

193. Ibid.

194. Al-Hindi, "Jaysh al-Inqadh (1948–1949), Part I," 51–52.

195. "Broadcast of the ALA Forces," *al-Difa'*, 8 April 1948; "A Party for the Opening of ALA Forces Broadcasting Station," *al-Difa'*, 12 April 1948.

196. "Party for the Opening of ALA Forces Broadcasting Station."

197. In late March 1948 Nasir al-Din attempted to find an Arab who spoke Hebrew and could take over the Hebrew language propaganda of the ALA. See "Document No. 1: File of the Supervisor on Security and Espionage in the Haifa HQ" [Hebrew translation], in IDFA 648/922/1975.

198. Al-Majlis al-Thaqafi al-Lubnani al-Shimali, *Trablus fi al-Dhakira* (Lebanon: Safadi Foundation, 2010), 121; Herf, *Nazi Propaganda for the Arab World*, 253.

199. "Al-Inqaz Broadcasts," 17 April 1948, al-Inqaz Radio, in SWB, no. 46, 15 April 1948, 67.

200. "A Notice from the Salvation Leadership on the Results of the Battle in Nuris," *al-Difaʿ*, 21 March 1948.

201. "Kawukji Says Zionism Will Be Crushed," 11 April 1948, al-Inqaz, Arab Liberation Army Station, in FBIS, Daily Report, no. 287, 12 April 1948, II6. A slightly different version of the text was published in *al-Difaʿ*. See "Party for the Opening of ALA Forces Broadcasting Station."

202. "Kawukji Says Zionism Will Be Crushed."

203. P. Crone, "Khālid b. al-Walīd," *Encyclopaedia of Islam*; D. S. Richards, "Salāḥ al-Dīn," *Encyclopaedia of Islam*.

204. "Kawukji Says Zionism Will Be Crushed." A Haganah informant reported that al-Qawuqji's views, in private, were different and that he realized the Zionists were a formidable enemy. See untitled report from 9 February 1948, in ISA MFA 4/2568.

205. For images of armored vehicles with the emblem and the Arabic inscriptions "Mishmar ha-ʿEmek" and "Zirʿin," two villages where major ALA attacks occurred, see IDFA Photo A/0/3310 and ISA Photo from Operation Dekel, accessed 27 April 2020, www.archives.gov.il/chapter/new-state-photo. The images were used for decades afterward by Israeli propaganda. See Alexander Dothan, *Milhemet Ha-ʿArvim Be-Yisraʾel (ba-Aspaklaryah ʾAarvit)* (Tel Aviv: N. Tverski, 1950), 58, 62.

206. "With Commander Fawzi al-Qawuqji in the Dangerous Triangle," *al-Difaʿ*, 8 April 1948.

207. Ibid.

208. Ibid.

209. Ibid. For a similar theme in the ALA radio, see "A Message from the Salvation Broadcasting Station . . . ," *al-Sarih*, 30 March 1948.

210. "Jews Will Accept Any Plan for State," 26 April 1948, al-Inqaz, Arab Liberation Army Station, in FBIS, Daily Report, no. 299, 28 April 1948, II2.

211. Morris, *1948*, 264–71.

212. Nasir al-Din, "The Suggestions of ALA Soldiers," clipped in IDFA 377/100001/1957; also in *Al-Yawm* [Beirut], 15 May 1948, reproduced in Badran, *Al-Ittijah al-Wahdawi fi Fikr ʿAli Nasir al-Din*, 148–49.

213. Ibid.

214. Ibid.

215. Ibid. The golden calf story is mentioned in both the Hebrew Bible (Exodus

32:4ff.) and the Qur'an (7:148ff.). According to the Qur'anic narrative, the Israelites on their way from Egypt to Canaan grew impatient when Moses failed to return to the camp because he was fasting, in obedience of God's order. Believing Moses had abandoned them, the Israelites smelted their golden jewelry into a calf figure and pronounced it as the God who took them out of Egypt. In the Qur'an, this was the sin of idolatry (*shirk*), one of the most serious sins; nevertheless, it was forgiven by God.

216. Nasir al-Din, "Suggestions of ALA Soldiers."

217. Ibid.

218. Shayyaa, *'Ali Nasir al-Din*, 20–25; Hourani, *Syria and Lebanon*, 197–98; Khoury, *Syria and the French Mandate*, 400–401; Cyrus Schayegh, The *Middle East and the Making of the Modern World* (Cambridge, MA: Harvard University Press, 2017), 225–26.

219. Youssef Chaitani, *Post-colonial Syria and Lebanon: The Decline of Arab Nationalism and the Triumph of the State* (London: I. B. Tauris, 2007), 67.

220. Relying on British sources, Haim Levenberg contended that as early as February 1948, al-Qawuqji secretly agreed to hand over the territory under ALA control to King Abdullah after the end of the British mandate. I find the evidence for a collusion between King Abdullah and al-Qawuqji weak; however, it does seem that their relationship improved when the latter entered Palestine, perhaps because of their mutual disdain for the mufti. In late April Abdullah was interviewed on the ALA radio. See Levenberg, *Military Preparations*, 196, 205; Parsons, *The Commander*, 217–18; "Abdullah Urges Jews to Cease Agression," 24 April 1948, al-Inqaz, Arab Liberation Army Station, in FBIS, Daily Report, no. 297, 26 April 1948, II4–II5.

221. Quoted in Landis, "Syria and the Palestine War," 195, and Sela, "Tsava ha-Hatsala ba-Galil," 211, respectively.

222. *Al-Hayat* [English translation], 10 March 1948, in American Legation–Beirut, *Review of the Local Arabic Press*, 10 March 1948, in HILA.

223. General Commander for Palestine Forces, "Special Operation Orders for the Haifa Area Commander" [Hebrew translation], 28 March 1948, in IDFA 648/922/1975.

224. Hani al-Khayyir, *Adib al-Shishikali: Sahib al-Inqilab al-Talit fi Suriya al-Bidaya wa-al-Nahaya* (Damascus: H. al-Khayr, 1994), 27; Al-Hindi, "Jaysh al-Inqadh (1948–1949), Part I," 38; Landis, "Syria and the Palestine War," 195.

225. The Associated Press reported in July 1947 that a senior commander from al-Najjada, Kamil 'Ariqat, said in a speech in Jaffa that he was "waiting for the order to throw the Jews into the sea." The purported quote was reprinted in the English and Arabic press. Moreover, in a study of the Egyptian participation in the 1948 war, a retired Egyptian

army general quoted Abd al-Rahman 'Azzam, the secretary-general of the Arab League, as saying in December 1947, "we will start [fighting] and won't stop until complete victory, and the throwing of our enemies into the sea." The quote was ostensibly taken from a daily publication of the Muslim Brotherhood (vols. 487–88, 3–4 December 1947). Despite an extensive search, I was unable to locate these statements in contemporaneous sources. In fact, Arabic press reports of the Jaffa gathering—where 'Ariqat spoke—made no mention of these comments. See "Decisions of the Youth Conference in Jaffa . . . ," *al-Difaʿ*, 14 July 1947; "The Youth Conference Is a New Page in the History of the National Movement in Palestine," *al-Shaʿb*, 14 July 1947; "To the Nation Only by Muhammad Saʿid al-Kashif," undated [ca. March 1948], in ISA P 16/1055; "More on the Jaffa Conference" [Haganah intelligence report], 15 July 1947, in HA 105/358; Ibrahim Shakib, *Harb Filastin, 1948: Ruʾya Misriya* (Cairo: al-Zahraʾ lil-Iʿlam al-ʿArabi, 1986), 63.

226. For Ben-Gurion's public speaking on the supposed Arab plan to exterminate the Jews during the war, see Ben-Gurion, *Be-Hilahem Yisraʾel*, 24, 129, 130–31, 226; Ben-Gurion, *Yoman ha-Milhamah*, vol. 2, 525; Ben-Gurion, *Yoman ha-Milhamah*, vol. 3, 729. For an ambiguous mention of extermination by al-Qawuqji, see propaganda surrounding the battle of Mishmar ha-ʿEmek in chapter 4.

227. Efraim Karsh, *Palestine Betrayed* (New Haven, CT: Yale University Press, 2011), 105, 209; David Barnett and Efraim Karsh, "Azzam's Genocidal Threat," *Middle East Forum*, Fall 2011, 85–88; Rubin and Schwanitz, *Nazis, Islamists, and the Making of the Modern Middle East*, 246. For a critical analysis, see Tom Segev, "The Makings of History: The Blind Misleading the Blind," *Haaretz* [English], 11 October 2011; Benny Morris, "Review: Revisionism on the West Bank," *National Report*, no. 108 (July/August 2010), 73–81.

228. Haganah Intelligence, "Developments in the Arab Army," 9 February 1948, in ISA MFA 4/2568. Another Haganah intelligence report stipulated that al-Qawuqji intended to level Tel Aviv. The report added that the inhabitants of all Jewish settlements would be moved into the Arab parts of Palestine. See Haganah Intelligence, untitled, 18 March 1948. According to Morris, in August 1948, shortly before the defeat of the ALA, al-Qawuqji was recorded by British intelligence as threatening, "We will have to initiate total war. We will murder, wreck and ruin everything standing in our way, be it English, American or Jewish." See Morris, *1948*, 61.

229. "Special Operation Orders for the Haifa Area Commander."

230. Quoted in "Document No. 3: Training Regime for Hittin Battalion" [Hebrew translation], in IDFA 648/922/1975.

231. "Document 101: Hittin Battalion HQ, Battalion Commander to Platoon Commanders" [Hebrew translation], 24 April 1948, in IDFA 648/922/1975.

232. A special committee was set up to deal with spoils taken from the enemy. "Document No. 3: Training Regime for Hittin Battalion"; "Special Operation Orders for the Haifa Area Commander"; ALA, Hittin Battalion HQ, Commander of the Hittin Battalion to Chairman of Spoils Committee, "Attn: Monetary Payment" [Hebrew translation], 11 May 1948, in KMA 15/2/4.

233. "Al-Inqaz Broadcasts," 18 May 1948, al-Inqaz Radio, in SWB, no. 52, 27 May 1948, 65. As for al-Qawuqji himself repeating similar accusations, see "With Commander Fawzi al-Qawuqji."

234. "A Collection of Arab News Reports," 18 April 1948, in HA 105/143.

235. "Special Operation Orders for the Haifa Area Commander." This order was repeated in several documents. See "Document No. 3: Training Regime for Hittin Battalion"; "Interrogation of a Prisoner."

236. General Command for the Defense of Palestine, "Circular to All Units" [Hebrew translation], 13 May 1948, in HA 105/132.

237. Undated letter from the Committee of Reform, Wadi Nisnas [Hebrew translation], ca. February 1948, in HA 105/358.

238. "Intelligence Report for the Period between 1–5 February 1948."

239. Ibid.

240. "Document 84: Administrative Order No. 7" [Hebrew translation], 26 February 1948, in IDFA 648/922/1975.

241. Ibid.

242. "Document 84."

243. For lists of soldiers recommended for decorations, see KMA 15/2/2 and KMA 15/2/3; "Attn: Monetary Payment."

244. Fawzi al-Qawuqji, "To My Brothers the Beloved Arabs of Palestine," undated, in IDFA 62/100001/1957.

245. "We Will Meet Next in Tel Aviv," April 1948, newspaper article clipped in HA 105/216B.

246. "To My Brothers."

247. "Fawzi Bek al-Qawuqji Enters Palestine," "Commander Fawzi Bek al-Qawuqji Makes His First Statement after Entrance . . . ," *al-Difaʿ*, 10 March 1948.

248. "The ALA Aims to Liberate the Country and Deliver It to the Arabs," *al-Difaʿ*, 29 March 1948.

249. Quoted in Parsons, *The Commander*, 212.

250. "Document 106/600: Commander of the First Company of the Iraqi Husayn Brigade to Chairman of the National Committee-Nablus," 19 February 1948, in Bahjat Husayn Sabri, *Watha'iq al-Lajna al-Qawmiyya al-'Arabiya bi-Nablus, 1947–1949* (Amman: al-Jami'ah al-Urduniyah, Markaz al-Watha'iq wa-al-Makhtutat, 1991), 138–39.

251. For testimonies pertaining to cases investigated by the battalion's military police, see KMA 15/2/4; NMA S/65.

252. "Intelligence Report for the Period between 1–5 February 1948," 5.

253. ALA, Hittin Battalion, letter from the National Committee to the Local Commander [Hebrew translation], 10 March 1948, in KMA 15/2/4.

254. "Three Messages from the Commander of the Salvation Forces to the Residents," *al-Difa'*, 24 March 1948.

255. "Document 102: Weekly Intelligence Report for the Hittin Battalion" [Hebrew translation], 25 April 1948, in IDFA 648/922/1975; Commander of Military Security in Nablus, "A Notice to the Noble Arab People" [Hebrew translation], 7 March 1948, in HA 105/216A.

256. "Notice to the Noble Arab People." The interest of the ALA in prices is not surprising given that some of its provisions were bought locally. See Muhammad 'Abd Wannan to the Commander of Hittin Battalion, 2 February 1948, in IDFA 292/100001/1957.

257. "Document 102"; "To Our Arab Brothers, God Bless Them," undated, in HA 105/216B; "Angel of Death to Dear Honorable," undated, in IDFA 565/100001/1957.

258. "Notice to the Noble Arab People."

259. "Document 165/655: ALA/The Jenin, Nablus, Tulkarm Area, Order to Hittin, Yarmuk, Circassian and Husayn Battalion Commanders," in Sabri, *Watha'iq al-Lajna al-Qawmiyya*, 151–52.

260. A member of the national committee explained to the local commander of the ALA that the accused refused to follow the customary law (*'urf*), which would have demanded that the thief return the cattle and submit to other punishments. See "Document 163/655: Chairman of the National Committee-Nablus to Commander of the Guarding Company, Ihsan Bek," 21 February 1948, in Sabri, *Watha'iq al-Lajna al-Qawmiyya*, 148. For another case where the customary law failed to achieve the desired outcome and the ALA was asked to intervene, see Sabri, *Watha'iq al-Lajna al-Qawmiyya*, 226–27.

261. "Notice No. 2 Published by the Salvation Forces in the Northern Front," *Filastin*,

11 March 1948; "Military Court in the HQ of the Salvation Forces," *al-Sarih*, 30 March 1948.

262. Alex Winder, "Policing and Crime in Mandate Palestine: Indigenous Policemen, British Colonial Control, and Palestinian Society, 1920–1948" (PhD diss., New York University, 2017), 168–218.

263. Ibid.

264. "Attn: A Court for the Bands," 20 February 1948, in ISA MFA 4/2568.

265. "Three Messages from the Commander of the Salvation."

266. Ibid. For a similar order see "Document 165/655."

267. For a case involving the confiscation of a car because the owner had failed to disclose he owned it, see "Document No. 44: ALA Court Martial Decision from 15 April 1948" [Hebrew translation], in IDFA 648/922/1975.

268. "The General Commander of the Palestine Forces to Battalion and Garrison Commanders" [Hebrew translation], 28 March 1948, in HA 105/216A.

269. "Administrative Order No. 1." According to an ALA volunteer, a Palestinian from Nablus approached the commander of the First Yarmuk battalion, Muhammad Safa, and told him he was paid to help the Jews plant a car bomb in Nablus in retaliation for the explosion on Ben Yehuda Street in Jerusalem on February 22, 1948, by 'Abd al-Qadir al-Husayni's men (which killed fifty-eight civilians, the majority of them Jewish). Apparently, the explosives were hidden under bags of oranges and flour, and the Palestinian's role was to sit next to the Jewish soldier when he drove the car into the city so as not to raise suspicion. See Khalid Arslan (Nablus) to Khuri Arslan (Damascus) [Hebrew translation], 20 March 1948, in HA 105/216G.

270. A Transjordanian sent his officer friend in the ALA a letter asking him to track down eight merchants from Iraq, Palestine, and Transjordan involved in selling cattle to Jews in Palestine. The officer was asked to threaten the eight with execution. See Letter to Rif'at Garib 'Awis (ALA), 4 January 1948, inside Haganah intelligence report, 26 March 1948, in HA 105/66.

271. "Document 172/655: Area Commander, Administrative Order," undated in Sabri, *Watha'iq al-Lajna al-Qawmiyya*, 160. Determining whether one was Jewish or Arab was a major concern for Arab forces. In Jaffa, two men with Iraqi Arabic accents were caught in December 1947 and thought to be Jewish spies after they could not perform the Islamic ritual washing for prayer. They were executed. See Matti Friedman, *Spies of No Country: Secret Lives at the Birth of Israel* (Chapel Hill, NC: Algonquin Books, 2019), 9–11.

272. Hillel Cohen, *Army of Shadows: Palestinian Collaboration with Zionism, 1917–1948* (Berkeley: University of California Press, 2009), 230–58; "Report from a Man Who Trained in the Qatana training Camp in Syria"; "According to Jonny [A report by a Palestinian informant for the Haganah]," 28 March 1948, in ISA MFA 4/2568; "Jonny Says."

273. General Command for the al-Inqadh Forces / Northern Front / Tulkarm Area, "Military Notice," undated, in IDFA 31/100001/1957.

274. "Turn to Arab Doctors," handwritten draft, undated, in IDFA 4/100001/1957.

275. Ibid.

276. "Document 102."

277. "To Our Arab Brothers."

278. "Document 165/655."

279. For the most part, local ALA commanders, even when sympathetic, had no equipment or weapons to provide to villagers who wanted to launch attacks on Jewish targets. See Jabal al-Arab Battalion/HQ, "Attn: Patrols," Shafa-'Amr 6 April 1948, in HA 105/132; Sela, "Tsava ha-Hatsala ba-Galil," 233.

280. Colonel Yehuda Wallach, "Soldiers' Education in View of Tactical Needs," 2 November 1952, 19, in *Education and Morale in the IDF*.

281. Colonel Yehuda Wallach in General Staff / Chief Education Officer-Hasbara, in *Education and Morale in the IDF*, 21.

282. During the month of September 1948, the Israeli postal censorship bureau intercepted a letter by an American who wrote to al-Qawuqji, requesting his autograph. She intended to add it to her collection of dignitaries' autographs. See "Intelligence Service HQ [Report]," 28 September 1948, 9–10, in IDFA 286/600137/1951.

CHAPTER 3

1. Untitled memos from the IDF Manpower Branch, 1949, in IDFA 14/6722/1949.

2. Ami Ayalon, *The Press in the Arab Middle East: A History* (New York: Oxford University Press, 1995), 142.

3. Ami Ayalon calculated 27 percent as the proximate literacy rate among Palestinians in 1948. Rosemarie Esber assessed, based on estimates prepared for the 1937 Peel Commission, that the number was 15 percent. See Ami Ayalon, *Reading Palestine: Printing and Literacy, 1900–1948* (Austin: University of Texas Press, 2004), 16–17; Rosemarie M. Esber, *Under the Cover of War: The Zionist Expulsion of the Palestinians* (Alexandria, VA: Arabicus Books & Media, 2008), 396.

4. See, for example, Yuval Ben-Bassat, *Petitioning the Sultan: Protests and Justice in Late Ottoman Palestine* (London: I. B. Tauris, 2013), 51n25; Ayalon, *Reading Palestine*, 131–53; Khalidi, *Palestinian Identity*, 57. For an example where the use of a scribe is mentioned, see Letter by Ahmad Ma'aruf to 'Ali Muhammad Isma'il, in IDFA 521/100001/1957.

5. Some of the questions Ella Shohat posed two decades ago inform this chapter: "Did Arab Jews want to stay? Did they want to leave? Did they exercise free will? Did they actually make a decision? Once in Israel, did they want to go back? Were they able to do so? And did they regret the impossibility of returning?" See Ella Shohat, "Rupture and Return: Zionist Discourse and the Study of Arab Jews," *Social Text* 21, no. 2 (2003): 55.

6. Matthew Hughes, "Collusion across the Litani? Lebanon and the 1948 War," in Rogan and Shlaim, *War for Palestine*, 215; Morris, *1948*, 394; Sela, "Tsava ha-Hatsala ba-Galil," 212–13; Arnon Golan, Jacob Peleg, Alon Kadish, and Yona Bandmann, *Ha-Ma'arakha 'al Yafo be-Tashah* (Sedeh Boker: Makhon Ben-Gurion le-Heker Yisra'el, 2017), 64–65. In his memoir, al-Qawuqji repeated a similar idea; see Fauzi al-Qawuqji, "Memoirs, 1948 Part I," *Journal of Palestine Studies* 1, no. 4 (Summer 1972): 48.

7. Shoko Watanabe demonstrated the diversity of the group of Tunisian Arabs who volunteered to fight alongside the Egyptian army in 1948. While some came because they could not find other employment, many were artisans, skilled workers, nurses, and students. See Shoko Watanabe, "A Forgotten Mobilization: The Tunisian Volunteer Movement for Palestine in 1948," *Journal of the Economic and Social History of the Orient* 60, no. 4 (2017): 488–523.

8. See Morris, *1948*, 394; Morris, "1948 as Jihad."

9. The sacredness of Palestine was a frequent theme in letters. See Abu Ibrahim al-Kasir (Damascus) to 'Umar al-Khatib (Palestine), 24 November 1947, in IDFA 565/100001/1957; "Memoirs of My Jihad—Memories of a *Mujahid* in Palestine" [Hebrew translation], in HA 105/124.

10. Zabun Husayn (Palestine) to Sawt Allah, 3 July 1948, in IDFA 565/100001/1957.
11. Ibid.

12. Letter to Ibrahim (Palestine) from unknown location, 14 April 1948, in IDFA 565/100001/1957.

13. Letter of Complaint by Nasib al-Abaza [Hebrew translation], 12 February 1948, in HA 105/132.

14. See, for example, HQ of the Regular Forces of Northern Palestine, Al-'Abd Abu

Muhammad and 'Ali Abu Khalid (Palestine) to Ibrahim 'Awdi Abu Ibrahim, undated, in IDFA 565/100001/1957. Many similar examples could be found in the file.

15. See, for example, letter by Jamil, 29 August 1948, in IDFA 565/100001/1957; letter by the parents of Mahmud Habib, in IDFA 521/100001/1957.

16. See, for example, a letter to Akram with concerns about his recent injury, 14 July 1947, in IDFA 565/100001/1957.

17. Jamil al-Hasan (Baghdad) to Madlul (Palestine), 25 March 1948, in IDFA 565/100001/1957.

18. Teacher in al-Zawra Elementary School (Baghdad) to Maki (Nablus), 25 March 1948, in IDFA 565/100001/1957.

19. Al-Hindi, "Jaysh al-Inqadh (1948–1949), Part I," 44–45; Yoav Gelber, *Komemi-yut ve-Nakbah: Yisra'el, ha-Falestinim u-Medinot 'Arav, 1948* (Or Yehuda: Devir, 2004), 121–22; Sela, "Tsava ha-Hatsala ba-Galil," 216–17. Although false reporting on the ALA was common, this was sometimes critiqued in the Arab press and there were also instances of accurate reporting on various problems within the volunteer army. The Lebanese *al-Hayat* newspaper, for example, reported on April 17, 1948, that the Arab League Military Committee was ignoring requests from the ALA for equipment, and that the Arab states did not supply the number of weapons to which they had committed. See *al-Hayat*, 17 April 1948, in American Legation–Beirut, *Review of the Local Arabic Press*, 17 April 1948, in HILA; report from *al-Sarih*, 15 January 1948, inside Haganah intelligence report, undated, in ISA P 16/1055.

20. Exaggerating the number of Jewish casualties in battle was common among both the rank-and-file and senior ALA officers. See Parsons, *The Commander*, 217.

21. Tim O'Brien, *The Things They Carried: A Work of Fiction* (Boston: Houghton Mifflin, 1990), 21; Diana C. Gill, *How We Are Changed by War: A Study of Letters and Diaries from Colonial Conflicts to Operation Iraqi Freedom* (New York: Routledge, 2010), 174–75.

22. Letter by an Iraqi volunteer [Hebrew translation], 11 April 1948, in HA 105/216B.

23. Ibid.

24. Jalal Ma'aruf (Jaffa) to Akram Nashat al-Qarawi (Baghdad–the military academy) [Hebrew translation], inside Haganah intelligence report, 24 March 1948, in HA 105/216B.

25. Ibid. For other reports, mentioning hundreds or thousands of Jewish casualties, see "Volunteer Diary from 1948" [Hebrew translation], in IDFA 648/922/1975; "Diary of Mar'i Hasan Hindawi," in IDFA 94/100001/1957; undated letter starting with "My Dear Brother," ca. March 1948, in ISA P 24/351.

26. For Alawite religious themes in letters, see letter by volunteer (Alawite battalion / Jaysh-Safad region) to his uncle, Mahmud al-Darubi, 21 August 1948, in IDFA 521/100001/1957.

27. Letter of a soldier from the Alawite Battalion to Abu Kamil, undated, in IDFA 435/100001/1957.

28. Ibid.

29. Ibid.

30. The urge to say farewell and capitalize on the danger of battle to help one's standing within the family also comes across in other letters. See al-Inqadh Forces / Second Yarmuk Battalion / Acre Garrison, Usama al-Kilani to Dear Mother (Bint Jbeil), undated, in IDFA 109/100001/1957.

31. Letter from parents to Mahmud Habib (Palestine), undated, in IDFA 521/100001/1957.

32. Letter from parents to Muhmmad S'aid (Palestine), 21 August 1948, in IDFA 521/100001/1957. On the theme of family agricultural work, see letter from parents to Ahmad As'ad (Palestine), 12 October 1948, in IDFA 521/100001/1957.

33. Letter from Kamas Saba' (Baghdad) to his son in Nablus [Hebrew translation dated 19 April 1948], in HA 105/216B. According to unsubstantiated rumors circulating at the time, al-Qawuqji showed disdain toward Iraqi volunteers and denied them proper medical care. This was allegedly because of the support of Iraqi volunteers for the mufti. See "Reports from the Pupil" [An informant for the Haganah]," 21 April 1948, in ISA MFA 4/2568.

34. Letter to Ibrahim (Palestine) from unknown location, 14 April 1948, in IDFA 565/100001/1957.

35. Ibid.

36. One of the letters sent to Mahmud includes an Islamic formulaic text praising 'Umar ibn al-Khattab, the second caliph who led the Muslim community from 586 to 590 after the death of Prophet Muhammad. 'Umar is viewed negatively in Shi'i Islam, and he is alleged to have suppressed views that supported 'Ali's succession rights. Although the letter mentioning 'Umar was not written by Mahmud but addressed to him, it is highly unlikely that a close friend would include Islamic formulaic remarks that might be considered offensive. This leads me to the conclusion that Mahmud was most likely Sunni. For the letter, see 'Abd al-Majid al-Salihi (Baghdad) to Maki Mahmud (Nablus), 18 March 1948, in IDFA 565/100001/1957 [hereafter "al-Salihi's Letter"].

37. In addition to the monthly salary paid by the ALA directly to the Iraqi volunteers, their families in Iraq also received a monthly stipend of two and a half dinars. Families of Iraqi volunteers who were killed in battle received a one-time severance payment of twenty dinars, in addition to a year's worth of salary. Wounded volunteers received six months' pay. See Jam'iyat Inqadh Filastin, *A'mal Jam'iyat Inqadh Filastin Khilal Sana 1948*, 16.

38. Maki Mahmud (Nablus) to Dear Mother (Baghdad), undated, in IDFA 565/100001/1957 [hereafter "Mahmud's Letter"].

39. After the Egyptians left the Sterling Zone in 1947, in 1948 one Egyptian pound was equal to 2.87 US dollars. Therefore, 15 Egyptian pounds equaled approximately 43 US dollars. The ALA monthly salary for second lieutenants (see below) was 350 Syrian lira, or approximately 160 US dollars, and a first lieutenant's monthly salary was approximately 400 Syrian lira, or around 180 US dollars. Therefore, 15 Egyptian pounds would be about 25–30 percent of Mahmud's monthly salary depending on his rank. See John Waterbury, *The Egypt of Nasser and Sadat: The Political Economy of Two Regimes* (Princeton, NJ: Princeton University Press, 1983), xxii.

40. Hanna Batatu, *The Old Social Classes and the Revolutionary Movements of Iraq: A Study of Iraq's Landed and Commercial Classes and of Its Communists, Ba'thists and Free Officers* (Princeton, NJ: Princeton University Press, 1978), 471–473.

41. "Mahmud's Letter."

42. Al-Hindi, "Jaysh al-Inqadh (1948–1949), Part I," 47.

43. If Mahmud had been married with children (something there is no evidence of), he would have received an additional 12–13 Iraqi dinars. See Batatu, *Old Social Classes,* 768–69.

44. The Syrian lira was pegged to the US dollar starting in 1947 at 2.19148 Syrian lira equal to 1 US dollar. The Iraqi dinar, meanwhile, was pegged to the British pound in 1947 at 1 dinar equal to 1 British pound. One British pound at that time was equal to 4.03 US dollars, so the exchange rate of Syrian pound to Iraqi dinar was 8.8316644 Syrian lira to 1 Iraqi dinar. An ALA second lieutenant earning 350 Syrian liras during that time period earned the equivalent of approximately 40 Iraqi dinars (350 / 8.8316644 = 39.6) and a first lieutenant earning 400 Syrian liras earned the equivalent of approximately 45 Iraqi dinars. See Edmond Y. Asfour, *Syria: Development and Monetary Policy* (Cambridge, MA: Harvard University Press, 1959), 52n21, 55.

45. One Iraqi volunteer indicated in a letter home that some of his friends returned to Iraq because their salary was inadequate and other promises made to them were

not kept. See "The Iraqi Fighters," a volunteer letter inside Haganah intelligence report, 11 April 1948, in HA 105/216B.

46. Gilad, "History of the ALA," 61.

47. "Mahmud's Letter."

48. Ibid.

49. In the letter, al-Salihi wrote Mahmud, "we collected the flowers of life together," to stress the degree of intimacy between the two; "Al-Salihi's Letter."

50. Ibid. See also Salih Yusuf to Mahadi, 26 April 1948, in IDFA 565/100001/1957.

51. "Al-Salihi's Letter."

52. Ibid. Jews were sometimes referred to as "disbelievers" or "infidels" in letters. See 'Adnan Shishkali to Adib Shiskali [Hebrew translation], inside Haganah intelligence report, 2 March 1948, in HA 105/216A.

53. "Mahmud's Letter."

54. "Al-Salihi's Letter."

55. Ibid.

56. This argument was made by Sylvia Haim. See Bashkin, "Iraqi Shadows, Iraqi Lights."

57. Peter Wien argued that many in Iraq looked up to Nazi Germany not because they supported the Nazi racial ideology—or Fascism more broadly—but because they believed in militarism. That Nazi Germany represented the main opposition to British hegemony was another major impetus. See Peter Wien, *Iraqi Arab Nationalism: Authoritarian, Totalitarian and Pro-Fascist Inclinations, 1932–1941* (London: Routledge, 2006), 113.

58. Sherifians were Sunni officers who participated in the Hashemite-led revolt against the Ottoman Empire during the First World War.

59. Orit Bashkin, *The Other Iraq: Pluralism and Culture in Hashemite Iraq* (Stanford, CA: Stanford University Press, 2009), 58–61, 84–86; Bashkin, "Iraqi Shadows," 152–63, 167–68.

60. Charles Tripp, "Iraq and the 1948 War: Mirror of Iraq's Disorder," in Rogan and Shlaim, *War for Palestine*, 128.

61. Susan Pedersen, "Getting Out of Iraq—in 1932: The League of Nations and the Road to Normative Statehood," *American Historical Review* 115, no. 4 (2010): 975–1000; Tripp, "Iraq and the 1948 War," 134; Batatu, *Old Social Classes,* 546, 550.

62. Tripp, "Iraq and the 1948 War," 130–32; Eric Davis, *Memories of State: Politics, History, and Collective Identity in Modern Iraq* (Berkeley: University of California Press,

2005), 87; Michael Eppel, "The Elite, the Effendiyya, and the Growth of Nationalism and Pan-Arabism in Hashemite Iraq, 1921–1958," *IJMES*, 30, no. 2 (May 1998): 241; "Other Developments in League States-Iraq," in SWB, no. 32, 8 January 1948, 56; "Iraq's Efforts for Palestine," "Iraqi United Front Leader's Statement," in SWB, no. 33, 15 January 1948, 55.

63. Teacher in al-Zawra' elementary school (Baghdad) to Maki (Nablus), 25 March 1948, Baghdad, in IDFA 565/100001/1957 [hereafter "Teacher's Letter 2"].

64. Teacher in al-Zawra' elementary school to Maki, 11 February 1948, Baghdad, in IDFA 565/100001/1957 [hereafter "Teacher's Letter 1"].

65. Ibid.

66. Batatu, *Old Social Classes*, 548–51; Davis, *Memories of State*, 86–87; Orit Bashkin, *New Babylonians: A History of Jews in Modern Iraq* (Stanford, CA: Stanford University Press, 2012), 149.

67. Marion Farouk-Sluglett and Peter Sluglett, *Iraq since 1958: From Revolution to Dictatorship* (New York: KPI, 1987), 39–40; Batatu, *Old Social Classes*, 551–52, 557.

68. Batatu, *Old Social Classes*, 552–53; Mahmud Shabib, *Wathba fi al-'Iraq wa-Suqut Salih Jabr* (Baghdad: Dar al-Thaqafa, 1988), 59; Orit Bashkin, "Lands, Hands and Sociocultural Boundaries: A Reading of Dhu Nun Ayyub's *The Hand, the Land and the Water* (1948)," *Middle Eastern Studies* 46, no. 3 (2010): 409–10.

69. Muhammad Mahdi Kubba, chairman of Istiqlal Party, "Bayan hizb al-Istiqlal," 2 January 1948, in Shabib, *Wathba fi al-'Iraq*, 45.

70. The National Democratic Party also mentioned Palestine in its propaganda, though only in passing. See Shabib, *Wathba fi al-'Iraq*, 45–46.

71. Shabib, *Wathba fi al-'Iraq*, 8, 60. While hell-bent on overthrowing the government, the protesters themselves—much like the teacher writing to Mahmud—did not call into question the existence of the monarchy. Several scholars have suggested that this was the first time that the group of army officers who brought down the monarchy in 1958 entertained such an idea. See Batatu, *Old Social Classes*, 554; Davis, *Memories of State*, 88.

72. Elie Kedourie, "The Break between Muslims and Jews in Iraq," in *Jews among Arabs: Contacts and Boundaries*, ed. Mark Cohen and Abraham Udovitch (Princeton, NJ: Darwin Press, 1989), 28–30; Bashkin, *New Babylonians*, 194–97.

73. "Teacher's Letter 1."

74. "Teacher's Letter 2."

75. It is also possible that by invoking a "sin," the teacher was referring to the Jews' supposed reluctance to obey God's command and enter the land of Canaan, a

tradition referenced in the Qur'an and many other Islamic texts. Alternatively, this may be a reference to the supposed betrayal of Prophet Muhammad by some of the Jewish tribes of Medina shortly after his arrival in 622 (the *Hijra*).

76. "Teacher's Letter 2." The disparaging references to Jews were repeated in several letters. See letter by Yusuf al-Saba'i, undated [Hebrew translation], in HA 105/124A; Al-'Afan Fahid to Shakib Wahab [Hebrew translation], inside Haganah intelligence report, 15 April 1948, in HA 105/216G.

77. "Complication from Letters" [Hebrew translation], inside Haganah intelligence report, 8 April 1948, in HA 105/216G.

78. Al-Qawuqji, "Memoirs, 1948 Part I," 37.

79. Ibid. I was unable to corroborate this story. It is possible this account refers to a meeting between Josh Palmon, a senior Haganah intelligence officer, and Gad Makhness, a political activist, with the Iraqi commander of the Hittin battalion, Mad-lul 'Abbas. The meeting was approved by Ben-Gurion and was apparently aimed at establishing contact with al-Qawuqji himself. See Gelber, *Komemiyut ve-Nakbah*, 114–15; Amiram Ezov, *Mishmar ha-'Emek Lo Tipol: Nekudat Mifneh be-Tashah* (Or Ye-hudah: Kineret, 2013), 66.

80. It is unclear if all of these quotes are by soldiers or other immigrants from Morocco to Israel. See Southern Censor, Internal Department, "Special Report: Mood among North African Immigrants," 31 July 1949, 4, in IDFA 18/621/1985. The report cites correspondence from the beginning of Moroccan immigration in late 1948 in addition to letters from 1949.

81. IS, "TSO Report No. 2," 10 October 1948, 3, in IDFA 353/535/2004. During one week in September 1948, 175 letters were sent by North African Gahal soldiers to North Africa. See Southern Censor (Tel Aviv) to Chief Censor, "Attn: Gahal Mail to North African Countries," 13 September 1948, in IDFA 13/621/1985.

82. TSO, no. 2, 4.

83. "Riots Again in Morocco against Jews," *Davar*, 14 June 1948; "Jewish Pogroms Again in Tripoli and Morocco," *Maariv*, 13 June 1948. Unless otherwise noted, all historic Hebrew press accounts were obtained from the Jewish Historical Press collection at the National Library of Israel, accessed 25 May 2020, www.jpress.org.il.

84. Shabtai Teveth, *Ha-Shanim ha-Ne'lamot ve-ha-Hor ha-Shahor* (Tel-Aviv: Devir, 1999), 151; Avi Picard *'Olim bi-Mesurah: Mediniyut Yisra'el Kelape 'Aliyatam shel Yehude Tsefon Afrikah, 1951–1956* (Sedeh Boker: Mekhon Ben-Gurion le-Heker Yisra'el, 2013), 180–82.

85. ID, "What Are They Writing in the Diaspora? (Mail to Nahal Soldiers)," 12 July 1949, 2, in IDFA 643/1470/2002.

86. Ibid.

87. ID, "TSO Report No. 13," 6 March 1949, 6–7, in IDFA 353/535/2004.

88. Henriette Dahan-Kalev, "You're So Pretty—You Don't Look Moroccan," *Israel Studies* 6, no. 1 (2001): 4.

89. Sami Shalom Chetrit, *Intra-Jewish Conflict in Israel: White Jews, Black Jews* (New York: Routledge, 2010), 57; "Special Report: Mood among North African Immigrants," 31 July 1949.

90. TSO, no. 13, 7.

91. Prosper Cohen, the former secretary of the Zionist federation in Morocco, also accused the Ashkenazi elite of antisemitism. See Yaron Tsur, "The Brief Career of Prosper Cohen: A Would-Be Leader of Moroccan Immigrants," in *Struggle and Survival in Palestine/Israel*, ed. Mark LeVine and Gershon Shafir (Berkeley: University of California Press, 2012), 79.

92. DI, "TSO Report No. 16," 26 April 1949, 6–7, in IDFA 353/535/2004.

93. Ibid., 9.

94. ID, "TSO Report No. 19," 5 June 1949, 8, in IDFA 353/535/2004.

95. ID, "TSO Report No. 20," 13 June 1949, 8, in IDFA 353/535/2004.

96. "Special Report: Mood among North African Immigrants," 31 July 1949, 4.

97. Operations Branch/Intelligence/4 [censorship bureau], "Censorship Report," 26 April 1949, in IDFA 875/1109/2005.

98. Unit for Psychological Research / Center for Research of Public Opinion, "Mahal Comes to Israel," 17–18, in IDFA 225/7/1955; TSO, no. 16, 6.

99. "The General Department—Report for January 1949 (Censor 11)," 3, in IDFA 13/621/1985.

100. IS, "TSO Report No. 14," 13 March 1949, 4, in IDFA 353/535/2004. For a similar sentiment: IS, "TSO Report No. 23," 22 September 1949, 8, in IDFA 353/535/2004; "Censorship Report," 26 April 1949, 15.

101. The author was apparently Canadian. IS, "TSO Report No. 19," 5 June 1949, 5, in IDFA 353/535/2004.

102. IS, "TSO Report No. 4," 20 October 1948, 3, in IDFA 353/535/2004.

103. TSO, no. 4, 3.

104. IS, "TSO Report No. 11," 31 January 1949, 4, in IDFA 353/535/2004.

105. Ibid. Weiss, "1948's Forgotten Soldiers?" 154.

106. Gshur, "Mitnadvey Huts la-Arets," 147.

107. Omer Bartov, "The Holocaust as Leitmotif of the Twentieth Century," in *Lessons and Legacies VII: The Holocaust in International Perspective*, ed. Dagmar Herzog (Evanston, IL: Northwestern University Press, 2006), 3–25.

CHAPTER 4

1. Parsons, *The Commander*, 218–20.

2. Khalid Arslan (Nablus) to Khuri Arslan (Damascus).

3. Ibid. On the crossing of ALA forces through Transjordanian territory, see Parsons, *The Commander*, 209–11.

4. "Diary of Mar'i Hasan Hindawi." Celebrations are also mentioned in press accounts: "The Arrival of Arab Volunteers to Nablus," *al-Sha'b*, 22 January 1948.

5. Khalid Arslan (Nablus) to Khuri Arslan (Damascus).

6. Ibid. Usama al-Kilani, the Lebanese volunteer, was also impressed with the British volunteers, and asked his friend in Bint Jbeil to help one of them since "we are good friends and he is my brother." See Usama al-Kilani (Acre) to Haytham (Bint Jbeil), undated, in IDFA 110/100001/1957.

7. Palestinians also wondered how British servicemen came to enlist in the ALA. Yusra Salah wrote her friend in Ramallah that Nablus was full of British volunteers, and that they looked odd wearing Arab garb. "What do you think? Why did they choose to serve in the Arab army? Is it their hatred for Jews?" wondered Salah in her letter. See Yusra Salah (Nablus) to 'A'ida 'Audi (Ramallah) [Hebrew translation], 14 April 1948, in Haganah Intelligence, "Letters' Censorship," 4 May 1948, in CZA S25/9209.

8. Khalid Arslan (Nablus) to Khuri Arslan (Damascus). Arslan's observation reflected the fact that before 1948, it was uncommon for female Palestinians to be employed as nurses, and the occupation was associated with a low social status. The war had increased the appeal of the profession. See Ellen L. Fleischman, *The Nation and Its "New" Women: The Palestinian Women's Movement, 1920–1948* (Berkeley: University of California Press, 2003), 55–56, 202.

9. Khalid Arslan (Nablus) to Khuri Arslan (Damascus). Writing from Nablus, an Egyptian volunteer, likely with the Muslim Brotherhood, echoed a similar impression after seeing Jewish women fighting alongside men in a battle inside the settlement of Hartuv, next to Jerusalem: "Among the 16 killed was a beautiful girl who held the first-aid [kit] in one hand, and the Sten [rifle] in the other." See unsigned letter from Nablus [Hebrew translation], 24 March 1948, in HA 105/216.

10. Shortly before these letters were written, in January 1948, the general sentiment was very different. The national committees in Nablus, Jenin, and Tulkarm
telegrammed the Arab prime ministers, speakers of parliament, local strongmen, and
the secretariat of the Arab League, asking "how long" the Palestinians would have to
wait for the rescue forces that the Arabs had pledged to send. This uncharacteristically
stern letter warned that by the time Arabs woke up, the only thing they could send
Palestinians would be flowers for the funerals of those killed in battle. This sentiment
changed by the time ALA volunteers started arriving in Palestine in great numbers.
"Everyone is optimistic about victory," wrote one Palestinian in March 1948, adding
that Europe would soon recognize the Palestinian victory as well. See undated letter
starting with "My Dear Brother," ca. March 1948, in ISA P 24/351; "Telegram of the
National Committees in Nablus, Tulkarm, and Jenin," *Filastin*, 7 January 1948.

11. Hani Abu-Jawala (Nablus) to ʿAdil Shahin (Tiberias) [Hebrew translation], 16
February 1948, in HA 105/215A.

12. The head of the Arab League Military Committee, Ismaʿil Safwat, also com-
plained that ʿAbd al-Qadir al-Husayni and his men tried to discredit the ALA in Nablus,
Jenin, and Tulkarm and dissuade Palestinians from joining it. See Khalaf, *Politics in
Palestine*, 191; Al-ʿArif, *Nakbat Filastin*, part I, 129–30.

13. Hani Abu-Jawala to ʿAdil Shahin. A similar sentiment is found in oral testimonies by Palestinians. The arrival of the ALA "lessened the inhabitants' sense of
responsibility for their own defense." See Esber, *Under the Cover of War*, 333–34.

14. Letter from Nazareth to Jaffa [Hebrew translation], 14 February 1948, inside
Haganah intelligence report, 12 March 1948, in HA 105/216A; undated letter starting
with "My Dear Brother," ca. March 1948. For propaganda disseminated by Arab leaders
about tens of thousands of volunteers coming to rescue Palestine, see "General Mobilization Predicated," in SWB, no. 30, 18 December 1947, 53; "Al-Kawukji's Activities," 11
March 1948, Arab News Agency, in SWB, no. 42, 18 March 1948, 59.

15. Undated letter starting with "My Dear Brother." Not everyone in Palestine
bought into the ALA propaganda or the sense of confidence conveyed by the AHC.
The Haganah intelligence obtained an essay circa March 1948, where the author, Muhammad Saʿid al-Kashif (about which nothing else is known), wrote a strongly worded
critique of the Arab leadership. It is unknown whether the essay was published, but
the Arabic copy in Haganah files criticized the "leaders who deceived the nation" by
boasting about thousands of volunteers and "weapons in abundance" that had arrived
in Palestine. Both the AHC and Arab League were blamed for failing the people, and

also the Arab press for echoing the leaders' false claims. Those Palestinians who fled the country were also reprimanded. The author's observations about Palestinian and Arab politics are quite perceptive considering when this essay was written. See "To the Nation Only by Muhammad Sa'id al-Kashif."

16. Dhib Ahmad al-Habibi (Bisan) to Salih Effendi [Hebrew translation], 11 March 1948, in HA 105/216A; Morris, *1948*, 106.

17. Al-Inqadh Forces / Second Yarmuk Battalion / Acre Garrison, Usama al-Kilani (Acre) to Haytham (Bint Jbeil), 11 April 1948, in IDFA 109/100001/1957; Zaki[?] to Omar S'aid, in IDFA 565/100001/1957; Shakib Wahab (Shafa-'Amr) to ALA HQ (Damascus), 17 April 1948, in HA 105/132.

18. Association for the Liberation of Palestine—Hama Branch, 'Uthman al-Hurani (Hama) to Hasan al-Qatan (Jaffa), 16 January 1948, in Abu 'Izza, "Mujahid Hasan al-Qatan."

19. When the ALA failed to respond to the pleas for weapons, other volunteers from Hama refused to leave the Qatana training camp and head for Palestine. Even the Hama volunteers who were already stationed in Jaffa eventually deserted. See Gilad, "History of the ALA," 84–86.

20. League for the Defense of Palestine—Hama, 'Uthman al-Hurani (Hama) to Hasan al-Qatan (Jaffa), 23 February 1948, in Abu 'Izza, "Mujahid Hasan al-Qatan."

21. "A Proclamation of the Welfare Committee in Tulkarm" [Hebrew translation], inside Haganah intelligence report, 26 February 1948, in HA 105/216A; "Commission for the Care if Mujahidin-Tulkarm to Commander of Second Hittin Battalion" [Hebrew translation], 15 May 1948, in KMA 15/2/4.

22. "Administrative Order No. 4/Sh"; "Administrative Order No. 1"; Morris, *1948*, 281; Parsons, *The Druze*, 76; "Document 106/604: Nablus National Committee to the Commander of the ALA, 5 May 1948, in Sabri, *Watha'iq al-Lajna al-Qawmiyya*, 90, 230–31; Al-Hindi, "Jaysh al-Inqadh (1948–1949), Part I," 55; Shoufani, "Fall of a Village, "110–12; "Jonny Says."

23. ALA HQ / Northern Front, Fawzi al-Qawuqji, "Movement Order (692)" [Hebrew translation], in KMA 15/2/2.

24. ALA/HQ, Fawzi al-Qawuqji to the Commanders of Division and Independent Units (No. 138), 25 July 1948, in IDFA 376/100001/1957.

25. Ghasan Jadid, Commander of the Alawite Battalion, "Administrative Order No. 13," 27 July 1948, in IDFA 435/100001/1957.

26. For incidents where ALA officers requested that soldiers who misbehaved

toward Palestinians be removed, see Commander of the First Battalion to Commander of Hittin Battalion, "The Guarding of the Garrisons," 4 May 1948, in IDFA 162/100001/1957; Jabal al-Arab Battalion to HQ, 24 May 1948, in HA 105/132.

27. HQ of al-Inqadh Force / Northern Front, Military Commander of Nablus, "Notice," 16 March 1948, in HA 105/216A.

28. Ibid.

29. Morris, *1948*, 91–92.

30. "Diary of Mar'i Hasan Hindawi."

31. Ibid.

32. Ibid. Commenting on the lack of training and prevalence of disobedience among his men, a company commander from the Hittin battalion warned the battalion commander in February 1948: "If anarchy prevails in the land of Palestine we have no hope of succeeding. I am pessimistic of the state of affairs." Commander of the First Company to Commander of Hittin Battalion, "Re: Your Letter from 12 February 1948," 13 February 1948, in IDFA 162/100001/1975.

33. Khalid Arslan (Nablus) to Khuri Arslan (Damascus).

34. Parsons, *The Commander*, 235–36; "Attn: Escaping from Bands," undated, in ISA MFA 4/2568. A Palestinian informant for the Haganah reported on a meeting between an ALA battalion commander and al-Qawuqji, where the defection of a high-ranking Iraqi officer was discussed: "This officer was known for his courage and valor. He came to Palestine with sincere intentions, to fight and save it, and not for economic reasons or because of adventurism. When he saw the mobs—those who came to Palestine for personal reasons—he was deeply disappointed and decided to flee." See "According to Jonny"; "Jonny Says"; "Reports from the Pupil."

35. Volunteers were taken off the ALA payroll after they defied a direct order and went to defend Palestinian villagers in Sha'b, next to Acre. See oral testimonies in Nafez Nazzal, *The Palestinian Exodus from Galilee, 1948* (Beirut: Institute for Palestine Studies, 1978), 88. For examples from other localities, see Esber, *Under the Cover of War*, 287; Shoufani, "Fall of a Village," 109.

36. Letter by Muhammad Salih Sa'id, undated, in IDFA 162/100001/1957.

37. Muhi al-Din al-Tayar (Nablus) to Father (Baghdad) [Hebrew translation], 4 April 1948, in HA 105/216A.

38. Ibid.

39. Hindawi's diary does not indicate dates. For a speculation on the date of the attack, see Gilad, "History of the ALA," 221; Tal, *War in Palestine*, 257–58.

40. "Diary of Mar'i Hasan Hindawi."

41. The commander of the unit that fought in Zir'in wrote to headquarters: "Only a few hours passed until the village returned to its pastoral quiet state ... Despite the mines which exploded and the many bombs falling, any trace of battle was [now] distant. But there, behind the walls of soil, [there is something] that offends the eye and cannot penetrate the soul, there lie the bodies of four Arab martyrs who were killed while defending Arab land." See Untitled Report on the Battle of Zir'in by an officer in the First Yarmuk Battalion, in IDFA 94/100001/1957.

42. "Diary of Mar'i Hasan Hindawi."

43. Gilad, "History of the ALA," 221–22; "A Notice from the Salvation Leadership"; "Seven of the Missing People from Beit Keshet Were Found Dead," *Davar*, 19 March 1948.

44. "Diary of Mar'i Hasan Hindawi."

45. For other instances where Jewish corpses were abused, see Sela, "Tsava ha-Hatsala ba-Galil," 217–18; Dr. Hochman, "Breaches of the Laws of War in the Arabs' War against Israel," 15 August 1948, in IDFA 120/4224/1949.

46. "We caught a hundred of them [Jewish civilians] who dropped their weapons and raised a white flag, and we returned them to Tel Aviv," Hajj Muhammad Salim al-Ma'ani, a Syrian volunteer, reported in his diary. In another instance, he delivered a captured Jew to the AHC. See "Volunteer Diary from 1948," 25–26 March 1948.

47. Mustafa Muhammad Fari'a to the Correspondent of al-Difa' in Tiberias, 27 February 1948, in HA 105/216G.

48. Hajj Shamil al-Samra'i (School of Medicine-Damascus) to Salman Salih Abu Hashim (Tubas) via 'Abd al-Halak al-'Anabtawi (Nablus) [Hebrew translation], 20 March 1948, in HA 105/216G.

49. Ibid.

50. Sela, "Tsava ha-Hatsala ba-Galil," 217–18; Morris, *1948*, 110–11.

51. Al-Hindi, "Jaysh al-Inqadh (1948–1949), Part II," 121.

52. Ezov, *Mishmar ha-'Emek*, 27–29, 71–88.

53. Al-Qawuqji, "Memoirs, 1948 Part I," 38–39; Ezov, *Mishmar ha-'Emek*, 88–94.

54. Burhan al-Din al-'Abbushi to Ahmad Hilmi Pasha, Jenin, 16 April 1948, in IDFA 98/100001/1957 [hereafter "al-'Abbushi's Letter"].

55. Al-Sayyid Najam, "*Shabah al-Andalus: 'Istahdara li-Suqut al-Andalus amama Nakbat Filastin*," 24 September 2006, in Burhan al-Din al-'Abbushi, Samak al-'Abbushi, and Hasan al-'Abbushi, *Faris al-Sayf wa-l-Qalam: al-A'mal al-Adabiya al-Kamila lil-Sha'ir al-Mujahid al-Rahil Burhan al-Din al-'Abbushi, 1911–1995* (Damascus: Mu'assasat Filastin lil-Thaqafah, 2009), 790, 792.

56. As a teacher in Iraq, al-ʿAbbushi tried to win hearts and minds for the Palestine cause, much like other Palestinian teachers and activists residing in Iraq at the time, including Amin al-Husayni, Darwish Miqdadi, Akram Zuʿaytir, and Muhammad ʿ Izzat Darwaza. See Wien, *Iraqi Arab Nationalism*, 32, 44–46, 110; Bashkin, *New Babylonians*, 132.

57. In the early 1940s, al-ʿAbbushi also wrote poems in praise of Hitler, wishing him victory over Britain and France. Victory of the Axis, he explained, would serve as punishment to the Allies for their support of Zionism. See Matti Peled, "Annals of Doom: Palestinian Literature—1917–1948," *Arabica*, T. 29, fasc. 2 (June 1982): 178–80.

58. Al-ʿAbbushi et al., *Faris al-Sayf,* 645, 656, 672, 684, 688–91, 798–99.

59. In his poem from the revolt, al-ʿAbbushi explained that success against the British in Iraq would enable al-Gaylani to march his army to Palestine and prevent the establishment of a Jewish state. See Peled, "Annals of Doom," 178–79.

60. ʿAbd al-Rahman Kayyali, *Al-Shiʿr al-Filastini fi Nakbat Filastin* (Beirut: al-Muʾassasah al-ʿArabiyah lil-Dirasat wa-al-Nashr, 1975), 116; Al-ʿAbbushi et al., *Faris al-Sayf,* 369. Also in Khalid A. Sulaiman, *Palestine and Modern Arab Poetry* (London: Zed Books, 1984), 34.

61. The poem is from 1946. See Kayyali, *Al-Shiʿr al-Filastini*, 109; Al-ʿAbbushi et al., *Faris al-Sayf,* 154. On the use of sex workers in land transactions, see Cohen, *Army of Shadows*, 200.

62. "Al-ʿAbbushi's Letter."

63. "List of Damages incurred in Mishmar ha-ʿEmek. . . . ," 17 April 1948, in IDFA 232/922/1975; Ezov, *Mishmar ha-ʿEmek*, 88–94.

64. Al-Hindi, "Jaysh al-Inqadh (1948–1949), Part II," 121–22. Al-Qawuqji claimed, years later: "I was afraid that our troops might suffer heavy casualties in the night, because they lacked discipline and experience in night fighting in rain and mud." See al-Qawuqji, "Memoirs, 1948—Part II," 39.

65. Ezov, *Mishmar ha-ʿEmek*, 104–6.

66. "Conversation with Carter Davidson, the National Director of Associated Press," 25 April 1948, in KMA 15/2/3; Al-Hindi, "Jaysh al-Inqadh (1948–1949), Part II," 121.

67. "Conversation with Carter Davidson." The remarks of the Iraqi officer were apparently candid. The British did arrive at the scene on April 6 and demanded that the ALA halt the attack for twenty-four hours, and al-Qawuqji consented, although not before the British threatened to use force if he did not. See Ezov, *Mishmar ha-ʿEmek*, 112–13, 130–31.

68. "After Requesting a 24-Hour Truce the Bands Dig In Next to Mishmar ha-ʿEmek,"

'Al ha-Mishmar, 9 April 1948; "How Was the 24-Hour Truce in Mishmar ha-'Emek Conducted," *Davar*, 9 April 1948; "Extending the Time for the Surrendering of Mishmar ha-'Emek," *al-Difa'*, 9 April 1948, clipped in HA 105/216G.

69. Ibid. "Mishmar ha-'Emek Rejects the Army's Demand Not to Attack the Bases of the Bands," *Maariv*, 8 April 1948; Ezov, *Mishmar ha-'Emek*, 135–36.

70. "A Notification by al-Inqadh Leadership on Mishmar ha-'Emek . . . ," *al-Difa'*, 11 April 1948, clipped in HA 105/216G; Parsons, *The Commander*, 227.

71. "Warning from the Commander to the Residents of Mishmar ha-'Emek," *al-Difa'*, 8 April 1948. These conditions were also published in the Hebrew press that evening, although they were attributed to "the Levantine imagination" of *al-Difa'*s correspondent. See "The Arab Press 'Conquered' Mishmar ha-'Emek," *Maariv*, 8 April 1948.

72. "Bulletin No. 1: Broadcasts of the al-Inqadh Forces (Hebrew Transmission)," 18 April 1948, in KMA 15/2/2. Cf. "Mismar Haemek Negotiations Explained," 18 April 1948, al-Inqaz, Arab Liberation Army Station, in FBIS, Daily Report, no. 293, 20 April 1948, II7.

73. "Arab Victory at Mishmar Ha-'Emek," 16 April 1948, in FBIS, in SWB, no. 47, 22 April 1948, 69.

74. "Arab Denial," 15 April 1948, al-Inqaz, Arab Liberation Army Station, in FBIS, Daily Report, no. 291, 16 April 1948, II1–II2.

75. The actual number of Jewish casualties was five civilians and thirteen Haganah men, and there were no captives. See "Reinforcement from Syria and Transjordan; Declaration by the Commander Fawzi al-Qawuqji; Travel by Commander Safwat Basha to Iraq," 18 April 1948, clipped in IDFA 4/100001/1957; "The Mishmar ha-'Emek Battle Reaches Its Peak and the Imprisonment of an Haganah Commander," *al-Difa'*, 14 April 1948; "The Defeat of the Enemy's Resistance in the Battle of Mishmar ha-'Emek," *al-Difa'*, 15 April 1948; "Extending the Time for the Surrendering of Mishmar ha-'Emek."

76. Haganah Intelligence, "The Battle of Mishmar ha-'Emek" [report on monitored transmissions], 8 May 1948, 2, in KMA 15/2/1. The claim that the Arab flag was flying over Mishmar ha-'Emek also appeared in letters by Palestinians. See Muhsin Fawaz to Abu 'Adnan, undated, in IDFA 98/100001/1957.

77. In order to drag out the negotiations, the representative for the kibbutz demanded that the ALA first pay for the damages it caused the kibbutz and then allow them more time to reach out to the Haganah. See Morris, *The Birth*, 240–41; Ezov, *Mishmar ha-'Emek*, 137–38.

78. The kibbutz representative explained that they could not commit in the name of the Haganah not to target the surrounding Palestinian villages, and the Haganah

command, shortly thereafter, officially rejected these terms. See: "Extending the Time for the Surrendering"; "Mishmar ha-'Emek Rejects the Army's Demand"; Ezov, *Mishmar ha-'Emek*, 148, 160, 164–65. ALA soldiers apparently saw the reinforcements arrive but were unable to stop them. See "Notifications of the Military HQ in Mishmar ha-'Emek on April 5 Regrading the Battle" [report on monitored transmissions], undated, in HA 105/216G.

79. Morris, *The Birth*, 240–41; Morris, *1948*, 134. According to Morris, the depopulation of villages in Marj Ibn 'Amir was the first time Ben-Gurion had sanctioned the forcible expulsion of Palestinians during the war. It is noteworthy, however, that 1948 was not the first instance when Zionist settlers forced residents of Marj Ibn 'Amir off their lands. In the 1930s and early 1940s, the JNF purchased lands in the region from absentee landlords and, with the help of the British authorities, evacuated Palestinian tenant farmers from several villages. See Areej Sabbagh-Khoury, "Lizkor Kedei Lehashkih: Kibbutzei Hashomer Hatsa'ir ve-Defusei ha-Yetsug shel ha-Kfarim ha-Falastinim," in Hirsch, *Mifgashim: Historyah ve-Antropologyah shel ha-Merhav ha-Yisra'eli-Falastini*, 176–204.

80. "Mountain after Mountain Was Captured and the Bands Were Driven Away: The Villages Next to Mishmar ha-'Emek Were Captured," *'Al ha-Mishmar*, 11 April 1948; Ezov, *Mishmar ha-'Emek*, 180–234; Al-Qawuqji, "Memoirs, 1948—Part I," 40–41. Concerning how residents of the surrounding kibbutzim narrated their participation in the depopulation of Marj Ibn 'Amir at the time, see Sabbagh-Khoury, "Lizkor Kedei Lehashkih," 176–204.

81. Uriel, "Day and Night in an Arab Village (Impressions from the Mishmar ha-'Emek Front)," *Ba-'Igud*, May–June 1948, vol. 12, 26, in IDFA 22/1147/2002.

82. Parsons, *The Commander*, 230. Al-Qawuqji also appealed to other ALA officers to come to his aid, but they were apparently reluctant. See Haganah Intelligence, "The Druze in the Palestine War," 1 August 1948, in IDFA 13/957/1952; "A Telegram from al-Qawuqji to Shakib Wahab during the Mishmar ha-'Emek Battle" [Hebrew translation], 18 May 1948, in HA 105/31.

83. "A Notification by al-Inqadh Leadership on Mishmar ha-'Emek . . . ," *al-Difa'*, 11 April 1948.

84. "Arab and Jewish Morale," al-Inqaz Radio, 15 April 1948, FBIS in SWB, no. 47, 22 April 1948, 70–71. On the reception of radio broadcasts by Palestinian villagers in 1948, see Shoufani, "Fall of a Village," 120.

85. "Notification by al-Inqadh Leadership on Mishmar ha-'Emek."

86. Parsons, *The Commander*, 231.

87. Haganah Intelligence, "The Battle of Mishmar ha-ʿEmek" [report on monitored transmissions], 4.

88. Haganah intelligence report from 19 April 1948, in HA 105/31. A slightly different version of this document appears in "The Battle of Mishmar ha-ʿEmek" [report on monitored transmissions].

89. Haganah Intelligence, "The Battle of Mishmar ha-ʿEmek" [report on monitored transmissions], 8 May 1948, 4.

90. Morris, The Birth, 242; Ezov, Mishmar ha-ʿEmek, 18; Walid Khalidi, *All That Remains: The Palestinian Villages Occupied and Depopulated by Israel in 1948* (Washington, DC: Institute for Palestine Studies, 1992), 143.

91. Morris, *The Birth*, 242.

92. *mufatit al-akbad*, literally "crushing to the liver."

93. "Al-ʿAbbushi's Letter." The final disintegration of al-Andalus, in southern Spain, came in 1492 after Queen Isabella and King Ferdinand concluded a ten-year war and conquered the city of Granada. Jews were expelled from Spain that year and Muslims were forced to convert to Christianity. By the early seventeenth century the remaining Muslims were expelled. See Jocelyn Hendrickson and Simon Barton, "Reconquista," in *The Oxford Encyclopedia of the Islamic World* (Oxford: Oxford University Press, 2009), accessed 3 May 2016, www.oxford-islamicworld.com/entry?entry=t236.e0976.

94. Burhan al-Din al-ʿAbbushi, "Al-Watan al-Mubiʿ," 23 January 1945, in al-ʿAbbushi et al., *Faris al-Sayf*, 50–51. Translated by Khalid A. Sulaiman in *Palestine and Modern Arab Poetry*, 38.

95. Khalid A. Sulaiman, *Palestine and Modern Arab Poetry*, 57–58. The theme of "Palestine as a second al-Andalus" was common in literary publications in Palestine and elsewhere in the Arab world throughout the 1930s and 1940s. See pamphlets included in the Library of Congress's Eltaher Collection: *Khatar al-Yahud ʿala Filastin al-Muqaddasa wa-al-Aqtar al-ʿArabiya: Nida' wa-Bayan min Filastin al-ʿArabiya al-Islamiya al-Mujahida ila Kull Muslim wa-ila Kull ʿArabi fi Mashariq al-Ard wa-Magharibiha* (undated), 7; Mahmud M. Sadiq, *Bi-al-Dimaʿ Tuharrar al-Awtan: Malhamat al-Harb al-Muqaddasa wa-Nashid al-ʿUruba fi Tahrir Filastin* (Cairo: Dar al-Maʿarif lil-Tibaʿah wa-al-Nashr, 1948), 6.

96. The play portrays the Mishmar ha-ʿEmek battle and another famous battle known as the Battle of Jenin, where Iraqi forces were able to stand up to the IDF. Al-Sayyid Najam, "*Shabah al-Andalus*: 'Istahdara li-Suqut al-Andalus Amama Nakbat

Filastin," 24 September 2006, in al-'Abbushi et al., *Faris al-Sayf*, 791; Shams al-Din Ghanim al-Qadir 'Asida, "Burhan al-Din al-'Abbushi Adiban" (master's thesis, Al-Najah National University–Nablus, 2012), 13.

97. Burhan al-Din, *Shabah al-Andalus*, in al-'Abbushi et al., *Faris al-Sayf*, 447.

98. It is possible that the girl in the play was alluding to acts of rape. In the stage directions, al-'Abbushi added that while the girl was speaking, the fighters were crying. Israeli sources suggest that there were instances of sexual abuse in the occupation of Marj Ibn 'Amir. See Hasso, "Modernity and Gender in Arab Accounts of the 1948 and 1967 Defeats," 492–500; Morris, *The Birth*, 242–43.

99. Burhan al-Din, *Shabah al-Andalus*, in al-'Abbushi et al., *Faris al-Sayf*, 427–28.

100. Ibid., 430.

101. Oz Almog, *The Sabra: The Creation of the New Jew* (Berkeley: University of California Press, 2000), 56–57. On a similar theme, see Anita Shapira, *Israel: A History* (Waltham, MA: Brandeis University Press, 2012), 150–51; Shapira, "Hirbet Hizah," 24–25.

102. Morris, *1948*, 298.

103. IS, "TSO Report No. 3," 14 October 1948, 2, in IDFA 353/535/2004.

104. Ibid.

105. Operation Yoav was launched to deal the last blow to the Bernadotte Plan, according to which Israel would lose the Negev. Four brigades were sent into battle on October 15, 1948, with the goal of disrupting the Egyptian lines of communication, isolating their brigades into pockets, and eventually driving them out of Palestine altogether. See Morris, *1948*, 321, 326–27.

106. IS, "TSO Report No. 5," 30 October 1948, 2, in IDFA 353/535/2004.

107. Ibid. An identical sentiment appears in one of the soldiers' bulletins. See Rozenson, *Kotvim 'ba-Mivtsa'*, 115–16.

108. TSO, no. 5, 2.

109. IS, "TSO Report No. 6," 14 November 1948, 3, in IDFA 353/535/2004.

110. Morris, *1948*, 328; Ariella Azoulay, *Alimut Mekhonenet, 1947–1950: Gene'alogyah Hazutit shel Mishtar va-Hafikhat ha-Ason le-Ason mi-Nekudat Mabatam'* (Tel Aviv: Resling, 2009), 26.

111. Morris, *1948*, 328.

112. Azoulay, *Alimut Mekhonenet*, 29–31.

113. "Apartments and Businesses under the Supervision of the Custodian for

Absentees' Property to Be Sold to Their Holders," *Haaretz*, 18 January 1953; Stein, "Israeli Routes through Nakba Landscapes," 6–15.

114. TSO, no. 6, 4.

115. A soldiers' publication from July 1948 included a humorous sketch in which a wife demanded that her husband bring back plunder from the conquered areas. The wife threatened the husband, "If you return tomorrow from Jaffa without bringing me anything—you can forget your address, understood?" See M. K., "The Tale of a Looter," *'Alim: The Newspaper of the Military Unit in Jaffa*, 25 July 1948, in IDFA 25/1147/2002.

116. TSO, no. 6, 4.

117. Ibid.

118. On modern Jewish biblical exegesis about pillage, which might have influenced this soldier, see Sokolow, "What Is This Bleeting [*sic*] of Sheep in My Ears," 145–49.

119. Gelber, *Komemiyut ve-Nakbah*, 348. In Dawayima soldiers found articles belonging to the Gush Etzion convoy, including army trousers, Palmach leaflets, and soldiers' letters. See Inbar, *Moznayim ve-Herev*, 1002.

120. IS, "TSO Report No. 8," 15 December 1948, 2, in IDFA 353/535/2004.

121. Ibid.

122. Several internal IDF investigations were launched, and a governmental committee was also set up to investigate the incidents. It recommended that a platoon commander be charged with murder, but this recommendation was never implemented, probably because of the general amnesty that was declared in February 1949. See Morris, *1948*, 333; Morris, *The Birth*, 470–71; Saleh Abd al-Jawad, "Zionist Massacres: The Creation of the Palestinian Refugee Problem in the 1948 War," in *Israel and the Palestinian Refugees*, ed. Eyal Benvenisti, Chaim Gans, and Sari Hanafi (Berlin: Springer, 2007), 67. On the general amnesty, see Inbar, *Moznayim ve-Herev*, 398, 1001–4.

123. TSO, no. 8, 2.

124. "A Special Annex to Operation Order Horev." See chapter 2 for Allon's directive.

125. *Daf Kravi*, no. 21.

126. Morris, *1948*, 331; Morris, *The Birth*, 472.

127. Rona Sela, *Le-'Iyun ha-Tsibur: Tatslume Falistinim be-Arkhiyonim Tseva'iyim be-Yisra'el* (Tel Aviv: Helenah, 2009), photograph no. 20.

128. TSO, no. 6, 3–4.

129. Penslar argued: "In military affairs, as in so many other respects, Israel represents a continuation of the diaspora via other means." I present a different view in

this chapter. I argue that the emergence of a *sovereign* Jewish armed force in Palestine/Israel constituted a break with earlier modern experiences of Jews with military service. See Penslar, *Jews and the Military*, 262.

130. Morris, *The Birth*, 528–29.

131. "Al-Inqaz Broadcasts," 29 April 1948, al-Inqaz Radio, in SWB, no. 49, 6 May 1948, 69.

132. According to some reports, by July 1948 there was a significant increase in the number of Palestinians who fought alongside ALA forces. See Sela, "Tsava ha-Hatsala ba-Galil," 239–40.

133. A report by a Palestinian informant—working for the Haganah—who trained in Qatana suggests that Palestinians trainees became resentful of the ALA because of the corporal punishment they suffered from commanding officers in the camp. "Many used to say, if we had known that this is why they brought us here, we would have never volunteered. Is this how our leaders think we would win the war against the Jews? If these are their ways and actions, we hope they fail." See "Report from a Man Who Trained in the Qatana training Camp in Syria."

134. "Letter to My Dear Sister" [Hebrew translation], 19 April 1948 in "Complication from Letters," 26 April 1948, in HA 105/216B.

135. Ibid.

136. There is no evidence of a nurse being killed in the al-Qastal battle. 'Abd al-Qadir al-Husayni's wife, Wajiha, is reported to have converted her house into a small army base, where she and other women treated the wounded. 'Abd al-Qadir al-Husayni himself, in a letter to his children several days before he was killed in battle, promised his daughter Hayfa' that if she excelled in school, he would buy her a first-aid kit so that she could treat the wounded fighters (he also promised his sons to buy them "real rifles and guns so that you can kill Jews with them"). See Asma Tubi, *'Abir wa-Majd* (Beirut, 1966), 314–15; letter from 'Abd al-Qadir al-Husayni to his children from 2 April 1948, in 'Isa K. Muhsin, *Filastin al-Umm wa-Ibnuha al-Barr, 'Abd al-Qadir al-Husayni* (Amman: Dar al-Jalil, 1986), 463.

137. Fleischman, *The Nation and Its "New" Women*, 202; Tubi, *'Abir wa-Majd*, 313–14.

138. "Commander al-Qawuqji Starts the March toward Disciplining the Haganah," 6 April 1948, *al-Sarih* (Jerusalem), clipped in ISA GL/13963/8.

139. Report from the Arabic press [Hebrew translation], inside Haganah intelligence report, 28 March 1948, in ISA P 19/10910.

140. Many Palestinian families feared their daughters would be sexually assaulted

and therefore forced them to leave the country. See Hasso, "Modernity and Gender in Arab Accounts of the 1948 and 1967 Defeats," 492–500.

141. Writing a week after the battle was over (and after the Dayr Yasin massacre and the death of 'Abd al-Qadir al-Husayni), a local Jerusalemite military leader, 'Irfan Salim al-Bitar, told Ahmad Hilmi 'Abd al-Baki from the AHC that the only way to save Palestine was to "say candidly to whoever promised [to save Palestine] that in the current conditions, the country (and especially Jerusalem) would only be saved by regular armies." See 'Irfan Salim al-Bitar to Ahmad Hilmi Pasha, 21 April 1948, in IDFA 2062/100001/1957.

142. As early as 1959, Walid Khalidi, a prominent Palestinian historian, demonstrated that the Israeli claim was a fallacy. Still, for decades later, scholarship appearing in the West repeated the myth that Palestinians were ordered to leave by Arab leaders. See Walid Khalidi, "Why Did the Palestinians Leave?" *Middle East Forum*, July 1959, 21–24, 35.

143. Data compiled from Abu-Sitta, *Atlas of Palestine*, 108–16; Itamar Radai, "The Collapse of the Palestinian-Arab Middle Class in 1948: The Case of Qatamon," *Middle Eastern Studies* 43, no. 6 (November 2007): 961–82. Abu Sitta's figure for Qatamon's population appears to be erroneous.

144. Al-Inqadh Forces HQ / Northern Front / Commander, Fawzi al-Qawuqji, "Notice No. 6," 24 April 1948, in IDFA 376/100001/1957.

145. Ibid. It is noteworthy that Morris has argued that on the same day al-Qawuqji published his message, April 24, the ALA instructed Palestinians from the village of al-Furaydis, south of Haifa, to evacuate. Morris based his claim on a Haganah intelligence briefing. See Morris, *The Birth*, 175.

146. "Arab Communique Warns against Rumors," 24 April 1948, al-Inqaz, Arab Liberation Army Station, in FBIS, Daily Report, no. 297, 26 April 1948, II4.

147. "Military Notice."

148. ALA / Safad Region / Alawite Battalion, Commander of the Safad Region to the Inhabitants of . . . 19 July 1948, in IDFA 435/100001/1957.

149. "Military Notice."

150. On May 13, ALA soldiers reportedly confiscated five pounds from each fleeing refugee on the road from Kafr Saba to Qalqilya. There are also reports of ALA retaliations against village heads who surrendered to Jewish forces. See Morris, *1948*, 164; 'Adil Manna, *Nakbah ve-Hisardut: Sipuram shel ha-Falestinim she-Notru be-Hefah uva-Galil, 1948–1956* (Jerusalem: Mekhon Van Lir, ha-Kibuts ha-Me'uhad, 2017), 76.

151. Morris, *1948*, 128–29. Regarding the influence of Dayr Yasin according to oral testimonies by Palestinians, see Esber, *Under the Cover of War*, 199, 214, 278, 296, 338.

152. Muhsin Fawaz to Abu Muhammad Qasim Zahadi, 18 April 1948 [?], in IDFA 2062/100001/1957.

153. Ibid. For a discussion of the number of casualties and the rumors about Dayr Yasin circulating at the time, see Benny Morris, "The Historiography of Deir Yassin," *Journal of Israeli History* 24, no. 1 (2005): 79–107; Walid Khalidi, *Dayr Yasin: al-Jum'a, 9 Nisan/April 1948* (Beirut: Mu'assasat al-Dirasat al-Filastiniya, 1998). For the inflated number circulating in the Arab press, see Gelber, *Palestine, 1948*, 315.

154. Jordan Fortwangler ('Ayn Karim) to Joseph Yos (Baden) [Hebrew translation], 25 April 1948, in Haganah Intelligence, "Censorship of Letters," 9 May 1948, in CZA S25/9209.

155. Tamir Goren, *Hefah ha-'Arvit be-Tashah: 'Otsmat ha-Ma'avak u-Memade ha-Hitmotetut* (Sedeh Boker: Makhon Ben-Gurion le-Heker Yisra'el, 2006), 189–90, 197, 233.

156. Abu Qasim (Kawkab Abu al-Hija) to Nimir al-Khatib (Haifa), 11 December 1947, in IDFA 565/100001/1957. Nimir al-Khatib was the author of one of the first books to discuss the Palestinian nakba; see *Min Athar al-Nakba* (Damascus: al-Matba'a al-Amumiya, 1951).

157. Abu Qasim (Kawkab Abu al-Hija) to Nimir al-Khatib (Haifa). For similar plans from elsewhere in Palestine, see Shoufani, "Fall of a Village," 121; "A Farce That Needs an End," *al-Mizan*, 28 February 1948, 6.

158. Goren, *Hefah ha-'Arvit*, 195–96.

159. Undated and unsigned letter starting with "After greetings and regards," in IDFA 565/100001/1957. The author of the letter was likely Christian because he referenced several family members with distinctly Christian names, such as Paulus and Joseph.

160. Ibid.

161. Undated letter titled "My dear brother *Hafdhat al-Mula*," in IDFA 565/100001 /1957.

162. Ibid. See also letter from Shafik As'ad 'Abd al-Hadi (Jenin) to his brother Kamil As'ad 'Abd al-Hadi (Haifa), 25 April 1948, in HA 105/252.

163. Letter from Haifa to Muhammad Dawud 'Abd al-Fatah (Beirut), 8 March 1948, in IDFA 565/100001/1957. Family and friends who had already left Palestine made the decision to stay in Haifa even harder. See Himmat Zubi, "The Ongoing Nakba: Urban Palestinian Survival in Haifa," in Abdo and Masalha, *Oral History of the Palestinian Nakba*, 182–208.

164. Goren, *Hefah ha-'Arvit*, 129–46; Walid Khalidi, "The Fall of Haifa Revisited," *Journal of Palestine Studies* 37, no. 3 (2008): 34–35; Shay Fogelman, "Port in a Storm," *Haaretz* [English], 3 June 2011.

165. For the historiographical debate on the depopulation of Haifa, see Khalidi, "Fall of Haifa Revisited"; Yfaat Weiss, *A Confiscated Memory: Wadi Salib and Haifa's Lost Heritage* (New York: Columbia University Press, 2011), 9–50.

166. Goren, *Hefah ha-'Arvit*, 220–27; Weiss, *Confiscated Memory*, 25.

167. Haganah Intelligence, "Translation of a Letter sent from Kafr Yasif to Acre" [Hebrew translation], 7 July 1948, in HA 105/154.

168. Ibid.

169. "Letter written on April 26 1948 by a Father to his Son, Munir Effendi Nur, an Inspector in the Police HQ in Nablus" [Hebrew translation], in HA 105/252.

170. Morris, *1948*, 164–66.

171. Ibid. Haganah agents may have poisoned the city's water supply, prompting the outbreak of typhus. According to one report, this was part of a larger initiative to engage in biological warfare. See Sara Leibovitz-Dar, "Microbes in State Service," *Hadashot*, 13 August 1993; Morris, *1948*, 465–66n270; letter by the city's mayor, in IDFA 273/100001/1957.

172. Gelber, *Komemiyut ve-Nakbah*, 236; Morris, *1948*, 338–39.

173. Morris, *1948*, 339.

174. "The Treatment of Sacred Places in the Occupied Territories," 27 October 1948, in IDFA 6/284/1949. As mentioned in chapter 2, the education officer of the Golani brigade was somewhat suspicious of hate indoctrination, but it is doubtful whether Golani's conduct was radically different than that of other units. See Manna, *Nakbah ve-Hisardut*, 92, 213.

175. Quoted in Benny Morris, "Revisiting the Palestinian Exodus of 1948," in Rogan and Shlaim, *War for Palestine*, 51, 54. Morris argued that while Carmel did not give explicit orders to carry out massacres, his officers interpreted his ambiguous commands "as an authorization to carry out murderous acts that would intimidate the population into flight." By the end of the operation, Carmel reversed his policy. He published a pamphlet that decried the "abuse of civilians, murder and robbery" that he discovered were still common following the Galilee's occupation. Like Karkoubi, Carmel was primarily concerned that "corruption and transgression from within" would come to define the new Israeli society. See Front A, "Day Order by Moshe Carmel, Commander of Front A," 25 November 1948, in IDFA 120/231/2015.

176. Morris, *The Birth*, 473. It is noteworthy that according to data presented by Salman Abu Sitta, the total of Palestinians who became refugees during Operation Hiram is about 13,000. The data set may be incomplete. See Abu Sitta, *Atlas of Palestine*, 90–96.

177. Gelber, *Komemiyut ve-Nakbah*, 352; Abu Sitta, *Atlas of Palestine*, 90–96, 106–8; Morris, *1948*, 345.

178. The exception was the fierce resistance put up by the Druze of Yanuh. See Morris, *The Birth*, 473; Gelber, *Komemiyut ve-Nakbah*, 236; Laila Parsons, "The Druze and the Birth of Israel," in Rogan and Shlaim, *War for Palestine*, 65–67; Geller, *Minorities in the Israeli Military*, 40–41.

179. Gelber, *Komemiyut ve-Nakbah*, 354; Morris, *The Birth*, 479–480; Abd al-Jawad, "Zionist Massacres," 119–20. For oral testimonies from the massacre, see Hisham Zreiq, "The Sons and Daughters of Eilaboun," in Abdo and Masalha, *Oral History of the Palestinian Nakba*, 227–44.

180. Gelber, *Komemiyut ve-Nakbah*, 239.

181. IDF records cite that thirty-three people were murdered, while Arif al-Arif argued the number was eighty-nine. See Abd al-Jawad, "Zionist Massacres," 120–21; Morris, *The Birth*, 481; "No Stigma Attached," *Journal of Palestine Studies* 7, no. 4 (Summer 1978): 144. The officer in charge of the massacre was prosecuted a month later and sentenced to seven years in prison, of which he served one, after a reduction of his sentence. He was eventually pardoned. See Morris, *The Birth*, 481n121; Inbar, *Moznayim ve-Herev*, 659–61.

182. The use of the feminine form in the Hebrew word "scout" (*sayeret*) in the letter indicates that the writer was a female soldier. Other words in the feminine form support this.

183. TSO, no. 6, 3–4. Unfortunately, this exceptionally long letter is the only one that specifically addresses the conquest of the Galilee in Operation Hiram.

184. Ibid.

185. Ibid.

186. Ibid. Eliezer is a common name for a Jewish male. The name appears in the original. It is impossible to identify with certainty who were the tortured soldiers in the reported incident. The ALA had Bosnian-Muslim officers from Yugoslavia who volunteered in an act of Islamic solidarity with Palestinians. According to one source, three Bosnian units arrived at the Middle East from Italy with hundreds of volunteers, all former soldiers in the 13th S.S. Handschar division. This division was mobilized

by Amin al-Husayni to fight alongside the Axis during the Second World War. An intelligence report from early 1948 indicated that at least one German officer also accompanied the Muslim volunteers. Testimonies by Bosnian officers suggest that the torture and murder described in the letter may have taken place in the Lebanese village of Mis al-Jabal (close to kibbutz Manara). See Seth J. Frantzman and Jovan Culibrk, "Strange Bedfellows: The Bosnians and Yugoslav Volunteers in the 1948 War in Israel/Palestine," *History of the 20th Century-Istorija 20. Veka*, no. 1 (2009): 189–201; Kaniuk, *Tashah*, 96.

187. Rivkah's response to the brutality of her male comrades was not necessarily influenced by her gender. While some scholars have argued that female soldiers in the Israeli army served as the moral compass of their units, reproving their male counterparts when they behaved immorally, there is not enough evidence to substantiate such a claim for the period under study. See Uta Klein, "'Our Best Boys': The Gendered Nature of Civil-Military Relations in Israel," *Men and Masculinities* 2 no. 1 (1999): 56; Shapira, *Land and Power*, 364.

188. See examples in Netiva Ben-Yehuda, *1948–Ben ha-Sefirot: Roman 'al Hathalat ha-Milhamah* (Jerusalem: Keter, 1981), 121–22, 197–98, 223, 228, 311–14; Mustafa Abbasi, "The Battle for Safad in the War of 1948: A Revised Study," *IJMES* 36, no. 1 (February 2004): 21–47.

189. TSO, no. 6, 3–4.

190. Al-Tira Youth Club to the General Commander of al-Inqadh Forces [Hebrew translation], 27 June 1948, in KMA 15/2/3.

191. Morris, *The Birth*, 355, 438.

192. Al-Inqadh Forces / Northern Front / The Commander, "No. 368" [Hebrew translation], 6 April 1948, in IDFA 648/922/1975.

193. Shoufani, "Fall of a Village," 110. The commander of the Druze battalion, Shakib Wahab, criticized the Arab League because it did not grant his request to supply his forces in Ramat Yohanan, east of Haifa. He wondered whether the league was truly interested in defeating Zionism, and accused Arab leaders of not taking the Jewish enemy seriously. "We must free a nation from a cruel enemy, and if God forbid the enemy wins, there would be no Arab left anywhere." When no response came to Wahab's first few letters, he sent another note to the headquarters, blaming them for "intentional lack of interest," and warning that he and his men felt "hopeless." Shortly after, Wahab's battalion defected to the Israeli side. See Shakib Wahab to ALA HQ [Hebrew translation], 17 April 1948 and 7 May 1948, in HA 105/132.

194. Commander of the Second Company to Commander of the Hittin Battalion, "Conclusions from the Mishmar ha-'Emek Battle," undated, in IDFA 373/100001/1957.

195. Ibid.

196. Shoufani, "Fall of a Village," 110–12. It was only after the war that several prominent Palestinian leaders and intellectuals pointed to the culpability of the ALA in the loss of Palestine. Among those were Musa Alami, Muhammad Nimr al-Khatib, and Taqi al-Din al-Nabhani. See Musa Alami, "The Lesson of Palestine," *Middle East Journal* 3, no. 4 (October 1949): 373–405; Nimr al-Khatib, *Min Athar al-Nakba*; Taqi al-Din al-Nabhani, *Inqadh Filastin* (Damascus: Ibn Zaydun, 1950). For a similar critique of the ALA in oral testimonies by Palestinians, see Esber, *Under the Cover of War*, 193, 195.

197. "Conclusions from the Mishmar ha-'Emek Battle."

198. Ibid.

199. This was a claim al-Qawuqji himself adopted. See Parsons, *The Commander*, 235.

200. Al-Qawuqji, for example, turned to blaming the volunteers themselves. He also blamed Taha al-Hashimi for failing to supply the ALA as promised. See al-Qawuqji, "Memoirs, 1948, Part I," 48; Sela, "Tsava ha-Hatsala ba-Galil," 240–43.

201. Morris, *1948*, 260, 282; Parsons, *The Commander*, 234–47.

202. Sela, "Tsava ha-Hatsala ba-Galil," 245–48.

203. "Order No. 37—To Deputy Hasan Zina," 28 October 1948, in IDFA 2062/100001/1957; Sela," Tsava ha-Hatsala ba-Galil," 246. It is unclear from which unit this order originated.

204. "Order No. 37—To Deputy Hasan Zina."

205. Sela, "Tsava ha-Hatsala ba-Galil," 248.

206. Sela, "Tsava ha-Hatsala ba-Galil," 248; Al-Hindi, "Jaysh al-Inqadh (1948–1949), Part II," 128; Batatu, *Syria's Peasantry*, 127.

207. Those targeted for their activism included not only Akram al-Hurani of Hama but also Wasfi al-Tal, who later rose to prominence in Jordanian politics. Political parties such as the Syrian Ba'ath and Egyptian Muslim Brotherhood were also targeted. Even tribes like the Arab al-Fadl of Amir Fa'ur were considered a threat to national security due to their activities in 1948. See Mandel, "Transnationalism and Its Discontents," 337; Chatty, "Leaders, Land, and Limousines," 394; Sela, "Tsava ha-Hatsala ba-Galil," 248; Al-Hindi, "Jaysh al-Inqadh (1948–1949), Part II," 128; Owen, "Akram al-Hourani," 59–62; Batatu, *Syria's Peasantry*, 127.

CHAPTER 5

1. Seikaly, "How I Met My Great-Grandfather," 10, 13–16.

2. TSO, no. 8, 6.

3. Some scholars argued that "the history" to which the Zionist movement wished to return was closely related to Protestant Christian ideas. See Amnon Raz-Krakotzkin, "Ha-Shivah el ha-Historiah shel ha-Geulah," in Eisenstadt and Lissak, *Ha-Tsyonut ve-ha- Hazara la-Historiyah*, 249–76.

4. TSO, no. 8, 6.

5. ID, "TSO Report No. 10," 15 January 1949, 2, in IDFA 353/535/2004.

6. Ibid.

7. ID, "TSO Report No. 12," 31 January 1949, 3, in IDFA 353/535/2004.

8. The number of POWs in Israeli captivity during the war is not entirely clear. In addition to five recognized camps for POWs, there were as many as seventeen unofficial camps during the war, making it especially difficult to give an accurate count. According to Mustafa Kabha and Wadiʻ Mahmud ʻAwawda, Israel detained anywhere from 7,000 to 12,000 Arabs in the period between 1947 and 1949, the majority of whom were Palestinians. See Mustafa Kabha and Wadiʻ Mahmud ʻAwawda, *Usra Bila Hirab: Al-Muʻtaqalun al-Filastiniya, wa-al-Muʻtaqalat al-Israʼiliya al-ʼ Ula: 1948–1949* (Beirut: Muʼassasat al-Dirasat al-Filastiniya 2013), 21; Salman Abu Sitta and Terry Rempel, "The ICRC and the Detention of Palestinian Civilians in Israel's 1948 POW/Labor Camps," *Journal of Palestine Studies* 43, no. 4 (Summer 2014): 17–18. For lower estimates, see Aharon Klein, "Ha-Shvuyim ha-ʻAravim be-Milhemet ha-ʻAtsmaʻut," in Kadish, *Milhemet haʻAtsmaʻut, Tashah-Tashat*, 571.

9. The IDF had placed several Jewish intelligence agents of Mizrahi origin among the POWs and they were transferred to Transjordan as part of a prisoner exchange. They were supposed to settle in Amman and report back to the IDF. One was quickly captured by the Transjordanian authorities and executed. See Friedman, *Spies of No Country*, 193–206.

10. IS HQ, "Bi-Weekly Report," 27 February 1949, 8, in IDFA 875/1109/2005. A list of the most popular recipients of POW letters in February 1949 included King Abdullah's sons, Talal and Nayif; Hussam al-Din Jarallah, the new mufti of Jerusalem appointed by King Abdullah; Abdullah al-Tal, governor of the old city of Jerusalem; Muhammad ʻAli Jaʻabari, mayor of Hebron; Suliman Tuqan, mayor of Nablus; ʻArif al-ʻArif, governor of Ramallah; Sulayman al-Taji al-Faruqi, a prominent Palestinian jurist, politician, and

poet; 'Azmi Nashashibi, head of the Palestine Broadcasting Service and a confidant of the Hashemites; Samir al-Rifa'i, Palestine-born former prime minister of Transjordan; Mithqal al-Fayiz, a prominent Transjordanian Bedouin shaykh; and Yussuf Haykal, former mayor of Jaffa.

11. Unless otherwise noted, Palestinian letters appearing in this chapter are the censor's Hebrew translations as they appeared in the censorship bureau's reports.

12. IS HQ, "Bi-Weekly Censorship Report No. 3," 6 February 1949, 6, in IDFA 875/1109/2005.

13. Avi Shlaim, *Collusion across the Jordan: King Abdullah, the Zionist Movement, and the Partition of Palestine* (Oxford: Clarendon Press, 1989).

14. Massad, *Colonial Effects*, 226–29; Mary C. Wilson, *King Abdullah, Britain, and the Making of Jordan* (Cambridge: Cambridge University Press, 1987), 182–84; Avi Plascov, *The Palestinian Refugees in Jordan 1948–1957* (London: Frank Cass, 1981), 1–28. Massad and Wilson argued that some of the Palestinian delegates were goaded by the Transjordanian army to attend the conference.

15. The All-Palestine Government had no sovereign power, even in the seat of the government in Gaza, which was exclusively controlled by the Egyptians. See Avi Shlaim, "The Rise and Fall of the All-Palestine Government in Gaza," *Journal of Palestine Studies* 20, no. 1 (Autumn 1990): 37–53; Plascov, *Palestinian Refugees in Jordan*, 7–9.

16. "Bi-Weekly Censorship Report No. 3," 6 February 1949, 7.

17. The International Committee of the Red Cross (ICRC) also tried to prevent the expulsion of Palestinian POWs upon their release but with little success. See Abu Sitta and Rempel, "The ICRC," 28–29.

18. IS HQ, "Censorship Report No. 1 for the Period 12/17–30 [1948]," 10 January 1949, 2, in IDFA 875/1109/2005.

19. "Bi-Weekly Report," 27 February 1949, 8. A similar sentiment appears in "Censorship Report," 14 March 1949, in IDFA 875/1109/2005.

20. The censor noted that often one POW would write letters for many of the others. See "Intelligence Service HQ [Report]," 28 September 1948, 8.

21. Abu Sitta and Rempel, "The ICRC," 29–30.

22. At the end of 1948, IDF authorities dismissed twenty-five to fifty volunteers for adjustment problems, as they were "bringing down the morale of other Mahal men who came in contact with them." See Gshur, "Mitnadvey Huts la-Arets," 249.

23. The "P" stands for *protektsya*, a Hebrew word borrowed from Russian, meaning cronyism or favoritism.

24. Unit for Psychological Research / Center for Research of Public Opinion, "Mahal Comes to Israel," 2–3, 14, 16, 18, in IDFA 225/7/1955. The poll suggested that, despite their dissatisfaction, 75 percent of volunteers wanted to stay in Israel after the war. For more on Mahal dissatisfaction, see Gshur, "Mitnadvey Huts la-Arets," 218–32, 273, 307–8.

25. "Instructions for Volunteers from Overseas," in IDFA 19/1042/1949.

26. The concern over Mahal letters defaming Israel was raised by IDF officials. See Gshur, "Mitnadvey Huts la-Arets," 168, 253.

27. IS, "TSO Report No. 7," 5 December 1948, 3, in IDFA 353/535/2004.

28. TSO, no. 7, 3.

29. Ibid., 4. This is an adaptation of the famous last words attributed to Trumpeldor.

30. "Report," ca. November 1948 [compiled by the civilian section of the Tel Aviv censorship bureau], 1, in IDFA 13/621/1985.

31. Quoted in Gshur, "Mitnadvey Huts la-Arets," 168.

32. "Mahal Comes to Israel," 17, 18.

33. TSO, no. 7, 4.

34. According to IDF regulations, "overseas volunteers have the right to return to their countries of origin at the expense of Government within six months after their release." See Brigade Seven, "HAMITNADEV-A Newsletter for the Volunteer" [English], no. 53, 20 March 1949, 4, in IDFA 48/1147/2002.

35. TSO, no. 7, 4.

36. Ibid.

37. The Talmud includes several exegeses that condemn the Israelites for resorting to militarism. One suggests that God punished Abraham and his descendants with 210 years of oppression in Egypt because Abraham "impressed [Torah] scholars (*talmidei hakhamim*) into military service." See Sokolow, "What Is This Bleeting [*sic*] of Sheep in My Ears," 145.

38. David Bridger and Samuel Wolk, eds., *The New Jewish Encyclopedia* (New York: Behrman House, 1976), 170; Moshe Idel, *Golem: Jewish Magical and Mystical Traditions on the Artificial Anthropoid* (Albany: State University of New York Press, 1990), 251–58; Maya Barzilai, *Golem: Modern Wars and Their Monsters* (New York: New York University Press, 2016), 1–26.

39. The golem myth was also depicted in popular culture in the early twentieth century, appearing in novels and even featured in the 1920 German film *Der Golem*. The film was also released in the United States. The golem trope in Israel following the war was most often associated with the Arab enemy. Still, several Israeli novelists

used the metaphor for self-reflection and "to expose the vulnerability of societies . . .
that rely on violent measures to achieve political goals"; see Barzilai, *Golem*, 107–44.

40. Derek Penslar, "Rebels without a Patron State: How Israel Financed the 1948
War," in *Purchasing Power: The Economics of Modern Jewish History*, ed. Rebecca Ko-
brin and Adam Teller, 171–91 (Philadelphia: University of Pennsylvania Press, 2015).

41. Alon Gan's survey of the views of American Jewish leaders and thinkers on the
question of the "return to history" shows that until the 1967 war, the overwhelming
majority of Jewish leaders expressed fear that the Yishuv and later the State of Israel
would resort to chauvinistic nationalism and an overreliance on military power and
abandon what they saw as Judaism's humanism and universal moral message. See Alon
Gan, "'Ha-Hazara ha-Yehudit la-Historyah' ba-Mahshava ha-Tsyonit ha-Amerikanit
(1897–1967)," in Eisenstadt and Lissak, *Ha-Tsyonut ve-ha-Hazara la-Historiya*, 361–88.

42. ID, "TSO Report No. 2," 10 October 1948, 4, in IDFA 353/535/2004.

43. Ibid.

44. The letter originated from Wadi Salib, a depopulated Arab neighborhood of
Haifa. By 1949 it was inhabited mostly by Mizrahi Jews, primarily North Africans.

45. Letter in French from [redacted name], 6230 Madregot Ajloun to [redacted
name] Hotel du Centre, Paris IX, 28 February, in Censorship Department, "Attn: Anti-
Jewish and Anti-Zionist Letters," 16 March 1948, in IDFA 2449/1433/2002. An annota-
tion on the report indicated that the letter was stopped.

46. In one censorship bureau report showcasing the writing of Sabra Jews residing
in the United States in an official capacity, the censor commented that the negative
opinion of American Jews was widespread. One letter noted: "The rich Jews, even if
they give money, are not good Zionists. They do not feel moved by our state. They
give money [to Israel] just as they give money to tuberculosis patients and others."
See "Censorship Report," 26 April 1949, 16.

47. The letter was written on October 30, 1948. Quoted in Tikva Honig-Parnass,
"Reflections of the '48 Generation," *Al-Ahram Weekly Online*, no. 586, 16–22 May 2002,
accessed 30 September 2013, http://weekly.ahram.org.eg/2002/586/sc4.htm.

48. Ibid. Not all Jewish volunteers from Western countries demonstrated the same
sentiment toward Arabs. One British volunteer, involved in transporting Arab POWs,
commented that the POW camp "made the impression of a zoo . . . full of monkeys."
See "Censorship Report," 10 February 1949, 10, in IDFA 875/1109/2005.

49. Mahal officers sometimes expressed similar sentiments. The commander of
the Seventh Brigade, Canadian officer Benjamin Dunkelman, famously refused an

order to expel Palestinians from Nazareth after the occupation of the city. He reportedly agreed to transfer the control of the city only when promised by Ben-Gurion that its inhabitants would not be expelled. See Penslar, *Jews and the Military*, 235–36.

50. As late as 1942, Jewish religious leaders from the Conservative and Reform movements in the United States reaffirmed the right of individuals to refuse army service for pacifist reasons. See Penslar, *Jews and the Military*, 209.

51. Gan, "'Ha-Hazara ha-Yehudit la-Historyah,'" 361–88.

52. ID, "TSO Report No. 14," 13 March 1949, 3, in IDFA 353/535/2004.

53. Southern Censor (Tel Aviv) to Chief Censor, "A Report for the Month of January," 2 February 1949, in IDFA 13/621/1985. It is likely that the writer was a Mahal volunteer; however, it is not specified in the report.

54. ID, "TSO Report No. 18," 20 May 1949, 1, in IDFA 353/535/2004.

55. This is a quotation by Moshe Shertok in an Education Service leaflet, undated, in IDFA 496/4944/1949.

56. Quoted in the Israel Institute for Applied Social Research, *Information Bulletin* 22, October 1969. I would like to thank Daphna and Nurit Guttman for providing me a copy of the publication.

57. The pollsters did not explain the reason for the reportedly unanimous opposition of Yemenites to the return of the refugees. One possible explanation is that Yemenites, some of whom were brought to Palestine to replace Arab laborers, came to view Palestinians as competition in the job market and therefore objected to their return. See Ari Ariel, *Jewish-Muslim Relations and Migration from Yemen to Palestine in the Late Nineteenth and Twentieth Centuries* (Leiden: Brill, 2014).

58. *Information Bulletin 22*.

59. See Cohen, *Good Arabs*; Jacob Tovi, *Israel and the Palestinian Refugee Issue: The Formulation of Policy, 1948–1956* (New York: Routledge, 2014). Israeli intelligence agents of Mizrahi origin disguised themselves as Palestinians and followed the stream of refugees fleeing Haifa to Beirut in April 1948. The intelligence agents settled among Palestinians and reported back on their sentiments and on other political and military developments. See Friedman, *Spies of No Country*, 100–126.

60. "Censorship Report," 14 March 1949, 8; "Censorship Report," 11 May 1949, in IDFA 875/1109/2005.

61. "Intelligence Service HQ [Report]," 28 September 1948, 8–9.

62. "Censorship Report No. 1 for the Period 12/17–30 [1948]," 3. On changes in gender roles among refugees, see Julie Peteet, *Landscape of Hope and Despair: Palestinian Refugee Camps* (Philadelphia: University of Pennsylvania Press, 2005), 118–20.

63. "Censorship Report No. 1 for the Period 12/17–30 [1948]," 3.

64. Military Censor, "Report on Smuggled Mail to Enemy Countries," May 1949, 3, in IDFA 8/621/1985. For the legal status of refugees after 1949, see Rony Gabbay, *Political Study of the Arab-Jewish Conflict: The Arab Refugee Problem, a Case Study* (Geneva: E. Droz, 1959), 206–15.

65. Gabbay, *Political Study,* 206–210; Peteet, *Landscape of Hope and Despair,* 120–124.

66. Gabbay, *Political Study,* 142; Plascov, *Palestinian Refugees in Jordan,* 10–28. "Intelligence Service HQ [Report]," 28 September 1948, 9; "Report on Smuggled Mail to Enemy Countries," May 1949, 3; IS, "On Arab Mail from Enemy Countries and Mail by Arab Israelis," 2, 15 September 1949, in IDFA 8/621/1985.

67. "Censorship Report," 10 February 1949, 7.

68. Ibid.

69. Ibid.

70. "Bi-Weekly Report," 27 February 1949, 9.

71. "Censorship Report," 10 February 1949, 7–8.

72. "There is hardly a letter that does not relate the death of a family member or this or that acquaintance," the censor noted in March 1949. See "Censorship Report," 14 March 1949, 8.

73. The literal translation of the phrase is "his death in the countries of exile [*bilād al-ghurba*]." See letter by Wadiʿ ʿAbd Allah al-Sulhan [Arabic], 21 June 1948, in IDFA 565/100001/1957.

74. "Censorship Report," 10 February 1949, 7; IS HQ, "Bi-Weekly Censorship Report No. 2," 20 January 1949, 3, in IDFA 875/1109/2005.

75. "Censorship Report No. 1 for the Period 12/17–30 [1948]," 3; see also Censor No. 3, "A Short Report on the Occupied Areas of Jaffa, Lydda and Ramle," 6 October 1948, in IDFA 14/621/1985.

76. IS HQ, "Bi-Weekly Censorship Report No. 2," 20 January 1949, 3.

77. "Bi-Weekly Report," 27 February 1949, 9; Plascov, *Palestinian Refugees in Jordan,* 21.

78. See letters in "Censorship Report," 11 May 1949.

79. Ben-Eliezer, *Making of Israeli Militarism,* 171.

80. Letter dated 14 August 1948 in "Short Report on the Occupied Areas of Jaffa, Lydda and Ramle," 1.

81. Ibid.

82. IS Base / Intelligence 4, "A Report on the Mail of the Conquered Areas in the Northern Part of the Country," 13 July 1949, 2, in IDFA 8/621/1985.

83. "Short Report on the Occupied Areas of Jaffa, Lydda and Ramle," 1–2. The censor lamented that businessmen from around the world were unaware that "Jaffa had been transformed" and kept sending mail to Jaffa's Arab merchants, not realizing they were no longer there. See Southern Censor (Tel Aviv) to Chief Censor, "A Report for the Month of November," 31 November 1948, 4, in IDFA 13/621/1985.

84. Indeed, by 1950, 95 percent of all olive groves and one half of all citrus groves in the part of Palestine that had become Israel had been transferred from Palestinian ownership to the Custodian for Absentees' Property and later sold by the state to the JNF. This essentially increased the land available for Jewish settlement by 250 percent. See Robinson, *Citizen Strangers*, 35–36, 47; Geremy Forman and Alexandre (Sandy) Kedar, "From Arab Land to 'Israel Lands': The Legal Dispossession," *Environment and Planning D: Society and Space* 22 (2004): 809–30.

85. One refugee from Lebanon asked a Palestinian in Jaffa to pay upwards of 500 Palestine liras to water his orchard so that it did not wilt. See "A Report on the Mail of the Conquered Areas in the Northern Part of the Country," 13 July 1949, 2; "Short Report on the Occupied Areas of Jaffa, Lydda and Ramle," 2.

86. "Intelligence 4 / Haifa District, "Attn: Letters Which Were Found with Infiltrators," 13 September 1951, in IDFA 660/1109/2005.

87. "Intelligence Report No. 8," 7 December 1948, 2, in IDFA 286/600137/1951.

88. "On Arab Mail from Enemy Countries and Mail by Arab Israelis," 15 September 1949, 2–3.

89. According to the censor, 2.5 percent of the 1,470 Palestinian letters that passed through the censorship bureau in September 1949 pertained to property. I was unable to locate similar figures for other months. See "On Arab Mail from Enemy Countries and Mail by Arab Israelis," 15 September 1949, 1.

90. "I tried to return to al-Ramla, but I was not given permission," wrote one refugee from Amman in May 1949. See "Censorship Report," 11 May 1949.

91. Ibid., 2; "Report on the Mail of the Conquered Areas in the Northern Part of the Country," 13 July 1949, 2.

92. Censorship Department, intercepted letter from Haifa to Lebanon (via Cyprus), 25 February 1949, inside report dated 17 March 1949, in IDFA 8/621/1985. Not all Palestinian refugees in Lebanon wished to return to Palestine/Israel. Several wealthy families were allowed to open businesses in Lebanon. They were not interested in returning, and in fact urged family members who remained in Israel to join them in Lebanon: "Why haven't you come? We already have sent you passports and visas two

and a half months ago at least," one letter stated. It appears that this family's relatives in Israel chose to remain where they were. See "Report on Smuggled Mail to Enemy Countries," May 1949, 3; "Censorship Report," 11 May 1949; Peteet, *Landscape of Hope and Despair*, 120–24.

93. "Report on the Mail of the Conquered Areas in the Northern Part of the Country," 4.

94. Ibid.

95. "Meetings in Tel Aviv 9–10 August 1949—Discharged Moroccan Gahal," in CZA S20/620.

96. TSO, no. 20, 9.

97. ID, "TSO Report No. 21," 3 July 1949, 4, in IDFA 353/535/2004.

98. ID, "A Report on the State of Mind among North African Immigrant Conscripts," 26 August 1949, 1, in IDFA 643/1470/2002.

99. Ibid., 2.

100. Ibid.

101. Ibid. Similar reports from September and November 1949 that analyzed an additional two thousand letters by North African soldiers reached the same conclusions: the majority wanted to leave Israel. According to September data based on 320 letters: 33 percent advised their family to immigrate to Israel immediately, 25 percent advised them to postpone immigration for the time being, and 42 percent advised them against immigrating to Israel. In 420 letters: 50 percent wanted to return to North Africa permanently, 17 percent wanted to return to North Africa but left open the option of immigrating to Israel once again (presumably when the economic situation improved), and 33 percent wanted to stay in Israel. According to November data, in 345 letters: 37 percent advised their family to immigrate to Israel immediately, 16 percent advised them to postpone immigration for the time being, and 47 percent advised them against immigrating to Israel. In 360 letters: 50 percent wanted to return to North Africa permanently, 18 percent wanted to return to North Africa but left open the option of immigrating to Israel once again, and 32 percent wanted to stay in Israel. See TSO, no. 23, 11; ID, "TSO Report No. 25," 29 November 1949, 6, in IDFA 353/535/2004.

102. "Special Report: Mood among North African Immigrants," 31 July 1949, 4–5. The survey was based on 1,440 letters examined between July 3, 1949, and August 5, 1949.

103. Ibid., 1.

104. Ben-Gurion's diary, entry for September 2, 1949, in Ben-Gurion Archives, Item no. 219927.

105. "Censorship Report," 26 April 1949, 16.

106. "Censorship Report No. 10," 13 June 1949, in IDFA 875/1109/2005. On discrimination in employment against Moroccan Jews, see Bryan K. Roby, *The Mizrahi Era of Rebellion: Israel's Forgotten Civil Rights Struggle, 1948–1966* (Syracuse, NY: Syracuse University Press 2015), 99.

107. "Censorship Report No. 10."

108. Ibid.

109. TSO, no. 25, 7.

110. TSO, no. 23, 12.

111. "Report on the State of Mind among North African Immigrant Conscripts," 3. Similar sentiments were recorded in letters by Turkish soldiers. See "Censorship Report," 26 April 1949.

112. Even within the army, discrimination was rampant, with European Gahal men being paid more than Moroccans. See "Intelligence Service HQ [Report]," 28 September 1948, 3.

113. TSO, no. 21, 7.

114. Quoted in Ella Shohat, "Sephardim in Israel: Zionism from the Standpoint of Its Jewish Victims," *Social Text*, nos. 19/20 (Autumn 1988): 4.

115. Ibid.

116. Tsur, *Kehilah Keru'ah*, 319. Tsur argued that Gelblum was channeling the views of Giora Yoseftal, head of the Jewish Agency's immigration department and one of the most important bureaucrats in setting Israeli immigration policy. According to Tsur, it was Yoseftal who allowed Gelblum into the transit camps in order to expose the true nature of the immigrants to the public. Yoseftal's views were similar to the views expressed in private by Israeli decision-makers, including Prime Minister Ben-Gurion and Foreign Minister Moshe Shertok. See Tsur, *Kehilah Keru'ah*, 269, 319; Shohat, "Sephardim in Israel," 4.

117. Yaron Tsur, "Carnival Fears: Moroccan Immigrants and the Ethnic Problem in the Young State of Israel," *Journal of Israeli History* 18, no. 1 (1997): 95.

118. Due to the publication of Gelblum's articles, even those Moroccan Jews who were adamant about staying in Israel found themselves in a precarious situation. One Moroccan immigrant, who was likely not a soldier, explained in his letter to Morocco that Gelblum's writing would serve as ammunition for those who called on

Jews not to leave Morocco. The immigrant urged that unless immediate action was taken to improve the integration of Moroccans in Israel, "major shocks will come to our country." See "Censorship Report No. 10," 13 June 1949.

119. "Special Report: Mood among North African Immigrants," 3.

120. Ibid.

121. Ibid., 4–5.

122. "North African Immigrants Narrate Their Bitterness," *Davar*, 24 June 1949; "Intelligence Service HQ [Report]," 28 September 1948, 4.

123. "Special Report: Mood among North African Immigrants," 2.

124. "Report on the State of Mind among North African Immigrant Conscripts," 3.

125. Ibid., 3. Another letter, directed to family in Morocco and intercepted by the civilian branch of the censorship bureau, stated that "it was better to suffer at the hands of a Moroccan Arab [the original has the word misspelled] than those of a Jewish Pole." See "Censorship Report," 26 April 1949, 16.

126. Shohat, "Rupture and Return," 52, 54.

127. The IDF archives redacted the writer's name during the declassification of the document, but the letter indicates that he was the son of the Palestinian representative to the UN, who was at the time Jamal al-Husayni (later the foreign minister of the All-Palestine Government).

128. "Bi-Weekly Report," 27 February 1949, 16.

129. Ibid. Similar optimism is displayed in a letter by the son of the Christian mayor of Bethlehem, Issa Basil Bandak. See IS HQ, "Report No. 7," 23 November 1948, 4, in IDFA 286/600137/1951.

130. Radai, *Palestinians in Jerusalem and Jaffa*, 67. The Albinas were a Catholic middle-class family of Italian descent. The family is believed to have immigrated to the Levant in the sixteenth or seventeenth century. They initially settled in the Musrara neighborhood in Jerusalem, but many members of the family later moved to Qatamon. See Iris Albina, "Souvenir from Gethsemane: Portrait of the Albina Brothers," *Jerusalem Quarterly* 60 (Autumn 2014): 59–76. (While most often written as Antoine Francis Albina, a more accurate transliteration of his name is Antun Franswa al-Bina.)

131. "Bi-Weekly Report," 27 February 1949, 16.

132. This criticism might have seemed odd to British officials in Palestine who corresponded with Albina only a year earlier in his capacity as a leader of the Qatamon neighborhood. In one letter to the British district governor from January 1948, Albina expressed his fear of retaliations by Jews inside Qatamon and requested that

the British help keep Arab fighters out of the neighborhood so that Jewish forces would not have a pretext to launch an offensive. See Radai, *Palestinians in Jerusalem and Jaffa*, 53–54.

133. For other accounts by Arab authors in the immediate aftermath of the nakba that critique Arab and Palestinian leaders, see Adnan Mohammad Abu-Ghazaleh, "The Impact of 1948 on Palestinian Arab Writers: The First Decade," *Middle East Forum* 66 (1970): 82–92; Alami, "Lesson of Palestine"; Qustantin Zurayq, *Ma'ana al-Nakba* (Beirut: Dar al-'Ilm li-al-Malayin, 1948).

134. "Bi-Weekly Report," 27 February 1949, 17.

135. "Censorship Report," 14 March 1949, 15.

136. For a more rigorous discussion of these questions, see Seikaly, "How I Met My Great-Grandfather," 13–19.

137. It is likely that the different views of about 30 percent of North African Jews in the IDF were related to class. However, since the intercepted letters do not normally provide the demographics of the authors, it is impossible to make such an assertion with certainty.

138. See Diana Fuss, "Interior Colonies: Frantz Fanon and the Politics of Identification," *Diacritics* 24, nos. 2/3 (Summer–Autumn 1994): 19–42.

139. Shohat, "Zionism from the Standpoint," 2; Yehouda Shenhav, *The Arab Jews: A Postcolonial Reading of Nationalism, Religion, and Ethnicity* (Stanford, CA: Stanford University Press, 2006), 70.

140. "Report on the State of Mind among North African Immigrant Conscripts," 3.

141. "Special Report: Mood among North African Immigrants," 5.

142. Edward W. Said, *Culture and Imperialism* (New York: Knopf, 1993), 245–60. Moroccan Jews were often described as lazy by Israeli officials. See Picard, *'Olim Bi-Mesurah*, 267.

143. On Homi Bhabha's and Frantz Fanon's idea of "mimicry of subjection" of the colonial power, see Fuss, "Interior Colonies," 19–42.

144. TSO, no. 25, 6.

145. The view that North Africans were hot-tempered and quick to resort to violence was popular among Zionist-Ashkenazi leaders and the general public. See Moshe Shokeid, "The Regulation of Aggression in Daily Life: Aggressive Relationships among Moroccan Immigrants in Israel," *Ethnology* 21, no. 3 (1982): 271–81; Gidi Weitz, "The Protocols of Wadi Salib," *Haaretz*, 13 February 2014.

146. Even some Jews in Morocco writing to family and friends in Israel adopted an Orientalist view, perhaps the result of decades under French colonialism. See "What Are They Writing in the Diaspora?," 2.

147. TSO, no. 16, 8. See also Southern Censor, Internal Department, "Special Report No. 44: This Is How Israel Is Described," 1949, 3, in IDFA 18/621/1985.

148. TSO, no. 23, 12; Tsur, *Kehilah Keruʻah*, 252.

149. TSO, no. 25, 7.

150. "What Are They Writing in the Diaspora?", 3.

151. "Censorship Report," 14 March 1949, 10.

152. "What Are They Writing in the Diaspora?", 3.

153. TSO, no. 21, 7.

154. Southern Censor to Chief Censor, "Special Report No. 39: The Mood among New Immigrants," 16 September 1949, 6, in IDFA 18/621/1985. Some Moroccan immigrants conceded that there was racism in Israel, but still urged their families to come. See "Censorship Report," 26 April 1949, 10.

155. Southern Censor, Economic Department, "Special Report No. 48: The State of Immigrants," January 1950, 5, in IDFA 18/821/1985.

156. "Report on the Mail of the Conquered Areas in the Northern Part of the Country," 4.

157. ʻAzmi Nashashibi, head of the Palestine Broadcasting Services, speaking on the radio from Ramallah in August 1948, accused the "Jewish censorship" of altering letters sent by Palestinians in Israel to their families abroad. See Yaacov Eyal (Landau), Middle East Department, Ministry of Foreign Affairs to General Staff / Personnel Department / 3, "Attn: Claims Against the Censorship of Arab Letters," 4 August 1948, in ISA G 19/303.

158. Cohen, *Good Arabs*, 27–28; Robinson, *Citizen Strangers*, 81.

159. "On Arab Mail from Enemy Countries and Mail by Arab Israelis," 15 September 1949, 1. For correspondence between the censorship bureau and the police on the transfer of such letters, see IDFA 8/621/1985. Another, more sophisticated method for smuggling mail in and out of Israel was by way of a third country. See "Report on Smuggled Mail to Enemy Countries," May 1949, 1.

160. The smugglers themselves were often caught by the Israeli police, put on trial, and jailed for extended periods of time; sometimes they were forced to work as informants for the Israeli intelligence. See Israel Police / Headquarters Unit / Investigation

Department, A. Shlush, Assistant Regional Supervisor (in the name of the Head of Investigation Department) to Intelligence 4, "Attn: Letters in the Hands of Infiltrators," 8 February 1951, in IDFA 8/621/1985; Cohen, *Good Arabs*, 28.

161. Robinson, *Citizen Strangers*, 74. For an example of redacted letters that deal with the return of refugees, see "Report on Smuggled Mail to Enemy Countries," May 1949.

162. ID, "A Report on Israeli Arab Mail and [Mail] from Enemy Territory for the Month of July 1949," 26 August 1949, 1, in IDFA 669/1109/2005.

163. "On Arab Mail from Enemy Countries and Mail by Arab Israelis," 15 September 1949, 1.

164. "Free-fire" policy refers to rules-of-engagement orders given to the soldiers that allowed them to shoot at suspicious characters without first giving a warning. See Benny Morris, *Israel's Border Wars, 1949–1956: Arab Infiltration, Israeli Retaliation, and the Countdown to the Suez War* (Oxford: Clarendon Press, 1993), 431–36; Cohen, *Good Arabs*, 85–94.

165. Cohen, *Good Arabs*, 71.

166. "On Arab Mail from Enemy Countries and Mail by Arab Israelis," 15 September 1949, 1. According to the censor, 1 percent of the 1,470 Palestinian letters that passed through the censorship bureau in September 1949 dealt with "infiltration," while another 4.5 percent of letters dealt with other issues pertaining to refugees. See also "Report on Israeli Arab Mail and [Mail] from Enemy Territory for the Month of July 1949."

167. "Meetings in Tel Aviv 9–10 August 1949—Discharged Moroccan Gahal"; Memo by the Secretary of the Zionist Federation in Paris, undated, ca. August 1948, in IDFA 8/1000827/1958.

168. "What Are They Writing in the Diaspora?"; Hatimi, "Al-Jama'at al-Yahudiya," 290–91.

169. H. M. Cohen, "Moroccan Jewry Is Watching Israel," *Hed Hamizrah*, 22 July 1949. See also Tsur, *Kehilah Keru'ah*, 301–11.

170. Tsur, *Kehilah Keru'ah*, 305–7.

171. See comments by censors in IDFA 13/621/1985; Southern Censor, Internal Department, "Special Report No. 4: What Foreign Correspondents Write in Their Personal Letters," April 1949, 1, in IDFA 14/621/1985. For a discussion of this practice from the 1950s, see Haifa Censor to Chief Censor, "Operation Pe and He," 29 August 1957, in IDFA 166/621/1985.

172. The meeting of the forum on July 31, 1949, was sponsored by the Department

for the Affairs of Jews in the Middle East at the Jewish Agency and attended by the director of the department. At the meeting, a forum member, who was a North African IDF officer, suggested drafting a letter that would be disguised to read as though written by an ordinary Moroccan immigrant residing in Israel. The letter itself was drafted seven days later and transferred to the Jewish Agency. See "The Department for the Affairs of Jews in the Middle East—A Meeting of the Forum for Veteran North Africans," 31 July 1949, in CZA S20/620; undated letter, Jerusalem 7 August 1949, in CZA S20/550/I; Hatimi, "Al-Jama'at al-Yahudiya," 290–91; Tsur, *Kehilah Keru'ah*, 307n195.

173. Undated letter, Jerusalem, 7 August 1949.

174. Ibid.

175. Ibid. The letter mentioned one of Morocco's wealthiest Jews, who returned to Morocco as well, but only so he could "get rid of his first wife 'A'isha who could not live without the meat pot [*sir ha-baśar*] and the bathhouses of Morocco."

176. Ibid.

177. Mandel, "Transnationalism and Its Discontents," 346.

178. Hatimi, "Al-Jama'at al-Yahudiya," 289; Mandel, "Transnationalism and Its Discontents," 348.

179. The French consul in Israel, Pierre Landy, met some of the returnees before their departure to Morocco. He wrote the foreign ministry in Paris that among Moroccan immigrants, "the Zionist ideal dissolves quickly . . . under the inclement sun of Palestine and in the brawling atmosphere of this unhappy country." See Maud, "Transnationalism and Its Discontents," 346.

180. Hatimi, "Al-Jama'at al-Yahudiya," 289n2.

181. Quoted in Hatimi, "Al-Jama'at al-Yahudiya," 329.

182. Voicing the desire to leave Israel was by no means exclusive to North Africans—some immigrants from Europe, the Americas, and Asia also chose to leave Israel. Nevertheless, it appears that those voices were much more prevalent among the communities of North African Jews than in Jewish communities from other areas, and especially communities of European-born Jews. Analysis of statistics of former immigrants who left Israel between 1948 and 1952 demonstrates two interesting trends. First, the number of those leaving Israel during that period who were from North African origin as a percent of the overall group's population in Israel was nearly 1.7 times that of emigrants of European and American origin. In other words, North Africans were nearly twice as likely to leave Israel compared with Ashkenazi Jews. Moreover, North Africans (along with Iranians and Turks) who emigrated from Israel during

this period returned predominantly to their country of birth, with nearly 70 percent of Moroccans, Algerians, and Tunisians emigrating from Israel during this period and returning to their land of birth. Considering the difficulty Moroccans faced in returning to Morocco, it is reasonable to assume the numbers would have been even greater had the immigrants who expressed a desire to return home were actually able to do so. See Hatimi, "Al-Jama'at al-Yahudiya," 287, 290; "Table A15. Jewish Population, by Country of Birth and Sex," "Table D5. Jewish Immigrants by Continent of Birth," "Table D20. Jewish Emigrants, (1) by Country of Birth," *Israel Statistical Yearbook* 9 (1958) (Jerusalem: Central Bureau of Statistics, 1959); Ori Yehudai, "Forth from Zion: Jewish Emigration from Palestine and Israel, 1945–1960" (PhD diss., University of Chicago, 2013); Southern Censor, Economic Department, "Special Report No. 48: The State of Immigrants," January 1950, in IDFA 18/821/1985.

183. A Google ngram chart reveals that the term "right of return" in English only started appearing in books around 1980. (It is hard to assess when the term was first introduced in Arabic.) This is likely due to the fact that the Palestinian struggle focused on "complete liberation" of Palestine well into the 1970s, and a return of the refugees was to be a natural consequence of such liberation. Khalidi noted that the Palestine National Council (PNC) had started as early as 1964 to refer to Palestinians who were forced out of Palestine in 1948 as "returnees" (*'a'idin*) rather than "refugees" (*laji'in*). See Rashid Khalidi, "Observations on the Right of Return," *Journal of Palestine Studies* 21, no. 2 (1992): 30, 34.

184. To aid in preventing "Levantinization," the government introduced selective immigration from Morocco in 1950 based on medical and social criteria. The youth became the primary candidates for immigration because it was believed they could more easily be socialized into Israeli culture, while the same socialization was impossible for their parents. This stirred up protests in Morocco itself, as family members of young men and women were not allowed to immigrate to Israel together with their children. See Tsur, *Kehilah Keru'ah*, 281–86, 302–6; Picard, *'Olim Bi-Mesurah*, 69–110.

185. For a similar theme in mobilization propaganda in DP camps, see *Anu ha-Homa* 3, 9–10.

CONCLUSION

1. IS, "TSO Report December 1960," 2, in IDFA 955/535/2004.

2. Education Department, Chapter Headings for Hasbara, "The Rhodes Talks," 16 January 1949, in IDFA 364/5254/1949, 3.

3. Ibid. Only a handful of pamphlets mentioned a yearning for peace. See *The Battalion: The Journal of Battalion 54*, vol. 9, 21 May 1948, in IDFA 13/1147/2002.

4. "Political Assassination in Israel," 4. Different themes were presented in those education materials prepared specifically for ultra-orthodox soldiers: "The people of Israel do not wish for war, but only for peace. . . . War is not but a corridor to the main room, a passage and a way towards peace." See "Shema Yisrael," *ha-Mivtsar*, vol. 1, August–September 1948, 5, in IDFA 63/1147/2002.

5. "Army Day." For how scorn directed at diplomacy evolved during the 1950s in the IDF, see Gil-li Vardi, "'Pounding Their Feet': Israeli Military Culture as Reflected in Early IDF Combat History," *Journal of Strategic Studies* 31, no. 2 (2008): 295–324.

6. The education officers concluded that they had to focus their efforts on the group of *"poshete yidden,"* Yiddish for simple Jews (literally, "beggars"),"who came because they felt it was their duty to do so, moved by a simple and uncomplicated feelings of Jewish loyalty." See Brigade Seven, "HAMITNADEV–A Newsletter for the Volunteer," no. 53, 1–2.

108–10, 125, 130, 149, 165, 169, 173–74, 185–87, 190, 201–2, 208, 216n33, 241nn197–98, 243n228, 300n85, 300n92; Arab Liberation Army (ALA) and, 1, 6, 14, 21–22, 61, 65–66, 103–4, 106, 109–10, 165, 169, 173–74, 186, 208, 269n19; Christians and, 241n197; ID cards and, 186; lira and, 185, 240n71; mobilization and, 33, 36, 61, 65–70, 74–75, 241nn197–98, 243n228; Mount Lebanon, 6, 216n33; nationalism and, 9, 11, 16, 36, 66, 74, 110, 208; al-Qawuqji and, 14, 21–22, 66, 104, 106, 108, 110, 173, 268n6; violence and, 149, 165, 169–70, 173–74, 276n6, 291n186

Lehi. *See* Stern Gang

Levantinization, 194, 206, 308n184

Library of Congress, 77

"light unto nations" (or la-goyim), 8, 93, 178, 182, 200, 206

literacy, 121, 267n3

looting, 24, 58, 83–84, 90–91, 94, 102, 112–13, 119, 128, 152, 157–59, 168–69, 188, 255n100, 286n118

Ma'ani, Hajj Muhammad Salim al-, 280n46

Maccabeans, 102

Ma'had, Al- (The Institute) [magazine], 65

Mahal, 48–49, 98–102, 119, 136, 138, 177, 180–83, 206, 210, 295n22, 296n24, 296n26, 297n49, 298n53

Mahmud, Maki, 126–32, 270n36, 272n49

Mahtar. See education department

Makhness, Gad, 274n79

Majdal, 115, 159–60, *161*

Makhzan (Morocco), 52, 54, 204

Malkiya battle, 173

al-Mansi, 152

Mandate for Palestine (Britain), 10, 12–13, 17, 20–22, 24, 38, 48, 50, 111, 262n220

Mapai. *See* Labor Zionism

Marcus, David, 49

Marj Ibn 'Amir, 148–49, 152, 154, 174, 283nn79–80, 285n98

Maronites, 67–68

Marseille, 47, 57, 232n54

Masada, 80

masculinity. *See* gender roles

massacres: Carmel and, 290n175; Dawayima, 158–59, 286n119; Dayr Yasin, 95, 151, 153, 161–64, 288n141, 289n151, 289n153; officer punishments for, 291n181; Oujda and Jerada, 51, 53–54, 57, 133, 236n118, 236n125; riots and, 53–54; surrender and, 111; Talmi on, 96

mellahs (Morocco), 136

Mesopotamia. *See* Iraq

Mizrahi Jews, 2–6, 8, 14, 49, 77, 89, 108, 116–18, 123, 132, 134–35, 185, 203, 294n9, 297n44, 298n57, 298n58, 298n5

"Morality in Israel's Army" (pamphlet), 82, 88, 249n40, 250n46

Moroccan Jews, 10–16, 26, 36, 40, 50–53, 62, 67, 74, 77, 80–85, 88, 91–92, 95–97, 101–2, 116–18, 122, 131, 133, 138,

133–35, 194, 198, 203, 206, 307n179;
kibbutzim and, 213n2; Labor, 13,
15, 33, 77, 85, 245n4, 248n26; land
purchases and, 6, 8, 12–13, 16, 148,
215n24, 283n79; messianism and, 6,
84; militarism and, 7–8, 12, 15, 17, 98,
182–83, 218n55; mobilization and, 32,
35–58, 61–75, 236nn127–28, 238n149,
243n228; Morocco and, 32, 51–56,
133–35, 176, 193, 195, 198, 203, 206,
208–9, 236n127, 237n129, 275n91,
304n145, 307n179; muscular Judaism
and, 7, 170, 175; nationalism and, 2, 5,
7–8, 10, 33, 36, 51–52, 54, 74, 129, 131,
184, 208, 307n179; Ottoman Empire
and, 8, 69, 215n24; propaganda and,
33, 42, 51, 56, 64, 72, 77, 98–101, 106,

108, 110, 133, 162, 193, 208–10, 245n4;
al-Qawuqji and, 40, 58, 70, 104–10,
151, 161, 261n204; religious, 6, 83–84,
251n48; returns and, 176, 179, 182–84,
193–200, 203, 206, 294n3, 297n46,
304n145, 307n179; "return to history"
and, 8, 157, 171, 176–77, 180, 182, 206,
297n41; Sabras and, 2, 15, 17, 209,
217n45, 218n55, 297n46; sacrifice
and, 7, 74; sovereignty and, 5, 8, 33,
108, 132, 160, 171, 286n129, 295n15; violence and, 140, 149, 151–52, 155–56,
160–62, 171, 218n55, 283n79, 292n193;
World War II and, 8, 16, 42, 45, 50, 74,
85, 98, 129, 208, 236n128

Zir'in, 145–47, 169, 261n205, 280n41
Zu'aytir, Akram, 11, 281n56

Heritage and the Cultural Struggle for Palestine 2019
CHIARA DE CESARI

Banking on the State: The Financial Foundations of Lebanon 2019
HICHAM SAFIEDDINE

Familiar Futures: Time, Selfhood, and Sovereignty in Iraq 2019
SARA PURSLEY

Hamas Contained: The Rise and Pacification of Palestinian Resistance 2018
TAREQ BACONI

*Hotels and Highways: The Construction of Modernization Theory
in Cold War Turkey* 2018
BEGÜM ADALET

Bureaucratic Intimacies: Human Rights in Turkey 2017
ELIF M. BABÜL

Impossible Exodus: Iraqi Jews in Israel 2017
ORIT BASHKIN

Brothers Apart: Palestinian Citizens of Israel and the Arab World 2017
MAHA NASSAR

Revolution without Revolutionaries: Making Sense of the Arab Spring 2017
ASEF BAYAT

Soundtrack of the Revolution: The Politics of Music in Iran 2017
NAHID SIAMDOUST

*Copts and the Security State: Violence, Coercion, and Sectarianism
in Contemporary Egypt* 2016
LAURE GUIRGUIS

Circuits of Faith: Migration, Education, and the Wahhabi Mission 2016
MICHAEL FARQUHAR

Morbid Symptoms: Relapse in the Arab Uprising 2016
GILBERT ACHCAR

*Imaginative Geographies of Algerian Violence: Conflict Science,
Conflict Management, Antipolitics* 2015
JACOB MUNDY

Police Encounters: Security and Surveillance in Gaza under Egyptian Rule 2015
ILANA FELDMAN

CPSIA information can be obtained
at www.ICGtesting.com
Printed in the USA
JSHW021238270321
12981JS00002B/137